TAROT COMPENDIUM

TAROT COMPENDIUM

Authors:
Giordano Berti,
Tali Goodwin,
Sasha Graham,
Marcus Katz,
Mark McElroy,
Riccardo Minetti,
Barbara Moore

Edited and compiled by
Sasha Graham

LO SCARABEO

Tarot Compendium

Edited and compiled by Sasha Graham

Authors:
Giordano Berti, Tali Goodwin, Sasha Graham, Marcus Katz, Mark McElroy, Riccardo Minetti, Barbara Moore

Graphic project:
Pietro Alligo, Santo Alligo

Editorial staff:
Chiara Demagistris, Riccardo Minetti, Alessandro Starrantino.

Editing:
Liz O'Neill

Marketing:
Mario Pignatiello, Andrea Chiarvesio

Special thanks:
Erik C. Dunne, Simon Altman

© 2017 by Lo Scarabeo srl
Via Cigna 110 – 10155 Torino – Italy
www.loscarabeo.com – www.facebook.com/LoScarabeoTarot

© images: Shutterstock.com; Lo Scarabeo; Right owners
© cover art: Erik C. Dunne

First edition – September 2017.

Printed by Shanghai Offset Printing Products Ltd.

About Sasha Graham

People visit Tarotists often with career questions. Young college grads and 20-somethings closing in on their Saturn Return frequently come my way because they are terrified of making the wrong decision. It's funny because when people come for love readings, all bets are off. Caution flies out the window. Outrageous behavior is justified. At the end of the day, the heart wants what the heart wants. People unquestioningly follow their heart's desire in love. But when it comes to career, people are often tentative and timid.

Focus on what thrills you I tell these clients before a single card flips. Focus on what makes your heart beat a bit faster (just like in love) even if it makes no sense. It will lead you to the right place amidst the confusion. Trusting what lights you up inside can be a scary prospect. But it yields massive dividends over a lifetime. I know this is true because I'm living proof.

I was born on Halloween just past midnight in the dark and chilly Adirondack mountains of upstate New York. Along with my mom and sister, I moved all around the country in a classic 70s scenario. We lived in craggy Colorado canyons and dusty Iowa pig farms. In Vermont's lush Green Mountains and on fertile New Jersey produce farms. Usually we were on our own, sometimes we lived with friends. Often my mother was married, other times not. Change was the only sure thing. But I knew what lit me up on the inside. It was living in New York City. I ran to the city as soon as I finished high school at age 17.

Fascinated with the occult and desperate to become anyone other than who I was,

I performed in live Vampire Theater, off-off-Broadway and became a B-movie star in straight to video horror films playing werewolves, aliens, gargoyles, mafia hit women and my perennial favorite, vampires. Feeling the intellectual deficit, I entered Hunter College and graduated with a BA in Literature and Comparative Religion. I joined the Tarot School and opened a private Tarot practice soon after

Beguiled by Tarot's history, I teamed up with curators and conceived and produced Tarot events at the Metropolitan Museum of Art and the Morgan Library. We examined rare Visconti, Marseille and Minchitate cards along with uncut Italian card sets. I regularly worked with New York's fashion and media set with clients like Christian Louboutin, M. Missoni, Burt's Bees, etc.

The Tarot Outreach Program was something I created for young adults transitioning out of the foster care system. I taught them how Tarot can be used to ignite and nurture personal intuition. Trust can be rebuilt and used to empower those who were robbed of stability and security as children.

For my Tarot books and work, I've been a guest on NPR's *Catskill Review of Books*, podcasts like *Love Bites* and on various Sirius XM Radio shows. Was the first Tarot Reader to grace the cover of *Crain's New York Business*, been written up in the *Wall Street Journal* and *The New York Daily News*. I enjoyed being a regular guest on the *Pix 11 Morning News* reading Tarot on pop culture topics and celebrities and wrote a weekly tarot column for *Marie Claire*.

Books include: *Tarot Diva, 365 Tarot Spreads* and *365 Tarot Spells*. I served as editor and contributing author of Lo Scarabeo's *Tarot Fundamentals*, *Tarot Experience* and *Tarot Compendium*. My first tarot deck, the *Haunted House Tarot* is due out in 2018 along with my latest book, *Llewellyn's Complete Book of the Rider Waite Smith Deck*.

My husband, daughter and I split our time between Manhattan and the eerily gothic Jane Eyre landscape of upstate NY.

Follow what excites you, thrills you and turns you on. I promise, it will never, ever steer you wrong.

About the authors

Giordano Berti is an Italian writer, and one of the greatest international experts on the connection between art and esotericism. A highly respected authority on the history of Tarot, his many books have been translated into English, French, Spanish, German, Dutch, Polish and Japanese. He is also the President of the Graf Institute in Bologna, Italy.

Tali Goodwin created the Tarosophy Tarot Association, Tarot Professionals, and Tarot Town with Marcus Katz. Together, Marcus and Tali have co-authored many books, including: *Secrets of the Waite-Smith Tarot, Around the Tarot in 78 Days, Tarot Face to Face* and *Easy Lenormand*.

Marcus Katz created the Tarosophy Tarot Association, Tarot Professionals, and Tarot Town with Tali Goodwin. Together, Tali and Marcus have co-authored many books, including: *Tarot Face to Face, Secrets of the Waite-Smith Tarot,* and *Around the Tarot in 78 Days*.

Mark McElroy is the author of *Putting the Tarot to Work, Taking the Tarot to Heart, What's in the Cards for You?, I Ching for Beginners* and *The Absolute Beginner's Guide to Tarot*. He calls Tarot "the ultimate visual brainstorming tool," and shares techniques designed to help others ask better questions, see more options, and achieve their goals. He holds a B.A. and M.A. in creative writing and composition from the Center for Writers at the University of Southern Mississippi. He has more than two decades of experience as a public speaker and corporate trainer. Today, he works as a writer, voice actor, and creativity consultant.

Riccardo Minetti is the Chief Editor of Lo Scarabeo for Tarot. Riccardo has a hand in the conception, design and direction of new Tarot decks and books and acts a mediator between writers, deck designers, artists and Lo Scarabeo. He has been involved in the creation of over 100 Tarot decks and books. Standouts include *Gothic Tarot of the Vampire, Etruscan Tarot, Manga Tarot, Fey Tarot* and the recently released *Epic Tarot*.

Barbara Moore is a leading expert in the field of Tarot and has published a number of Tarot books and decks, including: *Tarot for Beginners, Tarot Spreads, The Steampunk Tarot, The Gilded Tarot, The Mystic Dreamer*, and *Tarot of the Hidden Realm*. Writing is solitary work and is relieved by teaching Tarot at conferences around the world. Barbara also loves working with clients, using the Tarot to provide guidance and insight.

Letter from the Publisher

Dear readers,

With this third volume, *Tarot Compendium*, our *Tarot Encyclopedia* comes to its completion.

The path planned and foreseen by *Tarot Fundamentals* and carried forward by *Tarot Experience* finds its fulfillment with *Tarot Compendium*. The most advanced and dedicated aspects of Tarot knowledge are explored throughout its pages, deeply and largely.

It's the end of a wonderful journey, and we had great travel companions we would like to thank: starting with Sasha Graham, the book's Editor and main writer, continuing with our authors and writers Giordano Berti, Tali Goodwin, Marcus Katz, Mark McElroy, Barbara Moore and Riccardo Minetti.

We would like to include in these final thanks all the contributors (Lunaea Weatherstone, Richard Webster, Jenna Matlin, Jaymi Elford, Robert M. Place, Mary K. Greer, Kim Huggens, Theresa Reed, Nei Naiff and Erik C. Dunne) whose special contents gave us the opportunity to include additional points of view in an already choral book.

Another thank you goes to our editorial and marketing staff, to all the artists whose tarot artworks are a fundamental part of this opera, but—first and foremost—we want to say a huge "thank you" to our Kickstarter backers. Without your help and support, without your constant incitement and stimulus, this whole encyclopedia would have never been published, not in such a rich and gorgeous way.

This encyclopedia, now completed, already has its own special place in the history of Tarot.

Just as Lo Scarabeo has its special place in such history. As a happy, and not at all casual, coincidence, *Tarot Compendium* is being printed in the very same year our publishing house is celebrating its 30 years of existence, all dedicated to Tarot. This history of love and passion for Tarot is also celebrated by a unique exhibition, displaying both historical and modern Tarot decks, hosted here in Torino, where our publishing house has its offices, at the Ettore Fico Museum of Modern Arts.

This book is the end of our journey, but also the beginning of your journey in the Tarot world, with an increased awareness about everything related to Tarot, and of a journey in the world with Tarot by your side, and the Encyclopedia as a trusted companion.

Let's embrace the *Tarot Compendium* together, and show to the world our love and passion for Tarot.

Table of Contents

Preface by Sasha Graham

"I say patience, and shuffle the cards."
— Miguel de Cervantes, *Don Quixote*, Volume II

Dear Reader,
Welcome to *Tarot Compendium*. Taroists love to consider the nature of past, present, and future, don't we? The construct is always there, under the surface, deeply imbedded in the marrow of the thousands of Tarot spreads we use, create, and cast, even if we don't use the cards in a predictive way. As my fingers fly across the keyboard of a silver MacBook Air, I think about how past-me is communicating with future-you. Yes, you. If you are reading these words, I am reaching out from a blustery spring day in early 2017 and communicating with you in your present, your now. I like to speculate about where you are reading this. The special place you might be sitting, this book on your lap or a reading table, my words fresh in your mind. Writing and reading are truly metaphysical acts. Silent communication. A form of telepathy. They engage interior space. The moving, intimate, inner thought places. This private innermost space is the providence of a Tarotist. It is where we reach for meaning and engage in exploration into the unknown stretching beyond the borders of a Tarot card. Thank you for letting me in.

Past, present, and future link to another popular triad for cartomancers: fate, fortune, and destiny. In the old days, it was thought that fate, fortune, and destiny were written in the stars. Sealed and unalterable from the day of your birth. In parts of the world, this still rings true, especially if you live in an culture with a class system determined by birth.

In its original conception, fate was the agency that predetermined the course or plan of your entire life. Fortune dictated the specific events of your life, like striking it rich or making a good marriage. Destiny was ultimately where you were going, like it or not. It was believed diviners could look at cards, stones, or bones to discover where you were heading. Modern readers, like Caitlín Matthews and others, have redefined these terms. Fate in modern sensibility is the hand you were dealt. It is what you were born with, including things like parents, location, and physicality. Fortune is understood in the modern sense as innate talents or potentials you have. These talents and potentials can be honed or practiced for enjoyment or career. Destiny is something you carve out on your own using the gift of free will, i.e., personal choice. Tarot and free will are a winning combination as potentials are explored and options weighed so the best possible decisions can be made. Looking at the triplicity of ideas in past/present/future and fate/fortune/destiny, it becomes apparent that the third part of each triad is the most mysterious. Future and destiny both contain vast amounts of unknown. Examining triads in cross-cultural religions, we find the third remains the most mysterious of the bunch. The Pagan triple goddess triad of Maiden, Mother, and Crone presents the third and final evolution as the wise, sage Crone. The Crone has lived longest. She has garnered knowledge and experience. Christianity's triple deity, the Father, Son, and Holy Ghost, adhere to the same rule. The Holy Ghost is the most mysterious and metaphysical of the triad. The editorial team at Lo Scarabeo, following the tradition of great metaphysical trinities, decided to keep the juiciest high-level, advanced, and deeply spiritual knowledge for the last volume, *Tarot Compendium*.

This is not to say that you won't find incredible meaning and insights in *Tarot Fundamentals* and *Tarot Experience*. Besides, if you ask me off the record, I'd tell you the best experiences you will ever have with Tarot occur inside that beautiful mind of yours, that place where you are ingesting my words. The rich experiences occurring when you connect with a friend or querent over cards. The unique discoveries that you make for yourself, like my friend who tastes pineapple every time he pulls the Sun card. These things make for the vast firmament of Tarot.

Between the covers of this book you will find the scholarly stuff for the advanced reader and the curious soul. Take this information. Fly it to new heights. Rewrite your destiny. Create new spreads. Envision new mythologies. Cultivate new systems and definitions. Invent new archetypes. Take everything Tarot is or can be and push it into the future. Fate and fortune have set you up with extraordinary options and opportunities. I might be sitting here in the past, but I clearly see destiny twinkling inside you. It is blindingly brilliant. Just like its owner.

Cast your cards well,
Sasha Graham
New York City, 2017

INTRODUCTION

THE BOOK OF YOU

Welcome to *Tarot Compendium*, the third and final install-ment of Lo Scarabeo's *Tarot Trilogy*. In the pages of this book you, intrepid Reader, will find a jumping-off point for a broad range of esoteric knowledge associated with Tarot.

The introduction to *Tarot Fundamentals* proposed that you meet the Tarot inside Lo Scarabeo's trilogy the way you might explore a foreign city. It suggested you move through the deck like you might saunter down foreign streets for the very first time. These books are a guide, a passport to the wonders, beguilements, and strange places that the Tarot landscape unveils for the explorer.

Historical cities hold as many secrets as the Tarot. If you read the first two books, you explored the museums, met the archetypes, and enjoyed the artists. Those old occultists swept the graveyard dust off their shoulders and stood up to greet you. Dozens of divination techniques and applica-tions have been passed along. Spreads have been designed and offered for your enjoyment and enlightenment. The basics have been covered. You've made it this far. You've earned it.

Now you will discover the inner workings, the hidden city that the traveler rarely sees at first glance. Much of the information found inside *Tarot Compendium* is like the invisible networks of a great city. The occult knowledge in this book points toward regions that even lifelong residents remain blissfully unaware of. Esoteric information is like miles of electrical lines concealed under pavement. It is the water gushing through buried pipes so large you could walk through them with an elephant. It is the hidden network of tunnels speeding thousands of commuters over tracks to their station stops.

You have to go out of your way to think about it. Or someone needs to tell you about it or explain it in a way that makes sense to you. Once you become aware of secret, hidden things, occult knowledge can seem obvious after the fact. Like something you have always known. That's the way it is with learning. It's the High Priestess operating inside you. That knowledge is already there, you need only to uncover it, unroll her scroll or open the pages of a book.

Just as the basic elements are put in place to keep a city running, so the basic esoteric elements are the lineage of modern Tarot use. It is highly unlikely that Tarot derived or actually came from schools of deep esoteric thought. If it did, the traces are either hidden or were destroyed. Tarot's esoteric scholarship was placed on top of Tarot's ideal structure. Historical scholarship reveals that the first Tarot book was published in 1770 by Etteilla. A hundred years later Eliphas Lévi connects Tarot to Kabbalah (and subsequent esoteric disciplines), provoking a slew of influential Tarot texts from occultists and landmark work by the Golden Dawn's members. Their profound influence on Tarot is felt to this day. Tarot's ideal structure makes it possible for almost any system to be placed on top of it. The cards allow for an almost perfect syncopation of occult knowledge.

Tarot's esoterica is rooted in ancient times and predates all historical traces of Tarot. Astrology, the practice of scanning the sky for human meaning, dates back to Babylonian tablets circa 1700 BCE. The first text of magical Kabbalah, the mysterious Sepher Yetzirah, appeared between the third and sixth centuries. Pythagorean numerology dates to sixth-century BCE Greece with the philosopher who bears its name. Magical practice instinctively came to early man prior to organized religion as he began in earnest to attempt to affect the world around him in beneficial ways.

The field of modern psychology evolved right alongside the esoteric evolution of Tarot. Meaningful coincidence? Carl Jung would probably agree. Imagine for a moment what it would be like to understand your life without a psychological context. We have become so accustomed to personal psychology it is hard to imagine our lives or self-reflection without it. G. Stanley Hall, who founded the American Psychological Association, received the first American Ph.D. in psychology in 1878, ten years before the Golden Dawn formed. Sigmund Freud opened his therapy practice in Vienna just three years before Papus published his famous *Tarot of the Bohemians.* Carl Jung split with Freud and developed analytical psychology in 1913, four years after the publication of the Rider-Waite-Smith deck.

The evolutions of esoteric Tarot and modern psychology both examine the same thing. They seek to examine and expand the inner life of the individual. Both practices dive into the deep space of the psyche, the places where personalities are formed, where behavior is created, where dreams are born—the place from which an individual's experience springs. Each modality reaches into darkness and obscurity to seek light and illumination. It is no coincidence that each unfolded next to the other. And it is no coincidence that many therapists, counselors, and psychologists find Tarot a useful tool for their personal and/or professional practice.

Learning the esoteric value of Tarot will deepen and alter your practice forever. Tarot Compendium serves as a reference or jumping-off point. Like yoga, Reiki, or any other metaphysical practice, it is best to study with teachers, experiment with others, grow, learn, and share your knowledge with friends and colleagues. A personal practice is paramount, one made of dedication and commitment, even if it is only a single card a day.

All esoteric knowledge fits on Tarot because of Tarot's essential and basic structure. Tarot numbers, suits, and symbols echo and imitate our life on earth and in the physical world. Tarot usage mines the inner life so it expands the possibilities of our outer life. The card patterns repeat like our personal patterns. Tarot is truly a reflection of the universe. So when you gaze at the night sky or at an illustration of the Tree of Life or you find yourself counting up numbers and suits, what you are really doing is finding you. As always, we look closely at Tarot only to find ourselves reflected back.

KABBALAH

What Is the Kabbalah?

Kabbalah is a system of Jewish mysticism explaining the nature of the universe. Kabbalistic doctrine embraces all aspects of creation: the essence of God; the nature of angels, demons, and spirits; the mysteries of numbers and letters of the alphabet; the forces and laws of the universe and the human soul. It is the symbolic journey of the soul's return to divine grace. Kabbalah is a cornerstone of Western esoterica. It originated long before it was associated with Tarot. The word "Kabbalah" translates in Hebrew as "received tradition" and began as an oral communication to the initiated. It was taught and passed to a select few—usually Jewish men over the age of forty—and it was shrouded in secrecy.

Machzor Lemberg from year 1907 printed by David Balaban. The Machzor is a prayer book.

The origin of Kabbalah is steeped in Jewish tradition, yet it is as obscure as Tarot's origins. No single, agreed-upon,

concrete source or origin date for Kabbalah exists, though it is traced to the Hebrew Bible and rabbinic literature. One theory states that Kabbalah was given by God to Moses during his forty days on Mount Sinai. Another states that God taught the doctrine to angels who then passed the information on to man so that man could return to God.

What Does It Have to Do with Tarot?

Lon Milo DuQuette explains the connection between Tarot and Kabbalah perfectly in his book *The Chicken Qabalah of Rabbi Lamed Ben Clifford*. DuQuette points out that "Whether we realize it or not, when we work with the Tarot, we are working with the Qabalah. Tarot's like the DNA of the Qabalah—better than that—it's actually the picture-book of the Qabalah."

Tarot and Kabbalah have a nearly identical structure. In fact, the entire deck, each and every card and suit, can be associated with the Tree of Life. Early occultists realized they could connect the Tarot with Kabbalah. They could use the Tarot deck as a tool for describing the nature of the universe. Kabbalah's secret nature likely made it all the more attractive to occultists with a fondness for secret and hidden theories and a fascination with magic, alchemy, and divination.

The Tree of Life

The Tree of Life is the mystical symbol for the Kabbalah. Trees are a major archetypal symbol and are used cross-culturally. The Tree of Enlightenment, the Tree of Knowledge, and the World Tree exist as metaphors in Buddhism, Islam, Christianity, and other faiths. Charles Darwin explained the "tree of science" as the interconnectedness of all living things. Personal genealogy study and family history is referred to as the "family tree."

The Tree of Life with its 10 Sephirot is exclusive to the mystical Kabbalah. The connection between Tarot and Kabbalah is apparent when looking at a diagram of the Kabbalistic Tree of Life. It is exciting to discover how each metaphysical section connects to Tarot.

1858

The Tree of Life

The Tree of Life is the symbolic representation of Kabbalah. It is said to contain the map of humanity's fall from grace as depicted in the Book of Genesis. However, the Tree can also be used as a roadmap back into the Grace of the Diety. It is said that one who deciphers the Journey of Emergence and the Journey of Return will understand the Tree of Life and Kabbalah.

The names of the Sephirot may be slightly different depending on the text you find, as they were originally in Hebrew and have been translated to English alphabet.

On the previous page: Fresco of Moses by Joseph Schonman from year 1857 in Altlerchenfelder church, Wien.

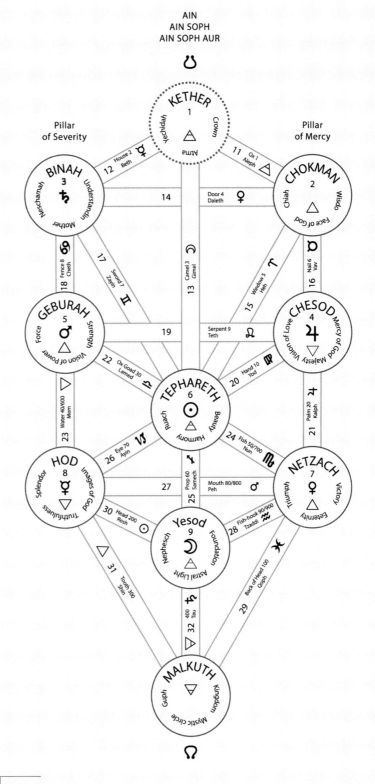

When to Use Kabbalistic Meanings

The Tree of Life's sections and paths, bits and pieces can all be connected to individual Tarot cards. Kabbalistic meanings will add immeasurable weight to the cartomancer's store of Tarot knowledge. It deepens the meaning behind each card. Practitioners often speak about how esoteric meanings alter their connection with the cards. A practitioner who reads cards to divine the future suddenly realizes he or she can use Tarot and esoteric meanings to unravel the meaning of life.

How Tarot corresponds to Kabbalah

22 Major Arcana	22 Hebrew letters
22 Major Arcana	22 Tree of Life paths
10 Numeral	10 Sephirot
16 Court Cards	16 Invisible Tree of Life paths

Portae Lucis, a Latin translation by Paulus Ricius of Joseph Gikatilla's most influential kabbalistic work, *Shaarel Ora*. Careful observers will note this image's similarity to Pamela Colman Smith's 10 of Pentacles card.

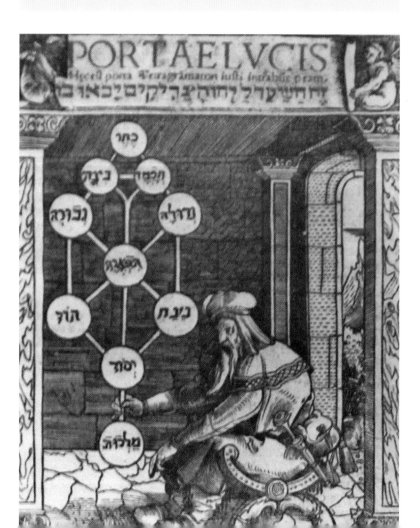

Why So Many Spellings?

Kabbalah is also spelled Kabalah, Kabala, and other K spellings, or Cabala, Cabbala, Cabbalah, and other C spellings, or Qabbala, Qaballah, and other Q spellings.

K — C — Q

Some say that the K spelling is used by those of the Jewish faith, that Christian kabbalists use the C spelling, and occultists use the Q spelling. None of these examples are hard and fast rules. Renaissance Christian and Hermetic scholars used the structure of Kabbalah to expound upon their own mystical understanding. This led to independent schools of Kabbalistic thought and multiple spellings of the title.

The 10 of Pentacles of the Waite Smith Tarot, by A. E. Waite and P. C. Smith.

History of the Kabbalah

The Early History

The first century CE is the approximate date for the *Sepher Yetzirah*, also known as the Book of Creation. This is a mystical text describing how God created the universe using the 22 letters of the Hebrew alphabet and the 10 primordial numbers. The Reader will immediately recognize that there are also 22 Major Arcana cards and 10 Minor Arcana cards (not including the court cards).

The *Sepher Yetzirah* is regarded as the first text to describe the Kabbalah. The 22 letters of the Hebrew alphabet describe the divine nature of God and the universe. The letters are broken down phonetically. There is a direct relation between the symbol, sound, and pronunciation. The idea of the creative power of sounds and letters can be traced to ancient Egypt, while the mystical use of numbers and letters can be traced to ancient Babylon.

During the Renaissance (14th through 17th centuries), Kabbalah entered non-Jewish culture when Christian and other religious mystics discovered how their dogmatic teachings could be integrated seamlessly onto a kabbalistic structure.

19th Century Occultism and the Golden Dawn

Alphonse Louis Constant (1810–1875), better known as Éliphas Lévi, was the first occultist to highlight the relationship between the Major Arcana and the Kabbalah. The famous French occultist highlighted the correspondences between the Arcana and Hebrew letters in the second volume of his *Dogme et Rituel de la Haute Magie* (*Dogma and Ritual of High Magic, 1855–56*).

The occultist Papus (Gérard Anaclet Vincent Encausse, 1865–1916) developed the doctrine of kabbalistic Tarot in three groups representing the creation of three worlds: divine, human, and cosmic. Papus saw the 22 figures of the Major Arcana as both allegories of the fall of Adam and Eve in the material world and the stages of man's possible return to paradise, an opportunity to return after original sin. This idea is often expressed as "the journey of emergence" and "the journey of return."

Samuel Liddell MacGregor Mathers (1854–1918), an English esoteric, further expressed these ideas while writing for the adepts (initiates) of the Hermetic Order of the Golden Dawn, a magical society he helped found. Mathers pointed out ideas implicit to Lévi and Papus but not yet fully formulated. He used the *Sepher Yetzirah* as the basis for his kabbalistic interpretation of the Tarot.

Book T, The Tarot was a Golden Dawn private manuscript secretly written by Mathers. Like other Golden Dawn documents, the back story of the manuscript was fabricated to give it an air of authenticity. The story went that the text was discovered in the tomb of Christian Rosenkreuz, the founder of the Rosicrucian Order. *Book T* contains Mather's kabbalistic connections. These associations would lay the groundwork for future Tarot texts, decks, and books, including those by Arthur Edward Waite, Aleister Crowley, and Paul Foster Case.

The biggest difference in the French system of esoteric Kabbalah is the positioning of the Fool. Lévi felt that the Magician card should lead the Tarot deck. He placed the Fool card, which was unnumbered, between the Judgment card and the World card. Mathers placed the Fool at the beginning of the deck with the number zero as that which precedes every other number. This links the Fool to the Hebrew letter aleph.

Alphonse Louis Constant, alias Éliphas Lévi. Photography.

Gérard Encausse, alias Papus. Photography.

Samuel Liddell Mathers. Photography.

There is no right or wrong between each of these systems, though it is widely agreed that the Golden Dawn system leads to deeper and more meaningful study.

Ein Sof and Sephirot

The Kabbalah describes the divine emanation of God—an abstract thing, action, or process stemming from a single source. **Ein Sof** ("the infinite") is the space of the universe that contains the nature of God, but the universe is not the Deity's space because God is beyond comprehension. The Deity itself cannot be named, described, or comprehended.

In order to be known, God made manifestations. These emanations or intelligences are called Sephirot (singular, Sephirah). It is important to understand that each Sephirah emanates from Ein Sof. Each represents a different aspect of the Deity. Ein Sof's light shines through each Sephirah. Each Sephirah is as perfect and infinite as Ein Sof because they are aspects of Ein Sof.

The light of the Ein Sof shines through each and every Sephirah.

The Ten Sephirot

Each Sephirah is explained below with examples of how the Reader can apply kabbalistic meanings to Tarot. Note that the Sephirot are attributed to body parts and, once complete, manifest a human being.

1. Crown (Kether)

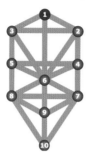    

Body part: Crown
Tarot Aces connect to the Crown Sephirah. Kether reflects Divine Will and is the very first emanation of the Deity or godhead. Like the first star appearing in the night sky, it is the first spark of the Tree, as the Aces are the spark of each suit. Kether is the beginning, start, and manifestation. This connects to and supports all traditional meanings of all Tarot Aces.

2. Wisdom (Chokhmah)

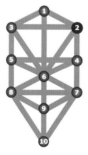    

Body part: Right side of the head
Tarot Twos connect to the Wisdom Sephirah. Chokhmah reflects intuition. This is spiritual wisdom in its highest expression. It is the top point on the masculine side/pillar of the Tree of Life. What was one has become two. Duality

now exists. Crown recognizes Wisdom and vice versa. In this way, one can consider the wisdom and duality of each suit.

- ○ **Two of Cups:** The Wisdom of water is the ability to absorb.
- ○ **Two of Wands:** The Wisdom of fire is the ability to purify.
- ○ **Two of Swords:** The Wisdom of air is the ability to bring clarity.
- ○ **Two of Pentacles:** The Wisdom of earth is the ability to grow and manifest.

3. Understanding (Binah)

Body part: Left side of the head
Tarot Threes connect to the Understanding Sephirah. Binah reflects the ability to analyze. With Binah, the first triad of the Tree appears. Understanding is the top point of the feminine side/pillar of the Tree of Life. Three now exist and in this triad, creativity is implicit. The first archetypal patterns and structures are found here.

- ○ **Three of Cups:** The Understanding of water is the ability to express emotion.
- ○ **Three of Wands:** The Understanding of fire is how it awakens the soul.
- ○ **Three of Swords:** The Understanding of air is the ability to be everywhere.
- ○ **Three of Pentacles:** The Understanding of earth is the ability to make manifest.

4. Mercy (Chesed)

Body part: Right arm

Tarot Fours connect to the Mercy Sephirah. Chesed reflects the ability to feel compassion. Mercy is the spot where Wisdom and Understanding collect from the supernal triad above (the first three Sephirot). A new triad is formed on the receptive masculine side/pillar of the Tree. It is a bridge between the spiritual and the beginning of manifestation. It is the place where the archetype in its purest form begins to form in the human and universal mind.

- **Four of Cups:** The Mercy of water is the ability to empathize.
- **Four of Wands:** The Mercy of fire is how it warms.
- **Four of Swords:** The Mercy of air is the ability to understand.
- **Four of Pentacles:** The Mercy of earth is the ability to nurture.

5. Strength (Gevurah)

Body part: Left arm

Tarot Fives connect to the Strength Sephirah. Gevurah reflects power and forces controlling strong emotion. It is the discipline required for manifestation. The explosion of compassion that comes from Mercy is contained in Strength. Strength is on the feminine side of the Tree and provides the needed balance as archetype, spirit, and form remain balanced.

- **Five of Cups:** The Strength of water is the ability to transform.
- **Five of Wands:** The Strength of fire is its enthusiasm.
- **Five of Swords:** The Strength of air is fluidity.
- **Five of Pentacles:** The Strength of earth is family.

6. Beauty (Tiferet)

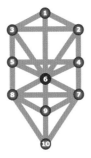    

Body part: Heart
Tarot Sixes connect to the Beauty Sephirah. Tiferet reflects truth and harmony. This Sephirah sits at the center of the Tree; it is the very heart. Inside the heart a synthesis of grace exists as energies are merged together. It is the heart of love and is thus called Beauty.

- **Six of Cups:** The Beauty of water is the ability to reflect.
- **Six of Wands:** The Beauty of fire is its ability to transfix.
- **Six of Swords:** The Beauty of air is its ability to caress.
- **Six of Pentacles:** The Beauty of earth is fecundity.

The key for understanding the Kabbalah is unlocking the symbolic power of abstraction.

7. Victory (Netzach)

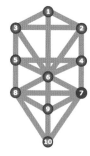    

Body part: Right leg

Tarot Sevens connect to the Victory Sephirah. Netzach contains the will to make things happen. It is where the creative mind emerges and occult thinking begins. It is the source of mystery. Netzach is spiritual experience as the Tree grows downward into physical manifestation.

- **Seven of Cups:** The Victory of water is the ability to become transparent.
- **Seven of Wands:** The Victory of fire is the urge toward spirituality.
- **Seven of Swords:** The Victory of air is articulation.
- **Seven of Pentacles:** The Victory of earth is its physicality.

8. Splendor (Hod)

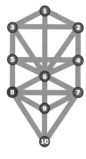    

Body part: Left leg

Tarot Eights connect to the Splendor Sephirah. Hod contains the basic structure of the entire universe. This is the window or kaleidoscope where one can look down to the physical molecular level and up to the highest forms of the godhead. It exists on the feminine side of the Tree and reflects persistence and humility.

- **Eight of Cups:** The Splendor of water is the ability to be buoyant.
- **Eight of Wands:** The Splendor of fire is its passion.
- **Eight of Swords:** The Splendor of air is its expansion.
- **Eight of Pentacles:** The Splendor of earth is its memory.

9. Foundation (Yesod)

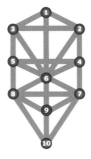    

Body part: Genitals/anus

Tarot Nines connect to the Foundation Sephirah. Yesod is the place through which everything is funneled as it becomes manifest in the material world. This is the skeletal structure upon which the physical world depends. It is where things become available and about to happen. The entirety of the Tree funnels into this Sephirah and, as such, things begin to take shape.

- **Nine of Cups:** The Foundation of water is the ability to transform.
- **Nine of Wands:** The Foundation of fire is its enthusiasm.
- **Nine of Swords:** The Foundation of air is fluidity.
- **Nine of Pentacles:** The Foundation of earth is its weight.

10. Kingdom (Malkuth)

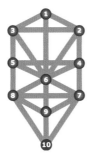    

33

Body part: Feet

Tarot Tens connect to the Kingdom Sephirah. Malkuth is the physical world. The Tree of Life is manifested here on earth. This is everything we can see, smell, hear, touch, taste, and intuit in the material world.

- **Ten of Cups:** The Kingdom of water is the element of water itself.
- **Ten of Wands:** The Kingdom of fire is the element of fire itself.
- **Ten of Swords:** The Kingdom of air is the element of air itself.
- **Ten of Pentacles:** The Kingdom of earth is the element of earth itself.

Triads and Pillars

The Three Triads

The first three Sephirot—Crown, Wisdom, and Understanding—make up the **first triad**, known as the archetypal or supernal triad. This can be understood as the intellectual world.

The **second triad** contains Mercy, Strength, and Beauty. This is known as the moral, ethical, and sensuous world.

The **third triad** comprises Splendor, Foundation, and Victory. This is the psychological and astral triad. This is called the material world.

The Three Pillars

The Tree of Life is held together by three strong pillars. These pillars have attributes of their own.

The three masculine Sephirot are 2, 4, and 7, located on the right side of the Tree. This is called the **Pillar of Mercy**.

The three feminine Sephirot are 3, 5, and 8, located on the left side of the Tree. This is called the **Pillar of Judgment**.

The four middle Sephirot—1, 6, 9, and 10—are located in the center of the Tree. This is called the **Pillar of Mildness**.

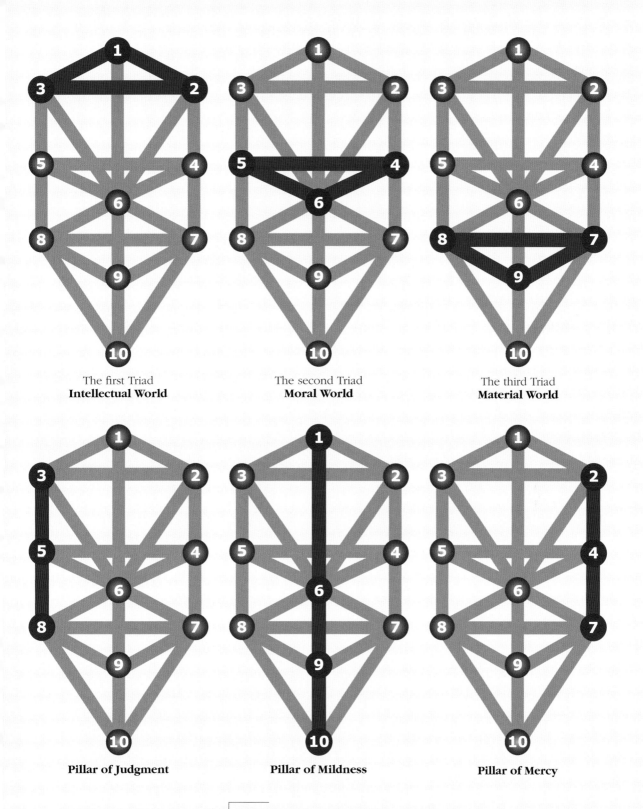

The first Triad
Intellectual World

The second Triad
Moral World

The third Triad
Material World

Pillar of Judgment

Pillar of Mildness

Pillar of Mercy

Hebrew Letters

Twenty-two paths connect the Sephirot on the Tree of Life. Each path is associated with a letter of the Hebrew alphabet, and each path is associated with a Major Arcana card. The 22 Hebrew alphabet letters, in a nutshell, contain the forces of the universe, the directions and spatial components of the universe, and the human component. They are broken down into three segments.

The Mother Letters

The three mother letters are universal forces that represent three primitive elements: air, water, and fire. It is said that fire created the heavens, air created air, and water created earth. Air is said to keep the balance between earth and the heavens.

Aleph: Air

Mem: Water

Shin: Fire

The Double Letters

The seven double letters are the forces of the universe that stand in opposition to one another. They are also connected to the directions or dimensions of the universe.

The seven double letters correspond to the seven visible heavenly bodies.

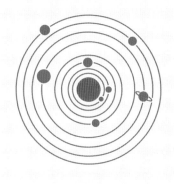

Bet: Mercury
Gimel: Moon
Dalet: Venus
Kaph: Jupiter
Peh: Mars
Resh: Sun
Tav: Saturn

Bet: Above

Gimel: Below

Dalet: East

Kaph: West

Peh: North

Resh: South

Tav: Center which holds everything together

The Simple Letters and Basic Human Attributes

The 12 simple letters are associated with human functioning. They also associate with the 12 signs of the zodiac, 12 months of the calendar year, and the limbs of the human body.

He: Sight

Vav: Hearing

Zayin: Smell

Het: Speech

Tet: Taste

Yod: Sexual love

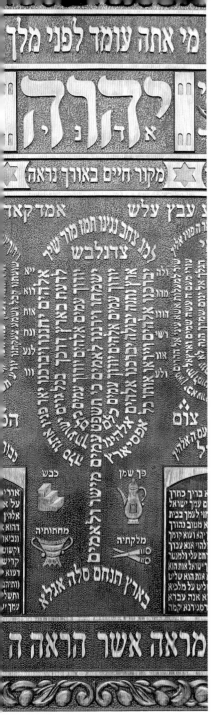

Lamed: Work

Nun: Movement

Samekh: Anger

Ayin: Mirth

Tzadc: Imagination

Qoph: Sleep

Cover of a Kabbalistic prayer book.

On the previous page: a modern and not esoteric rendition of the concept of the Tree of Life.

39

The Major Arcana Cards and Their Corresponding Kabbalistic Paths

The Fool

Letter: Aleph א
Path: 11
Connects Crown to
Wisdom
Element: Air
Mother letter
Translation: Ox

The Fool connects to the Hebrew letter Aleph. It highlights path number 11. This path connects Sephirot 1 and 2 (or a Tarot Ace and Tarot Two), which is Kether (Crown) to Chokhmah (Wisdom). Aleph is connected to the element of air and everything air represents.

Examine the path on the Tree leading from the Crown to Wisdom to its first movement downwards. The Fool is a gust of fresh air, the element it is assigned. It is the breath and animating principle of life. It is pranayama. It is divine prayer. Breath carries humanity's words. The word aleph translates to "ox." In early days, the ox made life, agriculture, and farming possible. Ox shoulders the heavy load and represents progress.

The Magician

Letter: Bet ב
Path: 12
Connects Crown to
Understanding
Planet: Mercury ☿
Double letter
Translation: House

The Magician connects to the Hebrew letter Bet. It highlights path number 12. This path connects Kether (Crown) and Binah (Understanding). Bet is one of the seven double letters. Bet is connected to the planet Mercury and all the qualities Mercury represents.

Examine the Fool and the Magician's path as a graphic. A roof has formed at the top of the Tree of Life. The word bet translates to "house." A house is forming inside the Tree. Its top is created by the Fool (Aleph) and the Magician (Bet). A house is a dwelling place for humanity. Humans' first homes were caves. Modern houses are built by man, who emulates the power of the Magician to create something new when a structure is erected. This reflects the ability to alter and manipulate the material world. On the deepest level, it is the house reflected in the body, the house that shelters the soul. It is our intimacy, our center, and our inner temple.

The High Priestess

Letter: Gimel ג
Path: 13
Connects Crown to Beauty
Planet: Moon ☽
Double letter
Translation: Camel

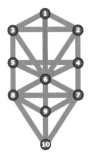

The High Priestess connects to the Hebrew letter Gimel. It highlights path number 13. This path connects Sephirot 1 and 6, which is Kether (Crown) to Tiferet (Beauty). Gimel is one of the seven double letters and represents the moon and all lunar qualities.

The path of the High Priestess moves down the center of the Tree from the Crown to the heart. This is why the High Priestess is often seen seated between two pillars. She is the center pillar. The word gimel translates to "camel." The camel stores water, life's sustaining element. Water connects to the moon, as the moon instigates tidal push and pull. Her path reaches from the Crown straight to the heart. It is the path which forges the authenticity and survival of the human soul.

The Empress

Letter: Dalet **ד**
Path: 14
Connects Wisdom to Understanding
Planet: Venus ♀
Double letter
Translation: Door

The Empress connects to the Hebrew letter Dalet. It highlights path number 14. This path connects Sephirot 3 and 2, which are Chokhmah (Wisdom) and Binah (Understanding). Dalet is one of the seven double letters and represents Venus and all associated qualities of the planet of love and beauty.

The roof of the Tree is now complete and constructed. The Empress's path is the first path to connect the right and left, masculine and feminine, pillars together. A trinity is formed at the top of the Tree, as in "Father, Son, Holy Spirit" or "Mother, Maiden, Crone." The word dalet translates as "door." A foundational meaning of the Empress is that of pregnancy—woman is the door to life. The Empress is the door through which all pass.

The Emperor

Letter: He **ה**
Path: 15
Connects Wisdom to Beauty
Zodiac: Aries ♈
Simple letter
Translation: Window

The Emperor connects to the Hebrew letter He. It highlights path number 15. This path connects Chokhmah (Wisdom) and Tiferet (Beauty). He is one of the 12 simple letters and it represents the zodiac sign of Aries.

The paths between the Tree of Life are well underway. The Hebrew word He translates as "window." The roof and interior of the structure is complete, and mankind is free to look outside itself into the world beyond. An essential meaning of

Emperor is empire. The Emperor is often seated on a throne and surveys all that is his. It is through the window of our eyes that mankind reaches the point of maturation. There is a big, wide world beyond the child. This marks an opening and is the place through which the light enters.

The Hierophant

Letter: Vav ו
Path: 16
Connects Wisdom to Mercy
Zodiac: Taurus ♉
Simple letter
Translation: Hook

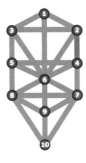

The Hierophant connects to the Hebrew letter Vav. It highlights path number 16. This path connects Chokhmah (Wisdom) to Chesed (Mercy). Vav is one of the 12 simple letters and it represents the zodiac sign of Taurus.

The path of the Hierophant is vertical, and the word vav translates as "hook," "spear," or "pin." Recall that an essential meaning of the Hierophant is the formal teachings of spirituality and religious dogma. It is through outer ritual and teachings that we become hooked or attached to the Deity from the inside. The path rests on the masculine pillar of the Tree and is phallic in its nature, as has been the dogmatic nature of masculine-dominated religion.

The Lovers

Letter: Zayin ז
Path: 17
Connects Understanding to Beauty
Zodiac: Gemini ♊
Simple letter
Translation: Sword

The Lovers connects to the Hebrew letter Zayin. It highlights path number 17. This path connects Binah

(Understanding) and Tiferet (Beauty). Zayin is one of the 12 simple letters, and it represents the zodiac sign of Gemini.

The path of the Lovers is diagonal, stemming from Understanding on the feminine side of the Tree to its heart center, Beauty. The word zayin translates as "sword." An essential meaning of the Lovers is sensual and physical love. Love is the sword by which we define our life, relationships, and decisions on every level. Love's sword may be used for destruction or protection.

The Chariot

Letter: Het ח
Path: 18
Connects Understanding to Strength
Zodiac: Cancer ♋
Simple letter
Translation: Enclosure

The Chariot connects to the Hebrew letter Het. It highlights path number 18. This path connects Binah (Understanding) to Gevurah (Strength). Het is one of the simple letters and it represents the zodiac sign of Cancer.

The path of the Chariot mirrors the path of the Hierophant but on the opposite side. The ways in which opposites blend, merge, and come together are of great importance, and much can be learned by comparing and contrasting. The Chariot's path is vertical and runs on the feminine side of the Tree from Understanding to Strength. Het translates from Hebrew as "enclosure." Look at all the paths up to this point. With the Chariot's path, a roof with two walls has appeared on the Tree. An enclosure exists. An enclosure is the dwelling space of the soul, the protected area defined by "interior" and "exterior." The Chariot card is often depicted as an enclosed vehicle protecting the driver.

Strength

Letter: Tet ט
Path: 19
Connects Mercy to Strength
Zodiac: Leo ♌
Simple letter
Translation: Serpent

The Strength card connects to the Hebrew letter Tet. It highlights path number 19. This path connects Chesed (Mercy) and Gevurah (Strength). Tet is one of the 12 simple letters and represents the zodiac sign of Leo.

The path of Strength runs horizontally across the breastplate of the Tree like a load-bearing beam in the structure of a house. The word tet translates as "serpent." The metaphor and meaning are immediately obvious. Serpent is a dual symbol of both fear and strength, of life and death, of temptation and freedom. It is the ability to take personal power and do something with it. The path moves from the masculine and feminine pillars demonstrating stark contrast and the blending of opposite energies into a single unifying force and display of Strength.

The Hermit

Letter: Yod י
Path: 20
Connects Mercy to Beauty
Zodiac: Virgo ♍
Simple letter
Translation: Hand

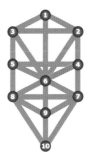

The Hermit card connects to the Hebrew letter Yod. It highlights path number 20. This path connects Chesed (Mercy) to Tiferet (Beauty). Yod is one of the 12 simple letters and represents the zodiac sign of Virgo.

The path of the Hermit runs diagonally from the masculine pillar to the Tree's heart center. The word yod translates as "hand." The hand and the Hermit reflect the work of man and the Deity. Consider the Sistine Chapel and Michelangelo's The Creation of Adam, where God sparks life in Adam by the touching of fingers. This path is the creativity, effort, and work of life. The Hebrew letter looks like a flickering flame, associated with the suit of Wands and the spark of life, commitment, and integrity.

The Wheel of Fortune

Letter: Kaph כ , ך
Path: 21
Connects Mercy to Victory
Planet: Jupiter ♃
Double letter
Translation: Palm

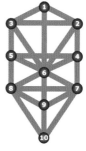

The Wheel of Fortune card connects to the Hebrew letter Kaph. It highlights path number 21. It joins Chesed (Mercy) and Netzach (Victory). Kaph is one of the seven double letters and connects to the planet Jupiter.

The Wheel of Fortune's path runs on the masculine side of the Tree vertically from Mercy to Victory. The word kaph means "palm." The palm is the sensitive and receptive part of the hand. It is the place where destiny is written on the body. The circular nature of the pictorial depiction of the Wheel of Fortune resounds with the palm of the hand.

Justice

Letter: Lamed ל
Path: 22
Connects Strength to Beauty
Zodiac: Libra ♎
Simple letter
Translation: Teach

The Justice card connects to the Hebrew letter Lamed. It highlights path number 22. It joins Gevurah (Strength) and

Tiferet (Beauty). Lamed is one of the 12 simple letters and connects to the zodiac sign of Libra.

The path of Justice moves on a diagonal from the feminine side of the Tree to the heart center. The word lamed translates as "ox goad," the stick used to prod animals while herding. This can also be understood as "to teach" or "discipline." This translation can be meditated upon in the context of the operations of the Justice card and its connections to work, fairness, and effort.

The Hanged Man

Letter: Mem מ , ם
Path: 23
Connects Strength to Splendor
Element: Water
Mother letter
Translation: Water

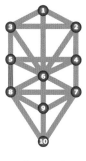

The Hanged Man card connects to the Hebrew letter Mem. It highlights path number 23. It joins Gevurah (Strength) and Hod (Splendor). Mem is one of the three mother letters and reflects the element of water.

The path of the Hanged Man is vertical and runs on the feminine side of the Tree. The word mem translates as "water." Examining the temporary nature of the suspended Hanged Man, we can make the correlation between this iconic symbol and the transformative nature of water, liquid, and the concept of flow.

Death

Letter: Nun נ , ן
Path: 24
Connects Beauty to Victory
Zodiac: Scorpio ♏
Simple letter
Translation: Fish

The Death card connects to the Hebrew letter Nun. It highlights path number 24. It joins Tiferet (Beauty) to Netzach (Victory). Nun is one of the 12 simple letters and represents the zodiac sign of Scorpio.

Death's path is the first path moving from the heart center of Beauty and extending down into the lower triad of the Tree. The word nun translates as "fish." The beauty of opposition is called into play when the life-giving nature of fish is coupled with the card reflecting Death.

Temperance

Letter: Samekh ס
Path: 25
Connects Beauty to Foundation
Zodiac: Sagittarius ♐
Simple letter
Translation: Prop

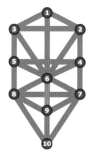 

The path of Temperance connects to the Hebrew letter Samekh. It highlights path number 25. It joins Tiferet (Beauty) and Yesod (Foundation). Samekh is one of the 12 simple letters and represents the zodiac sign of Sagittarius.

Temperance's path moves like a funnel directly down the lower spine of the Tree where it connects Beauty and Foundation. The word samekh translates as "prop" or "tent peg." Tents protecting against the elements must be fastened with the prop or tent peg. In this way, Samekh and Temperance are the way in which the individual is grounded and protected while reaching toward the divine. This idea of moving upward stems from the fact that tents are staked upward.

The Devil

The Devil card connects to the Hebrew letter Ayin. It highlights path number 26. It joins Tiferet (Beauty) to Hod (Splendor). Ayin is one of the 12 simple letters and represents the zodiac sign of Capricorn.

Letter: Ayin **ע**
Path: 26
Connects Beauty to
Splendor
Zodiac: Capricorn **♑**
Simple letter
Translation: Eye

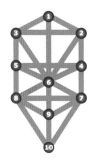

The Devil's path moves diagonally between the Tree's heart center and the feminine pillar The word ayin translates as "eye." The eye is where the individual receives the visual world. It is also where we look to see the nature of another person. Ayin has also been associated with the opening of the tip of the penis. All devilish implications may be inferred here.

The Tower

Letter: Peh **פ**, **ף**
Path: 27
Connects Victory to
Splendor
Planet: Mars **♂**
Double letter
Translation: Mouth

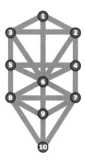

The Tower card connects to the Hebrew letter Peh. It highlights path number 27. It joins Netzach (Victory) to Hod (Splendor). Peh is one of the seven double letters and reflects the planet Mars.

The Tower's path runs horizontally across the lower triad of the Tree moving from Victory to Splendor. The word peh translates as "mouth." The symbol of mouth is rich as the place from which speech and expression spring forth. The mouth is used for breathing as well as for sustenance, drinking and eating food. The mouth is used for sexual and sensual pleasure. Tower-like power emulates from the choice and intention of the spoken word.

The Star

Letter: Tzade **צ** , **ץ**
Path: 28
Connects Victory to
Foundation
Zodiac: Aquarius ♒
Simple letter
Translation: Fishhook

The Star card connects to the Hebrew letter Tzade. It high-lights path number 28. It joins Netzach (Victory) to Yesod (Foundation). Tzade is one of the 12 simple letters and reflects the zodiac sign of Aquarius.

The Tarot cards marking the universe as seen from the earth reach toward the foundation of the Tree and the place where things become "real." The Star's path moves on a diagonal from the masculine pillar to the center. The word tzade translates as "fishhook." The path of the Death card connects to Nun, the Hebrew word for "fish." The path of the Star becomes the way of catching nourishment and life.

The Moon

Letter: Qoph **ק**
Path: 29
Connects Victory to Kingdom
Zodiac: Pisces ♓
Simple letter
Translation: Back of the
head

The Moon card connects to the Hebrew letter Qoph. It highlights path number 29. It joins Netzach (Victory) and Malkuth (Kingdom). Qoph is one of the 12 simple letters and represents the zodiac sign of Pisces.

The Moon's path shines on a diagonal from Victory to Kingdom, the place of the material world. The word qoph translates as "the back of the head." This can be placed in context with the Sun's path, Resh, meaning the "front of the head." The Moon's path connects to the place that is hidden from our own eyes. The image of a human being nears completion as the Tree is constructed.

The Sun

Letter: Resh ר
Path: 30
Connects Splendor to Foundation
Zodiac: The Sun ☉
Double letter
Translation: Face

The Sun card connects to the Hebrew letter Resh. It highlights path number 30. It joins Hod (Splendor) and Yesod (Foundation). Resh is a double letter and reflects its namesake, the Sun.

The Sun's path moves on a diagonal from the feminine pillar to Foundation, the spot where things are about to become manifest reality. The word resh translates as "face." The Sun brings us from the Moon, which reflected the back of the head, round to the front. The face is where we identify who someone is. Face is where we "face the world," feel the sun, and look to understand a person's intention.

Judgment

Letter: Shin ש
Path: 31
Connects Splendor to Kingdom
Elements: Fire and spirit
Mother letter
Translation: Tooth

The Judgment card connects to the Hebrew letter Shin. It highlights path number 31. It joins Hod (Splendor) and Malkuth (Kingdom). Shin is one of the three mother letters and reflects the elements of fire and spirit.

Judgment's path swings down from the lowest point on the feminine pillar and brings it home to Kingdom and the material world. The word shin translates as "tooth." Shin is considered to be the Holy Spirit.

The World

Letter: Tav ת
Path: 32
Connects Foundation to Kingdom
Element: Earth ⊕
Planet: Saturn ♄
Double letter
Translation: Mark

The World card connects to the Hebrew letter Tav. It highlights path number 32. This is the path between Yesod (Foundation) and Malkuth (Kingdom). Tav is one of the seven double letters and it reflects the element of earth and the planet Saturn.

The World's path is the final gateway straight into the world of the manifest, moving from Foundation to Kingdom. The word tav translates as "mark." The mark is made. Both the French and English schools of esoteric Kabbalah end with the World as Tav.

A traditional mechanical typewriter featuring Hebrew letters.

The Tetragrammaton and Tarot's Four Suits

The Tetragrammaton is a Hebrew name for God. It contains four Hebrew letters: Yod, He, Vav, He. If spoken aloud, the name is Yahweh or Jehovah. The Tetragrammaton contains four kabbalistic worlds, the four subtle bodies, the four parts of the soul, and last but not least, the four suits of Tarot. These four worlds or planes exist inside the Tree of Life and theoretically inside every human being.

Yod: Wands and the World of Atziluth

Archetypal world
Source of spiritual reality and impulse
Subtle body: Highest self
Soul part: Chayah (life force)
Element: Fire

To connect this esoteric theory to Tarot, imagine that each of the Wands cards (Ace through King) are set inside the

A modern computer keyboard, featuring Hebrew letters.

landscape of this kabbalistic world. In the simplest terms, the world of Atziluth can be understood as pure bliss. This is the home of the godhead or Deity. The Deity becomes aware of itself in this space. All primal, spiritual, physical urges blossom here. Yet it is a formless world, as elusive as a fire's flickering flames—observed, felt, yet unable to be held.

(first) He: Cups and the World of Beriah

Creative world
Source of relationship and meaning
Subtle body: Intuitive self
Soul part: Neshamah (spiritual awareness)
Element: Water

To connect this esoteric theory to Tarot, imagine that each of the Cups cards (Ace through King) are set inside the landscape of this kabbalistic world. In the simplest terms, the world of Beriah can be understood as the dreamy, angelic plane. This is the source of creative inspiration, where ideas spring forth. Angels exist here as agents of the Deity bringing messages and intuition to the worlds below. The landscape is as soft, transformative, and mutable as the ocean.

Vav: Swords and the World of Yetzirah

Formative world
Source of thought and structure
Subtle body: Mental self
Soul part: Ruach (intellect)
Element: Air

On the next page: Many different ways to express the name of God.

To connect this esoteric theory to Tarot, imagine that each of the Swords cards (Ace through King) are set inside the landscape of this kabbalistic world. In the simplest terms, the world of Yetzirah is the landscape of the mind. This is where ideas form and structures are put into place. This is the world of thought. The landscape is as exhilarating as the wind.

Material world
Source of matter and materialization
Subtle body: Physical self
Soul part: Nephesh (animal)
Element: Earth

To connect this esoteric theory to Tarot, imagine that each of the Pentacles cards (Ace through King) are set inside the landscape of this kabbalistic world. In the simplest terms, the world of Assiah is physical reality. The landscape of Assiah is everything you can see, feel, hear, touch, taste, and hold. The landscape is as real as your body.

Aces and Court Cards in the Kabbalah

Aces

Aces are called the spirit of each world's elemental attribute. Each Ace is the vitality and animation of its world. Each of the following cards live in that world.

- Ace of Wands is the Spirit of Fire.
- Ace of Cups is the Spirit of Water.
- Ace of Swords is the Spirit of Air.
- Ace of Pentacles is the Spirit of Earth.

Kabbalistic Court Card Names

The court cards are named like the Aces but differentiated with each court card's personality. This gives the Tarot reader more information on the nature of each court card and can be readily integrated.

- All Kings are fiery in nature and called Fire.
- All Queens are watery in nature and called Water.
- All Knights are airy in nature and called Air.
- All Pages are earthy in nature and called Earth.

The court card's nature is plugged into the element of each world. This creates its Kabbalistic name.

- King of Wands is Fire of Fire.
- Queen of Wands is Water of Fire.
- Knight of Wands is Air of Fire.
- Page of Wands is Earth of Fire.
- King of Cups is Fire of Water.
- Queen of Cups is Water of Water.
- Knight of Cups is Air of Water.
- Page of Cups is Earth of Water.
- King of Swords is Fire of Air.
- Queen of Swords is Water of Air.
- Knight of Swords is Air of Air.
- Page of Swords is Earth of Air.
- King of Pentacles is Fire of Earth.
- Queen of Pentacles is Water of Earth.
- Knight of Pentacles is Air of Earth.
- Page of Pentacles is Earth of Earth.

The Invisible Paths

What good would a secret esoteric system be without hidden paths? The following is a list of the invisible paths that correlate for the court cards.

- Knight of Wands connects 2 to 5 (path number 33).
- Queen of Wands connects 2 to 8 (path number 34).
- King of Wands connects 2 to 9 (path number 35).
- Page of Wands connects 2 to 10 (path number 36).
- Knight of Cups connects 3 to 4 (path number 37).
- Queen of Cups connects 3 to 7 (path number 38).
- King of Cups connects 3 to 9 (path number 39).
- Page of Cups connects 3 to 10 (path number 40).
- Knight of Swords connects 1 to 4 (path number 41).
- Queen of Swords connects 1 to 5 (path number 42).
- King of Swords connects 1 to 7 (path number 43).
- Page of Swords connects 1 to 8 (path number 44).
- Knight of Pentacles connects 4 to 9 (path number 45).
- Queen of Pentacles connects 4 to 10 (path number 46).
- King of Pentacles connects 5 to 9 (path number 47).
- Page of Pentacles connects 5 to 10 (path number 48).

ALCHEMY

Introduction

In this section, we will consider the correspondence between elements of alchemy and aspects of Tarot in both concept and practice. There is little direct association between the two subjects in their earlier history—although we can discern many overlaps and incidental reflections. Alchemy already had a long history prior to the first known versions of Tarot. However, in more recent years, there has been a direct placement and reading of alchemical symbolism in Tarot, from the early French occultists to contemporary decks such as the *Alchemical Tarot*.

We will also provide a reading list for those wishing to pursue the subject of alchemy more deeply, as there are many variations of alchemy, as with Tarot, and wide reading is to be recommended to the advanced Tarot reader. We will first sketch a brief outline of alchemy, regarding different aspects of the art and its relationship to symbolism, self-discovery and visionary experience—the main overlaps which we will then explore with Tarot.

Alchemy is the medieval version of modern chemistry.

A Brief Outline of Alchemy

In the monumental encyclopedia of Western esotericism, the *Dictionary of Gnosis and Western Esotericism* (Vol. 1), Alchemy is described foremost as "a subject of enormous intrinsic interest but one which has long proven difficult to grasp properly".[1] The authors identify four major problems in the treatment of alchemy: that there are many versions of alchemy, not just one; that a spiritual interpretation was applied to early alchemy, which was not demonstrable; that alchemy was a pseudo-science, when in fact, many scientists included it in their studies (notably, Isaac Newton); and that alchemy was different from chemistry, even though the terms were used interchangeably until the late 17th century.

When we look at studying alchemy, then, we should be most aware that there are many variations, in both approach and practice, and that the further back in history we go, it becomes increasingly difficult to discern what is physical and what is spiritual; what is alchemy and what is chemistry.

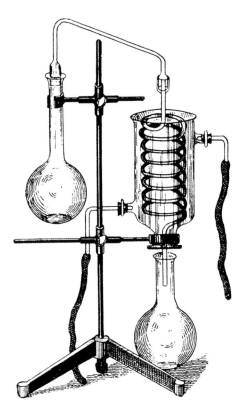

In ancient times, the tools used for alchemy and chemistry were the same. However, this is very different in modern times.

We do know that the first written evidence of alchemy in its commonly understood sense arises in the 3rd century A.D. in Greek and Egyptian writings such as the *Vision of Zosimos*.

The introduction of alchemy to the **Western** tradition can be dated to 11th February, 1144, when Robert of Chester's *Book of the Composition of Alchemy* was published. This book was part of a new current of free-thinkers, bringing Islamic thought to the West. As such, alchemy was already proving significant in cross-fertilising philosophies between East and West. Later, alchemy was also a publishing endeavour; more books on alchemy were published in England between 1650 and 1680 than before or afterwards.

Many such authors were monks, such as George Ripley, an Augustine canon. Western alchemy was often intertwined with Christian thought, comparing Christian doctrine to chemical processes. This began in the 14th century with Petrus Bonus[2] and continued throughout the 15th-17th centuries in the development of theosophical alchemy. It

61

was only in the Victorian resurgence of alchemical idealism that a wider "spiritual" gloss was applied to alchemy; pre-18th century alchemists were wedded to Christian doctrine far more intimately than the occult phase of interpretation discovers.

In alchemy, all things are considered in a state of evolution and transformation; everything is in an endless state of change from the basest of matter to the purest of metals. The seeds of the earth ultimately aspire to gold and even beyond, to the philosopher's stone. The stone is said to be capable of turning other metals into gold, and to heal, cure disease, and other miracles.

However, the basis of alchemy was chemical transformation. The word itself may likely come from the Greek word, *cheo*, meaning "to pour", as in the pouring of metals. It was only a later interpretation that suggested the word came from the word "Khem" (black) for Egypt. The earliest alchemists were chemists, metallurgists and physicians.

But the art was later also seen with a spiritual lens. Roger Bacon, writing in the 13th century, defined two forms of alchemy, the theoretical and the practical, both dealing in

Alchemy can be considered as a magical way to look at reality: everything in nature possesses hidden qualities and essences that can be transformed and refined to a higher, spiritual grade.

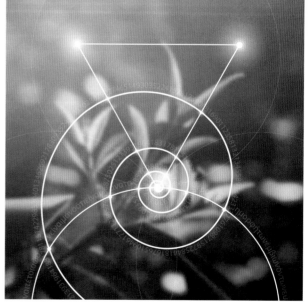

generation of products from the elements, but the latter more specifically which "teaches how to make... many other things better and more plentifully than they are made by nature."[3] Paracelsus wrote, "Alchemy is... to carry to its end something that has not yet been completed."[4]

In this concern, it was an example of a later philosophy which became known as *Naturphilosophie*, which in turn influenced C. G. Jung. In fact, an early author from this philosophy, Carl Gustav Carus, wrote his seminal book, *Psyche*, in 1846, which described the unconscious, ahead of Jung. The scholar Hanegraaf, quoting Coudert on alchemy, connects the practice of alchemy to Naturphilosophie and esotericism, but does question whether "spiritual" alchemy existed prior to the Renaissance.[5]

So, it is not just the spiritual realm to which alchemy significantly provides a bridge, but the psychological realm. Carus considered psychology as the science of the soul's development from the unconscious to the conscious, much as alchemy considers the development of matter. Jung wrote, "Alchemy, therefore, has performed for me the great and invaluable service of providing material in which my experience could find sufficient room."[6]

TYPES OF ALCHEMY

There are several ways of categorizing the types of alchemy that we encounter in our studies. Ponce suggests three *dialects*, or approaches to alchemy; psychological, mythological, and metaphysical, and we can also seek to examine the myth of the alchemist within the esoteric tradition, and its significance in the telling of the tradition itself.[7] As Norton wrote:

> *Also they wrote not every man to teach*
> *But to show themselves by secret speech.*
> *[...]*
> *Whereby each of his fellows were made certain:*
> *how that he was to them a brother,*
> *For every of them understood another.*[8]

In this extract we get a hint of a secret brotherhood, much like the Rosicrucians, whose manifestos included the "Chymical Wedding", one of the most significant allegorical tales of the initiatory system and significant in maintaining the myth of the Rosicrucians since its publication in 1616, following the *Fama* and *Confessio* manifestos in the prior years.

McLean suggests that this category of alchemical work embodies the Rosicrucianism that "is the esoteric philosophy lying at the heart of Western Hermeticism which provides a path for the balancing and integration of the masculine and feminine aspects of our souls, and the inner meeting of the lofty intellect with the primal earthy energies at the centre of our being".[9]

We can already see in this type of description that the metaphysical dimension of alchemy is illustrated in such Tarot cards as Temperance.

Alchemy also finds its correspondence in Kabbalah, prior to its inception into Tarot. By 1616, a degenerate form of Kabbalah as a generic term for elements of alchemy had surfaced, as evidenced by the appearance of such works as Steffan Michelspacher, *Cabala: Spiegel der Kunst und Natur*

On the previous page: a representation of psychological, mythological and metaphysical alchemy.

in Alchymia (Augsburg: David Frank, 1616). This alchemical work, which is often reprinted, draws primarily from Agrippa's conflated view of Kabbalah and magic. "The 'cabala' is referred to as mirror of Art and nature: in alchemy."[10]

However, Gershom Scholem in his essay "Alchemie und Kabbala,"[11] demonstrated that there was no genuine Hebrew alchemical-kabbalistic tradition in the Renaissance; before the 17th century, Jewish Kabbalists were hardly interested in the pursuit of alchemy (Hayyim Vital in Safed being one of the exceptions, and then only briefly) nor did the alchemical symbolism of gold as the purest metal find any correlative in Kabbalistic symbolism.

The golden age of alchemy was from the 15th to the 19th century.

It was the founders of the Golden Dawn who sought to bring alchemy into direct connection with Tarot, as we can see in this original paper by W. W. Westcott, one of the three S.R.I.A. (Societas Rosicruciana in Anglia) members who created the Order of the Golden Dawn in 1888. He categorized alchemy in four levels, according to the four worlds of Kabbalah:

- **Occult chemistry**
  Assiah

- **Psychic alchemy**
  Yetzirah

- **Mental alchemy**
  Briah

- **Spiritual alchemy**
  Atiziluth[12]

This type of correspondence between one system and another provides us the ability to map components across the different systems. When we make a correspondence between the attributes of occult chemistry as a level of alchemy and Assiah, the world of action in the Kabbalah, we can also make a mapping to the Pages of the Tarot court cards. This is because the court cards are also mapped to the Kabbalah, as follows:

- **Assiah**
  Pages (Princesses in the Golden Dawn and Thoth decks)

- **Yetzirah**
  Knights (Princes)

- **Briah**
  Queens (Queens)

- **Atziluth**
  Kings (Knights)

So "spiritual alchemy" would be the realm of the Kings of the court cards, and "mental" (or contemplative alchemy, the

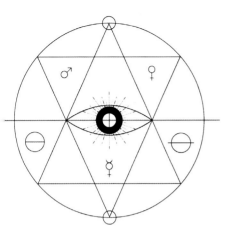

realm of the Queens. This is somewhat abstract, but we will also use this important approach of correspondences when we consider practical applications.

Alchemy is also built upon the fundamental notion of the four elements: earth, air, water and fire, which corresponds to the four suits of Tarot: Pentacles, Swords, Cups and Wands. In turn, these correspond to the four worlds of Kabbalah. These fundamental building blocks provide us a constant reminder that every map is of the same place. We will explore the four elements in a far more practical manner in our section on elemental dignities.

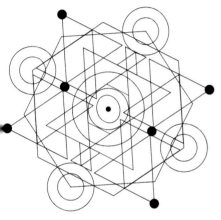

In summary, alchemy (in a variety of forms) can be seen to provide the esoteric tradition with the following tools, which can also be found in Tarot.

1 An allegorical language

2 A physical exemplar of hidden (occult) processes through mimesis

3 An interface to physical sciences and the scientific method

4 An interface to art

5 A mystical cosmology

6 A representation of the dynamic psyche

Similarly, both Tarot and alchemy share the same vision of a progressive evolution of the soul. As Gerry Gilchrist notes, "the Alchemist is described as the artist who, through his operations, brings nature to perfection."[13] In the case of Tarot, this follows the journey through the Major Arcana, as the Fool perfects himself in the World.

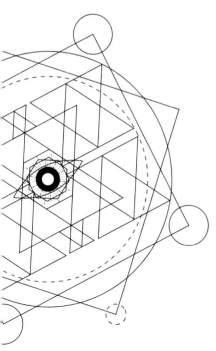

We will next present a brief piece of writing which has informed and inspired the alchemical and hermetic traditions since the 6th-8th centuries (and after its translation into Latin in the 12th century) before moving on to Tarot.

The Emerald Tablet

A foundation text of alchemical and hermetic thought is the Emerald Tablet. This short verse has several translations, this one is as used in the *Magister* (2016).

True, without falsehood, certain and most true, What is Below is like what is Above; and what is Above is like what is Below; for performing the miracles of the One Thing. And as all things were from the one, by the mediation of the one; so all things were born from this one thing by adaptation. Its Father is the Sun, its Mother is the Moon, the Wind carried it in its belly. Its Nurse is the Earth. It is the father of all the perfection of the whole world. Its power is Absolute. If it is turned into earth, you will separate the earth from the fire, the subtle from the gross, smoothly and with great cleverness. It ascends from earth into heaven, and again descends to earth, and receives the power of those things above and those below. In this way you will have the glory of the whole world!

Therefore all obscurity shall flee from you. It is the strong fortitude of all fortitude; because it will overcome every subtle thing and penetrate every solid. In this way the world was created. From it there will be wonderful adaptations, of which this is the method. And so I am called Hermes Trismegistus, having the three parts of the Philosophy of the whole world.

What I have said concerning the operation of the Sun is completed.[14]

We would suggest to the earnest Tarot practitioner who wishes to advance their contemplative work, that they should seek to consider which Major Tarot cards best illustrate the concepts in this verse, either individually or as a whole. This is not something that can be merely presented but rather, the work must be done by the person. As it is written, "by our work we are changed".

When you have selected the cards which correspond to the sections, verses or words, you can consider what connects the cards, what pattern they reveal, and perhaps, how they appear on the Tree of Life diagram. This type of work is an advanced form of Tarot which uses correspondences and contemplation in a form of re-arrangement, known as *Temura* or *Tzeruf*.[15]

The hidden symmetries of both alchemy and Kabbalah can often be found in nature, if one knows how to look.

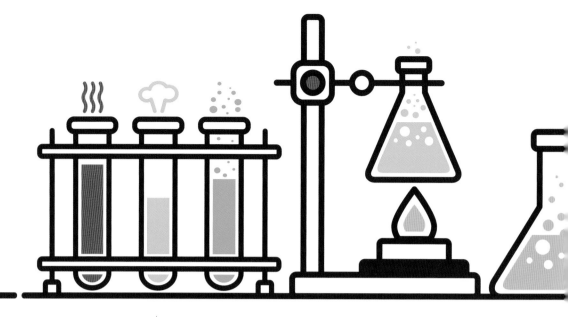

The Stages of Alchemy & The Fool's Journey

We have seen that alchemy regarded the universe in a constant state of evolutionary change—a change which could be hastened or provoked by the alchemist. This change was broken down into a sequence of explicit stages, each requiring success before the next stage could be attempted. The whole alchemical process was usually described as a sequence of seven, nine or twelve stages.[16] The list we provide here is from the alchemist George Ripley:

- **Calcination**
- **Solution**
- **Separation**
- **Conjunction**
- **Putrefaction**
- **Congelation**
- **Cibation**
- **Sublimation**
- **Fermentation**
- **Exaltation**
- **Multiplication**
- **Projection**

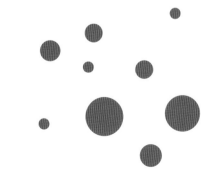

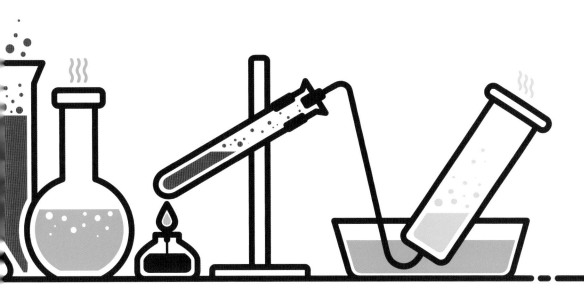

We can compare these stages perhaps to the procession of the Major Arcana cards, although we might wish to start the sequence from the World card (calcination) and return to the Magician (multiplication). These twelve stages might not directly fit the sequence as illustrated by the Tarot, but they can be grouped in generally similar sets, if we ascribe the first and final stage to one card and the intermediate stages to pairs of cards in sequence:

- Calcination: *World*
- Solution: *Judgement, Sun*
- Separation: *Moon, Star*
- Conjunction: *Tower, Devil*
- Putrefaction: *Temperance, Death*
- Congelation: *Hanged Man, Justice*
- Cibation: *Wheel, Hermit*
- Sublimation: *Strength, Chariot*
- Fermentation: *Hierophant, Emperor*
- Exaltation: *Empress, High Priestess*
- Multiplication: *Magician*

And that leaves us with the Fool as the final stage of Projection, which is a post-phase where the completed stone is used to project miracles into the world. The advanced student is encouraged to compare variations of the alchemical sequence to various arrangements of the Major Arcana.

We also take the stages to equate with stages of spiritual development or steps in the initiatory system of Western Esotericism. Whilst beyond the scope of this present book, let us look at the first two stages in this context.

The first two stages of alchemy according to Ripley are Calcination and Solution. The first is described as "the reduction of the matters used to a non-metallic condition" (usually by application of gentle, external, heat). In Richard Cavendish's interpretation of this process, he suggests:

> *Calcination probably stands for the purging fires of aspiration and self-discipline... The work begins with a burning discontent with oneself and one's life... Combined with a fierce determination to do better, the result is the disintegration of the natural self. The outer, surface aspects of the personality are burned away and what is left is the 'powder' of the inner man.*[17]

He also equates this process to the Tarot card of "The Day of Judgement," which is due to his use of an alternative alchemical sequence. Again, the reader is advised to explore different sets of correspondence which all provide alternative maps of the same landscape and a similar journey.

Alchemy, by its own nature, suggests a work in a linear sequence, where each process follows another in a specific order that cannot be changed.

ALCHEMY AND TAROT

Alchemy and Tarot as a Visionary State

It is not just in the illustration of a progressive and initiatory journey (of metals or the soul—or both) where there is a parallel between Tarot and alchemy. We also would suggest that many of the unique and specific qualities of alchemical illustration and writing are exactly those experienced in the hypnagogic state.[18] This is the state immediately prior to sleep where sometimes strange hallucinations or physical sensations can be experienced. One such specific quality of visions in this state is that spoken words are perceived as visual text, which is a situation often pictured in alchemical illustrations; often the words are spoken as a scroll emerging from the mouth of a character or animal. There are many similar conditions between the visionary state of alchemy and the hypnagogic state. In such, there is a parallel to the divinatory state of the Tarot reader when they access their specific oracular state.

Here is a poetic account given in the alchemical text *John Dastin's Dream*, published by Elias Ashmole (1652), which indicates the state in which the vision is received:

> *Not yet full sleping, nor yet full waking, But betweene twayne lying in a traunce;*
> *Halfe closed mine Eyne in my slumbering...* [19]

Most advanced Tarot readers will recognize this "in between state" which is similar to a "trance" as it is often where oracular messages are received beyond the cards themselves—yet entirely from the cards, when they have provoked this specific state.

Sometimes, either at the start of a lifetime of Tarot, or after many years, the reader can dream fluently in the language of Tarot. In this sense, too, we parallel the art of alchemy, dreaming of Tarot cards whose words flow as text, and strange repeating patterns or fractal loops.

Alchemy is like a visionary journey, full of symbolical meanings.

Alchemy and Tarot as a Guide

A further similarity between the practice of alchemy and Tarot as a long-time advanced work is the arising of a relationship between the practitioner and the spirit of the work. This is often sensed as a presence or guide—a personification of the whole of the work. This is also a key component of the hypnagogic state, further demonstrating the overlap between the two systems found in a particular state of consciousness.

The guide of alchemy was often embodied as Mercury or *Mercurious*, and sometimes appeared to challenge the alchemist or assist their ascent to a higher plane of understanding. This was sometimes depicted as a mountain—the same mountain of initiation found in hermetic lore and in the rituals of the Golden Dawn.

The guide of Tarot is often sensed as a spirit unique to a deck or to the Tarot as a whole. It guides our hands when we are shuffling, inspires us to certain words or messages, and has a unique character of its own. As with the alchemical guide, the Tarot guide is often mercurial, a trickster and one hell of a holy guru. There are also direct ways of contacting this guide which can be found in such works as the *Inner Guide Meditation* by Edwin Steinbrecher.[20]

One practitioner once dreamt they met the Fool as a mad jester at the top of a mountain, standing on the edge of a great chasm. The Fool said to them, "I say, I say, I say, what do you call two Kabbalists?" In the dream, the practitioner sighed and said by rote, "I don't know, what do you call two Kabbalists?" "Lost," answered the Fool.

Alchemy & Tarot as Gates

Both alchemical illustrations and Tarot cards may be used as gateways into which we can enter through active imagination. In contemplating the images, entering into them, and engaging with the landscapes, figures and processes which then open within the illustration, we make changes to our own inner landscape. As Adam McLean notes:

Alchemical emblems are not textual information encoded in symbols which can be precisely decrypted into a 'meaning', but they are instead dynamic gateways, before which we can stand and allow ourselves to enter into an inner dialogue with the imagery.[21]

There are several methods to enter a pictorial landscape, both by active imagination and by dream. In contemplating an image prior to sleep for several nights in a row, you may discover yourself within that image during a dream.

To enter a landscape by active imagination, practice visualizing the image for several minutes, by viewing it, closing your eyes and trying to recall as many details as possible. Open your eyes, compare your visualization to the real Tarot card or alchemical illustration, and then repeat this several times. When you have a reasonable internal image, place it upon a doorway or imagine it as a curtain or veil. Enter through that gateway or through the veil into whatever landscape awaits you on the other side.

If you have difficulties with this method, there are many online classes in improving your visualization or you can purchase an Inner Guide Meditation Workbook which sets your own astrological birth-chart into Tarot cards and provides instructions for the IGM technique.[22]

Waite-Smith

The Waite-Smith Tarot contains several explicit and implicit allusions to alchemy, particular in the Major Arcana. However, we also see likely alchemical (rather than merely hermetic) symbols in the Minor cards, such as the Two of Cups, where the head of lion arises between the wings of a caduceus wand. We have also proposed elsewhere that the Seven of Cups attempts an illustration of the seven stages of alchemy according to Michael Maier.[23]

A. E. Waite wrote a great deal on alchemy, translating and publishing substantial material, namely in 1893, twenty-two pieces originally compiled in 1678 in Latin, as *The Hermetic*

Museum. His earlier views were of a middle path between considering alchemy as a practical experimental art and as a "psycho-chemistry". However, after a hiatus of some three decades of not writing on alchemy, his 1926 *The Secret Tradition in Alchemy* took a surprising turn and stripped the subject of all mystical intent.

So, his first "delightful experiment" with Tarot includes a few hints of alchemy but there is little to be found ten years later in his second Tarot set, the *Waite-Trinick Tarot* which focused more on the mystical path of the heart and its unification to the divine through the *Shekinah.*[24]

Those hints include the Magician as an obvious mercurial figure, demonstrating the Emerald Tablet dictum of "as above, so below". The cubic stone of the Charioteer is both the box-like chariot found in the Italian procession of the *Triumphi* and the *prima materia* of the alchemists. Alchemical symbols are also to be located on the Wheel of Fortune card, following Éliphas Lévi.[25]

The Thoth Tarot

A second deck to be recommended for alchemical study is the *Thoth Tarot* by Aleister Crowley and Lady Frieda Harris.[26] However, here we see alchemy considered by Crowley as sexual symbolism—albeit that sexuality itself is also seen symbolic of initiatory work.

There are explicit references to alchemy throughout the deck, none more obvious than in the retitling of Temperance to Art, and the alchemical symbolism of that card. In fact, here Crowley has taken one of two alternative depictions of the card straight from the Golden Dawn—whereas Waite, several years earlier, had taken the other version from the Order.

The sexual chemistry of existence is built into the structure of the Thoth Tarot. We see this most clearly in the little-referenced "Appendix B" of the *Book of Thoth*. In Appendix B, a section on "Vital Triads", Crowley splits the Major Arcana into sets of three, assigned to his own cosmology.

The Adjustment card (Justice), for example, falls in the triad equated to "the woman, justified", and is symbolic of "the sexually joined". It is in this group with the Chariot, "the grail, the chariot of life", and Art (Temperance), "The Pregnant Womb preserving life".

The Liber T Tarot, by Roberto Negrini with artwork by Andrea Serio is a modern rendition of the Thoth Tarot.

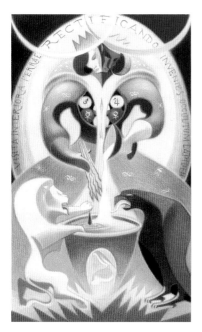

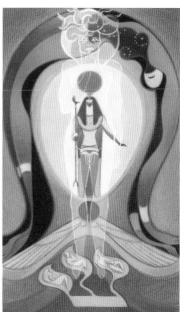

When we are aware of these alchemical patterns, structures and processes within the design of the deck, we can apply them to practical readings. We can see this triad of cards as three stages of pregnancy; the Chariot is the protective but (as yet) empty womb; the Art (Temperance) card is the preserving womb as the embryo develops (in the alchemical crucible) and the Adjustment (Justice) card is the sexual act that creates this new life. So, when these cards show up in a reading they can indicate the progress of any creative act, whether it be an actual birth, or a new project, relationship, lifestyle, etc.

It is worth exploring the "vital triads" to see how Crowley saw the patterns of creation, energy and the alchemical myths of all life—they underpin at the most profound level any aspect of everyday life. In knowing the deepest patterns, we can work up to illuminate even the most apparently mundane of questions. If someone is asking about whether they should change their job, this is entirely connected to their values, experience and sense of identity; their relationship to the entire universe. As it is said, "as above, so below".

The Emperor, from the Liber T Tarot. Artwork by Andrea Serio. Detail.

The Fool, from the Liber T Tarot.
Artwork by Andrea Serio. Detail.

Other Alchemical Decks

The most purely alchemical deck is the simply titled *Alchemical Tarot* by Robert M. Place. It is now in its fourth edition. The companion book for the deck is listed in our further reading section here and is essential reading for comparing alchemy and Tarot.

Although the various Golden Dawn decks have alchemical symbolism, we would recommend the *Golden Dawn Temple Tarot* deck by Nick Farrell, with art by Harry and Nicola Wendrich, for color symbolism alone, and the *Hermetic Tarot* by Godfrey Dowson for a black and white version of Golden Dawn symbolism.

The book *Tarot ReVisioned* (2003) by Leigh McCloskey has a deep alchemical aesthetic and is ideal for meditation and contemplation. The foreword is written by Stanislas Klossowski de Rola, whose work *The Golden Game* is an essential collation of alchemical images for the student.

ALCHEMICAL SPREADS

It is perhaps too basic a construct to include in this advanced book, but we can take any aspect of alchemical symbolism and illustration to produce a Tarot spread. We could place our cards out in a caduceus shape to read several distinct positions for how to elevate a situation from the mundane to the mystical. We could lay out our cards in a circle to represent the *Ouroboros*, the alchemical snake eating its own tail—and then lay three cards in the center to show how to escape that cycle in our lives by transforming the energy of the situation.

As in any spread, the shape to place the cards draws from the power of symbols.

Number of Cards: 7
Cards Used: Major and Minor Arcana
Time: 15 minutes
Objective: An alchemical vision of the future
Layout: Two lines of three cards and a seventh cards above them

We could lay out three cards to represent the Sulphur, Mercury and Salt of a situation; the Soul, Spirit and Body as a triad. A seven-card reading would correspond to the seven metals and their corresponding planets, in a progressive manner:

1. **Lead**: What is at the base of the situation, the primal nature of it.
2. **Mercury**: What is most able to be changed.
3. **Tin**: What it will cost.
4. **Iron**: What will be most challenging.
5. **Copper**: What can be rescued.
6. **Silver**: What this reflects outside of the situation throughout life.
7. **Gold**: The best possible outcome.

We leave the advanced reader to explore alchemy in more detail and generate their own alchemical spreads with a reading list and further recommendations for study.

Notes

1. Wouter J. Hanegraaf (ed.), *Dictionary of Gnosis & Western Esotericism*, 2 vols. (Boston: Brill, 2005), Vol. 1, p. 12.

2. Herwig Buntz, "Alchemy III: 12th/13th–15th Century," in Hanegraaf, *Dictionary of Gnosis & Western Esotericism*, Vol. 1, p. 36.

3. Quoted in William R. Newman, *Promethean Ambitions* (Chicago: University of Chicago Press, 2004), p. 117, which also discusses the tensions inherent in the "Neoplatonizing Aristotelianism of medieval and early modern natural philosophy."

4. Paracelsus, "De Natura Rerum" (1537) I/11, in Karl Sudhoff and Wilhelm Matthiessen (eds.), *Paracelsus, Samtliche Werke* (Munich: O. W. Barth, 1922–25), pp. 348–349, quoted in Jolande Jacobi (ed.), *Paracelsus: Selected Writings* (New Jersey: Princetown University Press, 1979), pp. 141–143.

5. Wouter J. Hanegraaff, *New Age Religion and Western Culture* (Leiden: Brill, 1996), pp. 395–395. This chapter also contains useful reference sources for the historical argument.

6. Edward F. Edinger, *Anatomy of the Psyche: Alchemical Symbolism in Psychotherapy* (Illinois: Open Court Press, 1994), p. 2. This is quoted from C. W. Jung, but Edinger's book gives a clearer depiction of the stages of alchemy corresponding to the individuation process, and hence, to some degree, the initiation system of the esoteric tradition.

7. C. Ponce, *Alchemy: Papers Toward a Radical Metaphysics* (Berkeley: North Atlantic Books, 1983).

8. Quoted in C. Henrich, *Strange Fruit* (London: Bloomsbury, 1995), p. 40. Originally in Thomas Norton, *Theatrum Chemicum Britannicum*, ed. Elias Ashmole.

9. G. Knight and A. McLean, *Commentary on the Chymical Wedding of Christian Rosenkreutz*, (Edinburgh: Magnum Opus Hermetic Sourceworks, 1984), p. 110.

10. Steffan Michelspacher, "Cabala" (1616) in Stanislas K. de Rola, *The Golden Game: Alchemical Engravings of the Seventeenth Century* (London: Thames & Hudson, 1988) p. 52 (text), pp. 54–55 (images).

11. Eranos Jahrbuch (46) 1977, pp. 1–96.

12. Notes on alchemy by N.O.M. [Non Omnis Moriar, William Wynn Westcott], Yorke Collection NS32.

13. C. Gilchrist, *The Elements of Alchemy* (Dorset: Element, 1998), p. 7.

14. New translation provided courtesy of Dr. Peter Forshaw, the Center for the History of Hermetic Philosophy and Related Currents, University of Amsterdam.

15. See A. Kaplan, *Meditation and the Kabbalah* (Boston: Weiser, 1982), p. 135.

16. F. S. Taylor, *The Alchemists* (London: The Scientific Book Club, [n.d.]), p. 142.

17. R. Cavendish, *The Black Arts* (London: Pan Books, 1967) p. 180–197. This book is titled for sensational value only, and the chapter on "The Making of the Stone" remains one of the few practical interpretations of alchemical processes in the context of the initiatory process in publication. However, there is now a more recent analysis, from a Jungian point of view, Edinger's *Anatomy of the Psyche.*

18. M. Katz, The Magister, Vol. 0 (Keswick: Forge Press, 2016).

19. J. Dastin, "Dastin's Dream." See www.alchemywebsite.com/tcbdastn.html.

20. Edwin Steinbrecher, *The Inner Guide Meditation* (Wellingborough: Aquarian Press, 1982).

21. A, McLean, *The Western Mandala* (Hermetic Research Series: Edinburgh, 1983). Also refer to McLean, *Study Course on Alchemical Symbolism*, available in print from www.alchemywebsite.com.

22. See IGM Workbook at www.lynbirkbeck.com and "Improve Your Visualisation" class at www.magickaschool.com.

23. M. Katz and T. Goodwin, *Secrets of the Waite-Smith Tarot* (Woodbury: Llewellyn Publications, 2015), pp. 271–272.

24. M. Katz and T. Goodwin, *Abiding in the Sanctuary: The Waite-Trinick Tarot* (Keswick: Forge Press, 2011.

25. See R. Place, *Tarot and Alchemy* (Saugerties: Hermes Publications, 2011) pp. 82–85.

26. M. Katz, *Secrets of the Thoth Tarot* (Keswick: Forge Press, 2017).

ASTROLOGY

Traditional and Modern Astrology

An 18th century writer on Tarot and the occult, Antoine Court de Gébelin, spread the romantic theory of Tarot's connection to ancient Egypt all over Paris when he began publishing. His theories of Tarot's Egyptian origin were eventually disproved. Yet, a remarkable divinatory system does date back to ancient Egypt, and even to Mesopotamia, Greece, and China. It is astrology. The astrological system fits perfectly over the framework of Tarot.

Astrology is one of the oldest forms of divination. It forecasts earthly and human events by interpreting and observing the motion of the sun, moon, planets, and fixed stars. Astrology posits that human personality and fate are foretold by examining the exact location of astral bodies at the time of birth. A natal star chart or astrological chart is like a snapshot of the sky. It recreates an exact picture of the solar system at the moment of an individual's birth.

The Dendera Temple, in Egypt, is decorated with many astrological notations and hieroglyphs.

For ages, there was no difference between astrology and astronomy. In modern times, however, the disciplines are utterly separated.

Astrology columns became ingrained in popular culture back in the 1930s when Britain's Sunday Express newspaper created the first regular astrology column. The column, hoping to appeal to a wide variety of readership, used the 12 familiar star or sun zodiac signs to make general predictions. Astrology caught on like wildfire on both sides of the Atlantic. Astrological Tarot associations foster new understanding and encourage fresh divinatory techniques for the cartomancer. Astrology offers deeper meaning and new lenses with which to internalize and understand Tarot cards. Astrology is ideal for those who want to offer predictive and precise timing and dates with Tarot. Astrology's nature is so vast that everything on earth can be placed in an astrological context. Everything aspected by a particular astrological sign, planet, or house may also be associated with the Tarot card associated with that particular sign, planet, or house.

Traditional vs. Modern Astrology

The differences between traditional and modern astrology are akin to the differences between traditional and modern Tarot. Traditional astrology is a combination of the multiple astrological schools from its ancient inception. Modern astrology is astrology practiced from the 19th century forward. The conflicting ways in which the systems are used also reflect how humanity has changed and evolved.

Predictive vs. Self-Directed

The greatest evolution between tradition and modern astrology (and an evolution holding true for Tarot usage as well) is that traditional and older schools use astrological systems in a predictive manner. Astrological readings, omens, and charts interpreted the fate of a person or society. Modern astrology makes use of self-direction, free will, and the idea that one has a direct impact on one's future. Modern ideas put forth the notion that an individual can look to the stars to garner personal information and understanding, then act accordingly. It posits that a person's destiny is not set in stone by the stars.

Astrology distanced itself from predictive "readings" in the same way Tarot did.

This evolution has much to do with the way we live our lives. In ancient times, individuals were likely to remain in the station to which they were born. If you were born a peasant, chances were you remained a peasant. This still holds true today in many developing countries and third-world countries. Yet, in the Western world it is possible for an individual to transcend the situation they are born into and reach toward any goal they choose. Women are no longer married off as assets or considered property but are now equal citizens worthy of human rights. This self-determination is reflected in our modern divinatory systems.

Separate Entity vs. You

The 12 houses of astrology are the sections or regions of human life, cut up like pieces of a pie. They reflect things like appearance, finance, and marriage. Traditional astrology views houses as entities completely separate from the individual. The houses are examined to see if they are well aspected—if they are "good" or "bad." Modern astrology differs. It posits that the houses reflect an individual's relationship with each house's subject. For example, the 7th house, which is the marriage house, would reflect the individual's perception of marriage and relationships. The house does not exist independently of the individual. It is like looking at flickering red candle on a table. Traditional astrology would examine that candle by itself. Modern astrology would examine the individual's relationship to the candle, considering thoughts, feelings, and preferences. Once again, the difference between external circumstances and the psychological state are apparent.

Good and Bad Planets vs. Holistic View

Traditional astrology assigned the qualities of good or bad, or even evil, to planets and houses. Modern astrologers have changed and challenged the idea of bad or evil aspects by calling them "energy." Sometimes, the modern view changed the house altogether. Modern usage changes the 6th house from "Disease, Slaves, and Pets" to "Health." This same evolution has occurred within Tarot. Many older Tarot books will reference "evil" cards. Most modern cartomancers will adamantly state there are no evil cards.

TAROT ASSOCIATIONS

Papus vs. Mathers

Tarot's astrological associations tend to be influenced by two esoteric schools. The French school was influenced by Papus (Gérard Anaclet Vincent Encausse) and the English school by Samuel Liddell MacGregor Mathers. Multiple varieties of Tarot decks have been created with alternative ways of understanding Tarot and astrology.

Gérard Anaclet Vincent Encausse on the left and Samuel Liddell MacGregor Mathers on the right.

On the previous page, an astrolo-ger/astronomer watches the stars in a 19th century print.

The first astrology-inspired Tarot deck dates back to the late 18th century when the French astrologer and fortuneteller Etteilla published a deck of cards he called The Book of Thoth. Etteilla was an astrologer as well as a card reader and saw a natural link between the two systems. This link was further explored by Papus, who wrote the famous Tarot treatise *Le Tarot des Bohémiens* or "Tarot of the Gypsies" in Paris in 1889. In England, the Hermetic Order of the Golden Dawn produced a text called the *Liber T* or *Book T* by co-founder Mathers in 1887.

Mathers places the Fool as the leading card of the Major Arcana. The English school switches the placement of Strength and Justice. The *Book T* system was the basis for Arthur Edward Waite's Rider-Waite-Smith Tarot (1910), Paul Foster Case's *The Tarot: A Key to the Wisdom of the Ages* (1947) and Aleister Crowley's *The Book of Thoth* (1944).

Post-War Astrological Decks

The first post-war astrology deck was the Zolar Tarot (1964), published by US Games in 1984 as Zolar's Astrological Tarot. This deck was produced by Robert Donald Papon, a student of the famous American astrologer Bruce King (1900–1976), aka Zolar. This deck was strongly influenced by the Rider-Waite-Smith deck and very difficult to link to the astrological associations. The Celestial Tarot (US Games, 2004), painted by Kay Steventon, designed by Brian Clark, put distance between the traditional images of the Arcana and the zodiac. This deck featured the zodiac, planets, and decans rather than Tarot archetypes. The deck is further supplemented with astrological and kabbalistic symbols. The deck is limited from a structural point of view without the innovations of Mathers's English school. The Initiatory Tarot of the Golden Dawn deck (Lo Scarabeo, 2008), designed by Giordano Berti and painted by Patrizio Evangelisti, embraces all aspects of the Golden Dawn.

Between Tradition and Modernity

The charm of ancient astrology is still alive in modern works. A perfect example is the Elemental Tarot (1988, reissued by St. Martins Press in 2001), by Caroline Smith and John Astrop, which displays a modern Art Deco style. Here, we find an author who deftly blends astrological myths of the Greeks, Egyptians, and Babylonians to create a complex system of 78 Tarot cards. The cards are recognizable even though the names are completely changed.

The Tarot of Cleopatra (Lo Scarabeo, 2006) is painted by Silvana Alasia and designed by Etta Stoico, who refer to the origins of Western astrology in their deck. The Minor Arcana

In modern times, the use of computers and even phone apps has made astrological calculations much easier.

On the previous page: the Hanged Man of the Initiatory Tarot of the Golden Dawn. Detail. Artwork by Patrizio Evangelisti.

are inspired by the spirits of each month and the Egyptian gods who oversaw each decan. The images depicted on the reliefs of the Temple of Dendera dating back to the 1st century BCE are also included. The Zodiac Tarot by Lee Bursten and Luca Raimondo (Lo Scarabeo, 2007) is one of the most complex astrological decks yet simple to use. This deck fits into the English school but suggests associations between Tarot secrets and astrology.

Alternatives to the French and English Schools

Authors in the 20th century have sought to build a personal system of attributions that is inclusive of both Papus and Mathers. Among these, the famous French astrologer Georges Muchery (1892–1981) published an important book, *Le Tarot Astrologique*, in 1927. Tarot is not mentioned directly within the pages of the volume, other than in the title, but there are 16 tables including 78 illustrations depicting the planets, their zodiacal signs, and different aspects. A work by Muchery entitled *La Synthèse du Tarot* devotes many pages to the relationship between Tarot and astrology. Stressing the importance of the number 12 in the Tarot (the sum of the numbers 1 through 12 is 78: 1+2+3+4+5+6+7+8+9+10+11+12 = 78), Muchery includes a diagram that outlines the associations between the 78 cards and the 12 zodiac signs. This interesting relationship between Tarot and astrology offered a modern twist to readers.

Reading the Astrological Chart

To understand Tarot's astrological associations it is important to understand the diagram explaining the geometrical and mathematical movement of the zodiac. The zodiac is the belt of the heavens around the earth where we find the paths of the sun, moon, and principal planets. It contains 12 constellations, and therefore there are 12 divisions or signs of the zodiac.

An Example of an Astrological Chart

Symbolic Chart of You

The astrological chart may look like a nautical map or compass at first glance. The chart pinpoints the exact location of the stars and planets at the moment of your birth. Use the chart to navigate uncharted waters, glean insight and locate true north in any situation.

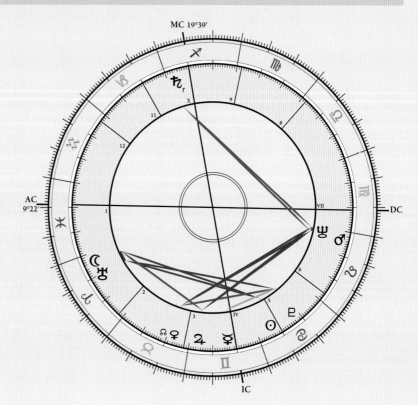

Cardinal, Fixed, and Mutable Signs

The astrological chart is a circle containing 360 degrees. The degrees are divided up into the 12 zodiac signs, like equal slices of a pie. Each of the four seasons of the year—spring, summer, autumn, winter—contain three signs each. Each astrological sign contains 30 degrees of the zodiac circle.

Cardinal Signs

The beginning of the circle is marked by Aries and indicates the spring equinox. It is simple to understand why spring was chosen to start the zodiac when recalling that spring is the season of rebirth. Directly across the pie from the spring equinox, at 180 degrees, lies the autumn equinox. The autumn equinox is heralded by the beginning of Libra.

A diagram showing the four cardinal signs: Aries, Libra, Cancer and Capricorn.

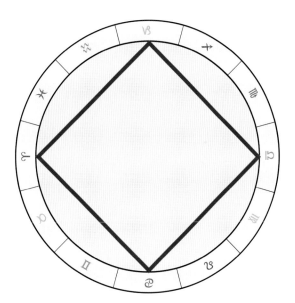

Aries and Libra are referred to as cardinal signs. These two cardinal signs are called this because they are the "hinges" upon which the solar year rotates. Can you guess what the other two cardinal signs are associated with? If you assumed they are the signs that begin at summer solstice (Cancer at 90 degrees) and winter solstice (Capricorn at 270 degrees), you are correct.

The stars were faithful companions of humanity and navigation, since the beginning of history.

To remember that cardinal sign energy represents that which is fresh, new, original thinking, like a burst of fresh air, think of the cardinal bird. Birds burst with song at the beginning of each day just as the cardinal signs begin each season.

Fixed Signs

A fixed sign follows the fresh cardinal energy, sandwiched between the cardinal and mutable signs. The fixed sign in spring is Taurus, while its opposite, the fixed sign of autumn, is Scorpio. Fixed is the energetic center of the season. The fixed sign of summer is Leo, and the fixed sign of winter is Aquarius. Fixed energy is the least likely to change and stays true to its name, intense and unwavering.

A diagram showing the four fixed signs: Taurus, Scorpio, Leo and Aquarius.

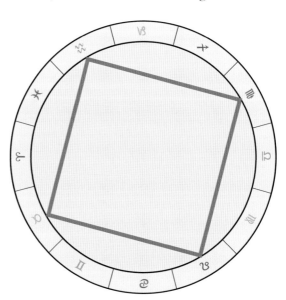

Mutable Signs

Mutable signs are like bookends marking the end of a season. Gemini ends spring, Virgo ends summer, Sagittarius ends autumn, and Pisces ends winter. Mutable energy is bendy, as its name suggests. It is flexible and likely to change.

A diagram showing the four mutable signs: Gemini, Virgo, Sagittarius and Pisces.

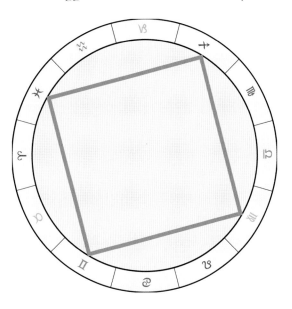

Decans

A simple diagram showing the relative position of the planets in the solar system. Planets of both classical and modern astrology can be seen.

On the astrological chart, you will always have a cardinal sign followed by a fixed sign and then a mutable sign, followed by cardinal, fixed, and mutable. The sequence keeps revolving like a wheel. Each individual sign is then divided into three intervals of 10 degrees each, which are called decans.

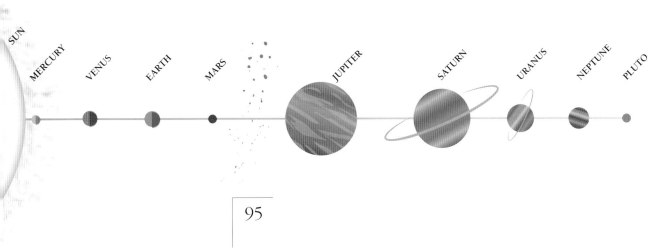

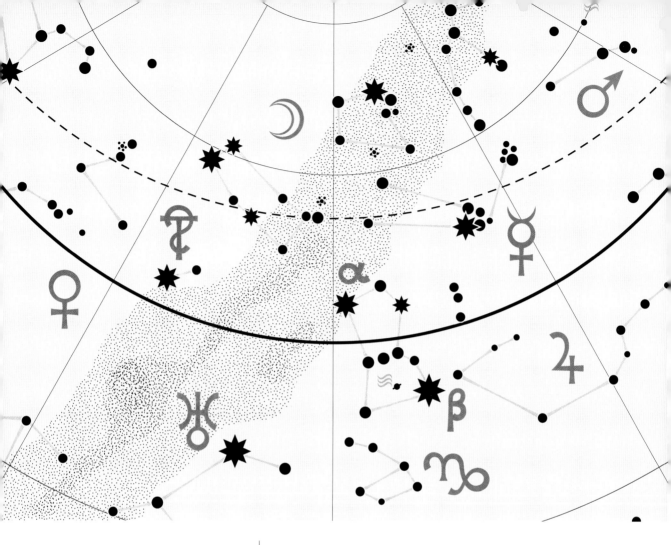

Character and Temperament

The zodiac signs are defined according to their "character," which is either male or female. Their "temperament" is directly related to the four elements. Masculine signs are associated with Fire (Wands) and Air (Swords). These masculine signs tend to be expansive and extroverted. Standing in contrast are the feminine signs of Earth (Pentacles) and Water (Cups), which tend to be receptive and introverted. Use the classic symbolism of the suit to recall their meaning. Swords and Wands are pointed, phallic, and extroverted, while the feminine suits of Cups and Pentacles are soft and receptive like containers.

Triplicities: Fire, Air, Earth, and Water

Each element corresponds with three signs; this is called the triplicity of the element.

The triplicity of Fire is Aries, Leo, and Sagittarius. Aries is a Fire force which is either creative or destructive. The Fire of Leo is an energy that is inexhaustible. The Fire of Sagittarius is like a burning ember surviving all weather conditions, staying alight, burning eternally.

FIRE

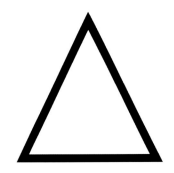

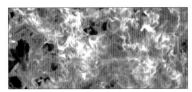

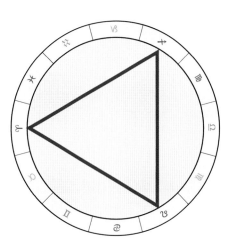

The triplicity of Air is Gemini, Libra, and Aquarius. Gemini is the Air of emotion, like a refreshing breeze that clears away fleeting negativity. The Air of Libra is the crisp refreshing autumn wind that lets us know something marvelous is soon to arrive. The Air of Aquarius is the silent, still air of white winter.

AIR

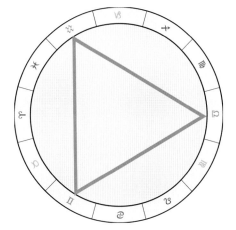

EARTH

The triplicity of Earth is Taurus, Virgo, and Capricorn. The Earth of Taurus is warm, open, and fertile like the tilled fields of spring. The Earth of Virgo is hot and productive, springing forth the flowers and vegetables of summer. The Earth of Capricorn is cold and frozen yet it preserves precious items, goods, and ideas.

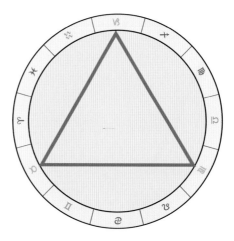

WATER

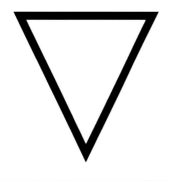

The triplicity of Water is Cancer, Scorpio, and Pisces. Cancer is the thoughtful, placid Water of a still pond. Scorpio is the churning, cloudy, dark and deep ocean Waters. The Water of Pisces is akin to streams of ideas, fantasies, and fancies, impossible to ever stop or slow.

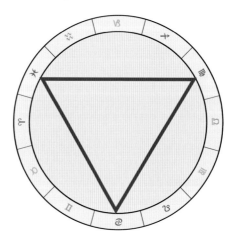

Astrological Symbols

To use astrology one must recognize its vocabulary of symbols.

Signs

♈	♉	♊	♋	♌	♍
Aries	Taurus	Gemini	Cancer	Leo	Virgo

♎	♏	♐	♑	♒	♓
Libra	Scorpio	Sagittarius	Capricorn	Aquarius	Pisces

Planets

☉	☽	☿	♀	♂
Sun	Moon	Mercury	Venus	Mars

♃	♄	♅	♆	♇
Jupiter	Saturn	Uranus	Neptune	Pluto

Elements

△	△	▽	▽
Fire	**Air**	**Earth**	**Water**

Astrology and the Body Parts

Traditionally, each astrological sign is connected to a specific part of the human body.

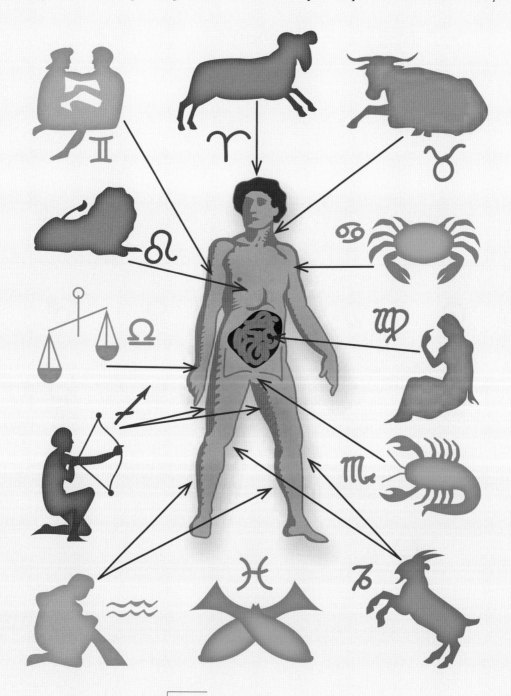

TAROT AND THE 12 ASTROLOGICAL SIGNS

The 12 signs of the zodiac and their associated Tarot cards deepen the cartomancer's practice. In addition to the signs, the 12 cards reflect the 12 astrological houses which can be integrated into the meaning of each card. Along with the house, days of the week, colors, flowers, metals, elements, ruling planets, and all their various aspects may be applied.

ARIES
THE EMPEROR

Aries is Latin for "the ram." Rams and/or horns are often ingrained into the imagery of various Emperor cards. Aries is the sign of bravery, laser-like focus, and confidence. Aries reflects the pioneering spirit. Honest and passionate, Aries displays leadership qualities. American President Thomas Jefferson, financier J.P. Morgan, and author Maya Angelou exemplify Aries qualities and were all born under the sign. Consider how these personalities integrate with the Emperor card.

Day: **Tuesday**

Color: **Red**

Flower: **Honeysuckle**
Metal: **Iron**
Quality: **Cardinal**

Element: **Fire**

Ruling Planet: **Mars**

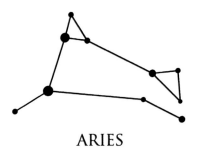

ARIES

Aries influences the 1st house of the self. According to Renaissance astrology, "It hath signification of the life of man, of the stature, color, complexion, form and shape of him." Look here to discover information regarding the physical body and outward traits. It also reflects who an individual is presently and who they will become in the future as well as the house of early childhood. How do an individual's outward projection and the nature of their juvenile influences contribute to your understanding of the Emperor card?

TAURUS
THE HIEROPHANT

Taurus comes from the Greek tauros which means " bull" or "steer." The symbol of Taurus can be found on various Hierophant cards. Dependable and stable qualities define the sign of Taurus. Taurus reflects a methodical and dedicated spirit. Consider the intersection of Taurus's qualities along with the Hierophant's meanings of tradition, order, and ritual. Taurus is also considered the most sensual sign of the zodiac and one who takes full command of the five senses. Pope John Paul II, William Shakespeare, and Sigmund Freud were all born under the sign. Consider how these personalities integrate with the Hierophant card.

Day: **Friday**

Color: **Earth tones**

Flower: **Poppy**
Metal: **Copper**
Quality: **Fixed**

Element: **Earth**

Ruling Planet: **Venus**

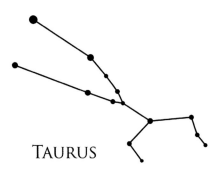

TAURUS

Taurus rules the 2nd house of money and possessions. According to Renaissance astrology, this house, "Is required judgment concerning the estate or fortune of him, his wealth or poverty, of all removable goods, money lent, profit or gains, loss or damage, it signifies a man's friends or assistants, in private duels." This house reflects what an individual values, the place from which their self-worth and self-value stem. It reflects what someone owns and how they choose to spend their money. How do an individual's possessions and financial structure contribute to your understanding of the Hierophant card?

GEMINI
THE LOVERS

Gemini is from the Latin word for "twins." Gemini twins represent the yin and yang of life and all it encompasses. A man and woman are almost always shown in the Lovers card, representing opposites who come together. Geminis are fiercely intellectual, playful, and curious. Gemini reflects an adaptable and imaginative spirit, delightful and flirtatious. Marilyn Monroe, Josephine Baker, and Harriet Beecher Stowe were all born under this sign. Consider how these personalities integrate with the Lovers card.

Day: **Wednesday**

Color: **Yellow**

Flower: **Lavender**
Metal: **Quicksilver**
Quality: **Fixed**

Element: **Air**

Ruling Planet: **Mercury**

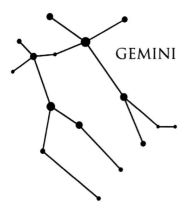

GEMINI

Gemini rules the 3rd house of communication, siblings, and elementary education. According to Renaissance astrology, this house "hath signification of brethren, sisters, cousins, kindred, neighbors, small journeys, or inland-journeys, oft removing from one place to another, epistles, letters, rumors, messengers." The manner in which individuals express themselves, the nature of brother and sister relationships, and early learning are found here. Expression is a verbal form of intercourse. How does an individual's relationship to communion and partnership contribute to your understanding of the Lovers card?

CANCER
THE CHARIOT

Cancer is the Latin word for "crab." The crab is a crustacean who lives under an exoskeleton in and near water. The Charioteer is often depicted inside a protective chariot. Cancers are considered moody and emotional as their watery nature would suggest. They tend to be sensitive and intuitive, which are traits closely linked to the element of Water. Malala Yousafzai, Frida Kahlo, and Helen Keller were all born under this sign. Consider how these personalities integrate with the Chariot card.

Day: **Monday**

Color: **Violet**

Flower: **Larkspur**
Metal: **Silver**
Quality: **Fixed**

Element: **Water**

Ruling Planet: **Moon**

CANCER

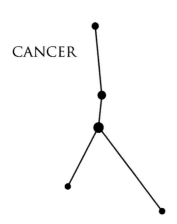

The 4th house of the zodiac reflects home life, family, and nurturing influences. According to Renaissance astrology, it is "of lands, houses, tenements, inheritances, tillage of the earth, treasures hidden, the determination or end of anything; towns, cities or castles, besieged or not besieged; all ancient dwellings, gardens, fields, pastures, orchards; the quality and nature of the grounds one purchases, whether vineyards, cornfield, whether the ground be woody, stony or barren." This is the place where one's family relationships are considered. How much influence does a family have on the ability of the individual to evolve? How do an individual's relationship with their family and the way in which they were nurtured and nurture others contribute to your understanding of the Chariot card?

LEO
STRENGTH

Leo comes from the Latin word for "lion." The archetype of lion has been associated with strength, agility, and royalty since the dawn of man. Creatures of such great power appear supernatural. Additionally, they contain the qualities of the cat, including stealth, cunning, cleverness, and elegance. Qualities of Leo include great determination and bravery in the face of all obstacles. Leo is the epitome of the energetic spirit. The fierce and charismatic Julia Child, Madonna, and Carl Jung were all born under the sign of Leo. Consider how these personalities integrate with the Strength card.

Day: **Sunday**

Color: **Orange**

Flower: **Sunflower**
Metal: **Gold**
Quality: **Fixed**

Element: **Fire**

Ruling Planet: **Sun**

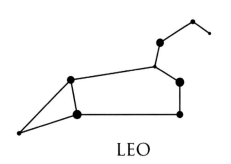

LEO

Leo influences the 5th house of pleasure and creativity. According to Renaissance astrology, "By this house we judge of children, of ambassadors, of the state of a woman with child, of banquets, of ale-houses, taverns, plays, of the wealth of the father, if the woman with child shall bring forth male or female." Ancient man used creativity to thrive and survive amidst many dangers. How does the creative spirit manifest in a modern world where everything is specialized, where others make our food, craft our clothing, build our houses, and teach our children? What is our relationship to pleasure? How do an individual's intrinsic level of satisfaction and the nature of creative expression contribute to your understanding of the Strength card?

VIRGO
THE HERMIT

Virgo comes from the Latin word for "virgin." Historically, the word virgin meant a woman who was not married and therefore not owned by any man. The archetype of the Hermit also implies a person (often depicted as male) who sequesters himself, avoiding all human contact in order to concentrate on spiritual pursuits. Virgo traits include deep loyalty and aching kindness. They possess a hardworking and practical spirit. The profound Mother Teresa, Greta Garbo, and Agatha Christie were all born under the sign of Virgo. Consider how these personalities integrate with the Hermit card.

Day: **Wednesday**

Color: **Dark blue**

Flower: **Narcissus**
Metal: **Quicksilver**
Quality: **Mutable**

Element: **Earth**

Ruling Planet: **Mercury**

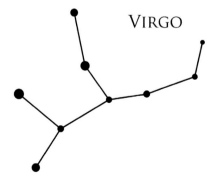

VIRGO

The 6th house of health is influenced by Virgo. According to Renaissance astrology, "It concerneth men and mid-servants, gallislaves, hogs, sheep, goats, hares, connies, all manner of lesser cattle, and profit and loss got thereby. Sickness, its quality and cause, principal humor offending, curable or not curable, whether the disease be short or long, day laborers, tenants, farmers, shepherds, and hogherds." This house has transformed since its birth in classical astrology, when people owned slaves, cattle, hogs, and sheep. However, it is still a way to examine the health of the house or all things connected to an individual. How do an individual's physical state and surroundings contribute to your understanding of the Hermit card?

LIBRA
JUSTICE

Libra derives from the Latin word for "balance." Scales represent the tension between two opposing forces. The sign of Libra comes at the season of autumn, and the figure can be understood as balancing light and darkness or day and night. Scales are the classic symbol of governmental justice. The qualities of Libra include an outgoing, social, and dynamic personality. The enigmatic John Lennon, Jesse Jackson, and Julie Andrews were all born under the sign of Libra. Consider how these personalities integrate with the Justice card. Harmony and peace are hallmarks of the Libra spirit.

Day: **Friday**

Color: **Indigo blue**

Flower: **Rose**
Metal: **Copper**
Quality: **Cardinal**

Element: **Air**

Ruling Planet: **Venus**

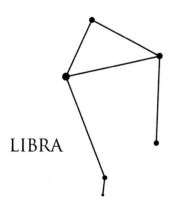

LIBRA

The 7th house rules partnerships and is influenced by Libra. According to Renaissance astrology, "It giveth judgment of marriage, and describes the person inquired after whether it be man or woman, all manner of love questions, our public enemies, all quarrels, duels, law-suits, thieves and thefts, the person stealing, whether man or woman, wives, sweethearts, their shape, description, condition." This house focuses on how you give to and take from another. How do interpersonal relationships and the tension of partnership contribute to your understanding of the Justice card?

SCORPIO
DEATH

Scorpio is Latin for "scorpion" and translates as the "creature with burning sting." The scorpion archetype bears ancient roots. The oldest arachnid fossil is a scorpion. It is the quintessential symbol of transformation, negotiating darkness in their burrows and hunting under night's darkness. Scorpio is legendary for its secretiveness and seduction. Resourceful and brave, Pablo Picasso, Martin Scorsese, and Theodore Roosevelt were all born under this sign. Consider how these personalities integrate with the Death card.

Day: **Tuesday**

Color: **Deep red**

Flower: **Chrysanthemum**
Metal: **Steel**
Quality: **Fixed**

Element: **Water**

Ruling Planet:
Pluto and Mars

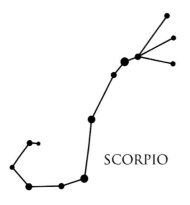

SCORPIO

The 8th house rules sex and death and is influenced by Scorpio. According to Renaissance astrology, "The estate of men deceased, death, its quality and nature; the wills, legacies and testaments of men deceased, dowry of the wife, portion of the maid, whether much or little, easy to be obtained or with difficulty. What kind of death a man shall die, it signifies fear and anguish of the mind. Who shall enjoy or be heir to deceased." This is the place of endings and beginnings, the cycles of human life, and the nature of human sexuality. How do an individual's sexual nature and relationship to deep transformation contribute to your understanding of the Death card?

SAGITTARIUS
TEMPERANCE

Sagittarius comes from the Latin for "archer" and "arrow." The archetype of the archer from early hunting man to the modern concept of a heart struck by love's arrow reminds us of the hunting magic inherent in this symbol. Sagittarians are considered curious and energetic. They embody the adventurous spirit. Innovative Ludwig van Beethoven, Winston Churchill, and Walt Disney were all born under the sign. Consider how these personalities integrate with the Temperance card.

Day: **Thursday**

Color: **Purple**

Flower: **Dandelion**
Metal: **Tin**
Quality: **Mutable**

Element: **Fire**

Ruling Planet: **Jupiter**

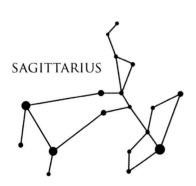

SAGITTARIUS

The 9th house, representing higher education, philosophy, and travel, is influenced by Sagittarius. According to Renaissance astrology, "By this house we give judgment of voyages or long journeys beyond … dreams, vision, foreign countries, of books, learning, church livings, or benefices." This is the place to examine an individual's dreams and aspirations. It is also the integration of what is learned and expressed at higher levels. How do an individual's personal philosophy and relationship to the world contribute to your understanding of the Temperance card?

CAPRICORN
THE DEVIL

Capricorn is from the Latin *capri cornus*, meaning "goat horns." Goats are known to be feisty, temperamental, and independent creatures. These qualities all apply to Capricorn, who are known as determined and ambitious. J.R.R. Tolkien, Richard Nixon, and Joan of Arc were all born under the sign. The ancient Greeks associated sexual virility and potency to the goat in the form of the god Pan. The Judeo-Christian West turned the goat into a devil-like figure, creating a cloven-footed, bearded, horned man who is associated with sexual lust and black magic. This wicked figure is seen or implied on many a Devil Tarot card.

Day: **Saturday**

Color:
Dark green and blue

Flower: **Carnation**
Metal: **Lead**
Quality: **Cardinal**

Element: **Earth**

Ruling Planet: **Saturn**

CAPRICORN

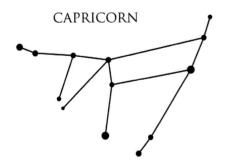

The 10th house reflects career and social status and is influenced by Capricorn. According to Renaissance astrology, "Commonly it personateth kings, princes, dukes, eagles, judges, prime officers, commanders in chief, whether in armies or towns, all sorts of magistracy and officers in authority, mothers, honour, preferment, dignity, office, lawyers, the profession or trade anyone useth." This house reflects the role we choose, how we inhabit it, and how our ego is massaged by others. It is also the house of the father figure. How do all of these relationships contribute to your understanding of the Devil card?

AQUARIUS
THE STAR

Aquarius is a Latin adjective like aquarium meaning "pertaining to water." Aquarius means "water carrier." The Star card almost always shows a person pouring water or next to a body of water. The sign of Aquarius is known for qualities of truth and imagination. Affection and intelligence shine through the Aquarius spirit. Revolutionaries Virginia Woolf, Rosa Parks, and Abraham Lincoln were all born under the sign. Consider how these personalities integrate with the Star card.

Day: **Wednesday**

Color: **Sky blue**

Flower: **Orchid**
Metal: **Uranium**
Quality: **Fixed**

Element: **Air**

Ruling Planet:
Uranus and Saturn

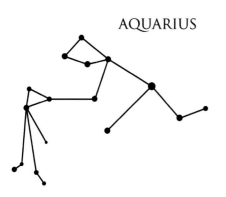

AQUARIUS

The 11th house of social groups, causes, and technology is influenced by Aquarius. According to Renaissance astrology, "It doth naturally represent friends and friendship, hope, trust, confidence, the praise or dispraise of anyone, the fidelity or flatness of friends." This is the house that reflects an individual's tribal sense and the ideas that bind people together. How do an individual's intimate relationships and peer group contribute to your understanding of the Star card?

PISCES
THE MOON

Pisces is from the Latin word for "fish." The Moon card often depicts a water creature emerging from a dark pool to greet the moon's rays. Imaginative and creative are words often used to describe Pisces. Pisces reflects a spiritual and transformative soul. Nurturing and intuitive Edgar Cayce, Auguste Renoir, and Elizabeth Taylor were all born under the sign. Consider how these personalities integrate with the Moon card.

Day: **Friday**

Element: **Water**

Color: **Lavender**

Flower: **Violet**
Metal: **Platinum**
Quality: **Mutable**

Ruling Planet:
Neptune and Jupiter

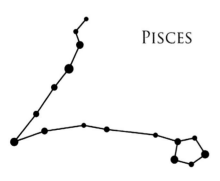

PISCES

The 12th house of secrets and desires is influenced by Pisces. According to Renaissance astrology, "It hath signification of private enemies, of witches, great cattle, as horses, oxen, elephants. Sorrow, tribulation, imprisonments, all manner of affliction, self-undoing and of such men as maliciously undermine their neighbors or inform secretly against them." How do an individual's shadow self, deepest nature, and hidden world contribute to your understanding of the Moon card?

TAROT AND THE 10 CELESTIAL BODIES

Celestial bodies are connected with Tarot's Major Arcana, sometimes with astonishing accuracy. Take note that early traditional astronomy could only make use of the visible planets in the night sky. Later, as technology blossomed, it was possible to see farther into the galaxy. This was when the planets Uranus, Neptune, and Pluto were discovered and integrated into modern astrology and assigned to the cards.

SUN
THE SUN

The sun is life. It is the center of the solar system. The sun is the sustaining force of the physical world as we know it. Sun symbolism is found in everything from golden royal crowns to fruit juice cartons. Solar rays are seen as containing the magical properties of life, birth, and possibility. Ancient rituals celebrated the return of the sun each year as the days grew longer. The sun is the star that makes all life possible.

The Sun, in astrology, reflects the ego and the self. The sun is the center of the solar system just as we are the center of our own lives. People and events revolve around us like a mini solar system. This is why the astrological Sun represents the will to live and the creative forces at play in an individual's life.

It is a safe bet that almost every Sun Tarot card has an image of the sun on it. How does the astrological meaning of the Sun deepen or transform your understanding of the traditional meanings of the Sun card as birth, health, growth, and expansion?

Classical Planet

Rules:
Leo (Strength)

Associated:
Heart and spine

Element:
Fire

SUN

MOON
THE HIGH PRIESTESS

The moon is the closest celestial body to our earth. It is the nocturnal reflector of the sun's light. The Sun and Moon are often paired together in astrology. The Moon reflects the shadow self, dreams, and nighttime visions. The moon controls the tides of the oceans.

The Moon, in astrology, is used to examine the depths of an individual's psychology. The Moon reflects personal habits that correspond to the moon's own cyclical habits of waxing, growing full, waning, and becoming dark. The Moon indicates unconscious needs which exert a gravitational pull in an individual's life toward the things that they most desire.

The High Priestess card is ruled by the Moon. She is often depicted with moon imagery and is often drawn close to water. How does the astrological meaning of the Moon apply to or transform your understanding of the High Priestess's traditional meanings of wisdom, self-knowledge, and truth?

Classical Planet

Rules:
Cancer (Chariot)

Associated:
Breasts, womb, stomach, and womb

Element:
Water

MOON

MERCURY
THE MAGICIAN

Mercury is the planet of communication. It is the winged messenger of the gods and sometimes portrayed as a trickster. Mercury's energy infuses everything it touches. It keeps things moving. Mercury represents the mind and how an individual perceives their life story.

Mercury acts as the messenger in astrology, ruling daily interpersonal correspondences. This includes writing, speech, media, emails, and contracts. Communication aspects of Mercury are perceived to go awry during a Mercury Retrograde when the planet appears to reverse its path across the sky. The Magician card is associated with Mercury. The Magician is seen as an agent of change and one who imposes his free will. How does the astrological meaning of Mercury apply to or transform your understanding of the Magician card's traditional meanings of mastery, charisma, and showmanship?

Classical Planet

Rules: **Gemini (Lovers) and Virgo (Hermit)**

Associated: **Brain, nervous system, sensory organs**

Element: **Air**

MERCURY

VENUS
THE EMPRESS

Venus is known as the evening star due to its brilliance in the night sky. It is the planet of love, romance, and harmony. It relates to shared pleasure, how pleasure to offered, and how it is received. Physical delights and all aspects of beauty connect to Venus.

Venus rules over love and money in astrology. Professional Tarot readers often state that love and finance are the two most popular topics of their readings and the top two reasons querents visit them.

The Empress card is associated with Venus. Venus symbols are found decorating this card in various decks. How does the astrological meaning of Venus enhance or transform your understanding of the Empress's traditional meanings of creativity, motherhood, and femininity?

Classical Planet

Rules:
**Taurus (Hierophant)
and Libra (Justice)**
Associated:
Throat

Element:
Earth

VENUS

MARS
THE TOWER

Fiery planet Mars is named after the Roman god of war. Mars, "the red planet," has inspired fascination and speculation as long as eyes have gazed upon it.

Mars in astrology is assigned all the attributes of the color red including passion and self-assertion. Animal nature and survival are key elements to this planet. Cartomancers familiar with the fiery aspects of the suit of Wands might look at Mars as a Wand planet full of explosive energy. Action and desire radiate from this fourth planet from the sun.

The Tower card is associated with Mars. How does the astrological meaning of Mars enhance or transform your understanding of the Tower card whose traditional meanings include upheaval, destruction, and explosion?

Classical Planet

Rules:
Aries (Emperor)
Associated:
Blood

Element:
Fire

MARS

JUPITER
THE WHEEL OF FORTUNE

Jupiter is named after the Roman king of the gods. It is the largest planet in the solar system, more than twice as big as all of the other planets combined. The ancients, interestingly, had no idea how large the planet was when they assigned the name and meaning to it.

Jupiter's role is astrology is one of expansion and high purpose. The planet signifies good luck, growth, and higher learning. Jupiter can be seen in opposition or in tandem with the planet Saturn which offers the oppositional force of boundaries.

Jupiter is associated with the Wheel of Fortune card. How does the astrological association of Jupiter enhance or deepen your understanding of the Wheel of Fortune, whose traditional meanings signify a change of luck for the better, revolution, and fate?

♃	Rules: **Sagittarius (Temperance)**	Element: **Fire**
Classical Planet	Associated: **Hips and thighs**	

JUPITER

THE UNIVERSE / EL UNIVERSO — **XXI** ♅ — L'UNIVERSO / L'UNIVERS

DAS UNIVERSUM — UNIVERSUM

Saturn
The World

Saturn is often called the "jewel of the solar system" due to its thousands of gorgeous rings which are made of ice and rock. It is named after the Roman god of agriculture. Saturn in astrology can be seen in opposition to Jupiter. Where Jupiter reflects expansion, Saturn brings restrictions and boundaries. Metaphorically, the two planets hold each other in check or balance each other like the Temperance card balances energies. Rather than looking at Saturn's restrictions as negative, recall that boundaries are required in life. They keep things from spinning out of control. One can also examine this from an artistic standpoint. An artist experiments, blurts, writes, rehearses, and plays with a variety of creative options. This is very Jupiter-like. Once the artist discovers what works and what doesn't, Saturn energy is brought in through editing, refinement, and finishing touches. This is how the two energies work in tandem.

Classical Planet

Rules:
Capricorn (Devil)
Associated:
Bones and skin

Element:
Earth

SATURN

URANUS
THE FOOL

Uranus is named for the Greek god of the heavens, Ouranos, and was discovered in 1781.

Astrologically, Uranus rules rebellion and revolution. Originality and individuality are its hallmarks and it loves to break with tradition. Uranus is a massive energy which provokes daring inventions and new technological breakthroughs.

The Fool is associated with Uranus. How does the astrological association of Uranus enhance or deepen your understanding of the Fool, whose traditional meanings include freedom, thinking outside the box, and potential?

Modern Planet

Rules:
Aquarius (Star)

Associated:
Lower legs, ankles, and circulatory system

Element:
Air

URANUS

NEPTUNE
THE HANGED MAN

Neptune is a watery planet with 14 known moons. It was discovered in 1846 and named for the Roman god of the sea. Astrologically, Neptune rules the dreamy aspects of the element of water. It contains illusion, inspiration, abstraction, and spirituality in its most sensual sense.

The Hanged Man is associated with Neptune. How does the astrological association of Neptune enhance or deepen your understanding of the Hanged Man, whose traditional meanings include enlightenment, a pause or limbo, and sacrifice?

Modern Planet

Rules:
Pisces (Moon)
Associated:
Illness and neuroses

Element:
Water

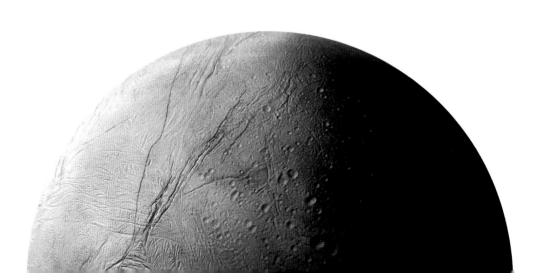

NEPTUNE

PLUTO
JUDGMENT

Scientists may have revoked Pluto's planetary status but that doesn't deter astrologers. They still count on this celestial body who rides on the far reaches of our solar system. It was discovered in 1930 and named after the Greek god Pluto, who rules the Underworld. Pluto takes about 248 years to complete its orbit around the sun.

Pluto rules the subconscious in astrology. Renewal and rebirth are all aspected by this transformative planet. This means that Pluto is the place of deep energetic reserves and surprising resources that make all transformations possible. It is a subtle yet wildly powerful planet.

The Judgment card is associated with Pluto. How does the astrological association of Pluto enhance or alter your understanding of Judgment's traditional meaning as the point of evolution and irreversible internal change before the glory of the World card is invoked?

♇

Modern Planet
Celestial Body

Rules:
Scorpio (Death)

Associated:
**Sex, death,
inheritance**

Element:
Fire

PLUTO

ACES AND ASTROLOGY

Aces are the root of the energy of an element. That energy is ready to connect with astrology.
In the following pages, the aces are taken from the Initiatory Tarot of the Golden Dawn, from the Liber T Tarot and from the Lo Scarabeo Tarot.

Tarot's four suits are based on the four elements: Fire, Earth, Air, and Water. Astrology also makes use of the four elements.
The Aces in astrology are the birthplace, the explosion of the element, just as they are the root or seed of the suit in Tarot.

Fire sign qualities: Passionate, daring, and driven

Ace of Wands is the Root of Fire

The Ace of Wands connects to the Root of Fire. The Ace of Wands is the seed of Fire and the explosion of the sustaining and destructive expansion of the element of Fire. It is the color of human blood. The warmth in human bones on cold winter nights. The instinct pointing us toward the things we want before we know we want them. It is the rush of animal attraction and stirrings of sexuality. It is the nerves in your belly when standing up for something you believe in. Everything that an individual feels passion, fire, and love for is found in Fire and the suit of Wands.

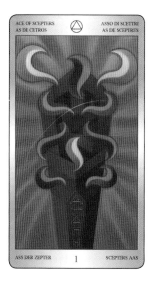

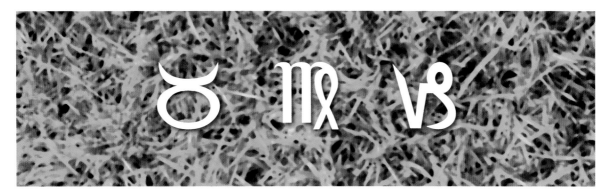

Earth sign qualities: Practical, hardworking, and logical

Ace of Pentacles is the Root of Earth

The Ace of Pentacles connects to the Root of Earth. The Ace of Pentacles is the seed containing everything that is manifested in the material reality of what an individual considers the concrete world. Bodies, houses, mud, dirt, mountains, furniture, cars, people, friends, family, foes, forests, books, computers, animals, cities, towns, and entire continents. Everything an individual can touch, taste, see, and feel is found in Earth and the suit of Pentacles.

Air sign qualities: Logical, witty, and independent

Ace of Swords is the Root of Air

The Ace of Swords connects to the Root of Air. The Ace of Swords is the seed that contains everything manifested in the world of thought, calculation, and mental acuity. The Root of Air contains the words spoken to other people and the narrative constructed inside an individual's head. Events play out in life, we decide what they mean or we react, all due to the element of Air. Communication forms here: letters, speeches, emails, and books. Everything the individual thinks and expresses is found in Air and the suit of Swords.

Water sign qualities: Emotional, empathetic, and artistic.

Ace of Cups is the Root of Water

The Ace of Cups connects to the Root of Water. The Ace of Cups is the seed that contains every feeling and emotion that a human can feel. The Root of Water is the transformative place of the human imagination and holds our capacity to dream, vision, and empathize. It is where we feel love and connection, anger and sadness, hope and joy, despair and boredom. Every emotional response is felt through the lens of Water and the suit of Cups.

TRIPLICITIES AND DECANS

◦— **Triplicities** are the three astrological signs assigned to each element.

◦— **Decans** are the 10-degree pieces of the astrological chart connecting to each Minor Arcana card.

◦— **Planetary subrulers** are the planets chosen by the Golden Dawn to rule the Minor Arcana. These planets are from an ancient form of astrology called the Chaldean order of planets, and this system fits seamlessly into the structure of Tarot.

◦— **Golden Dawn titles** are a way to remember the planetary subruler chosen for each card. Take note that these titles would have a profound impact on the pictures drawn to illustrate the decks springing from the Golden Dawn's members.

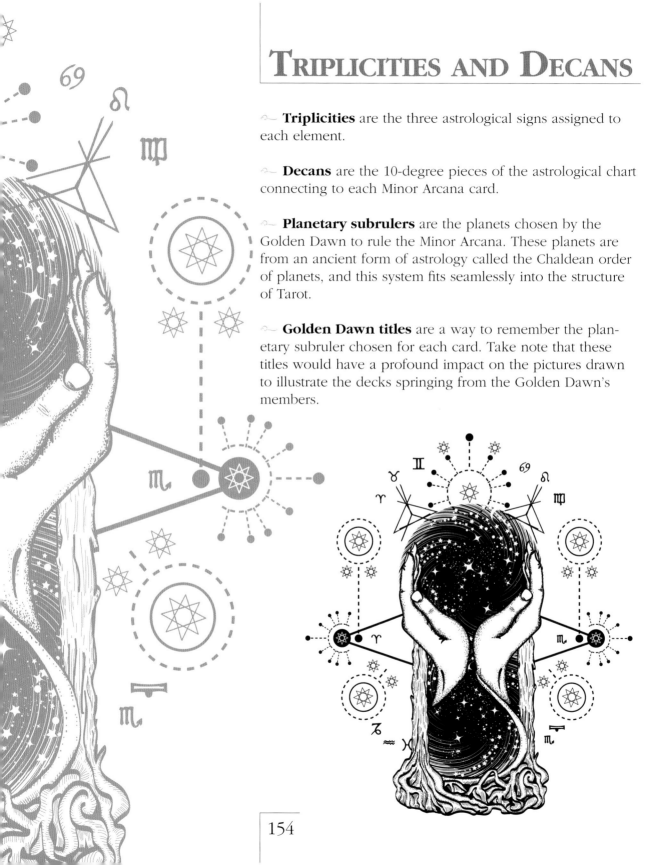

Aries

Explosion of Fire
(Cardinal Fire)

- **Two of Wands**
- **Mars in Aries**
- **Lord of Dominion**

Aggressive Mars meets assertive Aries, and the Lord of Dominion is born. To dominate is to take control, exercise influence, and make oneself and one's intentions clear. This card is often illustrated with an individual who is seen plotting and planning an enterprise.

- **Three of Wands**
- **Sun in Aries**
- **Lord of Established Strength**

The explosive and nuclear energy of the Sun meets independent Aries, and the Lord of Established Strength is born. Established strength reflects an individual who has already proved himself or herself worthy and powerful. This theme is often seen in the Three of Wands where a wealthy merchant sets his ships out into the world or conversely, is waiting for his ships to return with his riches.

- **Four of Wands**
- **Venus in Aries**
- **Lord of Perfected Work**

Beautiful Venus meets successful Aries, and the Lord of Perfected Work is born. There is inherent symmetry, beauty, and charm in any form of work done to the best of an individual's ability. The theme of perfected work is often seen in the Four of Wands in the construction of four Wands brought together in a celebratory canopy or chuppah.

155

Slow and Steady Wins the Race
(Fixed Earth)

- **Five of Pentacles**
- **Mercury in Taurus**
- **Lord of Material Trouble**

Perceptive Mercury meets stubborn Taurus, and the Lord of Material Trouble is born. Who and what we resist has a tendency to persist. The Five of Pentacles often portrays people who are fraught with peril or challenge.

- **Six of Pentacles**
- **Moon in Taurus**
- **Lord of Material Success**

The intuitive Moon meets pleasure-seeking Taurus, and the Lord of Material Success is born. How does intuition foster advancement? How does pleasure serve us in our professional lives? Images of charity are often found on this card.

- **Seven of Pentacles**
- **Saturn in Taurus**
- **Lord of Success Unfulfilled**

Restrictive Saturn meets down-to-earth Taurus, and the Lord of Success Unfulfilled is born. How do boundaries restrict us? Being grounded and focused can sometimes distract us from seeing the big picture. The Seven of Pentacles often shows a successful individual who desires more.

Rapidly Changing
(Mutable Air)

- **Eight of Swords**
- **Jupiter in Gemini**
- **Lord of Shortened Force**

Expansive Jupiter meets dynamic Gemini, and the Lord of Shortened Force is born. The electrifying energy radiating through this card means that it takes minimum effort for maximum effect. This card is often illustrated with an individual who is blindfolded and bound.

- **Nine of Swords**
- **Mars in Gemini**
- **Lord of Despair and Cruelty**

Powerful Mars meets mischievous Gemini, and the Lord of Despair and Cruelty is born. Omnipotent forces mingle with transgression, and the results are oftentimes disastrous, however fleeting. This card is often illustrated with late night mental suffering.

- **Ten of Swords**
- **Sun in Gemini**
- **Lord of Ruin**

The explosive Sun meets double-sided Gemini, and the Lord of Ruin is born. Duplicity often blows up when light is shone on it. This card is often illustrated with an individual who has been killed or stabbed, yet sometimes the card holds a secret clue or message revealing there is more to come.

Cancer

Bubbling Emotion
(Cardinal Water)

~ **Two of Cups**
~ **Venus in Cancer**
~ **Lord of Love**

Romantic Venus meets sensitive Cancer, and the Lord of Love is born. Enchantment and fascination ensue when two open souls meet. This card is often depicted with a romantic pair coming together in mutual admiration.

~ **Three of Cups**
~ **Mercury in Cancer**
~ **Lord of Abundance**

Communicative Mercury and friendly Cancer meet, and the Lord of Abundance is born. An expressive nature and openness is a recipe for growth which spurs more of the same. This card is often illustrated with three people dancing, celebrating and laughing.

~ **Four of Cups**
~ **Moon in Cancer**
~ **Lord of Blended Pleasure**

The moody Moon meets empathetic Cancer, and the Lord of Blended Pleasure is born. Cups dip into all sides of the emotional spectrum. This card is often illustrated with a person who is offered a cup of opportunity, however, they do not see it.

Stable Passion
(Fixed Fire)

- **Five of Wands**
- **Saturn in Leo**
- **Lord of Strife**

Laborious Saturn meets domineering Leo, and the Lord of Strife is born. Powerful personalities and highly charged energy can provoke conflict or disagreement, yet these are the very challenges that push an idea forward into required evolution. The Five of Wands is often portrayed with five youths sparring.

- **Six of Wands**
- **Jupiter in Leo**
- **Lord of Victory**

Exalted-thinking Jupiter meets charismatic Leo, and the Lord of Victory is born. Achievement and success require a combination of many elements. This card is often illustrated with a victory parade.

- **Seven of Wands**
- **Mars in Leo**
- **Lord of Valor**

Dynamic Mars meets action-oriented Leo, and the Lord of Valor is born. Courage lies dormant until it is called upon. We only know our strength when challenges test us. This card is often illustrated with an individual taking an offensive or defensive stance.

Virgo

Quakes and Tremors
(Mutable Earth)

~ **Eight of Pentacles**
~ **Sun in Virgo**
~ **Lord of Prudence**

The sustaining Sun meets Virgo the leader, and the Lord of Prudence is born. Sagacity and common sense infuse the word prudence, which is fueled by solar energy. This card is often illustrated with an individual deeply invested in work.

~ **Nine of Pentacles**
~ **Venus in Virgo**
~ **Lord of Material Gain**

Gorgeous Venus meets creative Virgo, and the Lord of Material Gain is born. The gathering of material possessions is a pleasing pursuit when we do not fall under the spell of believing that this is all there is. This card is often illustrated with an attractive woman lingering in a vineyard.

~ **Ten of Pentacles**
~ **Mercury in Virgo**
~ **Lord of Wealth**

Logical Mercury meets clever Virgo, and the Lord of Wealth is born. The nature of wealth goes beyond finance and includes people, animals, and the places we inhabit. This card is often illustrated with a multigenerational family.

Libra

Fresh Ideas
(Cardinal Air)

- **Two of Swords**
- **Moon in Libra**
- **Lord of Peace Restored**

The intuitive Moon and peaceful Libra meet, and the Lord of Peace Restored is born. A sensitive nature, treated with care and respect, will find its equilibrium and clarity ensues. This card is often illustrated with a person wearing a blindfold; it is not a prison, but rather, a gateway to inner peace.

- **Three of Swords**
- **Saturn in Libra**
- **Lord of Sorrow**

Restrictive Saturn meets harmonious Libra, and the Lord of Sorrow is born. The edge of harmony cuts like a knife. This card is often illustrated with a heart pierced by multiple swords.

- **Four of Swords**
- **Jupiter in Libra**
- **Lord of Rest from Strifc**

Fortunate Jupiter meets gracious Libra, and the Lord of Rest from Strife is born. Peace comes from stillness. This card is often illustrated with a resting knight or knight's effigy.

Deep and Eloquent
(Fixed Water)

- **Five of Cups**
- **Mars in Scorpio**
- **Lord of Loss of Pleasure**

Forceful Mars and hardcore Scorpio meet, and the Lord of Loss of Pleasure is born. Can two equally powerful energies cancel each other out? This card is often illustrated with a forlorn figure.

- **Six of Cups**
- **Sun in Scorpio**
- **Lord of Pleasure**

The glowing Sun meets sexual Scorpio, and the Lord of Pleasure is born. This combination magnifies the energy of the senses. This card is often illustrated with the giving of gifts.

- **Seven of Cups**
- **Venus in Scorpio**
- **Lord of Illusory Success**

Enchanting Venus meets deeply imaginative Scorpio, and the Lord of Illusory Success is born. Things that hypnotize us are not always what they seem. This card is often illustrated with cups floating in the air like a vision.

Sagittarius

Flickering Flames
(Mutable Fire)

- **Eight of Wands**
- **Mercury in Sagittarius**
- **Lord of Swiftness**

Perceptive Mercury meets extroverted Sagittarius, and the Lord of Swiftness is born. Speed of the mind and action of the heart make for great haste and the turning of events. This card is often illustrated with wands flying through the air to an unknown destination.

- **Nine of Wands**
- **Moon in Sagittarius**
- **Lord of Great Strength**

The subtle Moon meets enthusiastic Sagittarius, and the Lord of Great Strength is born. Energy bursting from unseen reserves can result in amazing feats. The card is often illustrated with the figure of a person moving through a gate.

- **Ten of Wands**
- **Saturn in Sagittarius**
- **Lord of Oppression**

Authoritarian Saturn meets optimistic Sagittarius, and the Lord of Oppression is born. A domineering personality can feel like death to a person who is open and free. This card is often illustrated with an individual who carries a very heavy load.

Capricorn

Fresh and Fecund
(Cardinal Earth)

- **Two of Pentacles**
- **Jupiter in Capricorn**
- **Lord of Harmonious Change**

Spiritual Jupiter meets helpful Capricorn, and the Lord of Harmonious Change is born. An effortless and pleasurable alteration is a joy to behold. This card is often illustrated with a juggler who balances two balls.

- **Three of Pentacles**
- **Mars in Capricorn**
- **Lord of Material Works**

Driving Mars meets determined Capricorn, and the Lord of Material Works is born. What type of effort is required to construct something in the material world? This card is usually expressed with three people collaborating.

- **Four of Pentacles**
- **Sun in Capricorn**
- **Lord of Earthly Power**

Regenerative Sun meets ambitious Capricorn, and the Lord of Earthly Power is born. The power of Earth lies in its ability to produce, nurture, and regenerate. This card is often illustrated with a figure who grasps his belongings.

Stillness
(Fixed Air)

- **Five of Swords**
- **Venus in Aquarius**
- **Lord of Defeat**

Stunning Venus meets imaginative Aquarius, and the Lord of Defeat is born. It is challenging to understand how the meeting of these two results in Defeat, but it does. Perhaps the two are so set in their ways that they refuse to budge or they are so protective that they become dangerous to themselves and others. Regardless of reason, the card is usually illustrated with a fight bearing clear winners and losers.

- **Six of Swords**
- **Mercury in Aquarius**
- **Lord of Earned Success**

Intellectual Mercury meets innovative Aquarius, and the Lord of Earned Success is born. How is earned success different from inherited or easy success, and which is more valuable? This card is often illustrated with figures crossing a body of water in a boat.

- **Seven of Swords**
- **Moon in Aquarius**
- **Lord of Unstable Effort**

The fickle Moon meets eccentric Aquarius meet, and the Lord of Unstable Effort is born. What makes an effort unstable? Is it lack of planning, bad luck, or something doomed from the beginning? This card is usually illustrated with a thieving figure.

Pisces

Rippling Waves
(Mutable Water)

- **Eight of Cups**
- **Saturn in Pisces**
- **Lord of Abandoned Success**

Authoritative Saturn meets gentle Pisces, and the Lord of Abandoned Success is born. What does it mean to abandon personal success? Can leaving achievements behind be a good thing? This card is often illustrated as a person beginning an uphill journey.

- **Nine of Cups**
- **Jupiter in Pisces**
- **Lord of Material Happiness**

Lucky Jupiter meets generous Pisces, and the Lord of Material Happiness is born. Luck and generosity meet with delicious results. This card is often illustrated with a magic genie who is about to grant a wish.

- **Ten of Cups**
- **Mars in Pisces**
- **Lord of Perfected Success**

Instinctual Mars meets compassionate Pisces, and the Lord of Perfected Success is born. Fire meets love with spectacular results. Usually, this card is illustrated as the "happily ever after" card.

Astrology
and Court Cards

The Golden Dawn astrological association is as follows:

Queens rule the cardinal signs:
- Aries
- Cancer
- Libra
- Capricorn

Recall that cardinal energy is fresh.

Kings rule the mutable signs:
- Gemini
- Virgo
- Sagittarius
- Pisces

Recall that mutable energy is malleable.

Knights rule the fixed signs:
- Taurus
- Leo
- Scorpio
- Aquarius

Recall that fixed energy is stable.

Pages are not assigned to any astrological suit by the Golden Dawn. They serve as the thrones or the seats of power for the aces.

Each court card rules over three decans, but the signs overlap. This means that each court card rules over a third of one sign and two thirds of the next. It also means that each court card has two Major Arcana cards and three Minor Arcana cards assigned to it (recall the Minor Arcana astrological decan associations). Additionally, the Golden Dawn assigned esoteric titles to each of the court cards. Timing is available using this system and can be especially helpful when seeking a court card significator.

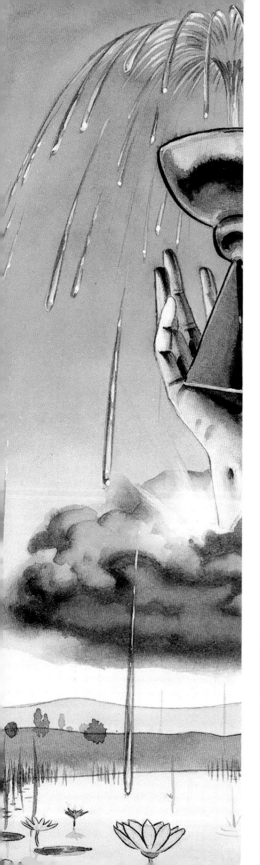

PRINCESS OF CHALICES — PRINCIPESSA DI COPPE
PRINCESA DE COPAS — PRINCESSE DE COUPES

PRINZESSIN DER KELCHE — BEKERS PRINSES

Page of Cups
*Princess
of the Waters*

Earth of Water

KNIGHT OF CHALICES — CAVALIERE DI COPPE
CABALLO DE COPAS — CHEVALIER DE COUPES

RITTER DER KELCHE — BEKERS RIDDER

Knight of Cups
*Prince of the Chariot
of Waters*

Air of Water

*Justice, Death
4 of Swords, 5 of Cups,
6 of Cups*

QUEEN OF CHALICES   REGINA DI COPPE
REINA DE COPAS   REINE DE COUPES

KÖNIGIN DER KELCHE   BEKERS KONINGIN

Queen of Cups
*Queen of the Thrones
of the Waters*

Water of Water

*Lovers, Chariot
10 of Swords, 2 of Cups,
3 of Cups*

PRINCE OF CHALICES   PRINCIPE DI COPPE
PRÍNCIPE DE COPAS   PRINCE DE COUPES

PRINZ DER KELCHE   BEKERS PRINS

King of Cups
*Lord of the Waves
and the Waters*

Fire of Water

*Star, Moon
7 of Swords, 8 of Cups,
9 of Cups*

169

PRINCESS OF PENTACLES   PRINCIPESSA DI PENTACOLI
PRINCESA DE PENTÁCULOS   PRINCESSE DE PENTACLES

PRINZESSIN DER PENTAKEL   PENTAGRAMMEN PRINSES

Page of Pentacles
*Princess
of the Echoing Hills*

Earth of Earth

KNIGHT OF PENTACLES   CAVALIERE DI PENTACOLI
CABALLO DE PENTÁCULOS   CHEVALIER DE PENTACLES

RITTER DER PENTAKEL   PENTAGRAMMEN RIDDER

Knight of Pentacles
*Prince of the Chariot
of Earth*

Air of Earth

*Emperor, Hierophant
4 of Wands, 5 of Pentacles,
6 of Pentacles*

170

QUEEN OF PENTACLES · REGINA DI PENTACOLI
REINA DE PENTÁCULOS · REINE DE PENTACLES

KÖNIGIN DER PENTAKEL · PENTAGRAMMEN KONINGIN

Queen of Pentacles
*Queen of the Thrones
of Earth*

Water of Earth

*Temperance, Devil
10 of Wands, 2 of Pentacles,
3 of Pentacles*

PRINCE OF PENTACLES · RE DI PENTACOLI
PRÍNCIPE DE PENTÁCULOS · PRINCE DE PENTACLES

PRINZ DER PENTAKEL · PENTAGRAMMEN PRINS

King of Pentacles
*Lord of the Wild
and Fertile Land*

Fire of Earth

*Strength, Hermit
7 of Wands, 8 of Pentacles,
9 of Pentacles*

PRINCESS OF WANDS   PRINCIPESSA DI BASTONI
PRINCESA DE BASTOS   PRINCESSE DE BÂTONS

PRINZESSIN DER STÄBE   STAVEN PRINSES

Page of Wands
*Princess
of the Shining Flame*

Earth of Fire

KNIGHT OF WANDS   CAVALIERE DI BASTONI
CABALLO DE BASTOS   CHEVALIER DE BÂTONS

RITTER DER STÄBE   STAVEN RIDDER

Knight of Wands
*Prince of the Chariots
of Fire*

Air of Fire

*Chariot, Strength
4 of Cups, 5 of Wands,
6 of Wands*

QUEEN OF WANDS   REGINA DI BASTONI
REINA DE BASTOS   REINE DE BÂTONS

KÖNIGIN DER STÄBE   STAVEN KONINGIN

Queen of Wands
*Queen of the Thrones
of Flame*

Water of Fire

*Moon, Emperor
10 of Cups, 2 of Wands,
3 of Wands*

PRINCE OF WANDS   PRINCIPE DI BASTONI
PRÍNCIPE DE BASTOS   PRINCE DE BÂTONS

PRINZ DER STÄBE   STAVEN PRINS

King of Wands
*Lord of the Flame
and the Lightning*

Fire of Fire

*Death, Temperance
7 of Cups, 8 of Wands,
9 of Wands*

173

PRINCESS OF SWORDS — PRINCIPESSA DI SPADE
PRINCESA DE ESPADAS — PRINCESSE D'ÉPÉES

PRINZESSIN DER SCHWERTER — ZWAARDEN PRINSES

Page of Swords
*Princess
of the Rushing Winds*

Earth of Air

KNIGHT OF SWORDS — CAVALIERE DI SPADE
CABALLO DE ESPADAS — CHEVALIER D'ÉPÉES

RITTER DER SCHWERTER — ZWAARDEN RIDDER

Knight of Swords
*Prince of the Chariot
of the Winds*

Air of Air

*Devil, Star
4 of Pentacles, 5 of Swords,
6 of Swords*

QUEEN OF SWORDS   REGINA DI SPADE
REINA DE ESPADAS   REINE D'ÉPÉES

KÖNIGIN DER SCHWERTER   ZWAARDEN KONINGIN

Queen of Swords
*Queen of the Thrones
of Air*

Water of Air

*Hermit, Justice
10 of Pentacles, 2 of Swords,
3 of Swords*

PRINCE OF SWORDS   PRINCIPE DI SPADE
PRÍNCIPE DE ESPADAS   PRINCE D'ÉPÉES

PRINZ DER SCHWERTER   ZWAARDEN PRINS

King of Swords
*Lord of the Winds
and Breezes*

Fire of Air

*Hierophant, Lovers
7 of Pentacles, 8 of Swords,
9 of Swords*

Tarot and Astrology Master Chart

Pinpoint the exact location of any Tarot card's position on the zodiac. Each card assumes the astrological attributions and qualities of its heavenly counterpart.

The zodiac and all 78 cards are reflected inside a sacred circle. The circle is an essential blueprint. It makes human life on the material plane possible. From the shape of the sun to earth's orbit, from the shape of bodily atoms to the shape of our eyes, from the scope of our experience to the track of our life, everything is contained in the circle and therefore in the Tarot.

Water/Cups

Earth/Pentacles

Fire/Wands

Air/Swords

Astrological Reference Sheet

Signs

♈ **Aries:** Exuberance, passion, impulse, spontaneity, individualism, domineering spirit.

♉ **Taurus:** A practical sense, discretion, love, beauty, nature and comfort, kindness, persistence, jealousy.

♊ **Gemini:** A brilliant intellect, curiosity, need, communicate, caustic wit, restlessness, inconstancy.

♋ **Cancer:** Union, association, gestation, maturation, fruits, recognition of their roots.

♌ **Leo:** Pride, dynamic, spirited, ambitious, generosity, loyalty, impulsiveness, exhibitionism.

♍ **Virgo:** Efficiency, hard work, foresight, attention to detail, love of order, critical spirit.

♎ **Libra:** Sensitivity, conciliatory spirit, kindness, diplomacy, sociability, hedonism, love of aesthetics.

♏ **Scorpio:** Passion, animosity, conflict between reason and emotion, self-centeredness, nonconformity, vanity.

♐ **Sagittarius:** Exuberant, adventurous spirit, a desire for knowledge, dreamer, poor pragmatism.

♑ **Capricorn:** Rationality, ambition, seeking security and stability, persistence, patience, diplomacy, utilitarianism.

♒ **Aquarius:** Creativity, kindness, generosity, spiritual innovator, an idealist and libertarian, changeability.

♓ **Pisces:** Inconsistency, unpredictability, spiritual dreamer, sensitivity, emotions, attraction to utopias.

Planets

☉ **Sun:** Clarity, tenderness, optimism, search for perfection, honesty, generosity, courage, creativity.

☽ **Moon:** Sensitivity, instinct, intuition, emotion, charm, imagination, illusions, unpredictability.

☿ **Mercury:** Mental alertness, creativity, skills, communication, diplomacy, love of travel, vested interests.

♀ **Venus:** Affectionate, sociable, romantic, love of harmony and beauty, sensuality, seduction.

♂ **Mars:** Energy, initiative, decisiveness, authoritarianism, competition, martial character, aggression.

♃ **Jupiter:** Affability, cheerfulness, confidence, generosity, physical growth, intellectual expansiveness, foresight.

♄ **Saturn:** Self-control, meditation, consistency, patience, critical sense, practicality, confidentiality, humility.

Astrological Correspondences: Numerals

	2	3	4	5
Cups	♀ ♋ Venus in Cancer	☿ ♋ Mercury in Cancer	☽ ♋ Moon in Cancer	♂ ♍ Mars in Scorpio
Pentacles	♃ ♑ Jupiter in Capricorn	♂ ♑ Mars in Capricorn	☉ ♑ Sun in Capricorn	☿ ♉ Mercury in Taurus
Wands	♂ ♈ Mars in Aries	☉ ♈ Sun in Aries	♀ ♈ Venus in Aries	♄ ♌ Saturn in Leo
Swords	☽ ♎ Moon in Libra	♄ ♎ Saturn in Libra	♃ ♎ Jupiter in Libra	♀ ♒ Venus in Aquarius

6	7	8	9	10
☉ ♏ Sun in Scorpio	♀ ♏ Venus in Scorpio	♄ ♓ Saturn in Pisces	♃ ♓ Jupiter in Pisces	♂ ♓ Mars in Pisces
☽ ♉ Moon in Taurus	♄ ♉ Saturn in Taurus	☉ ♍ Sun in Virgo	♀ ♍ Venus in Virgo	☿ ♍ Mercury in Virgo
♃ ♌ Jupiter in Leo	♂ ♌ Mars in Leo	☿ ♐ Mercury in Sagittarius	☽ ♐ Moon in Sagittarius	♄ ♐ Saturn in Sagittarius
☿ ♒ Mercury in Aquarius	☽ ♒ Moon in Aquarius	♃ ♊ Jupiter in Gemini	♂ ♊ Mars in Gemini	☉ ♊ Sun in Gemini

181

Astrological Correspondences: Court Cards

	Page	**Knight**	**Queen**	**King**
Cups	Winter solstice Capricorn ♑	♒ from 20° Aquarius to 20° Pisces ♓	♊ from 20° Gemini to 20° Cancer ♋	♎ from 20° Libra to 20° Scorpio ♏
Pentacles	Summer solstice Cancer ♋	♍ from 20° Virgo to 20° Leo ♌	♐ from 20° Sagittarius to 20° Capricorn ♑	♉ from 20° Taurus to 20° Aries ♈
Wands	Autumn equinox Libra ♎	♏ from 20° Scorpio to 20° Sagittarius ♐	♓ from 20° Pisces to 20° Aries ♈	♋ from 20° Cancer to 20° Leo ♌
Swords	Vernal equinox Aries ♈	♉ from 20° Taurus to 20° Gemini ♊	♍ from 20° Virgo to 20° Libra ♎	♑ from 20° Capricorn to 20° Aquarius ♒

Astrological Correspondences: Major Arcana

N°	Name	Astrology
0	The Fool	Air △
I	The Magician	Mercury ☿
II	The High Priestess	Moon ☽
III	The Empress	Venus ♀
IV	The Emperor	Aries ♈
V	The Hierophant	Taurus ♉
VI	The Lovers	Gemini ♊
VII	The Chariot	Cancer ♋
VIII	Justice	Libra ♎
IX	The Hermit	Virgo ♍
X	The Wheel of Fortune	Jupiter ♃

N°	Name	Astrology
XI	Strength	Leo ♌
XII	The Hanged Man	Water ▽
XIII	Death	Scorpio ♏
XIV	Temperance	Sagittarius ♐
XV	The Devil	Capricorn ♑
XVI	The Tower	Mars ♂
XVII	The Star	Aquarius ♒
XVIII	The Moon	Pisces ♓
XIX	The Sun	Sun ☉
XX	Judgment	Fire △
XXI	The World	Saturn ♄

A Pictorial Key to Astrology

The relation between astrology, Tarot and other disciplines is not set in stone. Actually there are many ways, theories and variations.

One of the main danger when approaching astrology with Tarot, is that the Reader will be locked into a mathematical correspondance between the Arcana and the relative astrological concept. A two-way connection that is too strict and rational to be actually useful in many circumstances.

What we would like to provide is a Pictorial Key to Astrology. In far 1909, the Pictorial Key to the Tarot, by A. E. Waite, was maybe the most important milestone to push Tarot beyond the limits of the esoteric sciences into the realm of the subjective, of intuition, and ultimately of modernity.

The pages that follow are meant to try to give a pictorial, intuitive vision of astrology and her correlations.

Symbols will be used, pictures, names, graphical expressions. They are not meant to be studied. Rather they are meant to be absorbed visually, like a free association, and potentially they will help to root the astrological meanings of Tarot within intuition and not just in the rational part of the mind, as knowledge.

Flower Attribution

Honeysuckle

Poppy

Lavender

Larkspur

Sunflower

Narcissus

Rose

Chrysanthemum

Dandelion

Carnation

Orchid

Violet

Aries

Ram

March 21
April 20

U+264S

Mars

Symbol

Diamond

Head,
Face

Fe

Fire

Lily

Taurus

Bull

April 21
May 20

U+2649

Venus

Agate

Throat,
Neck

Cu

Earth

Symbol

May's Lily

Gemini

Twins

May 21
June 21

Au Ag

Symbol

Mercury

♉ ♀ 2 6 4 ☿

Amethyst

Shoulders, Forearm

N

W

S

E

Aire

Narcissus

Cancer

Crab

June 22 July 22

Symbol

Moon

U+264B

Aeg

Emerald

Lungs. Stomach

Water

Jasmine

Leo Lion

Sun Symbol

July 23
August 22

U+264C

Au

Ruby

Heart

Fire

Peony

Virgin

Virgo

August 23
September 22

U+264D

Mercury

Symbol

Nephrite

Sn Cu

Liver,
Blood

Earth

Poppy

Scale

Libra

U+264E

September 23
October 22

Sapphire

Sn   Cu

♃

Venus
♀

Kidney,
Nerves

N
W   E
S

Air

Symbol

Iris

Scorpion

Scorpio

October 23
November 21

Pluto

Mars ♂

U+264F

Topaz

Fe

Steel

Genitals,
Backbone

Water

Symbol

Carnation

Sagittarius

Archer

November 23
December 21

Symbol

Opal

Zn

Jupiter

♃

U+2650

Hip Joints

Fire

Cornflower

Capricorn

Goat

December 22
January 19

Moonstone

U +2651

Saturn

♄

Gall Bladder
Liver

Earth

Pb

Symbol

Hyacinth

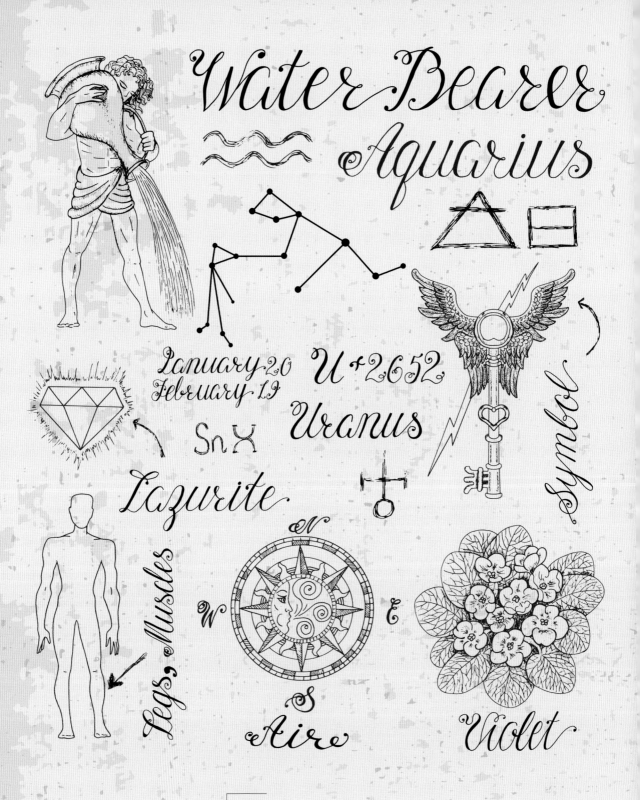

Water Bearer

Aquarius

January 20
February 19

Sn X

Lazurite

U +2652
Uranus

Legs, Muscles

N
W E
S
Air

Symbol

Violet

Pisces

Fish

February 20 March 20

Symbol

Pearl

U+2653

Zn

Neptune

Fingers, Nerves

Water

Crocus

NUMEROLOGY

What Is Numerology?

Numerology is a branch of knowledge derived from the occult significance of numbers. It is the study of the divine and mystical significance of the relationship between counting and measuring. Numerology can be used to describe a person's character or predict their future. However, as with Tarot, many find it more meaningful to use numerology to understand one's relationship to the universe rather than use it to simply forecast future events.

Numerology is the spiritual side of mathematics.

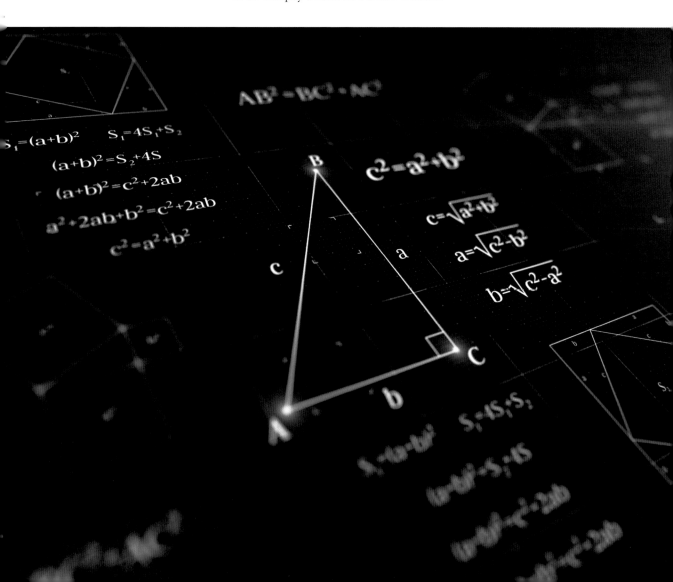

Before being overwhelmed by numbers, one should just focus on the first 10 figures.

Where Does It Come From?

Greek philosopher Pythagoras is called the "father of numerology." His theory states that everything in the material world can be expressed in numerical terms because all things can be reduced to numbers. However, the origin of this art and magical use of numbers can be traced back to ancient India, China, Egypt, Assyria, and prehistoric Europe. The moment people began to count they realized with this practical ability came power. Counting is a way of tracking and organizing the world. Early man counted the number of landmarks to reach a destination, counted and tracked stars and constellations in the sky. It was useful to count the days until crops bore fruit and how many hours of sunlight in a summer day. Greek and Hebrew alphabets contain letters that are attributed a numerical value. Numerology essentially comes from the human experience of the material world and can be found in differing forms across cultures.

How Does It Work?

Popular modern numerology uses an individual's birth date or attaches numerical significance to the letters of a person's name to describe the personality or predict the future. This is usually done by adding, subtracting, or reducing numbers. For instance, an individual's Life Path Number is usually calculated by adding the Month + Day + Year of birth and reducing the appropriate numbers.

Example

Birthday is October 12, 1974.
Reduces:
10 (October is 10th month) + 12 (12th day) + 21 (1 + 9 + 7 + 4)
10 + 12 + 21 = 63
6 + 3 = 9
9 is the Life Path Number and all 9 attributes would be assigned to that individual.
(The cartomancer may correlate this number with the Major Arcana as the querent's Life Path Card.)

How Does Numerology Connect to Tarot?

Numerology and Tarot merge seamlessly as the cards are finite, numbered, and countable. Every Tarot card has a numerological correspondence. A Reader can bring all the classic elements of numeric symbolism into a reading for added depth. They can also use numbers to gain greater insight from the cards. This practice helps the individual to discover secrets and observations about the world around them. To find the number, simply look to the card.

CHAL-
DEAN

PYTHA-
GORE-
AN

KAB-
BALIS-
TIC

Chaldean

Chaldean numerology originated in Mesopotamia and is related to Indian Vedic systems and Kabbalah. It is based on the vibrational quality and energies of numbers 1–8 with the number 9 set aside with special meaning. It is a complicated numerical system that reduces the letters of a person's name and assigns the hidden or occult influences in their life. Single numbers in Chaldean numerology reflect an individual's outer life, while double digits reflect the hidden or occult influences.

Pythagorean

Pythagoras was a 6th century BCE Greek mathematician who created the famous theorem describing modern geometry. Under this popular system of numerology, the numbers are assigned to letters of the Greek alphabet. Digits 1–9 are the basic numbers, while numbers 11 and 22 carry master vibrations. It uses name and date of birth to find an individual's numbers and examines the duality between the two.

Kabbalistic

Kabbalistic numerology connects to the twenty-two letters of the Hebrew alphabet, and was adapted for the Greek and then Roman alphabets. This is the system of numerology that merges perfectly with the structure of Tarot.

SACRED GEOMETRY

What Is Sacred Geometry?

Sacred geometry examines the mystical properties of patterns and shapes. The roots of sacred geometry are found in nature where repeating patterns are observed. It is used and/or observed in naturally occurring sacred space such as groves and holy wells. It is used by the architects of cathedrals, mosques, and temples to create awe-inspiring spiritual space. Sacred geometry is also beloved by Freemasons. It can be used by metaphysical practitioners to observe recurring patterns and themes in one's life path and to understand the nature of the physical universe.

How Does Sacred Geometry Apply to Tarot?

Sacred geometry exists inside the shapes and patterns used to illustrate the Tarot cards. The shapes are sometimes intentional, such as the six-pointed star often used inside the Hermit's lantern. However, occultists over the years have read into the proportions of the cards and their hidden symbolism, especially in older historical decks.

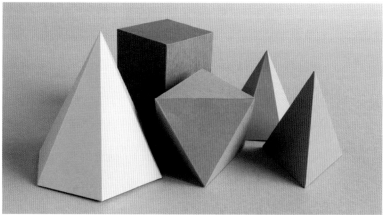

"We already know that the first card of the Tarot is completed by the twenty-first (21 + 1 = 22), and we see why, if this first card represents Microcosm, the last would represent Macrocosm, and the eleventh card, which serves as the universal link to all the complements of the Tarot, represents the Vital reflex Current, which serves as a link between the worlds."

Papus, The Tarot of the Bohemians (1892)

A Sacred Geometry Summary

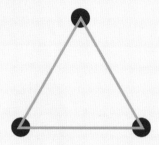

The single **point** is the symbol of unicity and of the self. Anything and everything is contained within a single point and it can be the origin of all.

Two points connecting make up the **line**. The line is the expression of duality, where male and female interact and complete each other.

Three points connecting create a **triangle**. The triangle is both the symbol of birth and of perfect balance. As birth, it is like the third point had been generated by the previous two points.

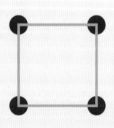

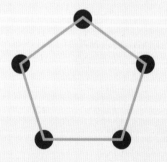

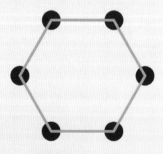

Four points give shape to a **square**. The square is solid, unwavering. It cannot be moved or breached. It is self contained and independent. It is the expression of stability.

Five points together form a **pentagon**, or a five-pointed star. The perfect balance of the square is abandoned to add something more and different, opening to change, transformation and mystique.

Six points create the **hexagon**. Usually all odd numbered figures express some kind of change and instability, while even numbered polygons express a stable and balanced situation. The hexagon is harmony.

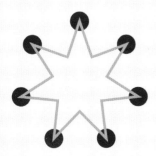

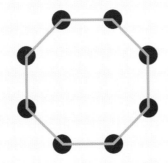

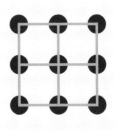

Seven points can be represented as the **heptagram** or a seven-points star. Going past the harmony of the six, the seven pierces through new dimensions and spiritual vision.

Eight points, or the **octagon**, is the symbol of complexity. Even if something is large and complicated, it is possible to perceive the beauty and balance of its inner workings.

Nine points can be used to create a **nine-points square**, or a nonagon . The nine-points square is the expression of the limits of our mind and perception and the key to go beyond them.

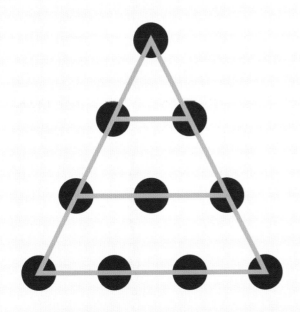

Ten points can be the decagon, but are more commonly represented as the **tetractys**. Shaped like a pyramid with a base of four points the tetractys is the symbolical peak of Sacred Geometry, expressing the perfection and completeness of the Divine.

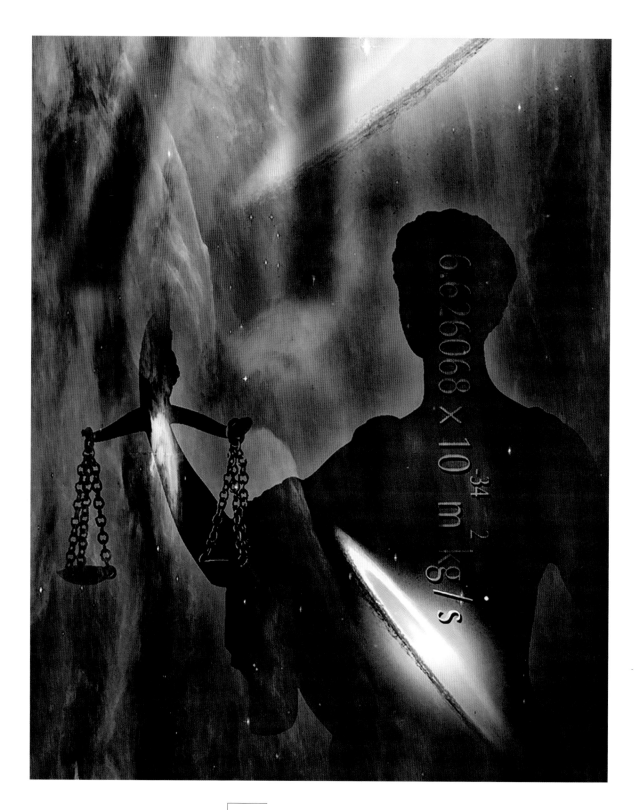

THE NUMBERS

The matrix of numbers encompasses the human system of symbols and figures used for counting, calculating and describing the seen and unseen world.

"Mathematics is the language with which God has written the universe."

- Galileo Galilei

NUMERAL ONE

Numerology: First

Number 1 is the first of all numbers. Every number multiplied or divided by the number 1 results in itself. Every number is also divisible by 1. Number 1 is the lowest common denominator of any sequence of numbers. It is a point of reference or measure for every number following number 1.

Various cultures connect number 1 to privilege. This is apparent in the idea of being the "chosen one." Number 1 symbolizes the top of a hierarchy, often associated with the supreme religious deity of any monotheistic religious system. Number 1 often symbolizes the act of creation. First there is nothing. Then there is one.

Number 1 symbolizes manifestation, assertion, the ego, selfhood, and isolation. Philosophically, it represents the synthesis and fundamental unity of things. Religiously, it represents the lord, god, or highest. Materialistically, it represents the individual. It is the symbol of the sun.

- *Keywords:* Monad, unity, principle, starting point, beginning of a cycle, potential, individual, self, leadership, yang, originality, inspiration.
- *Challenges:* Aggressive, single-minded, arrogant, stubborn.

Arcana

The Magician, Strength, The World, Ace of Cups, Ace of Pentacles, Ace of Wands, Ace of Swords.

The number 1 links seven Tarot cards: three Major Arcana and four Aces. The Magician's number 1 indicates the spark of creative potential. The Strength card (positioned at 11 in older decks) demonstrates the component of new beginnings and establishes a transition between the arcane related to the material world (cards 0–10) and those relating to the intellectual and spiritual (cards 12–21). The World card's 1 is understood as unity and a form of completeness that concludes the sequence of the Major Arcana.

Aces are the symbolic representation of all aspects related to the number 1. Each ace can be understood as the seed, the potential that all the other pip cards are born and

The number 1 is the divine origin of all things. At first there is nothing. Then there is something. It is the original, the first, the beginning.

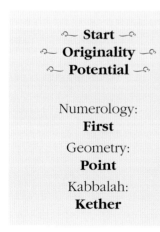

∽ **Start** ∽
∽ **Originality** ∽
∽ **Potential** ∽

Numerology:
First

Geometry:
Point

Kabbalah:
Kether

evolved from, gaining strength and momentum as they grow. Conversely, the ace and 1 can be understood as the pure concept, greatest strength, and manifestation. It is the maximum potential of each suit.

Geometry: Point

The number 1 represents the point. The point is the simplest geometric shape. It has no form or size. It is a monad. The point is the perfect symbol of eternity and individual time. The point has a lack of differentiation. It shows the absence of differences but also of possibilities and choices. Everything is perfect and fixed in the point. Nothing can be changed or transformed; it merely exists without intrusion of another.

Kabbalah: Kether

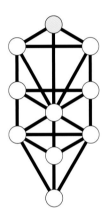

The Kabbalist number 1 on the Tree of Life refers to Kether, whose literal translation from Hebrew means "crown." The crown is the very top of the Tree of Life. It is the point of origin for cosmic creation, which originates from Ein Sof, "The End." Kabbalists call the first Sephirah the "Occult Occult," "Height Inscrutable," and "The head is not." This title demonstrates the idea that Kether is substantially different from all other numbers emanating from it. The crown is not part of the head. It is believed to be too sacred to be uttered. Like the ace, the crown transcends any form, created or uncreated, visible or invisible. In the intellectual world (Swords), this is the beginning of thought. In the physical world (Pentacles), this is the beginning of form. In the psychic world (Cups), this is the beginning of feeling. In the spiritual world (Wands), this is the beginning of desire. Kether sits high on the central column of the Tree of Life. It is represented with the color green.

NUMERAL TWO

Numerology: Second

Number 2 represents the idea that something has been duplicated. There is now division, two elements, and two things to be considered. The difference between two things creates conflict, dialogue, language, and exchange. You can understand number 2 as the start of something. While number 1 offers potential unexpressed, 2 suggests the start is underway, events are in motion. It represents a comparison between two elements. You may use this idea especially when discovering the idea of 2 among the suits of Tarot. The Roman numeral 2 was indicated by two parallel lines (II), the visual representation of binary. Binary means being composed of two pieces or two parts. According to Aristotelian philosophy (a philosophy based on the works of Aristotle) 2 is the choice of something which is either true or false, black or white, day or night. There can be no third possibility within a 2. Therefore, you either "do it" or "don't do it." The lines are clear. It is active and passive, male and female, plus and minus, both agreement and separation.

— *Keywords:* Duality, symmetry, attraction, partnership, encounter, harmony, charm, friendliness, understanding, receptivity, diplomacy, gentle, poised, cooperative, intuitive, sociable, comparison.

— *Challenges:* Repulsion, collision, indifferent, fearful, submissive, indecisiveness, unsteady, inflexible, inconsiderate, unstable, unsteady.

Arcana

The High Priestess, The Hanged Man, Two of Cups, Two of Pentacles, Two of Wands, Two of Swords.
Number 2 is connected to six Tarot cards, two Major Arcana and four Minors. The High Priestess's duality expresses the separation and coexistence of opposites. These two opposites contain matter and spirit, visible and invisible, white and black, masculinity and femininity, ying and yang. Number 2 also indicates conflict or opposition between two polarities or worlds and the equal amount of opposing energies.

*T*he number 2 describes duality. One becomes two and discernment is possible. Day finds night. Hot meets cold. Sweet balances sour. Midnight finds noon. Opposition takes shape.

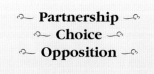

Partnership
Choice
Opposition

Numerology:
Second

Geometry:
Second

Kabbalah:
Chokhmah/Wisdom

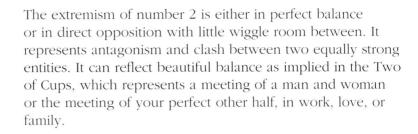

The extremism of number 2 is either in perfect balance or in direct opposition with little wiggle room between. It represents antagonism and clash between two equally strong entities. It can reflect beautiful balance as implied in the Two of Cups, which represents a meeting of a man and woman or the meeting of your perfect other half, in work, love, or family.

Geometry: Line

Number 2 represents the line or the shortest distance between two points. These two points and the line highlight the principles of equality, diversity, balance and imbalance, opposition and attraction.

Kabbalah: Chokhmah/Wisdom

The Kabbalist number 2 refers to Chokhmah, translating to "wisdom." It sits at the highest point of the right column of the Tree of Life and is connected to the first, third, fourth, and sixth Sephirot. Chokhmah's color is gray. Chokhmah expresses the cancellation of thought. Using mystical skills, through meditation, thoughts cancel themselves out and you may stand in line with the Deity. Chokhmah is emotional balance in the psychic world. It represents the union of wisdom and knowledge in the physical world. Chokhmah is intended as a gift of divine grace yet it requires deep maturity, experience, and humility to be fully experienced.

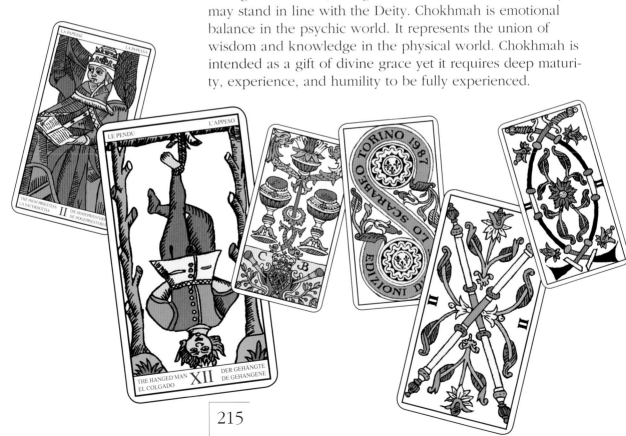

NUMERAL THREE

Numerology: Third

Number 3 represents coming to fruition. It is often referred to as the "perfect number." The perfection and equilibrium move beyond the conflict generated in the 2. It is the number of the Trinity and the ternary, alchemical mind-body-spirit. Number 3 is the result of the thought-action cycle, the man-woman-child cycle, and the creation of preservation and destruction. The number 3 has a deep mystical connection to Christianity because of its correlation with the Holy Trinity composed of the Father, Son, and Holy Spirit. The number 3 is connected to the Hindu Trimurti, composed of Brahma, Vishnu, and Shiva. Freud's famous trinity includes the id, ego, and superego. The number 3's solution of conflict between the balance of opposites can be understood in reference to human spatial dimensions: height, width, and depth.

- *Keywords:* Ternary, balance, symmetry, construction, perfection, birth, talent, imagination, visionary, communicative, energetic, expansion, kindness, spontaneous, assistance, humorous.
- *Challenges:* Moody, mania, instability, indifference, distracted.

Arcana

The Empress, Death, Three of Cups, Three of Pentacles, Three of Wands, Three of Swords.

Number 3 connects six tarot cards, two Majors and four Minors. The Empress expresses the number 3 as the passage of the virginity of the High Priestess to the femininity of the mother and on to the mystery of death as expressed by the Death card. She is often portrayed with the triple moon crown. Rebirth is the result of the Death card though it is the polar opposite of life as expressed by the Empress. Looking into the Minors, the idea of birth is continued as the expansion of the initial seed planted in the ace. A positive expansion is seen in the Three of Cups and a challenging one in the Three of Swords. The number 3 should be interpreted in all suits as the moment when the forces in play, after having

The number 3 creates a triplicity, the trinity and creative birth as the two combine to create a third. Complexity is now possible.

~ **Birth** ~
~ **Construction** ~
~ **Creativity** ~

Numerology:
Third
Geometry:
Equilateral triangle
Kabbalah:
Binah/Intelligence

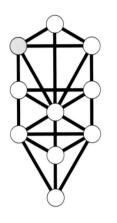

compared, measured, and resisted, result in the birth of a new situation. Number 3, regardless of suit, represents the solution to a problem or choice. It comes with a new set of consequences. It also represents mediation between two opposites.

Geometry: Equilateral Triangle

Number 3 is the equilateral triangle, a figure created by three points each connected to the other two. An equilateral triangle contains 3 equal sides and 3 equal angles. It is the basis of Pythagorean mystical inspiration. Alchemists use this figure as the representation of the forces of nature.

Kabbalah: Binah/Intelligence

The Kabbalist number 3 is Binah, whose literal translation is "intelligence." It is directly opposed to Chokhmah, the highest point of the left column of the Tree and connected to the first, second, fifth, and sixth Sephirot. The color representing this is black. Kabbalists refer to Binah as the "Great Sea" for its regenerative potential. Binah reflects the communication of ideas through the written word and the ability to integrate concepts and ideas from personalities and ideas. In the passionate world (Wands), Binah corresponds the vitality of spirit. Intellectually (Swords), it represents a well-made argument. In the psychic world (Cups), it represents the satisfaction after a difficult journey. In the physical world (Pentacles), Binah represents the powerful regeneration of life force.

NUMERAL FOUR

Numerology: Fourth

Number 4 is matter. It reflects purely physical issues as seen in the four cardinal points, the four seasons, and the four phases of the moon. Traditionally the number 4 is always used for physical manifestations as found in the alchemical elements (Water, Fire, Earth, Air) or according to medieval medicine (Phlegmatic, Sanguine, Choleric, Melancholic). The physical and material idea of the number 4 should not exclude from our understanding the idea of the number 4 as divine perfection. This idea is expressed in the appearance of the Tetragrammaton or the name of God expressed by the four Hebrew letter YHVH (Yod, He, Vav, He).

- *Keywords:* Quaternary, stability, static, concreteness, orientation, pause, perfection, reality, partition, order, classification, segmentation, reason, logic, pragmatic, disciplined.
- *Challenges:* Clumsy, conventional, dull, unadoptable, headstrong, stubborn.

Arcana

The Emperor, Temperance, Four of Cups, Four of Wands, Four of Pentacles, Four of Swords.

Number 4 is connected to six tarot cards, two Majors and four Minors. The Minor Arcana Fours express the consolidation of order and stability of the elements and temperaments that follow. Temperance is complementary to the Emperor by harmonizing tempers expressed by the four elements. The Emperor is immobile and rigid. Temperance is mobile and adaptable. The four elements reflect the manifestation of mental agility, physical strength, material achievements, and creativity in the translation of tangible works.

Number 4 can be considered an expression of stable order embracing every aspect of reality and human existence. This order can be the basis with which to build, metaphorically or literally. It is a constant reference point in the midst of the unavoidable change, turmoil, and readjustment of the universe.

Number 4 indicates perfection stemming from stability and order. It is the divine manifestation of the material plane and humans.

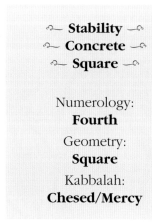

∾ **Stability** ∾
∾ **Concrete** ∾
∾ **Square** ∾

Numerology:
Fourth
Geometry:
Square
Kabbalah:
Chesed/Mercy

Geometry: Square

The number 4 is represented as a square in geometry. This figure represents the boundaries of space in a clean, clear, orderly way. At the same time, the square limits things, nudging them into a well-defined boundary. The phrase "squaring the circle" refers to the mathematical operations used to compare the area of a circle with that of a square. Symbolically, this expresses the unknowable nature of the divine—the circle—which manifests itself into a tangible and understandable form, the square.

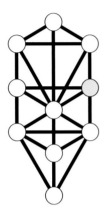

Kabbalah: Chesed/Mercy

The Kabbalist number 4 refers to Chesed, whose literal translation is kindness, benevolence, or "mercy." It is located on the right column of the Tree of Life, aligned with Chokhmah but at a lower level. Chesed is connected to the second, fifth, sixth, and seventh Sephirot. Its color is blue. Divine love (Wands) pardons and justifies all actions and is allied with humanity. Intellectually (Swords), Chesed expresses understanding, the ability to empathize and truly understand the problems of others. In the psychic world (Cups), Chesed expresses devotion and attachment to a situation or a person. In the physical world (Pentacles), Chesed reflects pity and the compassionate spirit that gives, pushes, and sacrifices to help others or the planet.

NUMERAL FIVE

Numerology: Fifth

The number 5 is the result of the equation and sum of 2 + 1 + 2. Understand this equation as a meditation of an individual (1) stuck between two complex (2) realities. The number 5 contains a lack of equilibrium. This is broken into 3 + 1 + 1 or 1 + 3 + 1, two combinations where one party dominates as much as the other.

Number 5 is the number of magic. Will and power form the basis of Western Esoteric magic. Number 5 is dynamic in nature and contains a potential destructiveness inside its expression of will and power.

- *Keywords:* Quinary, agitation, excitement, transformation, revolution, expansion, inclusiveness, comprehension, judgment, activity, vitality, release.
- *Challenges:* Rash, irresponsible, inconsistent, unreliable, restless, discord, upheaval.

Arcana

The Hierophant, The Devil, Five of Cups, Five of Diamonds, Five of Clubs, Five of Swords.

Number 5 is connected to six Tarot cards, two Major Arcana and four Minors. Both the Hierophant and the Devil express the influence of human nature. Both Arcana are conceived to mediate between the physical and divine. The difference between the two is the Hierophant demonstrating a willingness to accept moral responsibilities derived from the perception of divine influence. In contrast, the Devil accepts moral responsibility from the individual rather than the Deity. The Devil will always place passion ahead of responsibility. The Minor Arcana version of 5 represents a liberation of psychic energy (Cups), the explosion of physical strength (Pentacles), a rush of creativity (Wands), or an intense amount of intellectual reckoning (Swords). All suits reflect the 5 as restlessness and imperfection. This discomfort propels our search for a solution. It often looks or feels destructive in the short term, but it allows us to overcome limits and press forward.

*T*he number 5 indicates a lack of balance but also mediates between different realities. It is called the number of man because it reflects contradictions of human nature.

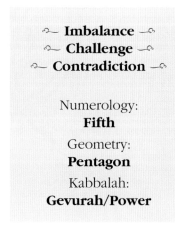

⌒— **Imbalance** —⌒
⌒— **Challenge** —⌒
⌒— **Contradiction** —⌒

Numerology:
Fifth

Geometry:
Pentagon

Kabbalah:
Gevurah/Power

Geometry: Pentagon

The number 5 represents a pentagon. The sides of a pentagon symbolically reflect the human body, head, legs, and arms. The pentagon also represents a five-pointed star. The five-pointed star inside a circle is called a pentacle. A star facing up is said to have the ascending voltage of spiritual nature. A star directed downward is said to have the electricity of a material nature.

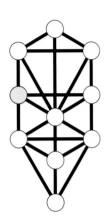

Kabbalah: Gevurah/Power

The Kabbalist number 5 is Gevurah, which is "power." This Sephirah sits opposite of Chesed, at the median of the left column of the Tree of Life. Gevurah is connected to the third, fourth, sixth, and eighth Sephirot. Gevurah's color is red. Spiritually (Wands), Gevurah represents the increase or decrease of power granted in other worlds. Intellectually (Swords), it represents fear of God but also how one addresses thoughts toward a goal. For the psyche (Cups), Gevurah expresses the psychological dynamics of emotion. It reminds that emotional excess can and will cloud your choices. Materially (Pentacles), Gevurah is linked with the left hand, which is the domain of matter. It reflects holding back and contracting.

NUMERAL SIX

Numerology: Sixth

The number 6 is the result of the sum 3 + 3. It represents union and perfection. It is the interaction of two entities equally attracting and repelling. Number 6 is the number of love and associated with Venus. Hindu symbolism places 6 as the union of the male lingam and the female yoni. Number 6 is balanced by two equals (3) of the same weight. This weight is dynamic and sometimes wishes to dominate the other, but they are stable and eternal: thus leading to a complementary situation without conflict.

— *Keywords:* Connection, weaving, imagination, love, discrimination, reconciliation, cooperation, marriage, parenthood, guardianship, healer, teacher, grace, balance, stability, music, art, dancing.
— *Challenges:* Impractical, shallow, restless, selfishness, unsupportive, weak willed.

Arcana

The Lovers, The Tower, Six of Cups, Six of Pentacles, Six of Wands, Six of Swords.

The number 6 connects two Majors and four Minors. The Lovers expresses 6 as a choice between two roads. One moves upward to enhance the spirit and the other moves downward to enhance the material. The Tower carries the 6 as personal choice. One side of the Tower represents personal ambitions and the abandonment of materiality and pride. The opposite side desires possession of individualistic will and pride. The four Minor Sixes are defined by the framework of their suit but represent the shape emerging from chaos or the equilibrium reached when turbulence subsides. To make a choice is to settle within the multiple possibilities that existed. Choice breeds order and allows you to have direction, make sense of what you want and where you are going.

Geometry: Hexagon

The hexagon is a regular polygon; all sides and all angles are equal. Hexagon angles are 60 degrees. It is possible to fill the

The number 6 represents the heart center. It is the balance that stems from the union of opposites.

— Beauty —
— Love —
— Light —

Numerology:
Sixth

Geometry:
Hexagon

Kabbalah:
Tiferet/Beauty

plane of the hexagon with other hexagons and not have any gaps. This further enhances the harmony of the geometric figure. Connecting the vertices of a hexagon will provide a six-pointed star consisting of two equilateral triangles. This shape can be called the Seal of Solomon and is a symbolic representation of physical and spiritual union.

Kabbalah: Tiferet/Beauty

The Kabbalist number 6 refers to Tiferet, which translates to "beauty." The Sephirah is located in the center column of the Tree of Life under the position of Kether. If Kether is understood as the head of the tree, then Tiferet can be understood as the heart. Note the first six Sephirot form the shape of a hexagon on the Tree of Life. Kabbalistic tradition holds Tiferet as the combination of six colors, which create overlapping infinite shades, expressions, and the variety of emotions an individual may experience.

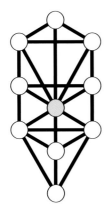

The intellectual world (Swords) expresses beauty through empowering words and statements of love. The psychic world (Cups) expresses beauty through the ecstasy of admiration for the beauty surrounding you. The spiritual world (Wands) is expressed through divine love that created all things, and the physical world (Pentacles) is expressed in the ability of nature to exist.

NUMERAL SEVEN

Numerology: Seventh

Number 7 is called "the number of the spheres." Since the Middle Ages it was thought Heaven was divided into seven concentric spheres, each connected to a planet. The number 7 is a prime number, divisible only by the number 1 and itself. This always gave 7 a mystical significance. It is the symbol of the individual's elevation toward the infinite. Examples include the seven chakras of the Hindu tradition, seven arms of the Jewish menorah, seven rungs of the ladder of Mithra (a mystery cult of antiquity). General examples include seven notes on a musical scale, seven visible planets, and seventh son of the seventh son.

- *Keywords:* Septenary, effort, development, raising, lowering, completion, time, space, duration, distance, immortality, thoughtfulness, mystic, philosophical, fortunate, secrets, alchemy, myth, religion, occult, deep seeing, endurance.
- *Challenge:* Hypercritical, morbid, silent, depression, stagnant, argumentative, limitations, misanthropic.

*T*he number 7 indicates the ability to rise and exceed limits by following ambitions and awareness. It represents the transition from physical to intellectual.

Arcana

The Chariot, The Star, Seven of Cups, Seven of Pentacles, Seven of Cups, Seven of Wands.

Number 7 is connected to six Tarot cards, two Majors and four Minors. It is expressed via the Chariot as the ability to have perfect knowledge of a desired goal and to reach it through the effort and habit of self-control and discipline. The Star represents the same process but on the other end of the spectrum. Rather than Chariot speed using strength and ambition, the Star is driven by an innocent and idealistic yearning to understand the world. The Chariot rises to dominate the world while the Star harmoniously merges with it.

The Minor cards are correlated with the seven planets, virtues, musical notes, and so on. Each of the suits demonstrates the ability to overcome limitations and transcend the material world.

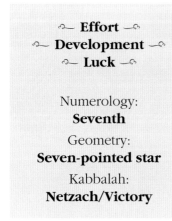

— Effort —
— Development —
— Luck —

Numerology:
Seventh

Geometry:
Seven-pointed star

Kabbalah:
Netzach/Victory

Geometry: Seven-pointed star

The seven-pointed star is also called a heptogram. This figure is traditionally associated with mystical symbols and represents the seven visible planets of astrology and the seven alchemical metals. The star is traditionally drawn with the tip upwards. In many depictions, there are also internal lines joining the vertices of the star. The heptogram is the symbol of Venus, Roman goddess of love. It is also used by the A A (sometimes called the Argentium Astrum), the brotherhood of magic founded by Aleister Crowley.

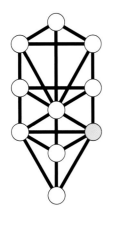

Kabbalah: Netzach/Victory

The Kabbalist number 7 refers to Netzach, whose translation is "victory." This Sephirah is located on the lower right column of the Tree of Life, the column of mercy. Netzach is connected to the fourth, sixth, eight, ninth, and tenth Sephirot. Because Netzach is located under the Sephirah Chesed, in the divine world it expresses the ability to extend the love of Chesed.

The spiritual world (Wands) expresses durability and stability, overcoming obstacles that hinder with good intentions. The intellectual world (Swords) represents consistency and a decision that leads to victory but also peace that guides the decision-making process. Psychologically (Cups) it is expressed by a sense of security allowing passion and emotion to overcome any fear. The physical world (Pentacles) is expressed with body control and absolute mastery over actions.

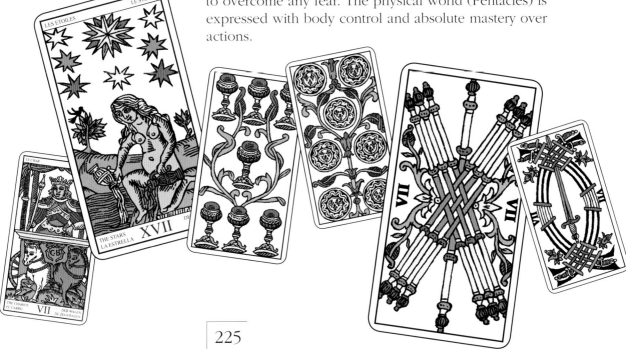

225

NUMERAL EIGHT

Numerology: Eighth

Number 8 is called an infinite number. The symbol of infinity is an 8 resting on its side in the form of a lemniscate. Observing 8's form, you can identify how the symbol manifests itself cyclically for an infinite amount of time. It is a cycle of perpetual motion. Number 8 also represents the stability obtained by change that is regular and constant.

— *Keywords:* Octosyllabic, cyclical, orderly, vision, subjectivity, active, decisive, dependability, trustworthy, status, wealth, executive, integrity, appearance.
— *Challenges:* Greedy, domineering, superior, tactless, snobby.

Arcana

Justice, The Moon, Eight of Cups, Eight of Diamonds, Eight of Wands, Eight of Swords

The number 8 is connected to six Tarot cards, two Majors and four Minors. Justice expresses the 8 via mental and physical balance. It is impartiality in judging and open to see in all directions while being able to assess the situation before acting. The Moon is constantly in flux, forever changing as it waxes and wanes. Justice reminds us that it is impossible to have every piece of information required to judge completely, while the Moon's limitations stem from the dependence of the creative imagination.

Minor card Eights are expressed via a continual renewal coming from the search for perfection when we look in different directions and find solutions to the unexpected obstacles we face.

Geometry: Octagon

Geometrically, the 8 is represented as an octagon. This figure is a graphic expression of the physical and spiritual balance of space. It symbolizes the four cardinal directions and four intermediate directions. This symbol is found frequently in Christian baptisteries and baptismal pools, domes of mosques, and churches. The octagon recalls the Ogdoad of

---

*T*he number 8 represents infinity expressed as a link between the individual and the harmony that is the underpinning of the universe. The number 8 indicates a presence of hidden order even when chaos reigns.

— **Vision** —
— **Power** —
— **Cyclic** —

Numerology:
Eighth

Geometry:
Octagon

Kabbalah:
Hod/Splendor

Gnostic philosophy, the eight arms of Vishnu in Hinduism, the eight spokes of the wheel of Buddhist law, and the eight trigrams of the Chinese I Ching.

Kabbalah: Hod/Splendor

The Kabbalist number 8 is Hod, whose literal translation is "splendor." This Sephirah is located on the lower point of the left column of the Tree of Life, beneath Gevurah. Hod is connected to the fifth, sixth, seventh, ninth, and tenth Sephirot.

Spiritually (Wands), Hod represents the omniscience of the light of truth. Intellectually (Swords), it represents reasoning rising from pure logic and free of emotion. Psychically (Cups), Hod is expressed as the equilibrium between the body and mind. Physically (Pentacles) it is the transfer of energy which provokes cellular growth on every level.

The number 9 represents the transition between the material and spiritual. It expresses the mystical threshold one can reach through, by direct experience, insight, or intuition. The number 9 represents how the divine permeates this world.

~ **Synchronicity** ~
~ **Karma** ~
~ **Transcendent** ~

Numerology:
Ninth
Geometry:
9-pointed square
Kabbalah:
Yesod/Foundation

NUMERAL NINE

Numerology: Ninth

Number 9 is called the magic number of the initiated due to its mystical properties. The multiplication of 3 times 3 is 9. The sum of our first ten numbers equals 45:

$0 + 1 + 2 + 3 + 4 + 5 + 6 + 7 + 8 + 9 = 45$

$4 + 5 = 9$

The number 9 is the last of ten digits and indicates the threshold between worlds and the ability to initiate, cross, experience, and enter the spiritual world. Christian traditions contain nine angels. Dante's Divine Comedy is divided into 99 cantos. The number 999 is considered sacred, while 666 is the number of the Antichrist.

~ *Keywords:* Experience, awareness, threshold, synchronicity, intuition, compassion, fulfillment, voyaging, humanitarian, freedom, wisdom, enlightenment, mysticism, sympathy, generous, genius.

~ *Challenges:* Lethargic, disconnected, confused, overwhelmed, lost.

Arcana

The Hermit, The Sun, Nine of Cups, Nine of Pentacles, Nine of Wands, Nine of Swords.

Number 9 is connected to six Tarot cards, two Majors and four Minors. The Hermit expresses the 9 as initiatory knowledge and the search for truth through meditation, solitude, and the ability to inhabit altered realities. The Sun is complementary to the Hermit in the sense that it expresses sharing knowledge with others based on a dialogue leading to action. While the Hermit lights the journey with the lamp of knowledge, the Sun illuminates the entire world with its light.

The Minor Nines contain something about to occur, awareness of what is to happen, the origins and intentions that place the individual in a situation of knowledge. New forces are taking shape.

Geometry: 9-pointed square

The number 9 is represented graphically by three rows of three points each, arranged to outline a square. The multiplication of 3 and 3 in this figure represents the symbolic transition between ground and space, between two and three dimensions, and between the square and the cube. The nine points refer to the Talisman of Saturn, also known as "square magic." This talisman and square magic occur when the figures are arranged in 9 so their sum, read horizontally, vertically, or diagonally is always 15.

Kabbalah: Yesod/Foundation

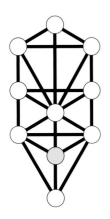

The Kabbalist number 9 refers to Yesod, whose literal meaning is "foundation." The Sephirah is located at the base of the central column of the Tree of Life, called the "column of temperance." Yesod is connected to the sixth, seventh, eighth, and tenth Sephirot. The 9 represents a diamond on the Tree of Life, and the representation of the tenth Sephirah is omitted as an expression of the pure material. The 9 represents that place on the Tree where everything is made material. It is the canal through which the spiritual becomes manifest and the conceptual becomes actual.

Intellectually (Swords), 9 represents the free exchange of thoughts flowing like water and perfectly articulated. Psychically (Cups), 9 is a new emotional understanding that opens the floodgates of possibility. Spiritually (Wands), the 9 suggests putting desire into action, passion, and enthusiasm that spreads past yourself and affects others. Physically (Pentacles), the 9 is expressed as being able to see the tangible results of your work in the world.

NUMERAL TEN

Numerology: Tenth

Number 10 is considered the number of knowledge. Adding the first 10 numbers:

1 + 2 + 3 + 4 + 5 + 6 + 7 + 8 + 9 + 10 = 55

5 + 5 = 10

Symbolically this reflects 10's ability to contain all numbers emerging before it and 10. It is a divine number, containing all the truth that came before, holding the beginning, end, and the journey in between.

- *Keywords:* Full, leadership, fulfillment, result, completeness, cycle, return, power.
- *Challenges:* Frustration, assertion, overwhelming, high expectations, competition, jealousy.

Arcana

The Wheel of Fortune, Judgment, The Fool, Ten of Cups, Ten of Wands, Ten of Pentacles, Ten of Swords.

Number 10 links seven Tarot cards, three Majors and four Minors. The Wheel of Fortune expresses a continuous and eternal flow of time, the cycle of life, and the reality of perpetual renewal. Judgment expresses the final awakening and the movement of the soul toward enlightenment. It is the Wheel completing its final turn in any transformation, be it psychical, mental, or spiritual. The Fool exists within the void, absent, empty, yet ingrained in the circle of renewal and birth.

Geometry: Tetractys

The tetractys is the graphic representation of the number 10 and features 10 points in a triangle of four rows. The ancient Pythagoreans attributed sacred value to it. They saw what they called the "the root of the eternal nature," containing the key to all things. They believed this diagram was a representation of the entire cosmos and a map of the human soul. Even the Kabbalistic Tree of Life is represented as a diagram of 10 points.

The number 10 represents both the completeness and the end of a cycle and the prospect of a new beginning. Number 10 ensures the continuity of stability that remains regardless of the passage of time and the waves of change.

∾ **Fulfillment** ∾
∾ **Cycle** ∾
∾ **Return** ∾

Numerology:
Tenth

Geometry:
Tetractys

Kabbalah:
Malkuth/Kingdom

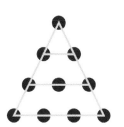

Kabbalah: Malkuth/Kingdom

The Kabbalist number 10 refers to Malkuth, whose literal translation is "kingdom." Kingdom is our physical reality. All points on the Tree of Life are spiritual except for Malkuth, which is grounded in physical reality here on earth. This is the divine world of creation.

In the spiritual world (Wands), this is the manifestation of an ideal. The physical (Pentacles) world shows our concrete results. Emotionally (Cups), we discover the world is created by the results of our emotions and perceptual abilities. Mentally (Swords), we see that what we speak and say becomes real, that our words contain power. Ultimately we discover in the 10 that the physical world is the domain of reality that springs from a mysterious, divine place.

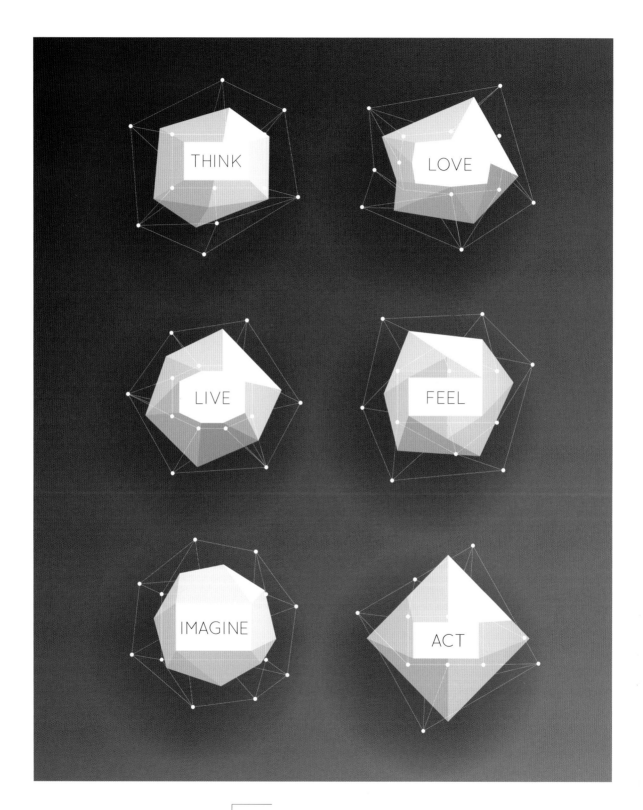

232

NUMERICAL TAROT SPREADS AND TECHNIQUES

Numerical techniques add fun and complexity to readings.
Major Arcana cards = 0 to 21
Pip cards = 1 to 10

The court cards are unnumbered. To calculate the court cards, simply follow the logical numerical association. Assign the following numbers, which follow the natural progression of the deck:
Page = 11
Knight = 12
Queen = 13
King = 14

Numerical spreads are definitely easier than advanced mathematics.

$$f(x) = \sum_{i=0}^{\alpha} \frac{f^{(i)}(0)}{i!} x^i$$

$$e = mc^2$$

$$\frac{1}{2}(\cos(ax-bx) - \cos(ax+bx)) -$$

$$\frac{k}{2}(\cos ax + bx) + (\cos ax - bx)) =$$

$$\nabla_A \vec{B}(x) = \lim_{\epsilon \to 0} \frac{\Pi_{(r,o,r)} \vec{B}(r(\epsilon)) - \vec{B}}{\epsilon}$$

$$c = \sqrt{a^2 + b^2}$$

$$-1$$

$$k > \nearrow$$

$$\sin \alpha = \frac{a}{c}$$

$$\ddot{x}^a + \Gamma^a_{bc} \dot{x}^b \dot{x}^c = 0$$

$$\cos \alpha = \frac{b}{c}$$

$$A \; tg\alpha = \frac{\sin \alpha}{\cos \alpha}$$

$$ctg\alpha = \frac{1}{tg\alpha} \sqrt{1 - \frac{v^2}{c^2}}$$

$$d/dT$$

$$\nabla \vec{x} = x^a_{;b} \frac{\partial}{\partial x^a} \otimes dx^b = (x^a_{;b} + \Gamma^a_{bc} x^c) \frac{\partial}{\partial x^a} \otimes dx^a$$

TRIGONOMETRY

$$\frac{\Delta t}{\sqrt{1 - \frac{v^2}{c^2}}}$$

$$\mathcal{L}_x g_{ab} = 0$$

$$\mathcal{L}_x T_{ab} = x^c \nabla_c T_{ab} + (\nabla_a x^c) T_{cb} + (\nabla_b x^c)$$

$$T_{ac} = x^c T_{ab,c} + x^c_{,a} T_{cb} + x^c_{,b} T_{ac}$$

$$\nabla_a x_b + \nabla_b x_a = 0 =$$

$$x^c_{,a} g_{abc} + x^c_{,a} g_{bc} + x^c_{,b} g_{ac} = 0$$

$$\nabla_{\vec{P}} \vec{x} = x^a_{;b} y^b \frac{\partial}{\partial x^a} = (x^a_{;b} + \Gamma^a_{bc} x^c) y^b \frac{\partial}{\partial x^a}$$

$$\frac{d}{dx} \int_a^x f(s) ds = f(x)$$

$$\frac{8 \Pi G}{c^4} T_{ab}$$

Before and After Spread

Number of Cards: 3
Cards Used: Major and
Minor Arcana
Time: 5 minutes
Objective: See the present
moment inside a sequence
from past to future
Layout: A simple line of 3
cards, with the first card at
the center

Once you fix a moment in time, it is useful to understand that any specific moment is but a single snapshot
inside a wider frame. Everything is part of a sequence
that has roots in the past and flows toward the future.
While we choose the direction of our individual actions,
we still swim in the river of life, made of causes and
consequences.

The Before and After Spread asks the Reader to pull a
single card at random and two more cards specifically as
determined by the first card. The resulting cards will create a
"run" or a logical sequence of cards.

∽ Pose a question.

1 Draw a card representing the present.

2 The Reader looks through the deck to find two more
cards. The previous card is chosen to represent the past. This
card is one digit lower than the present card.

3 The following card is chosen to represent the future.
This card has the value of one digit higher.

∽ The three cards are interpreted as the answer to the
question.

Example:

A question of personal authenticity and creativity is posed. "How can I best remain true to who I am and create valuable work that will empower others?"

- The Page of Wands is randomly drawn as the "present" card.
- The Ten of Wands is selected as the "past" card.
- The Knight of Wands is selected as the "future" card.

1 The Reader looks at the Ten of Wands (past) and says, "You have wrapped up many passion projects in the past. These are now finished."

2 The Reader looks the Page of Wands (present) and says, "You are playing with an amazing idea right now. Keep your eyes focused on the prize, remain mesmerized by passion. Trust your instincts: if it feels right, it is right. Remember the lessons of a child. In creative play there is discovery. A discovery for yourself will shed light for others."

3 The Reader looks at the Knight of Wands (future) card and says, "Soon it will be time to run with the greatest idea you have ever had. You will light up the world with your passion."

Note: For the Before and After technique, the highest possible numbers are Major Arcana 21 and Minor Arcana 10, or 14, if one assigns numbers to the court cards. If the highest number is pulled, "wrap around" and reconnect with the lowest (Major Arcana 0 or, in the Minors, the Ace of the same suit).

Intensity and Polarity Technique

Number of Cards: 1
Cards Used: Major and
Minor Arcana
Time: 2 minutes
Objective: Understand
how strong a force is and
if it's a positive or negative
force
Layout: A single card

Intensity and polarity are constructs taken from physics.
Each force can be represented by a vector and defined
by intensity (how strong is the force) and polarity (the
direction the force is pushing).

This simple technique was first presented by American
tarotist Tom Tadford Little to help students interpret the
minimally illustrated pips found in antique Tarot decks or
in any deck where the Minor Arcana is not illustrated with
pictures.

A The Reader gauges the intensity of a card; the higher the
number, the greater the intensity.

B The Reader considers the polarity of the card—whether
the number is odd (considered challenging) or even
(considered positive).

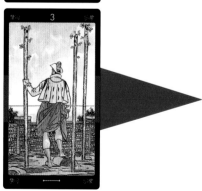

Intensity and polarity.

Example:

The Eight of Cups is:
- a strong force (8 out of 10)
- positive (even numbered)
- related to emotion or spirit (Cups)

The Eight of Cups signals a major positive emotional or spiritual event.

The Three of Wands is:
- a weak force (3 out of 10)
- negative (odd numbered)
- related to action and desires (Wands)

By contrast, the Three of Wands would signal a minor challenging action.

Number of Cards: 1
Cards Used: Major and Minor Arcana
Time: 1 minute
Objective: To identify how close the Querent is to her goal
Layout: A single card

Numerological readings are always very effective to give an answer to matters that can be quantified. Things like how strong is a feeling, how challanging is a task, or how close we are to a certain objective.

The Progression Technique is useful for Readers interested in timing. Progression assumes that the highest possible number (21 in the Majors, 10 or 14 in the Minors, depending on court card usage) represents the point at which a querent will achieve his or her goal.

A Reader draws a single card.

B The card's value reveals how close the querent is to reaching their goal.

Example:

If the Reader draws the High Priestess (2), the achievement of the goal lies far in the future (21).

By contrast, if the Reader draws the Nine of Swords, a decision (Swords) will be made almost immediately (9 out of 10)!

The 9 of Swords suggests an immediate decision, yes, but what kind of decision? The art of the card may suggest something, allowing the combination of a numerological reading with an intuitive reading.

Making a Difference Spread

Number of Cards: 2+
Cards Used: Major and Minor Arcana
Time: 5 minutes
Objective: Understanding the resources needed to reahc one objective
Layout: 2 cards drawn or selected. The difference between their numbers will cause the selection of additional cards

The first part of the spread can be used even without a numerological approach: However, adding numerology, the spread becomes immediately more interesting and gives a more accurate assessment of the situation.

The first two cards can be randomly drawn or selected, or even a mix of the two techniques, by selecting one and drawing the other. The choice depends on the Reader and on the clarity that the Querent has already regarding the present and on the goal she wishes to achieve.

A The Reader draws two cards:
- one to represent the present situation,
- the other to represent the desired goal.

Alternatively, these cards may be deliberately chosen to represent the present and desired future.

The Present

The Goal

B The Reader then subtracts the value of the lower-numbered card from the value of the higher-numbered card. The difference suggests a "**bridge**"—an action the querent can take to close the gap between where the querent is and where they want to be.

C The bridge card is chosen using numerology, but it can be interpreted normally. It answers the question "What can I do to make a difference and progress?" Usually this card indicates something to do, or something to let go and replace.

240

Example:

The Reader draws the Six of Swords (6) and the Emperor (4); the difference is 2. The querent should consider the strategies of reflection (High Priestess), ambition (2 of Wands), union (2 of Cups), discussion (2 of Swords), and flexibility (2 of Pentacles). These qualities will help bridge the querent to where they would like to be.

241

Early Christian Numerical Interpretation of Cards

Here is an early Christian interpretation of cards. *(Card images from the Tarot of the Tzar)*

represents

One or All
One God
One Universe

represents

God (Father) and Son

Three

represents

**God (Father), Son
and Holy Spirit**

Four

represents

**four "corners"
of the earth**

Five

represents

**God in the midst
of the world**

Six

represents

**the number of days
it took for Creation**

Seven

represents

**mystery
or the day of rest**

Eight

represents

**the seven visible planets
and the moon**

Nine

represents

**the major constellations
in the sky**

Ten

represents

**the completed universe
of 10 planets and satellites**

The Jack

represents

the court servant

The King

represents

**the male ruler
of the nation**

The suits

represent

**the four seasons
of the year**

The Queen

represents

**the female ruler
of the nation**

Hidden Number Technique

A Reader can discover hidden patterns and subtle connections by adding together the numbers of double-digit cards in the Major Arcana:

- **The Wheel of Fortune** (10)
  1 + 0 = 1 *Magician*

- **Justice** (11)
  1 = 1 = 2 *High Priestess*

- **Hanged Man** (12)
  1 + 2 = 3 *Empress*

- **Death** (13)
  1 + 3 = 4 *Emperor*

- **Temperance** (14)
  1 + 4 = 5 *Hierophant*

- **Devil** (15)
  1 + 5 = 6 *Lovers*

- **Tower** (16)
  1 + 6 = 7 *Chariot*

- **Star** (17)
  1 + 7 = 8 *Strength*

- **Moon** (18)
  1 + 8 = 9 *Hermit*

- **Sun** (19)
  1 + 9 = 10 *Wheel of Fortune*

- **Judgment** (20)
  2 + 0 = 2 *High Priestess*

- **World** (21)
  2 + 1 = 3 *Empress*

Adding together creates a progression.

Example:

Consider the Devil, with a value of 15:
15 = 1 + 5 = 6, the number of the Lovers
Is it a coincidence that, in traditional decks, the male and female figures strike similar poses at the feet of a powerful figure in both cards? Is it a coincidence that the purer emotions of love and unity (associated with the Lovers) are reflected, however darkly, in the addiction and hedonism of the Devil?

Quintessential Number Technique

The word "quintessential" is derived from the Latin word meaning "fifth essence." It implies a perfect example of fine quality. Imagine Picasso's finest painting or a classic dish served at your favorite Italian restaurant. Discover the quintessential number of a reading and use it as an overall guide for yourself or your querent.

To derive the quintessence, or overall theme, of any reading, the Reader adds together the values of all cards in the spread, then reduces that number (using a process called "mathematical reduction") to a number between 1 and 21, which correlates to a Major Arcana card. This card is the quintessence of the reading.

Example:

A three-card spread containing the Wheel (10), the Eight of Wands (8), and the Queen of Cups (13) has value of 31. Because 31 is higher than 21, the Reader employs mathematical reduction, adding the two digits in 31 to derive the quintessence ($3 + 1 = 4$).
4 = Emperor

The Reader may assume the reading will be colored by the themes of authority and rigidity.

Note: This technique can also be used to wrap up a reading. Once the reading has finished, add up the numbers to discover the essence of the reading as found in the corresponding Major Arcana card.

Personality Card Technique

A personality card is the purpose of an individual's current lifetime. It is what you've come into this lifetime to learn. Determine the personality card by adding the month, day, and year of your birth date.

Example:

A birth date of October 9, 1986:
10 + 9 + 1986 = 2005
Add this total together:
2 + 0 + 0 + 5 = 7
7 = The Chariot

Soul Card Technique

A soul card is the individual's purpose across many or all of their lifetimes. The soul card is calculated by adding the numbers of the personality card together.

Example:

An individual's personality card is the Moon (18).
Reduce further:
1 + 8 = 9 The Hermit

A personality card with a single digit cannot be reduced to a soul card number. In this case, the soul card and personality card are the same.
For example, a birth date reducing to 7 has the Chariot for both personality card and soul card.

TAROT CONSTELLATIONS

Tarot constellations are clusters of cards that share the same prime number. There are different ways to approach the Tarot constellations theories. The one we use in this book may seem like a simplified version, but it has the advantage of being totally mathematical.

There are nine Tarot constellations. Like a mythological constellation, they each symbolize particular qualities that mark the individual's path. The other cards inside the constellation serve to magnify the constellation's archetypal motifs.

Magician
Awareness, presence, external sense

High Priestess
Intuition, stillness, internal sense

Empress
Manifestation, creativity, mother

Emperor
Structure, strength, father

Hierophant
Mentor, ethics, spirituality

Lovers
Choice, discernment, opposition, union

Chariot
Quest, action, movement, hero

Strength
Might, power, animals, heroine

Hermit
Wisdom, experience, shamanistic experience

To see if a card belongs to a specific cluster it's necessary to add together all the figures composing the number of the card, like in the Hidden Number Technique. For instance Death is the Arcana number 13, and 1 + 3 = 4, so it belongs to the Emperor cluster.

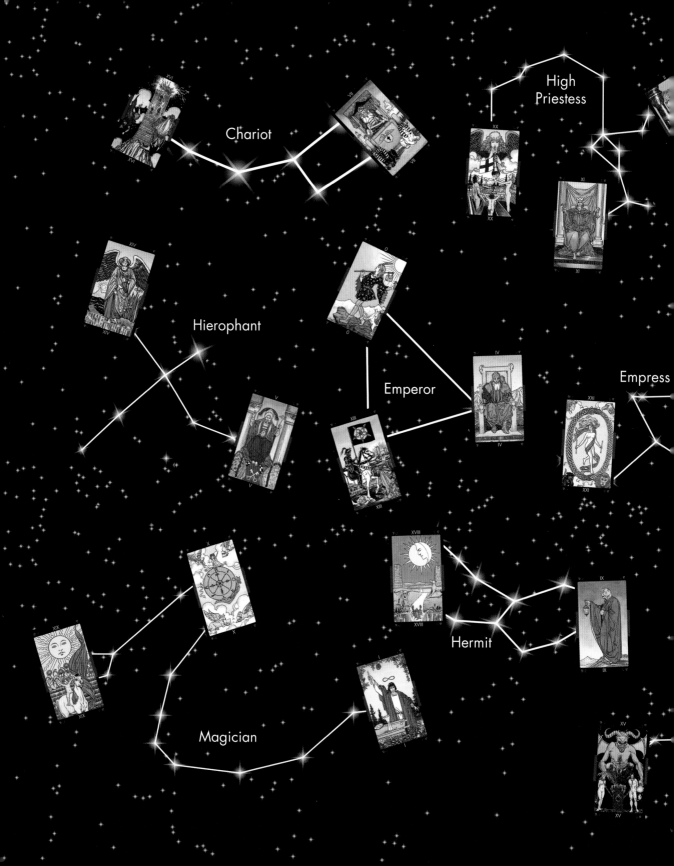

Strength

Lovers

Magician
Associated Majors Inside Cluster: Sun, Wheel of Fortune, Magician
Principle: Will and focused consciousness
Minor Arcana Cards: Tens, Aces

High Priestess
Associated Majors Inside Cluster: Judgment, Justice, High Priestess
Principle: Balanced judgment through intuitive awareness
Minor Arcana Cards: Twos, Pages

Empress
Associated Majors Inside Cluster: World, Hanged Man, Empress
Principle: Manifestation of the creative impulse
Minor Arcana Cards: Threes, Knights

Emperor
Associated Majors Inside Cluster: Fool, Death, Emperor
Principle: Life force and realization of power
Minor Arcana Cards: Fours, Queens

Hierophant
Associated Majors Inside Cluster: Temperance, Hierophant
Principle: Teaching and learning
Minor Arcana Cards: Fives, Kings

Lovers
Associated Majors Inside Cluster: Devil, Lovers
Principle: Relatedness and choice
Minor Arcana Cards: Sixes

Chariot
Associated Majors Inside Cluster: Tower, Chariot
Principle: Mastery through change
Minor Arcana Cards: Sevens

Strength
Associated Majors Inside Cluster: Star, Strength
Principle: Courage and self-esteem
Minor Arcana Cards: Eights

Hermit
Associated Majors Inside Cluster: Moon, Hermit
Principle: Introspection and personal integrity
Minor Arcana Cards: Nines

Thematic Constellations

The technique to gather cards into clusters is not necessarily useful only regarding numerology. The underlying concept is that cards are connected to each other and several cards are different manifestations of the same core concept, be it a number or something else.

Below you will see an example of constellations created using concepts, rather than numbers at the core.

1. Chaos
The Fool
The Wheel of Fortune
The Devil

2. Order
The Emperor
The Hierophant
Justice

3. Yang, Male
The Emperor
The Hierophant
The Sun

4. Yin, Female
The High Priestess
The Empress
The Moon

5. Expansion, growth
The Magician
The Chariot
The World

6. Reduction, blockage
The Hanged Man
The Tower
Judgement

7. Instinct, intuition, insight
The Empress
The Hanged Man
The Moon

8. Reason, logic, discipline
The High Priestess
Justice
The Sun

9. Solitude, silence, quiet
The Hermit
Temperance
The Star

10. Energy, movement, noise
The Chariot
The Devil
The Tower

11. Opening, beginnings
The Magician
Death
The Star

12. Closing, endings
Death
Judgement
The World

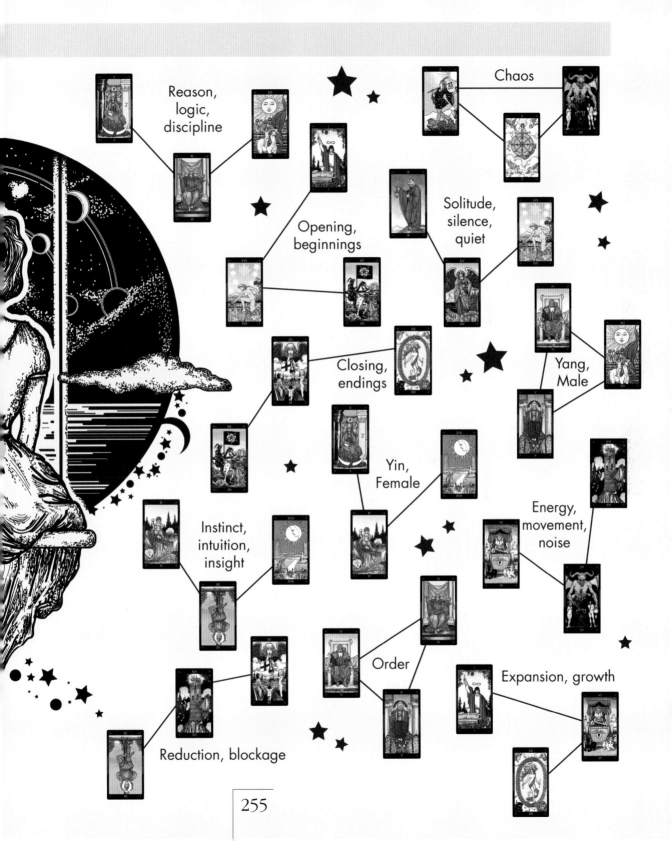

Reason, logic, discipline

Chaos

Opening, beginnings

Solitude, silence, quiet

Closing, endings

Yang, Male

Yin, Female

Instinct, intuition, insight

Energy, movement, noise

Order

Expansion, growth

Reduction, blockage

There may be a million leaves.
And each of them will always
be unique.

Welcome to Advanced Arcana

Page of Pentacles from the
Viceversa Tarot, by Massimiliano
Filadoro, artwork by Davide Corsi

"Not for a moment dare we succumb to the illusion that an archetype can be finally explained and disposed of."
— Carl Jung, *The Archetypes and the Collective Unconscious*

Readers wishing to explore the advanced meanings of the Arcana can educate themselves on the hidden structures and systems of Tarot. This will push the Reader past the boundaries of intuitive reading. The following pages are a highly advanced and technical guide to the cards yet the Reader should not be intimidated. Allow the information to sink in at your own pace. Open the book when you need reference or feel you are ready to incorporate esoteric information into your reading style.

You will discover a deepening web of interrelatedness capable of explaining the unexplainable.
The esoteric seeks to lift the veil of reality. They seek the mystical underpinnings of the universe by asking the most essential and important questions. Why are we here? Who are we? What is this crazy experience we call life? Tarot and its underlying systems will bring you further inside life's greatest questions. The images on the cards are complete insofar as the artist has put them down. What the images and systems reference is as vast as the ever expanding universe in which we all ride.

Lo Scarabeo's previous Tarot volumes provided essential information for each key. In the following pages you will find advanced associations including Kabbalah, numerology, psychology, colors, paths and alchemy. Each card connection can be used as a diving board so you may plunge yourself deeper into the Arcana and/or into each respective esoteric system.

0 THE FOOL

(1) *Spirit of Aether*

(2) Light
Innocence

(3) Shadow
Immobility

(4) Kabbalistic Path
Path 11, joining Kether and Chokhmah

(5) *Path Color: Bright pale yellow*

(6) Hebrew Letter

א

Aleph.

The first letter, like a barely audible whisper, represents the divine breath and prayer. The letter's meaning is "ox."

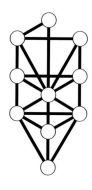

(7) 0
Zero is not nothingness.
Zero is the circle that encloses the universe without end.

(8) Alchemy
Alum.
It is the salt that generates the other salts, the substance of intangible materiality, the focus of intellectual life.

(9) Astrology
Air

(10) Esoteric Function
Breath of Life

(11) Musical Pitch
E natural

(12) Intelligence
Scintillating Intelligence.
It stands before the Face of the Cause of Causes.

(13) Magical Use
Fresh starts. New cycles. Journeys.

(14) Associated Ideas
Freedom, strangeness, incomprehensible action, carelessness, originality, creativity.

(15) Herbal Attribution
Ginseng

1 Esoteric Title

The esoteric title assigned to the Arcana by the Golden Dawn.

2 Light

Light is discovered by examining the Arcana holistically and entering each card as a world in and of itself. The light reflects the "bright" potential of the Arcana. The light stands in opposition to the shadow but is not its "opposite."

3 Shadow

Shadow is discovered by examining the Arcana holistically and entering each card as a world in and of itself. The shadow reflects the "hidden" potential of the Arcana. The shadow is what is discovered when the individual travels from the light into the unknown. The shadow stands in opposition to the light but is not its "opposite."

4 Kabbalistic Path

The associated Kabbalistic path found on the Tree of Life.

5 Path Color

The associated color of the Kabbalistic path found on the Tree of Life.

6 Hebrew Letter

The associated Hebrew letter and its meaning.

7 Number

The numerical representation of the card and the associated ideas that come with it.

8 Alchemy

The alchemical association of each Arcana.

9 Astrology

The astrological/planetary association of each Arcana.

10 Esoteric Function

The esoteric function assigned to the Arcana by the Golden Dawn.

11 Musical Pitch

The musical pitch associated with each Arcana by Paul Foster Case.

12 Intelligence

The Intelligence assigned to the Arcana by the Golden Dawn.

13 Magical Use

Suggested magical usage of the Arcana based on symbol and associated meaning.

14 Associated Ideas

A collection of familiar interpretations of each Arcana. The assemblage is meant to offer a jumping-off point into the endless wells of Tarot association and meaning.

15 Herbal Attribution

The herbal association of each Arcana based on the astrology and associations of the card.

Key to Minor Arcana

SEVEN OF CUPS

 (4) Element
Water

(1) Lord of Illusory Success

(2) Light
Fantasy

(3) Shadow
Dark - Temptation

(8) Astrology
Venus in Scorpio
(20° to 30° Scorpio)

(9) Sephirah
Netzach (Victory)

Venus: Affection, sociability, romance, love of harmony and beauty, sensuality and seduction. Scorpio: Passion, animosity, conflict between reason and feeling, egocentrism, nonconformity, vanity.

Meaning: The ability to coordinate, perseverance in adversity, stability, security and progress.

(5) Associated Ideas
Illusion, desire, vision, envy, false hope, deception.

(6) Magical Use
New possibilities.

(7) Herbal Attribution
Juniper berries

EIGHT OF CUPS

 Element
Water

Lord of Abandoned Success

Light
New direction.

Shadow
Repeat mistakes.

Astrology
Saturn in Pisces
(0° to 10° Pisces)

Sephirah
Hod (Splendor) in Beri'ah

*Saturn: Self-control, meditation, perseverance, patience, critical sense, concrete, confidence, humility.
Pisces: Inconsistency, unpredictability, dreamer spirit, sensitivity, emotions, attraction to utopias.*

Meaning: Dynamic, fast change, adaptability, socialization, business sense.

Associated Ideas
Change direction, start over, let it go, negative opinion.

Magical Use
Journeywork. Travel. Transcendence.

Herbal Attribution
Gravel root

1 Esoteric Title

The esoteric title assigned to the Arcana by the Golden Dawn.

2 Light

Light is discovered by examining the Arcana holistically and entering each card as a world in and of itself. The light reflects the "bright" potential of the Arcana. The light stands in opposition to the shadow but is not its "opposite."

3 Shadow

Shadow is discovered by examining the Arcana holistically and entering each card as a world in and of itself. The shadow reflects the "hidden" potential of the Arcana. The shadow is what is discovered when the individual travels from the light into the unknown. The shadow stands in opposition to the light but is not its "opposite."

4 Element

The Elemental attribution and the symbol representing it.

5 Associated Ideas

A collection of familiar interpretations of each Arcana. The assemblage is meant to offer a jumping-off point into the endless wells of Tarot association and meaning.

6 Magical Use

Suggested magical usage of the Arcana based on symbol and associated meaning.

7 Herbal Attribution

The herbal association of each Arcana based on the astrology and associations of the card.

8 Astrology

The astrological/planetary association of each Arcana.

9 Sephirah

Tree of Life placement corresponding with the Tetregrameton (Hebrew name of God).

KNIGHT OF CUPS

1 *Lord of the Waves and the Waters* ❧ *King of the Hosts of the Sea* ❧ *King of the Nymphs and Undines*

2 Light
Offering

3 Shadow
Hoarding

4 Elemental Counterchange
Fire of Water

△ ▽

6 Sephirah
Tiferet

5 Predominant Sun Sign
Pisces

♓

7 Approximate Time Period
February 9 – March 10

8 Timing
Rapid development and change, somewhat unstable and very unpredictable.

9 Aspect of Self
Personal mind/energies

10 Divinatory Personality
Will modifying Emotion

11 Family Position
Teenage child

12 Associated Tarot Cards
Seven of Swords, Eight of Cups, Nine of Cups

13 Activity
Triumphant, outgoing, speedy, fast moving.

14 Magical Use
Romance. Courting. Charm.

15 Herbal Attribution
Sarsaparilla

1   Esoteric Title

The esoteric title assigned to the Arcana by the Golden Dawn.

2   Light

The light reflects the "bright" potential of the Arcana. The light stands in opposition to the shadow but is not its "opposite."

3   Shadow

The shadow reflects the "hidden" potential of the Arcana. The shadow is what is discovered when the individual travels from the light into the unknown. The shadow stands in opposition to the light but is not its "opposite."

4   Elemental Counterchange

Kabbalistic associations of an elemental nature.

5   Predominant Sun Sign

Court cards rule various zodiac signs but always lean heavily into one particular sign, as listed here. Note: The Pages are not assigned to any astrological suit by the Golden Dawn. They serve as the thrones or the seats of power for the Aces and have no sun sign or time period.

6   Sephirah

Tree of Life placement corresponding with the Tetregrameton (Hebrew name of God).

7   Approximate Time Period

The approximate astrological time period of the court card.

8   Timing

Answers the time-honored questions of how to react and when it will happen.

9   Aspect of Self

Part of the body/self the card rules.

10   Divinatory Personality

Derived from the 16 basic elemental personalities based on the combination of two essential characteristics.

11   Family Position

Which part of the family unit the card represents. Also associated to the four letters of the sacred name of Jehovah.

12   Associated Tarot Cards

The Minor Arcana cards that are associated with each court card according to their Astrological Deacons.

13   Activity

The active parts of the card and how the personality type operates in the real world.

14   Magical Use

Suggested magical usage of the Arcana based on symbol and associated meaning.

15   Herbal Attribution

The herbal association of each Arcana based on the astrology and associations of the card.

0   THE FOOL

Spirit of Aether

Light
Innocence

Shadow
Immobility

Kabbalistic Path
Path 11, joining Kether and Chokhmah
Path Color: Bright pale yellow

Hebrew Letter

א

Aleph.

The first letter, like a barely audible whisper, represents the divine breath and prayer. The letter's meaning is "ox."

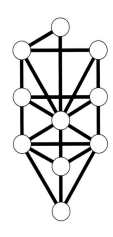

0
Zero is not nothingness.
Zero is the circle that encloses the universe without end.

Alchemy

Alum

It is the salt that generates the other salts, the substance of intangible materiality, the focus of intellectual life.

Astrology

Air

Esoteric Function
Breath of Life

Musical Pitch
E natural

Intelligence
Scintillating Intelligence.
It stands before the Face of the Cause of Causes.

Magical Use
Fresh starts. New cycles.
Journeys.

Associated Ideas
Freedom, strangeness, incomprehensible action, carelessness, originality, creativity.

Herbal Attribution
Ginseng

I THE MAGICIAN

Magus of Power

Light		Shadow
Ability		Stasis

Kabbalistic Path
Path 12, joining Kether and Binah
Path Color: Yellow

Hebrew Letter

Bet

Bet, which means "house," is the intimacy, the center, and the inner temple of every individual.

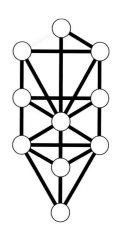

1
Number 1 is the first among all the numbers.

It expresses the beginning of everything, of every thought and every action. It also represents unity, the indivisible core, and the essence of every being.

Alchemy

The Alchemist

The operator who prepares tools necessary to achieve a great work.

Astrology

Mercury

Esoteric Function
Life/Death

Musical Pitch
E natural

Intelligence
Intelligence of Transparency.

The place issuing the visions and where prophesies are seen.

Magical Use
Increase charisma.
Invoke energy. Success.

Associated Ideas
Will, skill, spirit of initiative, communication, diplomacy, manipulation.

Herbal Attribution
Astragalus

II THE HIGH PRIESTESS

Princess of the Silver Star

Light
Knowledge

Shadow
Inauthentic

Kabbalistic Path
Path 13, joining Kether and Chokhmah
Path Color: Blue

Hebrew Letter

ג

Gimel:

Gimel, which means "camel," expresses the ability to survive thanks to one's resources.

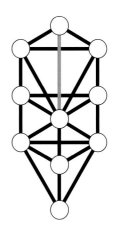

2

The number 2 is the natural continuation of something.

The duality is the equilibrium and energy between opposites.

Alchemy

Raw materials of the sages

The first puzzle is called the Path of the Alchemist.

Astrology

Black Moon

Esoteric Function
Peace/Strife

Musical Pitch
G sharp

Intelligence
Uniting Intelligence.

The essence of glory and consummation of all that is true in spirit.

Magical Use
Inner knowledge.
Journey work.
Highest and deepest self.

Associated Ideas
Study, faith, wisdom, intuition and femininity, confidentiality, self-control.

Herbal Attribution
Peony

269

THE EMPRESS

Daughter of the Mighty Ones

Light		Shadow
Creation		Destruction

Kabbalistic Path
Path 14, joining Chokhmah
and Binah
Path Color: Emerald green

Hebrew Letter

ד

Dalet

*Dalet, which means "door,"
represents the transition from
abstraction to concreteness.*

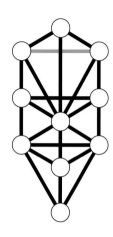

3
The number 3 is born
of the sum of the first
two numbers.
*Three expresses birth, the result
of fruitful union between the
two original elements.*

Alchemy

Salt, Sulfur, and Mercury
*The three parts—body, mind,
and soul—can evolve only in
harmony with each other.*

Astrology

Venus

Esoteric Function
Wisdom/Folly

Musical Pitch
F sharp

Intelligence
Illuminating Intelligence.
*The founder of the concealed and
fundamental ideas of holiness.*

Magical Use
Fertility. Femininity.
Creativity.

Associated Ideas
Intelligence, beneficial
influence, problem solver,
support, receptivity,
maternal instinct, protection.

Herbal Attribution
Dong quai

IV THE EMPEROR

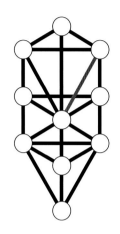

Sun of the Morning ☙ Chief Among the Mighty

Light		**Shadow**
Control		Irresponsibility

Kabbalistic Path
Path 15, joining Chokhmah
and Tiferet
Path Color: Scarlet

Hebrew Letter

ה

He

*He, which means "window,"
represents light that enters a
house, illuminating everything.*

4
The number 4 mirrors the
perfection of the square.

*Fours connects the cardinal points
to the seasons, the phases of the
moon, and the natural elements
in the Pythagorean tradition: air,
water, earth, and fire.*

Alchemy

The Adept

*He works on himself, and
transforms the
prima materia into the
Philosopher's Stone.*

Astrology

Aries

♈

Esoteric Function
Sight

Musical Pitch
C natural

Intelligence
Constituting Intelligence.
Creation in pure darkness.

Magical Use
Assertion. Creation.
Completion. Boundary work.

Associated Ideas
Authority, stability,
administration, control,
law, decisions, obligations.

Herbal Attribution
Atractylodes

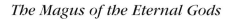

V THE HIEROPHANT

The Magus of the Eternal Gods

Light		**Shadow**
Guidance		Fear

Kabbalistic Path
Path 16, joining Chokhmah
and Chesel
Path Color: Red-orange

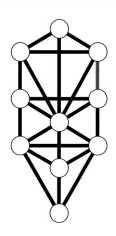

Hebrew Letter

ו

Vav

*Vav means "nail." Until it is
fixed there is no central pin or
equilibrium or perfection.*

5

The number 5 symbolizes
the human body.

*The head with arms and legs
open draws the vertices of a star
with five points. The number 5
is mediated and balanced. It is
the number of the five senses.*

Alchemy

Quintessence

*The essence of a deep
individual or a thought.*

Astrology

Taurus

Esoteric Function
Hearing

Intelligence
Triumphal and Eternal
Intelligence.
The glory above all other glories.

Associated Ideas
Inspiration, advice,
clemency, forgiveness,
peace, ritual, tradition,
hierarchy.

Musical Pitch
C sharp

Magical Use
Ritual. Doorway.

Herbal Attribution
Sage

VI | THE LOVERS

Children of the Voice Divine ☯ Oracles of the Mighty Gods

Light		Shadow
Choice		Nothingness

Kabbalistic Path
Path 17, joining Binah and Tiferet
Path Color: Orange

Hebrew Letter

ז

Zayin

Zayin means "sword" or "armor." The individual may obtain what he wants through battle.

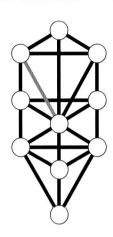

6

The number 6 is a number of harmony and equilibrium.

In ancient times the number 6 was sacred to Aphrodite, the goddess of love. The number 6 expresses the conjunction of opposites.

Alchemy

The Seal of Solomon

Two triangles crossed and opposed, express the perfect union of opposites.

Astrology

Gemini

♊

Esoteric Function
Smell

Musical Pitch
D natural

Intelligence
Disposing Intelligence.

Provides faith to the righteous, and they are clothed with the Holy Spirit by it.

Magical Use
Love. Sex. Romance.

Associated Ideas
Decision, examination, doubt, fork, attempt, oath, covenant.

Herbal Attribution
Parsley

273

VII | THE CHARIOT

Child of the Powers of Water *Lord of the Triumph of Light*

Light		**Shadow**
Conquest		Apathy

Kabbalistic Path

Path 18, joining Binah and Gevurah

Path Color: Red-orange

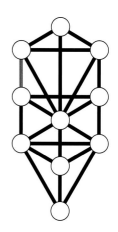

Hebrew Letter

ח

Het

Het means "enclosure" or "fence." A sacred space where the Deity's will reigns.

7

The number 7 expresses motions and transitions.

The number 7 connects to the astrological planets, the seven days of creation, metals in alchemy and the Christian Virtues.

Alchemy

Antimony

The square on a red triangle expresses the correct direction of any transformation.

Astrology

Cancer

Esoteric Function

Speech

Musical Pitch

C sharp

Intelligence

Intelligence of the House of Influence.

Good things are increased and hidden senses are drawn forth.

Magical Use

Movement. Initiative. Action.

Associated Ideas

Triumph, success, great ambition, ability, directive, progress.

Herbal Attribution

Cyperus

VIII | STRENGTH

Daughter of the Flaming Sword & Leader of the Lion

Light
Discipline

Shadow
Brutality

Kabbalistic Path
Path 19, joining Chesed and Gevurah
Path Color: Yellow-green

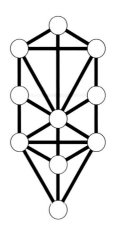

Hebrew Letter

ט

Tet

Tet, which means "serpent," expresses goodness, but goodness must act prudently.

8
The number 8 is about infinity.

The number 8 is a mathematical symbol as well as a symbol for the infinite and cyclical universal renewal. It is also represented as an octagon, or as an eight-pointed star.

Alchemy

Lead

The lion is the symbol for lead, the matter not yet transformed into alchemical gold.

Astrology

Leo

♌

Esoteric Function
Taste

Musical Pitch
E natural

Intelligence
Intelligence of the Secret of All Spiritual Activities.

The influence diffused by the most high and exalted sublime glory.

Magical Use
Perseverance. Strength. Resolve.

Associated Ideas
Energy, courage, self-mastery, work, conflict between opposites, overcome fear, relief.

Herbal Attribution
Cayenne

IX | THE HERMIT

Prophet of the Gods ~ Magus of the Voice of Light

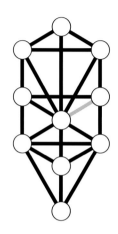

Light		Shadow
Withdrawal		Expulsion

Kabbalistic Path
Path 20, joining Chesed and Tiferet
Path Color: Green-yellow

Hebrew Letter

י

Yod

Yod, which means "hand," is a sign of authority but also represents individual limits.

9
The number 9 is threefold 3.

The number 9 is the result of the number 3 multiplied by itself. Perfection is projected in three dimensions: material, intellectual, and spiritual.

Alchemy

Hermes

The Hermit is the follower of Hermes, the alchemist supreme.

Astrology

Virgo

♍

Esoteric Function
Sexuality (Touch)

Musical Pitch
F natural

Intelligence
Intelligence of Will.

Through each and every person the Primordial Wisdom becomes known.

Magical Use
Contemplation. Spirituality. Wisdom.

Associated Ideas
Prudence, silence, loneliness, spiritual quest, meditation, austerity, humility.

Herbal Attribution
Licorice

X | THE WHEEL OF FORTUNE

Lord of the Forces of Life

Light
Fortune

Shadow
Stillness

Kabbalistic Path
Path 21, joining Chesed and Netzach

Path Color: Violet

Hebrew Letter

כ ך

Kaph

Kaph, which means "fist," is the hand that takes. Force must be tempered by morality.

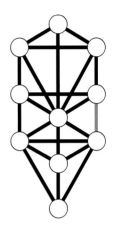

10

The number 10 represents the conclusion of a cycle.

It is the natural expression of the whole nature and its transformations.

Alchemy

The Azoth of the Sages

The vehicle of intelligence, or even the messenger of the upper and lower spirits.

Astrology

Jupiter

2

Esoteric Function
Riches/Poverty

Musical Pitch
A sharp

Intelligence
Intelligence of Conciliation.

Receives divine influence and lets it flows through all existence.

Magical Use
Luck. Action. Energy.

Associated Ideas
Alternating or cyclical opportunities, time (seasons, months or years), natural cycles.

Herbal Attribution
Slippery elm

JUSTICE

Daughter of the Lord of Truth *Holder of the Balances*

Light		Shadow
Equality		Cruelty

Kabbalistic Path
Path 22, joining Gevurah and Tiferet
Path Color: Emerald green

Hebrew Letter
ל
Lamed

Lamed, meaning "sting" or "ox goad," symbolizes the movement of man toward the Divine.

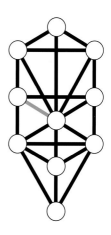

11
The number 11 represents a new cycle.
The number is composed of two ones and this indicates the duality leading to the inner harmonization of opposing principles.

Alchemy
The scales and the sword
These are the tools with which the alchemist doses between the elements and compounds.

Astrology
Libra

♎

Esoteric Function
Work

Musical Pitch
F sharp

Intelligence
Faithful Intelligence.
Every dweller of earth is under its spiritual shadow.

Magical Use
Legality. Work. Karma.

Associated Ideas
Balance, law, logic, rule, inflexibility, therefore, division, work.

Herbal Attribution
Plantain

THE HANGED MAN

Spirit of the Mighty Waters

Light		**Shadow**
Vision		Blindness

Kabbalistic Path
Path 23, joining Gevurah
and Hod
Path Color: Deep blue

Hebrew Letter

מ ם

Mem

*Mem, which means "water,"
represents the thirst for the deep
wisdom of the Creator.*

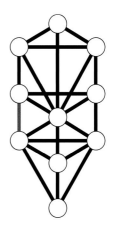

12

The number 12 is
all encompassing.

*The number 12 is seen in the 12
signs of the zodiac, 12 months
of the year, 12 tribes of Israel,
12 apostles, 12 hours of AM and
PM time.*

Alchemy

Purified sulfur

*Only through purification can
the element be used.*

Astrology

Water

Esoteric Function
Revelation/Concealment

Musical Pitch
G sharp

Intelligence
Stable Intelligence.

*It has sameness and consistency
through all numerations.*

Magical Use
Visions. Esoteric truth. Yoga.

Associated Ideas
Temporary difficulty, search,
inner idealism, detachment
from matter, transition.

Herbal Attribution
Kelp

XIII | DEATH

Child of the Great Transformers ☙ Lord of the Gates of Death

Light Transformation		**Shadow** Apathy

Kabbalistic Path
Path 24, joining Tiferet and Netzach

Path Color: Green-blue

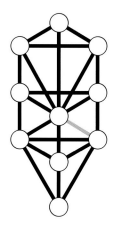

Hebrew Letter

נ ן

Nun

Nun, which means "fish" or "whale," represents the relationship between the mortal body and the immortal soul.

13
The number 13 represents a doorway or a gate.

The number 13 is considered lucky, unlucky, or uncanny depending on local traditions.

Alchemy
The Black Opus

It is where the consciousness of the Adept dies and decomposes to be born again.

Astrology
Scorpio

♏

Esoteric Function
Transformation

Musical Pitch
G natural

Intelligence
Imaginative Intelligence.

All the similitudes which are created in harmonious elegancies.

Magical Use
Change. Shadow work. Endings.

Associated Ideas
Threshold, sudden or unexpected change, radical change, irreversibility.

Herbal Attribution
Elderflower

TEMPERANCE

Daughter of the Reconcilers ❧ Bringer Forth of Life

Light		**Shadow**
Refinement		Imbalance

Kabbalistic Path

Path 25, joining Tiferet and Yesod

Path Color: Blue

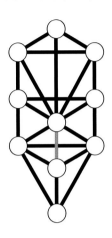

Hebrew Letter

Samekh

Samekh, which means "prop," the thing that keeps us grounded and supported.

14

The number 14 represents renewed balance and new beginnings.

Passover was celebrated 14 days after the spring equinox.

Alchemy

The White Opus

The ritual of death and resurrection.

Astrology

Sagittarius

Esoteric Function

Anger

Musical Pitch

G sharp

Intelligence

Intelligence of Probation or Tentative Intelligence.

The primary temptation by which all people are tested.

Magical Use

Balance. Excellence. Mastery.

Associated Ideas

Mixture, moderation, adaptation, translation, regeneration, care, gradual change.

Herbal Attribution

Echinacea

XV THE DEVIL

Lord of the Gates of Matter Child of the Forces of Time

Light		Shadow
Passion		Uninvolved

Kabbalistic Path

Path 26, joining Tiferet and Hod

Path Color: Indigo

Hebrew Letter

ע

Ayin

Ayin means "eye." Refers to both inward and outward perception.

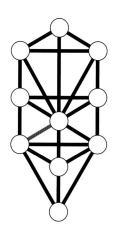

15

The number 15 represents imbalance and the "other side".

The 5 sensual ways are projected in the 3 worlds: physical, intellectual, and spiritual. According to St. Paul in Galatians, there are 15 fruits of sin.

Alchemy

The "Great Magical Agent"

The mean by which the Adept revives the inner spark.

Astrology

Capricorn

♑

Esoteric Function
Mirth

Musical Pitch
A natural

Intelligence
Renovating Intelligence.
God is thought to change things by renewing them.

Magical Use
Glee. Power. Intensity.

Associated Ideas
Instinct, attraction, sexual instinct, emotion, uncontrolled charm, suggestion, selfishness.

Herbal Attribution
Lobelia

THE TOWER

Lord of the Host of the Mighty

Light		**Shadow**
Collapse		Stillness

Kabbalistic Path

Path 27, joining Netzach and Hod

Path Color: Scarlet

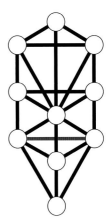

Hebrew Letter

פ ף

Peh

Peh, which means "mouth," refers to the power of speech and expression through words.

16

The number 16 is a prophetic number.

Multiply 2 by 8, the number of infinity. Multiply 4 by 4, the number of the sacred cube.

Alchemy

The "Fire of Heaven Below"

If fed too much it forces the Adept to begin again.

Astrology

Mars

♂

Esoteric Function

Grace/Sin

Musical Pitch

C natural

Intelligence

Active or Exciting Intelligence.

Through this, every being receives its spirit and motion.

Magical Use

Change. Alteration. Destruction.

Associated Ideas

Closing, prison, loss of safety, punishment, separation, removal.

Herbal Attribution

Garlic

XVII · THE STAR

Daughter of the Firmament *Dweller Between the Waters.*

Light		**Shadow**
Inspiration		Depression

Kabbalistic Path

Path 28, joining Netzach and Yesod

Path Color: Violet

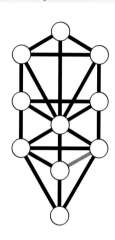

Hebrew Letter

צ ץ

Tzade

Tzade means "fish hook." It reflects divine imagination, faith, and perception.

17

The number 17 represents the human limits.

For the Romans, 17 was a symbol of a life reaching its end. For St. Augustine, 17 was a number related to the baptism and pointed to the passage from sin to purity.

Alchemy

Astral Influences

What the wise must learn to know and to dominate.

Astrology

Aquarius

Esoteric Function
Imagination

Musical Pitch
A sharp

Intelligence
Natural Intelligence.

The consummation of everything that is perfected in nature.

Magical Use
Muse. Inspiration.
Creative projects.

Associated Ideas
Foresight, favorable omen, purity, beauty.

Herbal Attribution
Skullcap

XVIII | THE MOON

Ruler of the Flux and Reflux *Child of the Sons of the Mighty*

Light		**Shadow**
Dream		Blindness

Kabbalistic Path
Path 29, joining Netzach and Malkuth
Path Color: Ultraviolet-crimson

Hebrew Letter

ק
Qoph

Qoph, which means "the back of the head," divides two opposite sides with an uncertain border.

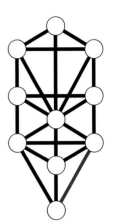

18

The number 18 is a mystery that cannot be solved by reason.

The number 18 is considered lucky, although it has no biblical or mythological meaning.

Alchemy

Astral Travel

When the soul leaves the body and ventures into the spiritual world.

Astrology

Pisces

Esoteric Function
Sleep

Intelligence
Corporeal Intelligence.
It forms beneath a new set of parameters.

Associated Ideas
Vision, intuition, application, research, mystery, sensitivity, ambiguity.

Musical Pitch
B natural

Magical Use
Dreamwork. Shadow work.

Herbal Attribution
Lemon balm

XIX | THE SUN

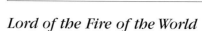

Lord of the Fire of the World

Light		**Shadow**
Energy		Nothingness

Kabbalistic Path

Path 30, joining Hod and Yesod

Path Color: Orange

Hebrew Letter

Resh

Resh, which means "head," symbolizes the place where thought is born and expands by invoking clarity.

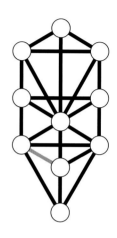

19

The number 19 is about insight, understanding and clarity.

The number 19 is the sum of 12 (zodiac signs) plus 7 (the planets in classical astrology). It represents the sky as a whole.

Alchemy

Gold of the Philosophers

The Sun is the gold of the philosophers or the light that brings understanding to the Adept.

Astrology

The Sun

Esoteric Function
Fertility/Barrenness

Musical Pitch
D natural

Intelligence
Collecting Intelligence.

The culmination of the celestial signs and the perfection of the astrologer's science.

Magical Use
Healing. Fertility. Manifestation.

Associated Ideas
Harmony, friendship, solidarity, honesty, generosity, expansiveness, clarity.

Herbal Attribution
Angelica

JUDGMENT

Spirit of the Primal Fire

Light		**Shadow**
Rebirth		Stuck

Kabbalistic Path

Path 31, joining Hod and Malkuth

Path Color: Glowing orange-scarlet

Hebrew Letter

ש

Shin

Shin, which means "tooth," represents the senses and matter and the cyclical movements of existence.

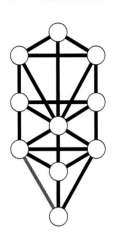

20

The number 20 is the end, or perfect completition.

The number 20 is composed of 2, expressing complementary opposition, and 0, which expands the value of every number it is placed with.

Alchemy

Awakening of Consciousness

The harmony between the parties, such as body, mind, and spirit, which leads to the awakening of consciousness.

Astrology

Fire

Esoteric Function
Realization

Musical Pitch
C natural

Intelligence
Perpetual Intelligence.

Regulates the motions of the Sun and Moon in their proper order.

Magical Use
Purification. Finding forgiveness. Self-esteem.

Associated Ideas
Renewal, awakening, important moment, examination of conscience.

Herbal Attribution
Goldenseal

XXI | THE WORLD

The Great One of the Night of Time

Light		Shadow
Completeness		Reversal

Kabbalistic Path

Path 32, joining Yesod and Malkuth

Path Color: Indigo

Hebrew Letter

ת

Tav

Tav, which means "mark" or "seal," represents truth and perfection. It is the initial Torah, divine law.

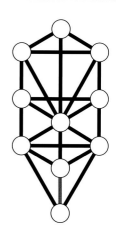

21

The number 21 is totality, and mystic completion.

The Book of Wisdom contains 21 attributes. It also mirrors the number 12 and thus becomes the engine of the universe in a higher dimension.

Alchemy

The Great Work

The consciousness of the Adept has achieved harmony with the entire universe.

Astrology

Saturn

Esoteric Function
Power/Servitude

Musical Pitch
A natural

Intelligence
Administrative Intelligence.

It directs and associates the seven planets in all their operations and all in their due course.

Magical Use
Success. Travel. Completion.

Associated Ideas
Reward, success, crowning, reintegration, happiness, fulfillment.

Herbal Attribution
Comfrey

The Four Kabbalistic Worlds

The four Kabbalistic Worlds associate with the Tetragrammaton (Hebrew name of God: *Yod, Heh, Vav, Heh*).

Each World contains its own Tree. They are placed in a linear arrangement and it begins at the top with:

Atziluth
The World of Emanation

Yetzirah
The World of Formation

Beriah
The World of Creation

Assiah
The World of Action

יהוה

Each world also connects to an element and a suit of Tarot.

- **Assiah (Heh)**
  is the Material World
  (Pentacles/Earth)

- **Yetzirah (Vav)**
  is the Formative World
  (Swords/Air)

- **Beriah (Heh)**
  is the Creative World
  (Cups/Water)

- **Atziluth (Yod)**
  is the Archetypal World
  (Wands/Fire)

ACE OF CUPS

Element
Rules the element of Water

Associated Ideas
The source of life, the Holy Grail, the heart, the human soul.

Magical Use
Forgiveness

Herbal Attribution
Lotus

Root of the Powers of Water

Light		**Shadow**
Flow		Blockage

Astrology
Water

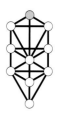

Sephirah
Kether (Crown)

Origin, the root of thought and action, superior knowledge, creativity, clarity, will.

TWO OF CUPS

Element
Water

Associated Ideas
Affection, connection, friendship, business contract, emotions, similar intentions.

Magical Use
Connection. Companionship.

Herbal Attribution
Uva ursi

Lord of Love

Light		**Shadow**
Greeting		Farewell

Astrology
Venus in Cancer
(0° to 10° Cancer)

Venus: *Affection, sociability, romance, love of harmony and beauty, sensuality and seduction.*
Cancer: *Union, association, gestation, fruit ripening, recognition of their roots.*

Sephirah
Chokhmah (Wisdom)

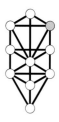

Intuition, seed idea, revealing paradox, incomprehensible, ineffable.

THREE OF CUPS

Element
Water

Associated Ideas
Sharing, joy, exhilaration, celebration, dance.

Magical Use
Happiness

Herbal Attribution
Trillium

Lord of Abundance

Light
Creativity

Shadow
Fear

Astrology
Mercury in Cancer
(10° to 20° Cancer)

☿ ♋

Mercury: *Mental alertness, imagination, communication skills, diplomacy, love of travel, occult interests.*
Cancer: *Union, association, gestation, fruit ripening, recognition of their roots.*

Sephirah
Binah (Understanding)

Analysis, rationality, logic, concreteness, clarity of language, ability to communicate.

FOUR OF CUPS

Element
Water

Associated Ideas
New idea, waiting, disappointment, boredom.

Magical Use
New possibility. Emotional stabilizer.

Herbal Attribution
Burdock

The Lord of Blended Pleasures

Light
Omen

Shadow
Blindness

Astrology
Moon in Cancer
(20° to 30° Cancer)

☽ ♋

Moon: *Sensitivity, instinct, intuition, emotion, seduction, imagination, illusions, unpredictability.*
Cancer: *Union, association, gestation, fruit ripening, recognition of their roots.*

Sephirah
Chesed (Mercy)

Sentiment, mercy, devotion, kindness, generosity, ability to forgive.

FIVE OF CUPS

Element
Water

Associated Ideas
Shortages, difficulties, regret, remorse, pessimism, self-sacrifice.

Magical Use
Breaking habits.

Herbal Attribution
Horsetail

Lord of Loss of Material Pleasure

Light		**Shadow**
Repentance		Loss

Astrology
Mars in Scorpio
(0° to 10° Scorpio)

Mars: *Energy, initiative, resolution, authoritarianism, competition, martial character, aggressiveness.*
Scorpio: *Passion, animosity, conflict between reason and feeling, egocentrism, nonconformity, vanity.*

Sephirah
Gevurah (Strength)

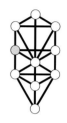

Discipline, rigor, severity rating, control, containment, moderation, limitation.

SIX OF CUPS

Element
Water

Associated Ideas
Gift, offering, message, peace, remembering, looking back.

Magical Use
Compassion. Love. Memory.

Herbal Attribution
Watermelon

Lord of Pleasure

Light		**Shadow**
Sharing		Nostalgia

Astrology
Sun in Scorpio
(10° to 20° Scorpio)

Sun: *Sensitivity, instinct, intuition, emotion, seduction, imagination, illusions, unpredictability.*
Scorpio: *Passion, animosity, conflict between reason and feeling, egocentrism, nonconformity, vanity.*

Sephirah
Tiferet (Beauty)

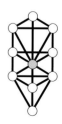

Aesthetics, sensitivity, love of nature, mediation, harmony, measure, balance, compassion.

SEVEN OF CUPS

Element
Water

Associated Ideas
Illusion, desire, vision, envy, false hope, deception.

Magical Use
New possibilities.

Herbal Attribution
Juniper berries

Lord of Illusory Success

Light		**Shadow**
Fantasy		Dark - Temptation

Astrology
Venus in Scorpio
(20° to 30° Scorpio)

♀ ♏

Venus: *Affection, sociability, romance, love of harmony and beauty, sensuality and seduction.*
Scorpio: *Passion, animosity, conflict between reason and feeling, egocentrism, nonconformity, vanity.*

Sephirah
Netzach (Victory)

The ability to coordinate, perseverance in adversity, stability, security and progress.

EIGHT OF CUPS

Element
Water

Associated Ideas
Change direction, start over, letting go, negative opinion.

Magical Use
Journeywork. Travel.
Transcendence.

Herbal Attribution
Gravel root

Lord of Abandoned Success

Light		**Shadow**
New direction.		Repeat mistakes.

Astrology
Saturn in Pisces
(0° to 10° Pisces)

♄ ♓

Saturn: *Self-control, meditation, perseverance, patience, critical sense, concrete, confidence, humility.*
Pisces: *Inconsistency, unpredictability, dreamer spirit, sensitivity, emotions, attraction to utopias.*

Sephirah
Hod (Splendor)

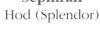

Dynamic, fast change, adaptability, socialization, business sense.

293

NINE OF CUPS

Lord of Material Happiness

Element
Water

Associated Ideas
Well-being, satisfaction, pleasure, fullness, apathy, saturation.

Magical Use
Wish fulfillment

Herbal Attribution
Squaw vine

Light		**Shadow**
Contentment		Loss

Astrology
Jupiter in Pisces
(10° to 20° Pisces)

♃ ♓

Jupiter: *Affability, cheerfulness, confidence, generosity, intellectual and physical growth, expansive, farsightedness.*
Pisces: *Inconsistency, unpredictability, dreamer spirit, sensitivity, emotions, attraction to utopias.*

Sephirah
Yesod (Foundation)

Character, personality, awareness of possibilities, hidden aspirations.

TEN OF CUPS

Lord of Perfected Success

Element
Water

Associated Ideas
Happiness, success, family harmony, happy moment.

Magical Use
Happy family.

Herbal Attribution
Marijuana

Light		**Shadow**
Happiness		Depression

Astrology
Mars in Pisces
(20° to 30° Pisces)

♂ ♓

Mars: *Self-control, meditation, perseverance, patience, critical sense, concrete, confidence, humility.*
Pisces: *Inconsistency, unpredictability, dreamer spirit, sensitivity, emotions, attraction to utopias.*

Sephirah
Malkuth (Kingdom)

Possession, subject, desires, perceptions of need, need of protection.

ACE OF PENTACLES

Element
Rules the element of Earth.

Associated Ideas
Acquisition, success, possession matter, physicality.

Magical Use
Financial issues.

Herbal Attribution
Whole grains

Root of the Powers of Air

| **Light** | | **Shadow** |
| Potential | | End |

Astrology
Earth

Sephirah
Kether (Crown)

Origin, the root of thought and action, knowledge, higher creativity, clarity, will.

TWO OF PENTACLES

Element
Earth

Associated Ideas
Gaiety, dance, speed, adaptability, indecision, vacillation.

Magical Use
Attraction magic.

Herbal Attribution
Yellow dock

Lord of Harmonious Change

| **Light** | | **Shadow** |
| Duality | | Inconsistency |

Astrology
Jupiter in Capricorn
(0° to 10° Capricorn)

♃ ♑

Jupiter: *Affability, cheerfulness, confidence, generosity, intellectual and physical growth, expansive, farsightedness.*
Capricorn: *Rationality, ambition, search for security and stability, tenacity, patience, diplomacy, utilitarianism.*

Sephirah
Chokhmah (Wisdom)

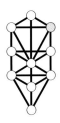

Intuition, beginning idea, revealing paradox, incomprehensible, ineffable.

THREE OF PENTACLES

Element
Earth

Associated Ideas
Craft, talent, proceed in stages, follow a project, inspiration, art.

Magical Use
Creative works.

Herbal Attribution
Gentian

Lord of Material Works

Light Collaboration		**Shadow** Destruction

Astrology
Mars in Capricorn
(10° to 20° Capricorn)

♂ ♑

Mars: *energy, initiative, resolution, authoritarianism, competition, martial character, aggressiveness.*
Capricorn: *Rationality, ambition, search for security and stability, tenacity, patience, diplomacy, utilitarianism.*

Sephirah
Binah (Understanding)

Analysis, rationality, logical, concreteness, clarity of language, ability to communicate.

FOUR OF PENTACLES

Element
Earth

Associated Ideas
Stinginess, parsimony, savings, greed, concentration, distrust.

Magical Use
Financial stability.

Herbal Attribution
Cascara bark

Lord of Earthly Power

Light Stability		**Shadow** Instability

Astrology
Sun in Capricorn
(20° to 30° Capricorn)

☉ ♑

Sun: *Clarity, tenderness, optimism, pursuit of perfection, purity, generosity, courage, creativity.*
Capricorn: *Rationality, ambition, search for security and stability, tenacity, patience, diplomacy, utilitarianism.*

Sephirah
Chesed (Mercy)

Sentiment, mercy, devotion, kindness, generosity, ability to forgive.

FIVE OF PENTACLES

Lord of Material Trouble

Element
Earth

Associated Ideas
Poverty, lack, needs, shortages, difficulty on material plane, looking for help.

Magical Use
Hidden gifts.

Herbal Attribution
Mugwort

Light
Consistency

Shadow
Separation

Astrology
Mercury in Taurus
(0° to 10° Taurus)

☿ ♉

Mercury: *Mental alertness, imagination, communication skills, diplomacy, love of travel, occult interests.*
Taurus: *A practical sense, confidentiality, love of beauty, nature and ease, sweetness, stubbornness, jealousy.*

Sephirah
Gevurah (Strength)

Discipline, rigor, severity rating, control, containment, moderation, limitation.

SIX OF PENTACLES

Lord of Material Success

Element
Earth

Associated Ideas
Generosity, gift, support, equitable distribution, sense of superiority.

Magical Use
Gifts.

Herbal Attribution
Hops

Light
Charity

Shadow
Selfishness

Astrology
Moon in Taurus
(10° to 20° Taurus)

 ☽ ♉

Moon: *Sensitivity, instinct, intuition, emotion, seduction, imagination, illusions, unpredictability.*
Taurus: *A practical sense, confidentiality, love of beauty, nature and ease, sweetness, stubbornness, jealousy.*

Sephirah
Tiferet (Beauty)

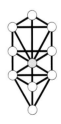

Aesthetics, sensitivity, love of nature, mediation, harmony, measure, balance, compassion.

SEVEN OF PENTACLES

Element
Earth

Lord of Unfulfilled Success

Light		**Shadow**
Evaluation		Dissatisfaction

Associated Ideas
Deal, counting, control, exchange, disinterest, noninvolvement.

Magical Use
Manifestation.

Herbal Attribution
Rhubarb

Astrology
Saturn in Taurus
(20° to 30° Taurus)

♄ ♉

Saturn: *Self-control, meditation, perseverance, patience, critical sense, concrete, confidence, humility.*
Taurus: *A practical sense, confidentiality, love of beauty, nature and ease, sweetness, stubbornness, jealousy.*

Sephirah
Netzach (Victory)

The ability to coordinate, perseverance in adversity, stability, security and progress

EIGHT OF PENTACLES

Element
Earth

Lord of Prudence

Light		**Shadow**
Work	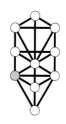	Slave

Associated Ideas
Commitment, dedication, manual skills, employment, routine, repetitive.

Magical Use
Career.

Herbal Attribution
Ginger

Astrology
Sun in Virgo
(0° to 10° Virgo)

☉ ♍

Sun: *Clarity, tenderness, optimism, pursuit of perfection, purity, generosity, courage, creativity.*
Virgo: *Efficiency, industriousness, security, attention to detail, love of order, critical spirit.*

Sephirah
Hod (Splendor)

Dynamic, fast change, adaptability, socialization, business sense.

NINE OF PENTACLES

Lord of Material Gain

Element
Earth

Associated Ideas
Discernment, prudence, material safety and serenity, elegance, pride.

Magical Use
Pleasure in all things.

Herbal Attribution
Dark grapes

Light
Pleasure

Shadow
Vanity

Astrology
Venus in Virgo
(10° to 20° Virgo)

♀ ♍

Venus: *Affection, sociability, romance, love of harmony and beauty, sensuality and seduction.*
Virgo: *Efficiency, industriousness, security, attention to detail, love of order, critical spirit.*

Sephirah
Yesod (Foundation)

Character, personality, awareness of possibilities, hidden aspirations.

TEN OF PENTACLES

Lord of Wealth

Element
Earth

Associated Ideas
Home, house, family life, package deliveries, links.

Magical Use
Family. Stability.

Herbal Attribution
Wild yam

Light
Wealth

Shadow
Inheritance

Astrology
Mercury in Virgo
(20° to 30° Virgo)

☿ ♍

Mercury: *Mental alertness, imagination, communication skills, diplomacy, love of travel, occult interests.*
Virgo: *Efficiency, industriousness, security, attention to detail, love of order, critical spirit.*

Sephirah
Malkuth (Kingdom)

Possession, subject, desires, perceptions of need, need of protection.

ACE OF WANDS

Root of the Powers of Fire

Element
Rules the
element of Fire

Associated Ideas
Flash, ignition, spark, flame,
idea, kindle, flare.

Magical Use
Energy.

Herbal Attribution
Yarrow

Light Initiative		**Shadow** Deadening

Astrology
Fire

Sephirah
Kether (Crown)

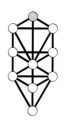

*Origin, the root of thought
and action, knowledge, higher
creativity, clarity, will.*

TWO OF WANDS

Lord of Dominion

Element
Fire

Associated Ideas
Project, expectations, desire,
doubt, indecision, risk.

Magical Use
Collaboration.

Herbal Attribution
Basil

Light Ambition		**Shadow** Restlessness

Astrology
Mars in Aries
(0° to 10° Aries)

Mars: *Energy, initiative,
resolution, authoritarianism,
competition, martial character,
aggressiveness.*
Aries: *Exuberance, passion,
impulses, spontaneity, individuality, domineering spirit.*

Sephirah
Chokhmah (Wisdom)

*Intuition, seed idea,
revealing paradox,
incomprehensible, ineffable.*

THREE OF WANDS

Element
Fire

Associated Ideas
Observation, patience, attention, hope, anticipation.

Magical Use
Creativity

Herbal Attribution
Saffron

Lord of Established Strength

Light		**Shadow**
Waiting		Delay

Astrology
Sun in Aries
(10° to 20° Aries)

☉ ♈

Sun: *Clarity, tenderness, optimism, pursuit of perfection, purity, generosity, courage, creativity.*
Aries: *Exuberance, passion, impulses, spontaneity, individuality, domineering spirit.*

Sephirah
Binah (Understanding)

Analysis, rationality, logical, concreteness, clarity of language, ability to communicate.

FOUR OF WANDS

Element
Fire

Associated Ideas
Tranquility, celebration, preliminary, detail, editing.

Magical Use
Ceremonial magic.

Herbal Attribution
Fennel seed

Lord of Perfected Work

Light		**Shadow**
Preparation		Perfectionism

Astrology
Venus in Aries
(20° to 30° Aries)

♀ ♈

Venus: *Affection, sociability, romance, love of harmony and beauty, sensuality and seduction.*
Aries: *Exuberance, passion, impulses, spontaneity, individuality, domineering spirit.*

Sephirah
Chesed (Mercy)

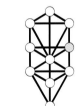

Sentiment, mercy, devotion, kindness, generosity, ability to forgive.

301

FIVE OF WANDS

Element
Fire

Associated Ideas
Imitation, simulation, training, fight, quarrel, rivalry.

Magical Use
Tests. Competitions.

Herbal Attribution
Turmeric

Lord of Strife

Light		Shadow
Competition		Conflict

Astrology
Saturn in Leo (0° to 10° Leo)

♄ ♌

Saturn: *Self-control, meditation, perseverance, patience, critical sense, concrete, confidence, humility.*
Leo: *Pride, dynamism, fiery, ambition, generosity, loyalty, impulsiveness, exhibitionism.*

Sephirah
Gevurah (Strength)

Discipline, rigor, severity rating, control, containment, moderation, limitation.

SIX OF WANDS

Element
Fire

Associated Ideas
Fame, the limelight, success, honor, arrival of a rival.

Magical Use
Campaigns. Career advancement.

Herbal Attribution
Hawthorn

Lord of Victory

Light		Shadow
Victory		Vanity

Astrology
Jupiter in Leo
(10° to 20° Leo)

♃ ♌

Jupiter: *Affability, cheerfulness, confidence, generosity, intellectual and physical growth, expansive, farsightedness.*
Leo: *Pride, dynamism, fiery, ambition, generosity, loyalty, impulsiveness, exhibitionism.*

Sephirah
Tiferet (Beauty)

Aesthetics, sensitivity, love of nature, mediation, harmony, measure, balance, compassion.

SEVEN OF WANDS

Element
Fire

Associated Ideas
Value, opinion, unconventionality, competition, self-confidence.

Magical Use
Defense

Herbal Attribution
Wild ginger

Lord of Valor

Light		**Shadow**
Opposition		Defense

Astrology
Mars in Leo (20° to 30° Leo)

♂ ♌

Mars: *Energy, initiative, resolution, authoritarianism, competition, martial character, aggressiveness.*
Leo: *Pride, dynamism, fiery, ambition, generosity, loyalty, impulsiveness, exhibitionism.*

Sephirah
Netzach (Victory)

The ability to coordinate, perseverance in adversity, stability, security and progress.

EIGHT OF WANDS

Element
Fire

Associated Ideas
Fast, action, movement, climax, tension order, instinctive reaction.

Magical Use
Stalled endeavors.

Herbal Attribution
Sassafras

Lord of Swiftness

Light		**Shadow**
Speed		Stuck

Astrology
Mercury in Sagittarius
(0° to 10° Sagittarius)

☿ ♐

Mercury: *Mental alertness, imagination, communication skills, diplomacy, love of travel, occult interests.*
Sagittarius: *Exuberance, spirit of adventure, desire for knowledge, dreamer, lack of pragmatism.*

Sephirah
Hod (Splendor)

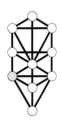

Dynamic, fast change, adaptability, socialization, business sense.

NINE OF WANDS

Element
Fire

Associated Ideas
Tenacity, guard, defense, border.

Magical Use
Gateways and threshold magic.

Herbal Attribution
Bayberry bark

Lord of Wands

Light		**Shadow**
Pushing forward		Fear

Astrology
Moon in Sagittarius
(10° to 20° Sagittarius)

☽ ♐

Moon: *Sensitivity, instinct, intuition, emotion, seduction, imagination, illusions, unpredictability.*
Sagittarius: *Exuberance, spirit of adventure, desire for knowledge, dreamer, lack of pragmatism.*

Sephirah
Yesod (Foundation)

Character, personality, awareness of possibilities, hidden aspirations.

TEN OF WANDS

Element
Fire

Associated Ideas
Oppression, fatigue, tiredness, direction, strength.

Magical Use
Project completion.

Herbal Attribution
Prickly ash bark

Lord of Oppression

Light		**Shadow**
Fatigue		Incomplete

Astrology
Saturn in Sagittarius
(20° to 30° Sagittarius)

♄ ♐

Saturn: *Self-control, meditation, perseverance, patience, critical sense, concrete, confidentiality, humility.*
Sagittarius: *Exuberance, spirit of adventure, desire for knowledge, dreamer, lack of pragmatism.*

Sephirah
Malkuth (Kingdom)

Possession, subject, desires, perceptions of need, need of protection.

ACE OF SWORDS

Root of the Powers of Air

Element
Rules the element of Air.

Light
Power

Shadow
Conflict

Astrology
Air

Sephirah
Kether (Crown)

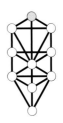

Associated Ideas
Responsibility, achievement, test of strength, conviction.

Magical Use
To nail it!

Herbal Attribution
Chamomile

Origin, the root of thought and action, knowledge, higher creativity, clarity, will.

TWO OF SWORDS

Lord of Peace Restored

Element
Air

Light
Discussion

Shadow
Arbitration

Astrology
Moon in Libra
(0° to 10° Libra)

Sephirah
Chokhmah (Wisdom)

Moon: *Sensitivity, instinct, intuition, emotion, seduction, imagination, illusions, unpredictability.*
Libra: *Sensitivity, conciliatory spirit, kindness, diplomacy, sociability, hedonism, love of aesthetics.*

Associated Ideas
Balance adjustment, duel, mediation, interposition.

Magical Use
To gain equilibrium.

Herbal Attribution
Passionflower

Intuition, seed idea, revealing paradox, incomprehensible, ineffable.

THREE OF SWORDS

Element
Air

Associated Ideas
Pain, injury, difficult time, communication difficulties, lack of support.

Magical Use
Heal the heart.

Herbal Attribution
Pleurisy root

Lord of Sorrow

Light		**Shadow**
Vulnerability		Blockage

Astrology
Saturn in Libra
(10° to 20° Libra)

♄ ♎

Saturn: *Self-control, meditation, perseverance, patience, critical sense, concrete, confidence, humility.*
Libra: *Sensitivity, conciliatory spirit, kindness, diplomacy, social, hedonism, love of aesthetics.*

Sephirah
Binah (Understanding)

Analysis, rationality, logical, concreteness, clarity, language, ability to communicate.

FOUR OF SWORDS

Element
Air

Associated Ideas
Resting, waking, loneliness, reflection, waiting, closing.

Magical Use
Restorative sleep.

Herbal Attribution
Mullein

Lord of Rest from Strife

Light		**Shadow**
Meditation		Incommunicability

Astrology
Jupiter in Libra
(20° to 30° Libra)

♃ ♎

Jupiter: *Affability, cheerfulness, confidence, generosity, intellectual and physical growth, expansive, farsightedness.*
Libra: *Sensitivity, conciliatory spirit, kindness, diplomacy, social, hedonism, love of aesthetics.*

Sephirah
Chesed (Mercy)

Sentiment, mercy, devotion, kindness, generosity, ability to forgive.

FIVE OF SWORDS

Lord of Defeat

Element
Air

Associated Ideas
Disgrace, exile, defeat, revocation of privileges, negative power over others, revenge.

Magical Use
End a quarrel.

Herbal Attribution
European mistletoe

Light
Selfishness

Shadow
Complacency

Astrology
Venus in Aquarius
(0° to 10° Aquarius)

♀ ♒

Venus: *Affection, sociability, romance, love of harmony and beauty, sensuality and seduction.*
Aquarius: *Creativity, kindness, generosity, innovative spirit, idealist, libertarian, changeability.*

Sephirah
Gevurah (Strength)

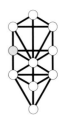

Discipline, rigor, severity rating, control, containment, moderation, limitation.

SIX OF SWORDS

Lord of Earned Success

Element
Air

Associated Ideas
Transition, reasoning, curiosity, transfer, exploration.

Magical Use
New beginnings.

Herbal Attribution
Vervain

Light
Journey

Shadow
Escape

Astrology
Mercury in Aquarius
(10° to 20° Aquarius)

☿ ♒

Mercury: *Mental alertness, imagination, communication skills, diplomacy, love of travel, occult interests.*
Aquarius: *Creativity, kindness, generosity, innovative spirit, idealist, libertarian, changeability.*

Sephirah
Tiferet (Beauty)

Aesthetics, sensitivity, love of nature, mediation, harmony, measure, balance, compassion.

SEVEN OF SWORDS

Element
Air

Associated Ideas
Dodge, hidden design, confidentiality, talk, try.

Magical Use
Cut ties.

Herbal Attribution
Wood betony

Lord of Unstable Effort

Light		Shadow
Subterfuge		Rumors

Astrology
Moon in Aquarius
(20° to 30° Aquarius)

☽ ♒

Moon: *Sensitivity, instinct, intuition, emotion, seduction, imagination, illusions, unpredictability.*
Aquarius: *creativity, kindness, generosity, innovative spirit, idealist, libertarian, changeability.*

Sephirah
Netzach (Victory)

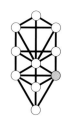

The ability to coordinate, perseverance in adversity, stability, security and progress.

EIGHT OF SWORDS

Element
Air

Associated Ideas
Trap, fear, difficulty of reasoning, impediment, obstacle.

Magical Use
Initiation.

Herbal Attribution
Black cohosh

Lord of Shortened Force

Light		Shadow
Limits		Bondage

Astrology
Jupiter in Gemini
(0° to 10° Gemini)

♃ ♊

Jupiter: *Affability, cheerfulness, confidence, generosity, intellectual and physical growth, expansive, farsightedness.*
Gemini: *Quick-wittedness, curiosity, need to communicate, caustic wit, restlessness, inconstancy.*

Sephirah
Hod (Splendor)

Dynamic, fast change, adaptability, socialization, business sense.

NINE OF SWORDS

Lord of Despair and Cruelty

Element
Air

Associated Ideas
Despair, nightmares, guilt, difficulties in dealing with things.

Magical Use
Stop troublesome thoughts.

Herbal Attribution
Valerian

Light
Sleeplessness

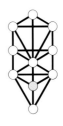

Shadow
Crisis

Astrology
Mars in Gemini
(10° to 20° Gemini)

♂ ♊

Mars: *Energy, initiative, resolution, authoritarianism, competition, martial character, aggressiveness.*
Gemini: *Quick-wittedness, curiosity, need to communicate, caustic wit, restlessness, inconstancy.*

Sephirah
Yesod (Foundation)

Character, personality, awareness of possibilities, hidden aspirations.

TEN OF SWORDS

Lord of Ruin

Element
Air

Associated Ideas
Sorrow, inevitability, tears, desolation, emptiness, sadness.

Magical Use
To end something completely.

Herbal Attribution
Ephedra

Light
Transcendence

Shadow
Ruin

Astrology
Sun in Gemini
(20° to 30° Gemini)

☉ ♊

Sun: *Clarity, tenderness, optimism, pursuit of perfection, purity, generosity, courage, creativity.*
Gemini: *Quick-wittedness, curiosity, need to communicate, caustic wit, restlessness, inconstancy.*

Sephirah
Malkuth (Kingdom)

Possession, subject, desires, perceptions of need, need of protection.

PAGE OF CUPS

Princess of the Waters *Lotus of the Palace of Floods*
Princess and Empress of the Nymphs and Undines

Light		**Shadow**
Playful		Sarcastic

Elemental Counterchange
Earth of Water

No Sun Sign
Personification
of the element of Water

Sephirah
Malkuth

**Approximate
Time Period**

Cancer, Scorpio, Pisces

Timing
The time is not yet right.
Do not rush, wait and let
things develop as they will
without interfering. More
must evolve before you
act. Patience, prudence and
study are necessary.

Aspect of Self
Body

Divinatory Personality
Senses modifying
Emotion

Family Position
Youngest child

Associated Tarot Cards
Ace of Cups, Ten of Cups

Activity
Absorption, study, watching,
learning.

Magical Use
Psychic power.

Herbal Attribution
Damiana

KNIGHT OF CUPS

Lord of the Waves and the Waters *King of the Hosts of the Sea*
King of the Nymphs and Undines

Light
Offering

Shadow
Hoarding

Elemental Counterchange
Fire of Water

Sephirah
Tiferet

Predominant Sun Sign
Pisces

**Approximate
Time Period**
February 9 – March 10

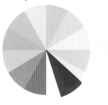

Timing
Rapid development and change, somewhat unstable and very unpredictable.

Aspect of Self
Personal mind/energies

Divinatory Personality
Will modifying
Emotion

Family Position
Teenage child

Associated Tarot Cards
Seven of Swords, Eight of Cups, Nine of Cups

Activity
Triumphant, outgoing, speedy, fast moving.

Magical Use
Romance. Courting. Charm.

Herbal Attribution
Sarsaparilla

QUEEN OF CUPS

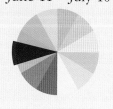

Queen of the Thrones of Waters
Queen of the Nymphs and Undines

Light		Shadow
Empathic		Judgmental

Elemental Counterchange
Water of Water

Sephirah
Binah

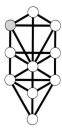

Predominant Sun Sign
Cancer

Approximate Time Period
June 11 – July 10

Timing
It is time to reflect.

Aspect of Self
Soul/heart

Divinatory Personality
Emotion reinforcing
Emotion

Family Position
Mother

Associated Tarot Cards
Ten of Swords, Two of
Cups, Three of Cups

Activity
Nurturing, encompassing,
sensitive, intuitive,
embracing.

Magical Use
Sensitivity.
Emotional support.

Herbal Attribution
Lady's mantle

KING OF CUPS

Prince of the Chariot of Waters
Prince and Emperor of the Nymphs and Undines

Light
Creative intelligence

Shadow
Creative destruction

Elemental Counterchange
Air of Water

Sephirah
Chokhmah

Predominant Sun Sign
Scorpio

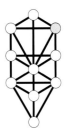

**Approximate
Time Period**
October 14 – November 12

Timing
Time for resolute and
distinctive action.

Aspect of Self
Spirit

Divinatory Personality
Intellect modifying
Emotion

Family Position
Father

Associated Tarot Cards
Four of Swords, Five of
Cups, Six of Cups

Activity
Active, success,
achievement, dispenses
order and keeps the peace.

Magical Use
Creative completion.

Herbal Attribution
Saw palmetto

PAGE OF PENTACLES

Princess of the Echoing Hills ⚜ *Rose of the Palace of Earth*
⚜ *Princess and Empress of the Gnomes*

Light		**Shadow**
Curious		Disinterested

Elemental Counterchange
Earth of Earth

No Sun Sign
Personification
of the element of Earth

Sephirah
Malkuth

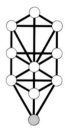

**Approximate
Time Period**
Taurus, Virgo, Capricorn

Timing
The time is not yet right, so do not rush. Wait and let things develop as they will without interfering. More must evolve before you act. Patience, prudence and study are necessary.

Aspect of Self
Body

Divinatory Personality
Senses reinforcing
Senses

Family Position
Youngest child

Associated Tarot Cards
Ace of Pentacles,
Ten of Pentacles

Activity
Absorption, study, watching,
learning.

Magical Use
Study. Apprenticeship.

Herbal Attribution
Blue flag

KNIGHT OF PENTACLES

๕ Lord of the Wide and Fertile Land
๕ King of the Spirits of Earth ๕ King of the Gnomes

Light
Gift

Shadow
Greedy

Elemental Counterchange
Fire of Earth

Sephirah
Tiferet

Predominant Sun Sign
Virgo

♍

**Approximate
Time Period**
August 13 – October 13

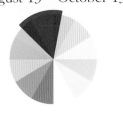

Timing
Rapid development and
change, somewhat unstable
and very unpredictable.

Aspect of Self
Personal mind/energies

Divinatory Personality
Will modifying
Senses

Family Position
Teenage child

Associated Tarot Cards
Seven of Wands, Eight of
Pentacles, Nine of Pentacles

Activity
Triumphant, outgoing,
speedy, fast moving.

Magical Use
Finance.

Herbal Attribution
Elecampane

QUEEN OF PENTACLES

❧ *Queen of the Thrones of Earth*
❧ *Queen of the Gnomes*

Light		Shadow
Sensual		Rejecting

Elemental Counterchange
Water of Earth

Predominant Sun Sign
Capricorn

Sephirah
Binah

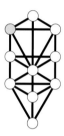

Approximate Time Period
December 12 - January 10

Timing
It is time to reflect.

Aspect of Self
Soul/heart

Divinatory Personality
Emotion modifying
Senses

Family Position
Mother

Associated Tarot Cards
Ten of Wands, Two of
Pentacles, Three of Pentacles

Activity
Nurturing, encompassing,
sensitive, intuitive and
embracing.

Magical Use
House. Home.

Herbal Attribution
Marshmallow

KING OF PENTACLES

☙ Prince of the Chariot of Earth
☙ Prince and Emperor of the Gnomes

Light		**Shadow**
Material success		Loss

Elemental Counterchange
Fire of Earth

Sephirah
Chokhmah

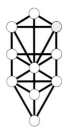

Predominant Sun Sign
Taurus

Approximate Time Period
April 10 – May 10

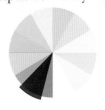

Timing
It is time for resolute and distinctive action.

Aspect of Self
Spirit

Divinatory Personality
Intellect modifying Senses

Family Position
Father

Associated Tarot Cards
Four of Wands, Five of Pentacles, Six of Pentacles

Activity
Active, success, achievement, dispenses order and keeps the peace.

Magical Use
Growth. Abundance.

Herbal Attribution
Alfalfa

PAGE OF WANDS

Princess of the Shining Flame *Rose of the Palace of Fire*
Princess and Empress of the Salamanders

Light		**Shadow**
Daring		Trepidation

Elemental Counterchange
Earth of Fire

No Sun Sign
Personification
of the element of Fire

Sephirah
Malkuth

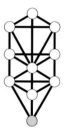

Approximate Time Period	**Timing**	**Aspect of Self**
Aries, Leo, Sagittarius	The time is not yet right, so do not rush. Wait and let things develop as they will without interfering. More must evolve before you act. Patience, prudence and study are necessary.	Body

Divinatory Personality
Senses modifying
Will

Family Position	**Associated Tarot Cards**	**Magical Use**
Youngest child	Ace of Wands, Ten of Wands	Travel.

Activity
Absorption, study,
watching, learning.

Herbal Attribution
Shepherd's purse

KNIGHT OF WANDS

Lord of the Flame and the Lightning
*King of the Spirits of Fire * King of the Salamanders*

Light		Shadow
Passion		Reserve

Elemental Counterchange
Fire of Fire

Sephirah
Tiferet

Predominant Sun Sign
Sagittarius

**Approximate
Time Period**
November 13 – December 11

Timing
Rapid development and
change, somewhat unstable
and very unpredictable.

Aspect of Self
Personal mind/energies

Divinatory Personality
Will reinforcing
Will.

Family Position
Teenage child

Associated Tarot Cards
Seven of Cups, Eight of
Wands, Nine of Wands

Activity
Triumphant, outgoing,
speedy, fast moving.

Magical Use
Change.

Herbal Attribution
Aconite

QUEEN OF WANDS

🪶 *Queen of the Thrones of Flames*
🪶 *Queen of the Salamanders*

Light		**Shadow**
Charisma		Shyness

Elemental Counterchange
Water of Fire

Sephirah
Binah

Predominant Sun Sign
Aries

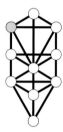

**Approximate
Time Period**
March 11 – April 9

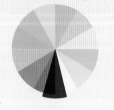

Timing
It is time to reflect.

Aspect of Self
Soul/heart

Divinatory Personality
Emotion modifying
Will

Family Position
Mother

Associated Tarot Cards
Ten of Cups, Two of Wands,
Three of Wands

Activity
Nurturing, encompassing,
sensitive, intuitive and
embracing.

Magical Use
Sex.

Herbal Attribution
Raspberry leaf

KING OF WANDS

Prince of the Chariot of Fire
Prince and Emperor of the Salamanders

Light
Animated

Shadow
Meek

Elemental Counterchange
Air of Fire

Sephirah
Chokhmah

Predominant Sun Sign
Leo

**Approximate
Time Period**
July 13 – August 12

Timing
It is time for resolute and
distinctive action.

Aspect of Self
Spirit

Divinatory Personality
Intellect modifying
Will

Family Position
Father

Associated Tarot Cards
Four of Cups, Five of
Wands, Six of Wands

Activity
Active, success,
achievement, dispenses
order and keeps the peace.

Magical Use
Challenge.

Herbal Attribution
Cinnamon

PAGE OF SWORDS

Princess of the Rushing Winds *Lotus of the Palace of Air*
Princess and Empress of the Sylphs and Sylphides

Light		**Shadow**
Cleverness		Dullness

Elemental Counterchange
Earth of Air

No Sun Sign
Personification
of the element of Air

Sephirah
Malkuth

Approximate Time Period	**Timing**	**Aspect of Self**
Gemini, Libra, Aquarius	The time is not yet right. Do not rush, wait and let things develop as they will without interfering. More must evolve before you act. Patience, prudence and study are necessary.	Body
♊ ♎ ♒		**Divinatory Personality** Senses modifying Intellect

Family Position
Youngest child

Associated Tarot Cards
Ace of Swords,
Ten of Swords

Activity
Absorption, study,
watching, learning.

Magical Use
Detective work.

Herbal Attribution
Dill

322

KNIGHT OF SWORDS

❧ Lord of the Winds and Breezes ❧ King of the Spirits of Air
❧ King of the Sylphs and Sylphides

Light
Bravery

Shadow
Fear

Elemental Counterchange
Fire of Air

Sephirah
Tiferet

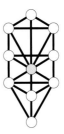

Predominant Sun Sign
Gemini

Approximate Time Period
May 11 – June 10

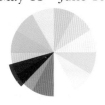

Timing
Rapid development and change, somewhat unstable and very unpredictable.

Aspect of Self
Personal mind/energies

Divinatory Personality
Will modifying Intellect

Family Position
Teenage child

Associated Tarot Cards
Seven of Pentacles, Eight of Swords, Nine of Swords

Activity
Triumphant, outgoing, speedy, fast moving.

Magical Use
Directness.

Herbal Attribution
Wild cherry bark

QUEEN OF SWORDS

Queen of the Thrones of Air
Queen of the Sylphs and Sylphides

Light		Shadow
Articulation		Immobile

Elemental Counterchange
Water of Air

Predominant Sun Sign
Libra

Ω

Sephirah
Binah

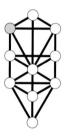

Approximate Time Period
September 13 – October 13

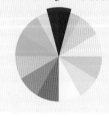

Timing
It is time to reflect.

Aspect of Self
Soul/heart

Divinatory Personality
Emotion modifying
Intellect

Family Position
Mother

Associated Tarot Cards
Ten of Pentacles, Two of Swords, Three of Swords

Activity
Nurturing, encompassing, sensitive, intuitive and embracing.

Magical Use
Precision.

Herbal Attribution
Lady's slipper

KING OF SWORDS

Prince of the Chariot of the Winds
Prince and Emperor of Sylphs and Sylphides

Light		**Shadow**
Mental power		Mental frailty

Elemental Counterchange
Air of Air

Sephirah
Chokhmah

Predominant Sun Sign
Aquarius

**Approximate
Time Period**
January 11 – February 8

Timing
It is time for resolute and
distinctive action.

Aspect of Self
Spirit

Divinatory Personality
Intellect reinforcing
Intellect

Family Position
Father

Associated Tarot Cards
Four of Pentacles, Five of
Swords, Six of Swords

Activity
Active, success,
achievement, dispenses
order and keeps the peace.

Magical Use
Genius.

Herbal Attribution
St. John's wort

WIRTH

The Structure of the Major Arcana

The most interesting and complete study of the structure of the Major Arcana was done by Wirth, a Swiss occultist who made connections between the cards using a complex system of relationships.

Structure can be seen as looking at the building blocks of a greater item. It's not about any single Arcana, but about the Arcana as a whole.

One of the most important studies on the Major Arcana can be found in the works of Oswald Wirth (1860-1943). With a deck of Tarot designed by himself, Wirth summarized the esoteric doctrines elaborated within the Cabalistic Order of the Rose + Cross, of which he was one of the most highly regarded exponents. Wirth's thinking can be applied to almost all Tarot decks and remains today one of the most lucid and complete analysis of the internal structure of the Major Arcana.

The Dry Path and the Humid Path of the Arcana are two halves of a single sequence.

The Dry Path and the Humid Path of the Arcana

According to Wirth, a first structural definition of the Major Arcana occurs by dividing these cards into two groups, called "paths" and placing them in two parallel lines. The Arcana from I to XI are the so-called "Dry Path" or the "Doric Path" and tend to be rational and active. The Arcana from XII to 0 make up the so-called "Humid Path" or "Ionic Path" and tend to be intuitive and passive. The Dry Path indicates the journey of an extremely active, logical and systematic individual. From this point of view for example, the High Priestess, while a representative of the mysteries, possesses a rational nature, as demonstrated by the book she has in hand. At the same time the Lovers, while overcome by passions, are obliged to lucidly and reasonably decide what path to take, and the Wheel, even though it is an inanimate object, must respond to a rigorous law of action and reaction.

On the contrary, the Humid Path indicates a journey of an extremely receptive, intuitive and mystical individual. For example Temperance, who appears active in the gesture of pouring liquid from one jug into another, tends towards a passive nature, as shown by the liquid which adapts to the shape and the circumstances it is given. In the same way, the Devil, master of materiality, is passive with respect to his condition, which renders him a slave to his own ambitions and therefore limited in his ability to act.

Branches, Transition Arcana and Pairs

In order to better understand the meaning of the two paths, according to Wirth it was necessary to divide them into two Branches. Each Branch is composed of five Arcana (of which one is dominant) and is separated by a Transition Arcana from the other Branch. The same schematic way that allows for the division of the Major Arcana into four groups also allows for the Arcana to be placed in a relationship between them in pairs. Each pair is formed by two Arcana that are complementary and that occupy equivalent positions within the Dry Path and the Humid Path.

Each Arcana pair is formed by two complementary and connected concepts. The Arcana IV and XIX, for example, represent two cards that are strongly masculine, that both express control, strength, authority, security and clarity. The essence of this pair could be summarized in the dichotomy between mental illumination (the Emperor) and spiritual illumination (the Sun).

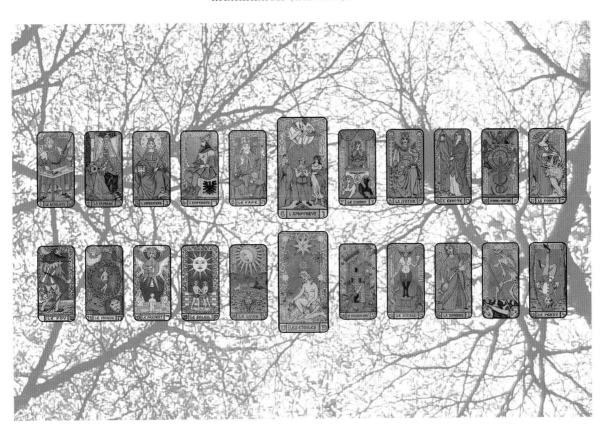

The Transition Arcana

As the expression "Transition Arcana" suggests, these two cards represent a choice or a junction within the different journeys delineated by the two Paths and the four Branches.

The Lovers card, for example, expresses an active choice between two paths that go in different directions, but neither of the two paths is right or wrong in an absolute sense. The card indicates, in fact, the need to identify the behavior capable of mediating one's personal aspirations with virtue.

The card of the Stars, however, expresses a passive tendency that it brings with it, even in this case, in different directions, neither right nor wrong. This means identifying one's own journey keeping in mind the celestial influences received at the moment of birth or, in a metaphoric sense, the influences of the environment and the circumstances. From this knowledge individual desires and aspirations are born, that should be both noble and virtuous.

Transition Arcana can be seen as thresholds or gates, but they can also be seen as standing between the Arcana as Solstices and Equinoxes stand between seasons.

The First Branch: Arcana from I to V

The First Branch is dominated by the Magician, followed by two pairs of Arcana: the Hierophant – the High Priestess and Emperor – Empress. The Magician is known in his solitude as an individual who possesses all the qualities expressed in the other four Arcana, regardless of gender (male and female) and function (religious or secular). Both genders express deductive knowledge (masculine) and inductive (feminine). The functions express physical (secular) and metaphysical (religious) knowledge.

The Second Branch: Arcana from VII to XI

The Second Branch is guided by the Chariot followed by two pairs of Arcana: Justice – Strength and the Hermit – the Wheel. The Chariot possesses all the qualities of the other four following Arcana that are neutral in terms of gender and function. Justice expresses the law of equilibrium, in any area of life (social, scientific, and so on). The Wheel expresses the cycles imposed by the applications of the laws, in any area of life. The Hermit represents the study of the laws, in every area of life, and Strength expresses the application of the subject matter of the laws.

The Third Branch: Arcana from XII to XVI

The Third Branch begins with the Hanged Man, a totally passive Arcana, that possesses all of the qualities of the four following Arcana, which are also neutral in terms of gender and function. Death expresses the complete absence of activity. Temperance represents a necessary transformation and a simple mix of elements. The Devil indicates slavery and submission to a superior will. The Tower expresses the cancellation of all ambition due to a crushing power.

The Fourth Branch: Arcana from XVIII to 0

The Fourth Branch is dominated by the Fool, a basically passive character in gathering together within him the qualities of the four Arcana in this group. In the "clear madness" of The Fool the luminous ideas of the Sun are established (male, rational and static) and the ambiguities suggested by the Moon (female, intuitive and dynamic), as is the mystic ecstasy (static and introversive) expressed by Judgement and the cosmic vision (dynamic and extroversive) contained in the World.

It is very important to remember that Wirth, who first theorized this Tarot structure, belongs to the French school of Tarot. One of the main differences from the more familiar English school is the numbering of Strength and Justice.

If using an English school deck (as most modern decks follow the English school) it is important to take the change in the sequence into account and modify the position of these two cards.

LA JVSTICE

VIIII - STRENGTH

LA FORCE

XI - JUSTICE

The Division of the Arcana into Dry Path and Humid Path

By placing the 22 major Arcana in two parallel lines, the two Paths of Tarot can be identified. The Arcana from I to XI represent the Dry Path, otherwise known as the rational journey, whereas the Arcana from XII to 0 represent the Humid Path, known also as the intuitive journey.

Dry Path

Humid Path

The Separation of the Paths into Branches

Separating each of the Paths into two Branches, it is possible to organize the Arcana into four groups of five Arcana, each one separated by two Transition Arcana: the Lovers and the Stars.

First Branch

Fourth Branch

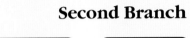

The Relationships between Pairs of Arcana

Each Arcana of a Path can be placed in relation to an Arcana of another Path: each Arcana of one Path corresponds to the equivalent Arcana belonging to the opposite Path. For example, the Arcana IV (the Emperor) is connected to the Arcana XIX (the Sun).

Each of the eleven pairs of Arcana has a fundamental theme:
- **Arcana I and 0:** reason and madness
- **Arcana II and XXI:** perception of the unknown and the infinite
- **Arcana III and XX:** birth and rebirth
- **Arcana IV and XIX:** mental and spiritual illumination
- **Arcana V and XVIII:** philosophical and mystical abstractions

- Arcana VI and XVII: choice and destiny
- Arcana VII and XVI: control and abandon
- Arcana VIII and XV: order and disorder
- Arcana IX and XIV: researcher and object of research
- Arcana X and XIII: cycle and end of cycle
- Arcana XI and XII: power and impotency

MYERS-BRIGGS

Psychological Mode and the Court Cards

The Myers-Briggs Type Indicator is a psychological system that can be integrated with Tarot to understand court cards and Tarot suit personality traits and psychological constructs.

Katherine Briggs and Isabel Briggs Myers were an American mother-daughter team who were self taught in the field of personality theory when the field of psychology was in its infancy. They created a groundbreaking psychological indicator based on the research and introspective theories found in Carl Jung's book *Psychological Types*, 1921. The Myers-Briggs indicator was used during World War II for women entering the industrial workforce for the first time. The system helped women single out the correct jobs for their personality types. The system is still used to describe modern day personality types. The system integrates seamlessly into Tarot's court cards and suits.

A psychological system does not fully describe the complexity of the individual. It is more like a portrait of a personality type.

Myers and Briggs used Jung's theoretical personality basis and outlined 16 possible personality types. Each of these types matches up to a court card. Once a Reader understands the model, it is a simple technique to apply to the court cards. It fosters a deeper understanding of Tarot's royal family and helps us understand the way we and the individuals around us behave.

Myers and Briggs's work centers around the core idea that people are consistent in their behavior. An individual's behavior consists of two pairs of **cognitive styles**:

- Perception: sensation and intuition (the "irrational" functions)
- Judgment: thinking and feeling (the "rational" functions)

Perception describes how an individual experiences the world around them. Perception is linked to the senses, explaining how people, places, events and experience enter the sensory facilities of sight, touch, taste, etc. It the sensual interaction and reaction to the physical world. For example, how hot sunlight feels on the skin.

Judgment describes how individuals interpret and infuse meaning into what they have perceived. Individuals reach conclusions and translate their experience into words and feelings. For example, an individual decides the hot sunlight is annoying because they are on their way to a job interview and don't want to sweat.

A graphical cloud built using the Myers-Briggs keywords for the description of personality types.

Each individual expresses their cognitive functions with an **attitude** that can be described as "introverted" or "extroverted."

The four codes of the Myers-Briggs indicators fill up the blank space with 16 different possible personality types.

An **Introverted** form describes how one keeps issues, ideas, feelings to oneself and on an internal level. An individual with this preference would likely keep their opinion of hot sunlight to themselves.

A **Extroverted** form describes how one expresses their ideas, issues and feelings. An individual with this preference would complain out loud about the hot sunlight.

Four Dimensions of Personality

The 16 personality types stem from four dimensions, four aspects of personality defined by two opposites. Each individual will have a preference which defines their personality.

1. Attitude (Introvert vs. Extrovert)

Explains where your focus lies. Do you focus on your inner or the outer world? Extroversion describes an individual who acts first and reflects afterwards. He acts, thinks, and returns to action. Introversion describes an individual who reflects on a situation, acts out and reflects. He reflects, acts and reflects again.

Putting any two dimensions into a graphic it is possible to understand intuitively the meaning behind the descriptors.

From the graphic is also clear that, for instance, a person may be Introvert and Sensing, or Introvert and Intuitive, but cannot be Introvert and Extrovert at the same time.

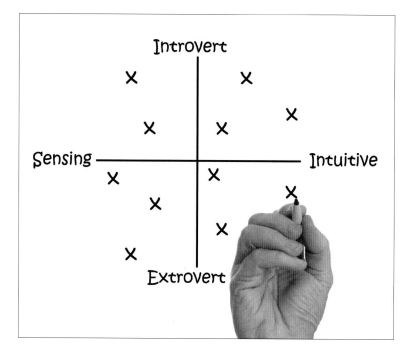

⌒ 2. Information (Sensing vs. Intuition)

Explains the process of how you react to basic information and stimuli. Do you prefer facts or metaphors? Sensing describes an individual who looks for tangible and concrete information in an ordered and sequential manner. Intuition describes an individual who looks for meanings and associations to provide insight.

⌒ 3. Decision Making (Thinking vs. Feeling)

Explains your process of decision making. Are you logical and pragmatic or do you focus on your own feelings and emotions regarding the situation? Thinking describes someone who makes decisions in an orderly, objective way. Feeling describes someone who is spontaneous, emotional and empathetic.

⌒ 4. Cognitive Style (Judging vs. Perceiving)

Explains how you embrace complexity. Do you crave organization or excitement? Judging describes an individual who thrives under circumstances where information is structured and organized. Perceiving describes an individual who thrives in flexible circumstances where information is fresh and stimulating.

Each Myers-Briggs dichotomy carries a letter assigned to it, and each letter relates to a court rank or a court suit:

- Extraversion = **E**
- Introversion = **I**

- Sensing = **S**
- Intuition = **N**

- Thinking = **T**
- Feeling = **F**

- Judging = **J**
- Perceiving = **P**

Each personality is represented by a combination of four letters. For example, an individual who is partial to Extraversion, Sensing, Thinking and Judging is ESTJ.

Each of these combinations is associated with the court cards:

- Page of Cups: INFP
- Knight of Cups: ENFP
- Queen of Cups: INFJ
- King of Cups: ENFJ
- Page of Pentacles: ISFP
- Knight of Pentacles: ESFP
- Queen of Pentacles: ISFJ
- King of Pentacles: ESFJ
- Page of Wands: INTP
- Knight of Wands: ENTP
- Queen of Wands: INTJ
- King of Wands: ENTJ
- Page of Swords: ISTP
- Knight of Swords: ESTP
- Queen of Swords: ISTJ
- King of Swords: ESTJ

Mutual Similarities

Examine the associations of the 16 personalities of the court cards and you will notice that some of the qualities intersect and stay the same while others change. This depends on the rank. For example, all Pages are Introverted and Perceiving. Thinking or Feeling and Intuition and Sensing are the changing qualities. The stable traits reflect attitude and lifestyle while changing traits reflect suit.

Group Structures

The court cards; Page, Knight, Queen and King, will be analyzed through the structural interpretation of the Myers-Briggs model.

Graphic depictions of court card are divided into five different sections: 1. Nature 2. Code 3. Traits 4. Transformations 5. Comparison cards.

For each card:

1. Nature: A brief summary of the nature of the court card will be provided.

The nature will include a verb expressing an action as a descriptor of the personality type related to the card, and the roles the personality type can take, depending on the different suits.

Both the verb and the roles can be used directly when interpretating court cards, as they can describe a personality type, a strategy or even a course of action.

People who share the same four codes of the Myers-Briggs have a similar personality to one another, and may be represented by the same court card. But they may still be very different people.

2. Code: The four letters of the Myers-Briggs system will be supplied alongside an image of the court card taken from the Tarot of Marseille.

Looking at the four letters it's possible to notice how two letters are always the same in any court card (these two letters indicates the stable traits) while the other two (referred to the changing traits) will change depending on the suit.

3. Traits: Stable and changing traits will be identified and explained. The changing traits will be related to the corresponding suit.

4. Transformations: The possible evolutions and transformation of a personality type will be displayed by changing one or two of the stable traits. With the transformation of a stable trait, the court card of reference will also change and, for instance, the Page will transform into a Knight, Queen or King. The transformations are very useful to understand the connection between different court cards.

5. Comparison Cards: From four different decks, the Universal Tarot, Liber T Tarot, Wiccan Tarot, and the Tarot of the Zodiac. Each deck expresses the court card according to a different perspective.

Personality

Each aspect of human personality affects the others. It is more clear to see them as independent constructs, but when they combine together, the result is more than the sum of the simple parts.

Integrating Myers-Briggs into Tarot is a recent innovation and is still under development. United States and Italy are at the forefront of cartomancy and pushing the practice forward with books and papers.

To reap the benefits of applying Myers-Briggs, a few elements must be considered:

- It allows the interpretation of Tarot suits with a psychological construct.
- Excludes gender and age
- Allows you to clearly define the differences and similarities between the court cards.
- The system is independent of the deck used.

However, there are also disadvantages using this model. For instance, the model connects the four suits to partial personality types. Such attributions would also affect the structure of the numerals and can impair the interpretation.

Ultimately, it is up to the Reader, as always, to choose which model and technique she will apply to the Tarot.

THE PAGES

Page of Cups

INFP

- Introversion
- Intuition
- Feeling
- Perceiving

Page of Pentacles

ISFP

- Introversion
- Sensing
- Feeling
- Perceiving

Page of Wands

INTP

- Introversion
- Intuition
- Thinking
- Perceiving

Page of Swords

ISTP

- Introversion
- Sensing
- Thinking
- Perceiving

An enthusiastic and youthful nature. Their emotional and receptive nature makes them attentive students but also dreamers. Pages are highly adaptive to any situation and carry playful qualities.

Verb	Roles
Explore	⌒ *Wands: inventor, advocate*
Learning the	⌒ *Cups: dreamer, idealist*
nature of your	⌒ *Pentacles: student, researcher*
element.	⌒ *Swords: player, apprentice*

Stable Traits

Introversion

The introverted Page can be determined with a dreamlike spirit and with interests that require solitude and intense ability like creative pursuits or study and an innate shyness.

Perception

Pages can be defined as passive. They receive information rather than pushing it out onto the world. They are actively selective and this is what provides incredible learning capability. It is without limits but also without direction.

Changing Traits

Functions
- ⌒ **Sensing** – Semi-rational: Swords and Pentacles.
- ⌒ **Intuition** – Irrational: Wands and Cups

Swords and Pentacles are focused on the physical and concrete aspects of reality while Wands and Cups focus on the spiritual and abstract.

Functions
- ⌒ **Thinking** – Semi-rational: Wands and Swords
- ⌒ **Feeling** – Irrational: Cups and Pentacles

Wands and Swords rely on their analytical and intellectual skills while Cups and Pentacles move from intuition and instinct.

The Page evolves into a Knight

Attitude transformation
Introversion ➡ Extraversion

An inward turning individual turns outward. They express themselves, acting instead of reflecting. They present ideas to peers rather than holding them close. They voice opinions and become action oriented. The Page becomes the Knight.

The Page evolves into a Queen

Cognitive Style transformation
Perceiving ➡ Judging

The Page moves from student to teacher. She learns but also evaluates and questions the systems presented to her. She thinks through complex ideas independently. The Page becomes the Queen.

The Page evolves into a King

Cognitive Style transformation
Perceiving ➡ Judging
Attitude transformation
Introversion ➡ Extraversion

The Page transforms herself completely. When both Attitude and Cognitive Style are changed, she becomes the King.

All Pages carry an introverted and receptive character which places them in a continuous condition of absorption and analysis of circumstances surrounding them. The main features are privacy, shyness and melancholia. They stand out for their great learning ability and adaptation to the people around them.

Universal Tarot Pages

The Pages represent a youthful spirit:

Idealistic, active, curious and enthusiastic yet also impulsive, inconsistent and easily influenced.

Liber T Tarot Pages

Pages represent Princesses:

The Princess represents absolute potential which results in action and results but also deep silence.

Wiccan Tarot Pages

Pages as the Elements

The Pages represent the energy of the suit expressed in a natural and pure fashion without the influence of human mind or soul.

Tarot of the Zodiac Pages

Pages as the Air

Pages share common Air elements as a basis for mobility, adaptability, growth and ambition.

353

THE KNIGHTS

Knight of Cups

ENFP

- Extraversion
- Intuition
- Feeling
- Perceiving

Knight of Pentacles

ESFP

- Extraversion
- Sensing
- Feeling
- Perceiving

Knight of Wands

ENTP

- Extraversion
- Intuition
- Thinking
- Perceiving

Knight of Swords

ESTP

- Extraversion
- Sensing
- Thinking
- Perceiving

The nature of the Knights pushes them to move in every direction, both physical and intellectual. They leave their mark on people, places and ideas.

Verb	Roles
Do Apply the nature of your element.	◦ *Knight of Wands:* actor, entertainer ◦ *Knight of Cups:* lover, artist ◦ *Knight of Wands:* promoter, activist ◦ *Knight of Pentacles:* worker, builder

Stable Traits

Extraverted Attitude
The extroversion of the Knights is determined for practical and intellectual reasons as both are their emotional motives. Direct contact is the preferred method of contact with the Knights.

Perceptive Cognitive Style
The perception of the Knights can be defined as passive because they try to receive more information from people and the world and are uncritical and appear superficial.

Changing Traits

Information
◦ **Sensing** – Rational Suits: Swords and Pentacles
◦ **Intuition** – Irrational Suits: Wands and Cups
Knights of Pentacles and Swords focus on physical and concrete aspects of reality while the Knights of Cups and Wands favor sentimental, philosophical and spiritual aspects.

Decision Making
◦ **Thinking** – Rational Suits: Wands and Spades
◦ **Feeling** – Irrational Suits: Cups and Pentacles
The Knights of Wands and Swords rely on the analytical and intellectual skills while the Knights of Cups and Pentacles rely on following intuition and instinct.

TRANSFORMATION OF THE KNIGHT

The Knight
evolves into the Page

Attitude Transformation
Extraversion ➤ Introversion
The Knight learns to look
inside himself before reacting
to the situations around him.
He reflects before acting and
transforms into the Page.

The Knight
evolves into the King

Cognitive Style Transformation
Judging ➤ Perceiving
The Knight elaborates upon
his opinions rather than settling
upon a single answer. He moves
toward complexity and
transforms into the King.

The Knight
evolves into the Queen

Attitude Transformation
Extraversion ➤ Introversion
Cognitive Style Transformation
Judging ➤ Perceiving
The Knight transforms himself
completely by reflecting on his inner thoughts
and becomes adept at intricacy and he
transforms into the Queen.

Knight share the common attitude of Extroversion which put them in a continuous state of physical and intellectual movement. This perpetual style creates an extraordinary energy towards any aspect of reality. The features include exuberance, irritation, fearfulness, aggression or detachment.

Universal Tarot Knights

The Knights represent young men/Knights:

The Knights reflect the transition from adolescence to maturity. They are in constant movement, active and influencing the world around them.

Liber T Tarot Knights

Knights represent Forces:

The Knights represent a powerful, violent and rapid force in action which comes and goes quickly yet leaves a deep impression on the interior of any situation.

Wiccan Tarot Knights

Knights as the Novice

The Knights represent the energy of the suit developing its own path but still expressing its own potential.

Tarot of the Zodiac Knights

Knights as Earth

Knights share common Earth elements as a basis of strong physicality even when attracted to intellectual strength, emotions and spiritual issues.

THE QUEENS

Queen of Cups

INFJ

- Introversion
- Intuition
- Feeling
- Judging

Queen of Pentacles

ISFJ

- Introversion
- Sensing
- Feeling
- Judging

Queen of Wands

INTJ

- Introversion
- Intuition
- Thinking
- Judging

Queen of Swords

ISTJ

- Introversion
- Sensing
- Thinking
- Judging

The Queen's nature is introverted and attentive leading to deep issues and an understanding of human nature, capable of perceiving all things hiding behind appearance.

Verb	Roles
To be	⌒ *Queen of Wands:* visionary, muse
Nurture the	⌒ *Queen of Cups:* empath, seer
nature of your	⌒ *Queen of Swords:* critic, analyst
element	⌒ *Queen of Pentacles:* parent, guardian

Stable Traits

Introverted Attitude
The introverted Queen is marked by the tendency to internalize any information and feel through reason. This makes them particularly suited to listening and giving excellent advice.

Judging Cognitive Style
The Queen's rational style is active. They receive as much information as possible from people and the world and translate it into concrete actions and problem solving.

Changing Traits

Information
⌒ **Sensing** – Rational Suits: Swords and Pentacles
⌒ **Intuition** – Irrational Suits: Wands and Cups
Pentacles and Sword Queens concentrate on the maternal aspects of everyday life while the Queens of Cups and Wands prefer the active and spiritual dimensions.

Decision Making
⌒ **Thinking** – Rational Suits: Wands and Swords
⌒ **Feeling** – Irrational Suits: Cups and Pentacles
The Queens of Swords and Wands rely on rational evaluation while the Queens of Cups and Pentacles rely on feelings.

**The Queen evolves
into the King**
Attitude transformation
(Introversion ➡ Extraversion)
The Queen moves from a depth
of knowledge and influence to
a breadth of knowledge and
influence transforming into the
King.

**The Queen evolves
into the Page**
Cognitive Style transformation
(Judging ➡ Perceiving)
The Queen moves from logic
into a display of abstraction and
transforms into the Page.

**The Queen evolves
into the Knight**
Attitude transformation
(Introversion ➡ Extraversion)
Cognitive Style transformation
(Judging ➡ Perceiving)
The Queen transforms herself
completely in the Attitude and
Cognitive Style and becomes the Knight

The Queens have a common introverted attitude that allows them to be reflective while deciphering external and internal movements of the mind. Their ability to listen while retaining retrospective communication gives a sense of detachment and gives them an air of maturity older than their years. Queens show themselves as trusted friends and well-balanced people.

Universal Tarot Queens

The Queens represent maturity/Queens:

The Queens reflect the maturity of those who have found balance and yet continue to make friends and learn from their own mistakes.

Liber T Tarot Queens

The Queens as the Mother

The Queens represent the energy of the Mother in every suit. Material force, firm and unshakable, and one whose effects are lasting.

Wiccan Tarot Queens

Queens as the Initiated

The Queens represent strength of knowledge in a mature woman who is active, fertile and constant.

Tarot of the Zodiac Queens

Queens as Water

Queens share common Water elements as a basis of great adaptability. At times it is wild and irrational energy, other times it is calm and quiet energy.

THE KINGS

King of Cups

ENFJ

- Extraversion
- Intuition
- Feeling
- Judging

King of Pentacles

ESFJ

- Extraversion
- Sensing
- Feeling
- Judging

King of Wands

ENTJ

- Extraversion
- Intuition
- Thinking
- Judging

King of Swords

ESTJ

- Extraversion
- Sensing
- Thinking
- Judging

The King's nature is outspoken and attentive and leads them to control the environment, surroundings and allows them to interact with reality through intermediaries. They coordinate and organize many toward a common goal.

Verb	Roles
Leading Manifesting the nature of the element	ᴑ *King of Wands:* leader, lawyer ᴑ *King of Cups:* counselor, doctor ᴑ *King of Swords:* teacher, consultant ᴑ *King of Pentacles:* father, mentor

Stable Traits

Extroverted Attitude
The extroversion of the King is expressed in the tendency to analyze every person and situation based on rationality, pragmatism and utilitarism. This rigidity reflects the aptitude of extreme focus and responsibility of decision making.

Judging Cognitive Style
The valuation style implemented by Kings is active. They collect information from outside themselves, process and return to people with practical actions.

Changing Traits

Information
ᴑ **Sensing** – Rational Suits: Swords and Pentacles
ᴑ **Intuition** – Irrational Suits: Wands and Cups
The Kings of Pentacles and Swords focus on objective and pragmatic data while the Kings of Cups and Wands are attracted to abstraction and intellectual speculation.

Decision Making
ᴑ **Thinking** – Rational Suits: Wands and Swords
ᴑ **Feeling** – Irrational Suits: Cups and Pentacles
The Kings of Swords and Wands rely on the criteria of convenience while the Kings of Cups and Pentacles allow guidance from ethical, philosophical and aesthetic principles.

**The King evolves
into the Queen**

Attitude transformation
(Extraversion ➡ Introversion)
The King eagerly speaks
and acts with others, becomes
curious about himself,
self reflective and transforms
into the Queen.

**The King evolves
into the Knight**

Cognitive Style transformation
(Judging ➡ Perceiving)
The King who strives
to control the world
loosens his grip, renounces
control and transforms
into the Knight.

**The King evolves
into the Page**

Attitude transformation
(Extraversion ➡ Introversion)
Cognitive Style transformation
(Judging ➡ Perceiving)
The King who transforms himself
entirely in Attitude and Cognitive Style
completely transforms into the Page.

The Kings share an attitude that characterizes constant intellectual work directed at controlling the reality about them using carefully selected intermediaries. The King's style includes humor and but also a testing of his minions who feel constantly put to the test. The Kings mix paternalism and severity, understanding and authoritarianism.

Universal Tarot Kings

The Kings represent maturity/Kings:

The Kings reflect consolidated power that wishes to expand further and expects servants, disciples and salaried workers to service his desires.

Liber T Tarot Kings

The Kings as the Father

The Kings represent the force of a concentrated and well defined space, quick and violent when manifesting yet their effects are long lasting.

Wiccan Tarot Kings

Kings as the Sage

The King is representative of power, knowledge at the highest level and one who will convey his knowledge in order to make the world a better place.

Tarot of the Zodiac Kings

Kings as Fire

Kings share common Fire elements as a basis of exuberance and heat that can invoke or destroy.

Transformation of the Suits

The transformation of Tarot suits is a subtle, yet fascinating experience. Observe, ponder and consider the transformation inside yourself on a daily basis or observe it in others. We, like the tides of the ocean, are always in a state of flux.

We move through the elemental attributes on a daily basis and/or we act out of character when differing scenarios are presented to us. The staunch and controlling CEO becomes mush in the hands in his grandchildren. The dreamy, intuitive artist becomes sharp and logical when balancing her checkbook.

Transformation is the nature of life.

It's important to remember that the Stable Traits and the Changing Traits between the ranks and the suits are inversed.

CUPS

Page of Cups

INFP

- Introversion
- Intuition
- Feeling
- Perceiving

Knight of Cups

ENFP

- Extraversion
- Intuition
- Feeling
- Perceiving

Queen of Cups

INFJ

- Introversion
- Intuition
- Feeling
- Judging

King of Cups

ENFJ

- Extraversion
- Intuition
- Feeling
- Judging

Cups express spiritual and emotional aspects of reality and the way we perceive it. It is a profoundly empathetic vision and interaction based on intuitions and feelings. Cups focus their attention on uniqueness, individuals, intentions and delve deep into the human mind.

Element	Roles
Water	⟳— *Receptive*
	⟳— *Subjective*
	⟳— *Abstract*
	⟳— *Radiant*

Stable Traits

Information
⟳— **Intuition**

Cups favor intuition as a tool for understanding and interpreting reality. Intuition is used like an information gathering tool.

Decision making
⟳— **Feeling**

Cups use sensations and feeling in deciding how to act. They move from the heart and process information from a subjective to an empathetic point of view.

Changing Traits

Attitude

Cups experience extroverted emotions and feelings in the Knight and King. They free their feelings in the introverted Page and Queen where the inner world is protected.

Cognitive Style

Cups are passive (Page and Knight) when they are paths and absorb feelings and emotions from others and the environment. External and active (Queen and King) can be picky and choose emotions and feelings.

**Cups change
into Pentacles**
Information transformation
(Intuition ➡ Sensing)
Cups move from misty
intuitiveness to a preference
for concrete and tangible
information and transform
into Pentacles.

**Cups change
into Wands**
Decision Making transformation
(Feeling ➡ Thinking)
Cups who become adept at
the use of logic and deduction,
without relying solely
on emotions, transform
into Wands.

**Cup change
into Swords**
Information transformation
(Intuition ➡ Sensing)
Decision Making transformation
(Feeling ➡ Thinking)
Cups abandoning their abstract nature to take
refuge in physical perceptions, logic and the
rational transform into Swords.

Cups express the spiritual and emotional currents of reality, and they focus on the way the human spirit perceives them. This results in a deeply empathetic relationship with reality, filled with feelings and insights. Cups draw forth and see the uniqueness of each existence, and they can relate to the deeper parts of the human mind.

Universal Tarot

Cups as Cups

Cups represent female qualities and the sacred nature of the human soul. They are the source of the emotions.

Liber T Tarot

Cups as Chalices

Cups represent psychic activity, human emotion and emotional and spiritual wealth.

Tarot of the Metamorphosis

Cups seen as myths

Cups represent the way humans see themselves inside a metaphysical framework.

Tarot of the Zodiac

Cups as Waves

Cups represent adaptability, absorption, the silence of one who lives in continual transformation.

PENTACLES

Page of Pentacles

ISFP

- Introversion
- Sensing
- Feeling
- Perceiving

Knight of Pentacles

ESFP

- Extraversion
- Sensing
- Feeling
- Perceiving

Queen of Pentacles

ISFJ

- Introversion
- Sensing
- Feeling
- Judging

King of Pentacles

ESFJ

- Extraversion
- Sensing
- Feeling
- Judging

Pentacles highlight female receptive qualities. They rely on the physical and material perception of the surrounding world, are capable of creating a strong sense of place and sense of belonging and empathy towards the environment and objects.

Element
Earth

Roles
- *Receptive*
- *Objective*
- *Material*
- *Radiant*

Stable Traits

Information
Sensing
Pentacles prefer sensory perceptions as a tool for interpreting and assessing everyday reality. The extraordinary spirit of observation that distinguishes this suit is the use of the five senses.

Decision Making
Feeling
The Pentacles have a strong sense of belonging to community which includes people and places and the objects they come into contact with. This rootedness to the physical is the link to a strong emotional center.

Changing Traits

Attitude
Pentacles express their emotions in active Extroverted form (King and Knight) or in a subtle Introverted form (Queen and Page).

Cognitive Style
Pentacles can be passive (Page and Knight) when they focus on receiving information from their surrounding environment or active (Queen and King) when they filter feelings received through their emotions or intuitions.

**Pentacles change
into Cups**

Information transformation
(Sensing ➤ Intuition)
Pentacles release their grasp on
reality and the physical, turn to
visions of the imagination and
transform into Cups.

**Pentacles change
into Swords**

Decision Making transformation
(Feeling ➤ Thinking)
Pentacles moving from
personalized issues into clear
cut truth and logical deductions
transform into Swords.

**Pentacles change
into Wands**

Information transformation
(Sensing ➤ Intuition)
Decision Making transformation
(Feeling ➤ Thinking)
Pentacles who abandon practicality and delve
into the passionate nature of truth completely
transform into the suit of Wands.

Pentacles express bodies, land, material assets and everything falling under the
domain of the senses. This creates a foundation of profound internal consistency
and a deep sense of belonging and community.

Universal Tarot

Pentacles as Pentacles

Pentacles represent the duality of the human soul comprised of various degrees from sacred to profane, light to dark, rational to intuitive.

Liber T Tarot

Pentacles as Discs

Pentacles represent thought towards materiality, concreteness, and the accumulation of goods and external signs of wellbeing.

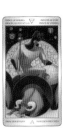

Tarot of the Metamorphosis

Pentacles seen as Science

Pentacles represent the individual's relationship to technology and how it relates to the ego.

Tarot of the Zodiac

Pentacles as Stones

Pentacles represent the ability to understand basic matter and are able to remain stable even as other things transform and change.

369

WANDS

Wands are the suit highlighting active male qualities based on strength, physical and psychic intensity. The relationship with reality is born from intuition and translated into rational expression.

Element	Roles
Fire	⌒ *Creative*
	⌒ *Subjective*
	⌒ *Material*
	⌒ *Directional*

Page of Wands

INTP

- Introversion
- Intuition
- Thinking
- Perceiving

Knight of Wands

ENTP

- Extraversion
- Intuition
- Thinking
- Perceiving

Queen of Wands

INTJ

- Introversion
- Intuition
- Thinking
- Judging

King of Wands

ENTJ

- Extraversion
- Intuition
- Thinking
- Judging

Stable Traits

Information
⌒ **Intuition**

Wands face reality from the simple and immediate insights that arise spontaneously and unpredictably thus making them an inconsistent and unpredictable suit.

Decision Making
⌒ **Thinking**

Wands transpose their intuitions and impulses onto practical plans using intellectual and analytical abilities which offers them control and awareness in every choice, even when the option is a surprise.

Changing Traits

Attitude

Wands hold emotions and feelings inside in the introverted form (Page and Queen) and involve others in an extraverted form (Knight and King).

Cognitive Style

Wands are passive (Page and Knight) when concentrating on absorbing and understanding the emotions of others. They are active (Queen and King) when digging into others to understand reasons and motivations.

**Wands change
into Swords**
Information transformation
(Intuition ➡ Sensing)
Wands moving from
insight and gut feelings into
clear focus on the present
transform into Swords.

**Wands change
into Cups**
Decision Making transformation
(Thinking ➡ Feeling)
Wands moving from
precise beliefs into empathic
attitudes towards others
transform into Cups.

**Wands change
into Pentacles**
Information transformation
(Intuition ➡ Sensing)
Decision Making transformation
(Thinking ➡ Feeling)
Wands who reverse their preferences
completely, rely upon their senses and are
conscious of others become completely
transformed into Pentacles.

Wands express actions and activities related to morality and tradition such as family care and education, teaching, prudence and religion. Wands express evolution and growth. Ethics are ruled by Wands along with lawful behavior, civic duty and responsibility to family.

Universal Tarot

Wands as Wands

Wands represent growth, maturation, aging, evolution and the evolutionary aspect of every human being.

Liber T Tarot

Wands as Scepters

Wands represent the energy of growth and power over reality, material constructions and development. It is the physical vigor of an individual.

Tarot of the Metamorphosis

Wands seen as Nature

Wands represent the individual's relationship to living in harmony with the natural energies and cycles of other people and the universe at large.

Tarot of the Zodiac

Wands as Flames

Wands represent the ability to understand and express ambition, will, passion and how people mold themselves and the world with image and ideals. It is also constant human activity.

SWORDS

Page of Swords

ISTP

- Introversion
- Sensing
- Thinking
- Perceiving

Knight of Swords

ESTP

- Extraversion
- Sensing
- Thinking
- Perceiving

Queen of Swords

ISTJ

- Introversion
- Sensing
- Thinking
- Judging

King of Swords

ESTJ

- Extraversion
- Sensing
- Thinking
- Judging

Swords are the suit highlighting rational male characteristics that are based on strong pragmatism and the service of intellectual facilities. It is communication and mental articulation.

Element
Air

Roles
- *Creative*
- *Objective*
- *Abstract*
- *Directional*

Stable Traits

Information
- **Sensing**

Swords prefer objectivity and security over complete reliance on the senses when facing everyday reality and making decisions.

Decision Making
- **Thinking**

Swords focus on rational and analytic ideas when evaluating a situation. The intellect is the guide so a balanced and logical conclusion is reached.

Changing Traits

Attitude

Swords express themselves in arguments and extroversion (Knight and King) and will communicate by holding back in the introverted form (Page and Queen).

Cognitive Style

Swords are passive (Page and Knight) when thinking and speculating or active (Queen and King) when using intellect for a specific and precise purpose.

**Sword change
into Wands**

Information transformation
(Sensing ➡ Intuition)
Swords swapping their level
headed objectivity in favor of
fiery intuition become Wands.

**Swords change
into Pentacles**

Decision Making transformation
(Thinking ➡ Feeling)
Swords grounded in reality yet
moving into feelings of empathy
transform into Pentacles.

**Swords change
into Cups**

Information transformation
(Sensing ➡ Intuition)
Decision Making transformation
(Thinking ➡ Feeling)
The Swords who release materiality
to embrace the subjective, emotional
aspects of life completely
transform into Cups.

Swords represent intellectual and analytical activities, speculative abstraction and rational reflections. They also refer to communication, language, conflicts, societal law and rules. Swords often sacrifice personal desire in favor of responsibilities and focus. It is the suit of troubleshooting and efficiency.

Universal Tarot

Swords as Swords

Swords represent the will to express ideas onto reality by supporting them with determination, intellectual and moral strength.

Liber T Tarot

Swords as Blades

Swords represent the energy to let go of what is not needed so the important things can be focused upon.

Tarot of the Metamorphosis

Swords seen as Thoughts

Swords represent materialization of humanity's collective unconscious through art, myth and literature.

Tarot of the Zodiac

Swords as Air

Swords represent the ability to analyze problems, to judge one or another's actions against the established rules of society.

ADVANCED TECHNIQUES

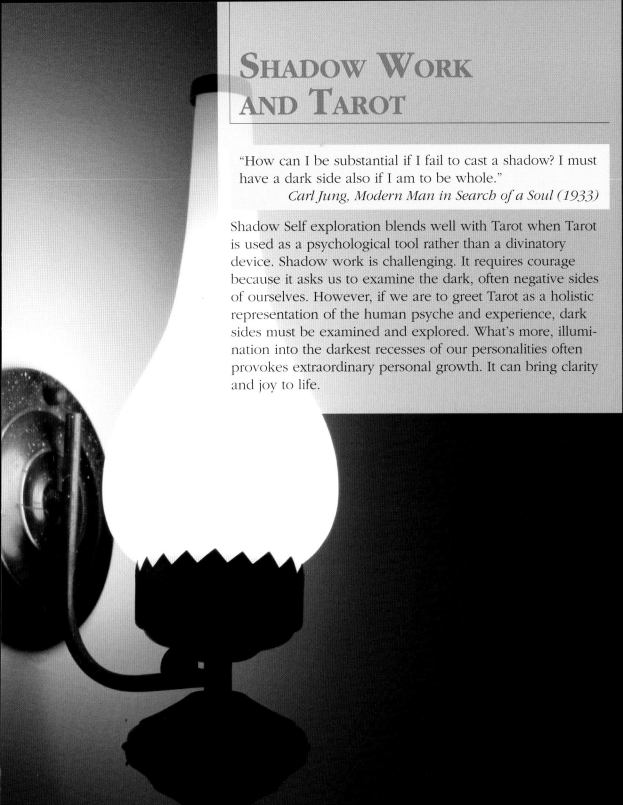

Shadow Work and Tarot

"How can I be substantial if I fail to cast a shadow? I must have a dark side also if I am to be whole."
Carl Jung, Modern Man in Search of a Soul (1933)

Shadow Self exploration blends well with Tarot when Tarot is used as a psychological tool rather than a divinatory device. Shadow work is challenging. It requires courage because it asks us to examine the dark, often negative sides of ourselves. However, if we are to greet Tarot as a holistic representation of the human psyche and experience, dark sides must be examined and explored. What's more, illumination into the darkest recesses of our personalities often provokes extraordinary personal growth. It can bring clarity and joy to life.

The Shadows Self always hides hidden depths that cannot be perceived from outside.

The Shadow Self is a psychological term coined by the great Carl Jung. It is used to describe the place where we store away all the things about ourselves and our personality that we do not like, approve of, or want to acknowledge. The Shadow Self is like a musty closet most people would rather avoid. Human impulses become stored in the Shadow when an emotion is felt but not acknowledged.

Example

Sarah feels extreme jealousy when she sees her co-worker, the seemingly successful and creative Jill. It appears to Sarah that Jill's life is perfect. Rather than deal with her jealous impulses, she shoves them inside herself and feigns sweetness to Jill. Deep down Sarah is consumed with a hate and annoyance that continues to grow with every interaction with Jill. What she doesn't realize if that her jealousy can be used as compass, pointing Sarah toward the life qualities she desires and could have if she wanted. Once identified as a Shadow trait, Sarah could unpack her impulse, figure out what it truly means, and then make strides to accomplishing and satisfying her desires.

Qualities stored in the Shadow Self

The emotions usually confined within the Shadow Self are those which are usually described as negative emotions. As these emotions are often socially negative, it's common to repress them inside the Shadow.

JEALOUSY

HATRED

ANGER

PASSION

SEXUALITY

RAGE

Good and Bad Qualities Exist in Your Shadow

It may seem counterintuitive, but good qualities and talents are often stored inside the Shadow Self along with darker impulses, especially those things we are ashamed of or qualities we have been told are not valuable. For example, Sarah demonstrated great aptitude for poetry and art when she was a teenager. Her domineering and scientifically minded parents told her art was a waste of time. They made fun of her art while only giving positive feedback when she received high marks in math and science. As a result, she shoved her artistic expression into her Shadow where it lay dormant. We place qualities we don't think we deserve or should express into our Shadow.

Positive qualities stored in the Shadow Self can include:

- Personal passions
- Creativity
- Extraordinary qualities
- Unique abilities
- Talents

The Shadow is not a negative landscape. Many complicated emotions and attitudes that are positive in nature but difficult to handle are confined within the Shadow Self.

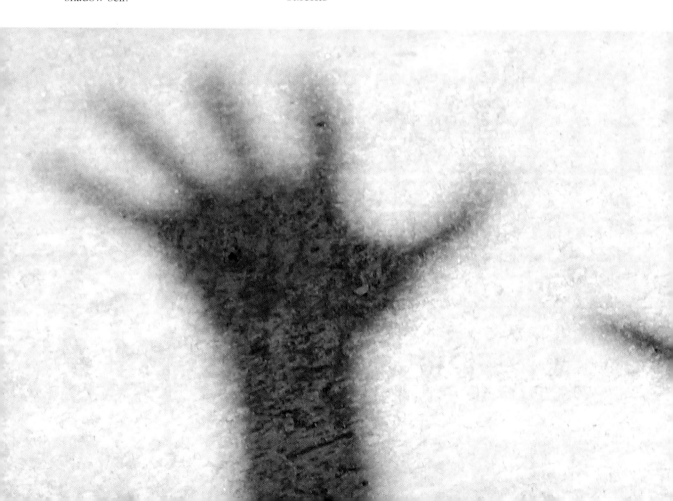

Dealing with the Shadow Self

Repressed issues can cause discomfort and sometimes blossom into serious issues.

Why?

Shadow issues will be projected onto others when not dealt with. This causes serious conflict and crisis for individuals and sometimes even societies at large. There are often stories in the news of politicians or prosecutors becoming convicted for the very crimes they fought against. This was their Shadow projection. The Nazi persecution of Jews is an extreme example of a society projecting its Shadow onto a group of people. Shadow Self projections are fascinating and teach us what many Tarot Readers already realize—that the world exists inside of us.

Want to discover what rests in your Shadow Self? Simple. Identify what ticks you off about others with the following exercise.

THE WHEEL OF FORTUNE

Shadow Self Exercise

1. Write a list of five people, real or fictional, you dislike or who annoy you.
2. Write the reason they irritate you next to their name.
3. Select five Tarot cards representing these people and/or their annoying qualities.
5. Write a list of five people, real or fictional, you admire.
6. Write the reason you admire them next to their name.
7. Select the Tarot cards that represent them and/or their qualities.
8. Circle all of the annoying and admirable qualities and the 10 Tarot cards.
9. These are the qualities and cards of your Shadow Self.
10. Consider how you display or have trouble displaying these qualities yourself.

Remember, Shadow Self exercises are meant to be metaphorical and allegorical.

Negative Cards Exercise

1. Select five Tarot cards you strongly dislike.
2. Pull them face up from the deck and place in front of you.
3. Write three ways each card could be the most powerful, useful agent of positive change. How could these cards be of service to you?

Positive Cards Exercise

Exploring the entire realm of Tarot, including the light and dark side of each card, adds depth to the Tarot practice.

1. Select a card you are fond of.
2. Write down the reason you like it.
3. Now write how that same card might be used as in greedy, selfish, and self-indulgent way.

Dark decks may be very useful when exploring the Shadow Self. It is the case, for instance, of the grim but colorful Santa Muerte Tarot, by Fabio Listrani.

Example

Susan loves the Ten of Cups. She is always happy when the card pops up in a reading. She selects the Ten of Cups as her card for this exercise and notes that the Ten of Cups reflects a happy family. She considers how this card could apply to her Shadow side. She laughs and thinks of the times she's been so annoyed by everyone that she wished her family would just disappear. Even though her thought was fleeting, she realizes this is a valid Shadow side of the Ten of Cups.

FREE ASSOCIATION MEETS TAROT

Free association techniques merge well with Tarot whenever Tarot is used as a psychological tool rather than a divinatory device. Legendary psychoanalyst Sigmund Freud invented free association to reach into a patient's psyche. Traditionally it is used in psychotherapy. The point of free association is help people uncover their true feelings and unconscious thoughts. It is not meant to uncover repressed incidents such as buried childhood memories but rather to seek an individual's authentic truth and underlying issues. For instance, a woman tells herself she loves and adores her in-laws. However, at every family dinner, she suffers from extreme anxiety. Free association in therapy might reveal that she's been telling herself she loves her in-laws, perhaps for her husband's sake, but deep down she despises them. Thanks to this revelation, she is free to explore and examine the conflict between her two emotions. She can now work to find productive ways to sooth her anxiety.

Why Free Association Works

Free association works when the individual does not self-censor. Truth, honesty, and trust are key. Freely stating what is on the mind, without judgment, can reveal unexpected outcomes. Traditionally, the client sits in a relaxed position and begins to articulate stream of consciousness thinking with their therapist. In a space of complete trust, and as relaxed as possible, the client speaks freely of anything that crosses their mind while the therapist makes notes. Further analysis of the stream of consciousness conversation reveals patterns and symbols open for interpretation. This same technique seams beautifully with Tarot for learning, discovery, and revelation. A Tarotist may embark on free association techniques alone or with a partner. They may use the techniques to deepen their Tarot practice or share with students and Querents.

On the left: Sigmund Freud, father of psychoanalysis.

Everything can be used for free associations. However, it's much easier by using words or images. Tarot cards, obviously, provide both.

Moving into the Free Association Mental State

The free association mental state is coincidentally similar to the frame of mind that many, but not all, Readers like to be in when they are performing a reading for themselves or others. This relaxed state of mind allows for intuitive impressions and deep listening. This ideal mental state comes from a place of security, relaxation, yet heightened awareness. Choose any meditative technique you like. Here's an example:

1. Choose a simple mantra such as "I speak the truth" or "authentic truth."

2. Close your eyes and sit comfortably with feet on the floor or with legs crossed.

3. Align the spine.

4. Breathe deeply, in through the nose, out through the mouth.

5. Focus on the breath to clear the mind.

6. Remind yourself to stay open and alert to any impulse.

7. Silently repeat the mantra for a few minutes.

8. Open your eyes and begin free association/Tarot reading.

THE SUN

General Free Association for Yourself with Tarot

Below is a list of Tarot-related words with common symbols found on a variety of decks. Copy five of the words onto a piece of paper. Next to each one, write the first word that comes to mind.

Choose one of the following exercises:

- Describe how the pairs of words make you feel.
- Write a short poem using the word pairs.
- Write the simple essay paragraph about each word pairing.
- Write the first paragraph of a fairy tale about each word pairing.

After completing the written exercise, sift through a Tarot deck. Pull out all the cards that correspond with the word pairings. It is okay if some repeat. Examine what new revelations have occurred in your Tarot journal or notebook.

A list of Tarot related words

ANGEL

BIRD

BOY

BRIDGE

BUTTERFLY

CLOUD

CROWN

FIRE

GIRL

GOWN

HIDDEN

LEAF

PILLAR

ROSE

SHADOW

SNAKE

SNOW

STAGE

SUN

UNIVERSE

WATER

WIND

WINGS

The Reversal Technique can be used to complement and make the free associations more varied and effective.

Free Association to Cultivate Deeper Tarot Meanings

1. Shuffle the deck.

2. Select one card at random.

3. Without censoring yourself, select three symbols (throne, flower, child, etc.) that you observe on the card.

4. Write those three symbols down on a piece of paper.

5. Put the card away or turn it over.

6. Focus on your three words. Without censoring yourself, write at least one paragraph about what each symbol means to you. Validate any stream of consciousness impulses while writing.

7. Bring the original card out or turn it over. Consider what you've written in the context of the card. What new discoveries have you made?

Free Association for a New Student of Tarot

The biggest barrier for new students of Tarot is fear of "getting it wrong." In free association there is no wrong. Everything is right. All is acceptable. New students should be encouraged to write about and explore the cards and perform the free association exercise above. Once they have associated into the symbol(s) of a card, they can cross-check and look up traditional card meanings. This leads to a personal connection and a rich and visceral experience of the Tarot.

Card Connections with Free Association

Learning how cards relate to one another, how to connect the meanings of a Tarot spread, can befuddle or intimidate new students. New students, either alone or with their teachers or friends, should:

1. Shuffle the deck.

2. Pull two random cards and place side by side.

3. Throw everything they think they know about Tarot out the window, beginning with a fresh slate. Write or articulate the story they see unfolding before them as if the cards were stills in a movie frame or in a graphic novel.

Another very useful technique to combine with free association is Tarot journaling.

Free Association with Querents

Querents often struggle to articulate the problem that brought them to the Reader. Often, the issue rests just below their subconscious. The Querent will often move faster to identify the base root of their problem or issue using free association with the cards. A Querent's lack of Tarot knowledge becomes helpful because there are no preconceived notions. The Querent can freely project their situation onto the cards.

To freely associate with a Querent, select a card that coincides with the Querent's issue at hand. Ask the Querent to describe their situation in the context of the image they observe. Remind them there is no wrong answer. Always ask the Querent which person/symbol on the card they identify with.

Romantic Issues
- Devil
- Lovers
- Seven of Swords
- Two of Cups

Financial Issues
- Ace of Pentacles
- Four of Pentacles
- Five of Pentacles
- Ten of Pentacles

Personal Path Issues
- Temperance
- Eight of Pentacles
- Eight of Cups
- World

Family Issues
- Emperor
- Four of Wands
- Ten of Pentacles
- Ten of Cups

Career Issues
- Two of Wands
- Three of Wands
- Three of Pentacles
- Emperor

SPIRIT COMMUNICATION BOARD

Romantic Issues

Financial Issues

Personal Path Issues

Family Issues

Career Issues

GOOD BYE

ELEMENTAL DIGNITIES

When the Hermetic Order of the Golden Dawn was founded in 1888, there was little material on the Tarot cards as an esoteric device. The French occultists such as Papus and Etteilla had begun to overlay the occult subjects upon the cards, taken up by Éliphas Lévi, but it would be the Golden Dawn that would build upon this foundation and in turn provide the bedrock for both Waite and Crowley, whose decks would then become arguably two of the three pillars of the Tarot temple – the third being the Tarot de Marseille.

From the beginning, W. W. Westcott, one of the three founders of the Order, had been keen to develop a full curriculum from the rudiments of the "cypher manuscripts." These manuscripts, now generally accepted to have been created by Freemason Kenneth MacKenzie, included basic ritual notes and sketch outlines of the Tarot, influenced by Lévi, whom MacKenzie had met in Paris in 1861.

Each element influences and reacts to the other elements in a different way.

Kabbalah, numerology, ancient Egyptian myth, psychology, Tarot, geomancy, alchemy, astrology...

Westcott had written to another of the founders, Samuel Liddell MacGregor Mathers, in 1887 that once the cypher was written up and a third Chief was chosen, they must "endeavour to spread a complete scheme of initiation".[1]

One aspect of that "complete scheme" was to be the Tarot, which Westcott had earlier described as:

> ...that enticing subject, the origin and meaning of the 22 Trumps or symbolic designs of the "Tarocchi" or pack of Tarot cards, which Eliphaz Lévi says form a group of keys which will unlock every secret of Theology and Cosmology.[2]

The result of their endeavours was to be the most comprehensive system of esotericism ever devised, creating correspondences between Kabbalah, numerology, ancient Egyptian myth, psychology, Tarot, geomancy, alchemy, astrology and a range of other esoteric subjects. In fact,

396

the result would be "a symbolic synthesis so complex and extensive as to stagger the imagination".[3]

We must go back to this original conception of the Order to fully appreciate how the method of "elemental dignities", the method we examine in this section, was conceived and utilized in practical Tarot reading. We will then provide several ways in which the reader may usefully apply elemental dignities to their own readings. Most importantly, we must recognize how closely the Tarot was linked to astrology at the time the method was produced, even more so than Kabbalah. Mathers describes the section on the Minor Arcana as a "description of the thirty-six decanates of the zodiac".[4]

First, we present the original *Book T* section on dignities, likely written by Mathers (this is not in the original cipher manuscript) and then we will briefly return to the concept as it is considered in astrology.

A **CARD** is strong or weak, well dignified or ill dignified, according to the cards next to it on either side.

Cards of the same suit on either side strengthen it greatly, for good or evil according to their nature.

Cards of opposite natures on either side weaken it greatly, for either good or evil.

- *Swords* are **inimical** to *Pentacles*
- *Wands* are **inimical** to *Cups*

- *Swords* are **friendly** with *Cups* and *Wands*
- *Wands* are **friendly** with *Swords* and *Pentacles*

If a card fall between two other which are mutually contrary, it is not much affected by either.[5]

Swords are friendly with Cups and Wands.

Mathers also provides us with more details:

If a card of the suit of wands falls between a cup and a sword, the sword modifies and connects the wand with the cup, so that it is not weakened by its vicinity, but is modified by the influence of both cards, therefore fairly strong. But if a card passes between two which are naturally contrary, it is not affected by either much, as a wand between a sword and a pentacle, which latter, being air and earth, are contrary and therefore weaken each other.[6]

Here we see two **measurements** of the cards: strong (well dignified) or weak (ill dignified), and two **relationships**: friendly or inimical. We also have a further suggestion of a card being moved more towards "good or evil" depending on the measurement and relationship of the two cards which lie on either side.

At the same time, Swords are enemies to Pentacles.

This notion of **dignity** derives from astrology, and *Book T*, whilst mainly dealing with Tarot, is dense with astrology, in addition to Kabbalah and geomancy (divination by casting stones or observing patterns in earth) which provides the pattern of the arrangement of the symbols on the Minor Arcana.

In astrology, dignity is a technical and potentially complex subject, however, it essentially describes the **measurement** of strength of a planet in itself (an "essential" dignity) and in **relationship** to its placement in a chart, other planets, etc. which is an "accidental" dignity.

Dignities are about relationships: affinity, empathy, mutual connection.

It is the "accidental" dignity that considers how a planet may be impacted with regard, for example, to a *triplicity* in which it finds itself – a triangular relationship in the chart with two other planets. This notion goes as far back as Ptolemy, who produced a table of dignities, and William Lilly, who in the 17th century wrote of the "strength, fortitude or debility" of planets according to dignity.

So, the application of this notion in astrology to Tarot is to be found in the relationship (accidental dignity) of a card

to two other cards in a triplicity. As the main Golden Dawn method in the inner Order was the "Opening of the Key"—a series of linked readings which lay out cards in a line (or circle) and read them in a counted order—this would always provide two cards either side of any chosen card.

If we now look further at *Book T*, taking the descriptions of three Minor cards and a court card, we can see that the authors have provided us a straight interpretation of an individual card, and suggested how it might be read if "ill dignified".

Two of Cups: Harmony of masculine and feminine united. Harmony, pleasure, mirth, subtlety: but if ill dignified—folly, dissipation, waste, silly actions.

Ten of Swords, Lord of Ruin: Almost a worse symbol than the Nine of Swords. Undisciplined, warring force, complete disruption and failure. Ruin of all plans and projects. Disdain, insolence and impertinence, yet mirth and jollity therewith. A marplot, loving to overthrow the happiness of others; a repeater of things; given to much unprofitable speech, and of many words. Yet clever, eloquent, etc., according to dignity.

Five of Wands, Lord of Strife: Violent strife and boldness, rashness, cruelty, violence, lust, desire, prodigality and generosity, depending on whether the card is well or ill dignified.

The Knave (Page or Princess) **of Wands**: Brilliance, courage, beauty, force, sudden in anger or love, desire of power, enthusiasm, revenge. If ill dignified, she is superficial, theatrical, cruel, unstable, domineering.

This provides us with a rough guide, but it is confusing. The dignity of each card is described as being "well" which is the normal interpretation (not a "strengthening" of it) and the "ill" dignity appears to be merely the reversal of the straight reading – what we would now simply say is a reversed reading, i.e., if the card appeared in the reading in a reversed manner, upside-down.

Further, there is no indication of how the Major Arcana may be considered in terms of dignity. So, let us return to the original text and provide a guide as to the application of dignities.

The Table of Dignities

As we saw in the *Book T* list, the dignities are determined by the relationship of the elements which correspond to the cards through their suits; this goes back to the earliest concepts of the four elements proposed by the Greek philosopher Empedocles.

We also find in history the notion of particular relationships between these elements:

> Of living things, my son, some are made friends with fire, and some with water, some with air, and some with earth, and some with two or three of these, and some with all. And, on the contrary, again some are made enemies of fire, and some of water, some of earth, and some of air, and some of two of them, and some of three, and some of all. For instance, son, the locust and all flies flee fire; the eagle and the hawk and all high-flying birds flee water, fish, air and earth; the snake avoids the open air. Whereas snakes and all creeping things love earth, all swimming things love water; winged things, air, of which they are the citizens; while those that fly still higher love the fire and have the habitat near it. Not that some of the animals as well do not love fire; for instance salamanders, for they even have their homes in it.[7]

When we now apply the elements to the suits of the Tarot through correspondence, we can see how these relationships map across to the Tarot.

- **Pentacles** = Earth
  Passive, dry, cold

- **Swords** = Air
  Active, wet, hot

- **Cups** = Water
  Passive, wet, cold

- **Wands** = Fire
  Active, dry, hot

The elements have relationships as follows:

INIMICAL
Wands/Fire – *Cups*/Water
Swords/Air – *Pentacles*/Earth

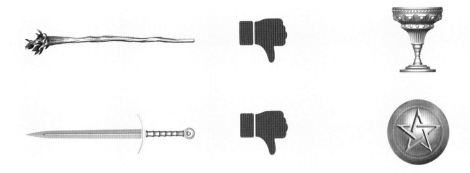

FRIENDLY
Swords/Air - *Wands*/Fire (strong)
Pentacles/Earth – *Cups*/Water (strong)
Swords/Air – *Cups*/Water (weak)
Wands/Fire – *Pentacles*/Earth (weak)

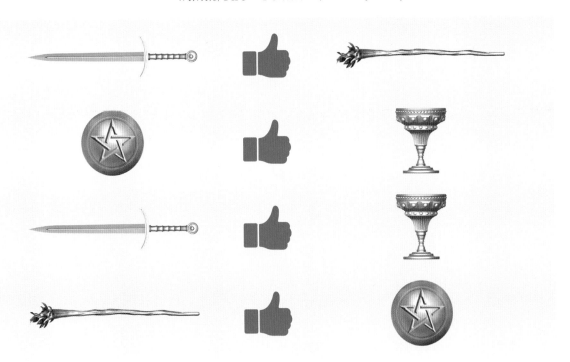

If we consider the basic qualities of the elements, whether they are dry/wet, hot/cold, passive/active, or simply their natural manifestation, we can see how these relationships are determined.

The active, dry and hot fire is totally opposite to the passive, cold, wet water – it is not that they put each other out, but they create a lot of conflict and steam when they try to co-exist. Similarly, the lofty heights of the air are opposite to the sullen depths of the earth – and stones cannot fly, they crash to the ground if they are lifted out of their natural place.

The desert may be defined as hot and dry. What would happen if you put the energies of Pentacles and Cups close to the desert?

We know that the active air and the active fire get on, literally, like a house on fire. What happens when you blow

on embers? Conversely, you put out a fire by removing any oxygen from it. They really are close friends and build each other up.

But what about water and earth? The Cups and Pentacles? They simply bog each other down, make things a bit muddier together. They are strong in relationship but both passive, so drag things down.

When we consider the elements in their everyday manifestation, as did Hermes in the Book of the Virgin, when he saw them as living creatures, we can quickly understand their likely relationship.

An artic glacier may be defined as cold and wet. What would happen if you put the energies of Swords and Wands in contact with the ice?

Applying Elemental Dignities

The most effective way to practice elemental dignities is in a three-card spread where we only read the central card. This in effect is a "segment" in the Golden Dawn method of Opening the Key. If you prefer, you can simply prepare an Opening of the Key (OOTK) reading and work through it in detail, practising with each counted card.

As the OOTK has no fixed spread positions, it is helpful to the reader when certain cards are highlighted or downgraded in importance by their elemental dignity. This again is a case of using earlier cartomantic (playing card reading) methods with an added esoteric rationale. Many of the early cartomantic books had tables of three card combinations to explain the relationship between the suits.[8]

Mathers at least gave us many examples of the application of the method.[9]

Imagine the Ten of Swords between the Nine of Swords and the Five of Swords.

He called this "very strong and potent in action. Very evil". We can see that the Swords here are strengthening each other, but for evil rather than good, given their own essential nature.

Suppose we had two Pentacles either side of a card, these are more positive but passive.

Mathers writes, "Fairly strong. Good. Considerable gain and glory". This is the usual reading of the Two of Wands being somewhat bolstered by the two earth cards.

We can also see how the court cards are given more nuance by the elemental dignities of the two cards either side of them in a reading.

Mathers says of this triplicity, "a rather fair man but very deceitful and malicious". Here the Cups (passive water) and the Swords (active air) have a weak strengthening of the central card, so bring it down somewhat to its more negative reading. The words "deceit" and "malice" derive from the reading of the Seven of Cups with its illusionary nature and the Five of Swords with its malicious intent.

In applying the elemental dignities to the cards, we also receive a far clearer measurement of "good" and "bad" meanings in addition to additional nuance upon their interpretation.

Let us look at a final example from Mathers.

Mathers says of this, "very weak, evil, slight loss in material things, but more anxiety than actual loss". The two cards to either side of the Ten of Swords are earth and water, so a strong relationship, but both passive. This leads to a weaker interpretation of the usually more tragic Ten of Swords, denigrated here to more anxiety than actual tragic loss. Sometimes it is good to pull a bad card down.

We have several examples of members of the Golden Dawn performing sections of the OOTK, and they utilized elemental dignities in pairs and in triplicity. We see in an example recorded by Annie Horniman and sent to W. B. Yeats in 1903 that she followed the *Book T* instructions.[10]

Table of Dignities & Keywords

In this table, we provide a general sense of each combination of dignities, noting that the arrangement of the two elements either side of the central card is considered the same, whichever side each of the two elements are placed. So, Air – Earth – Water is considered in the same way as Water – Earth – Air.

To use the table, determine the elements of the three cards (see also the following table of correspondences for the Major Arcana) and locate the central element. Then locate the line for that element which has the two side elements, whichever way they are arranged.

Example
Page of Wands + Three of Cups + Empress = Fire/Water/Earth which appears in the table as Earth/Water/Fire and is considered the same relationship.

We have then provided a suggestive keyword which can be applied to the overall reading of the central card. If you refer to the keywords for the cards provided in *Tarot Fundamentals*, you can now prefix the keyword from the elemental dignity table to add nuance to your readings. You may wish to expand these keywords with your own studies of the elements and their relationships, in addition to your experience as you experiment with the method in your own readings.

Example
Empress + Five of Pentacles + Six of Pentacles
= Earth/Earth/Earth.
We are reading the Five of Pentacles, which has the keywords (*Tarot Fundamentals*, p. 227) of poverty, hardship and struggle.
We can now see that this would be prefixed by "enduring" in terms of the elemental dignities. The two Earth cards either side of the Earth card result in a strong negative triplicity, "enduring poverty".

Earth	Earth	Earth	Strong influence, stable, somewhat fixed and cold.	Enduring
Earth	Earth	Air	Weak "as if they were not there".[11]	Weakening
Earth	Earth	Water	Weak influence, but slightly stronger earth.	Dragging
Earth	Earth	Fire	Positive influence, dynamic, greenhouse.	Cultivating
Air	Earth	Air	Ill dignified, conflicting, resistance to movement, a sandbag in a balloon (ballast).	Braking
Air	Earth	Water	Air and earth are opposite, but water in the vicinity provides some chance of movement. Air and water are weak friends. A little rain on the ground, but the seeds must be there first.	Opening
Air	Earth	Fire	Opposite to the above, the air and fire cannot agree how to support the earth, which is neither one nor the other.	Confusing
Water	Earth	Water	The two passive water cards cannot support the passive earth. They are strong in relationship, but downwards.	Sinking
Water	Earth	Fire	A resistance stuck in the middle of a conflict with no result.	Holding
Fire	Earth	Fire	Whilst weak friends, having an identical pair makes the fire quicken the earth, despite itself.	Shifting

Earth	Air	Earth	A yearning to reach upwards and beyond, and likely the means to do so, as ever, depending on the central card.	Aspiring
Earth	Air	Air	The air attempts to rescue itself from the inimical earth and air combination, but it struggles with itself.	Doubting
Earth	Air	Water	A strong affinity between experience and the emotions (earth and water) might overrule the mind.	Escaping
Earth	Air	Fire	Seismic activity shifts the mind which can respond well to creative disruption.	Creating
Air	Air	Air	Active and hot, tripled, a realm of violent or ruthless thought depending on the central card. Abstract.	Idealizing
Air	Air	Water	A good and creative opportunity arises from somewhere above. The central card has a lot of potential.	Inspiring
Air	Air	Fire	A spark inside ignites a sudden thought, although not yet manifest, it can be recognized.	Realization
Water	Air	Water	The feeling of what happens. An idea that has emotional meaning and feels right.	Compelling
Water	Air	Fire	A strong push and pull which can potentially be harnessed, if the mind remains clear of both emotions and desires.	Focusing
Fire	Air	Fire	The volatile air is lifted by the surrounding fires. Dignity.	Uplifting

411

Earth	Water	Air	A reasonably stable compromise between thought, reality and the emotions. Well dignified.	Assuring
Earth	Water	Water	The earth and water may muddy the waters. No real impact, merely a call for a double-check or caution.	Convincing
Earth	Water	Fire	The earth and fire weakly relate and have little impact on the water, which is only gently warmed, like a stove.	Encouraging
Air	Water	Air	Adrift in thought, nothing bad, but neither good. The central card is the feeling which the thoughts are recognizing.	Dreaming
Air	Water	Water	There may be clouds of illusion in the emotional content of the central card – certainly a little confusion.	Idling
Air	Water	Fire	A strong relationship between the air and fire serve to cook up something more powerful in the central water card.	Quickening
Water	Water	Water	The depth of passive water, surrounded by water. An ocean with no boundaries or bottom. Lack of boundaries.	Deepening
Fire	Water	Water	Here the water and fire put each other out, with little effect on the remaining central water card.	Rippling
Fire	Water	Fire	A troubling combination, where the emotions may be enflamed or otherwise out of control.	Inciting

Earth	Fire	Earth	The paired earth cards provide a stable base for the will of the flame. The card gets to express its essential nature.	Determining
Earth	Fire	Air	The air and earth catch the fire between, which is neutral. It is a perfect balance if the will is held.	Willing
Earth	Fire	Water	The fire stops the muddiness of the earth and water, resulting in a generally positive dignity for the central card.	Working
Earth	Fire	Fire	The fire and earth have a weak bond but this is uplifted by the additional fire of the central card, to effect positive change.	Igniting
Air	Fire	Air	Simple well-dignified, the air cards provide space for the fire card.	Empowering
Air	Fire	Water	The clouds are burnt through by the sun, a good triplicity where the central card shines through.	Emerging
Air	Fire	Fire	The air and fire support more fire, bringing positive and graduated growth.	Advancing
Water	Fire	Water	Poorly placed, the fire is frustrated by the lack of support.	Dampening
Water	Fire	Fire	Somewhat neutral, this combination suggests a slight disappointment but overall success in the central card.	Disappointing
Fire	Fire	Fire	Intense and rapid combustion and possibly destruction, depending on the central card.	Consuming

We would recommend the advanced student also journal a range of circumstances that correspond to each of these combinations, for example, a "troublesome bank loan" for Earth + Earth + Earth (particularly if the central card was the Five of Pentacles).

The reader might also create I Ching style poems or Haiku for each triplicity, such as:

~ Earth + Air + Water

Heaven above the swampland,
mud sticks to our shoes,
walking under empty sky.

The I Ching can be a strong source of inspiration for expressing Tarot images via words.

The Elemental Correspondences of the Major Arcana

We have so far ignored the Major Arcana; however, they have straightforward elemental correspondences based on their planetary, zodiacal or elemental correspondence. We provide here a table of the Major Arcana considered elementally:

Fool	Air	◓
Magician	Air	◓
High Priestess	Water	●
Empress	Earth	●
Emperor	Fire	●
Hierophant	Earth	●
Lovers	Air	◓
Chariot	Water	●
Strength	Fire	●
Hermit	Earth	●
Wheel of Fortune	Fire	●
Justice	Air	◓
Hanged Man	Water	●
Death	Water	●
Temperance	Fire	●
Devil	Earth	●
Tower	Fire	●
Star	Air	◓
Moon	Water	●
Sun	Fire	●
Judgement	Water	●
World	Earth	●

Once you have mastered the elemental dignities, you can also consider adding planetary dignities, to which we refer you to the reading list for further study.

Pairing Cards

It is also possible to utilize dignities in a lesser fashion when reading pairs of cards. In this case, it is suggested that opposite (inimical) cards mutually weaken each other, whereas identical elements strengthen each other. We can further suggest that where the paired cards are of the same element, they can be interpreted by adding the appropriate descriptive keywords:

- Fire = Swiftly
- Water = Responsibly
- Air = Thoughtfully
- Earth = Practically

Example
Five of Swords + Eight of Swords (both air) = "Defeat (5 of Swords) through betrayal (8 of Swords)... thoughtfully" suggesting that the defeat will come through a planned betrayal, likely already in motion, one that has been thought about by someone for some time.[12]

The environment defined by the four elements can be easily applied to many life experiences, such as office and work.
Fire may suggest to work fast, water to work well, air to work organized and earth to work sensibly.

We can also see that the sub-elements will add another layer to the reading of two cards.

Sub-Elements

The Golden Dawn, following the grimoire tradition and earlier philosophers, saw that when the elements were mixed, they produced different qualities. This provides another layer to our readings if we wish to consider a pair of cards rather than a triplicity.

The Qualities of the Elements

Fire and Water *Wands and Cups*	Slight weight, some subtlety, intense and rapid motion.
Fire and Air *Wands and Swords*	Great heat, intense lightness, slight brilliance, intense subtlety, tense motion.
Fire and Earth *Wands and Pentacles*	Great dryness, slight obscurity.
Water and Air *Cups and Swords*	Great moisture, intense motion.
Water and Earth *Cups and Pentacles*	Great cold, intense weight, intense obscurity, intense solidity.
Air and Earth *Swords and Pentacles*	Some weight, intense obscurity, little solidity, little motion.

When we appreciate these combinations of elements in pairs, we can assess in a simple two-card reading the measures of the importance of the situation (weight), the obviousness of it, or otherwise (obscurity), the speed in which it is likely to transpire (motion), and how fluid or fixed it might be (solidity).

All about the elements is a constant changing relationship. Each element is connected to the other so they affect a situation portrayed by a reading as a whole and not as single entities.

Example

In a question about timing, or speed of resolution of a situation, we draw two cards; the King of Swords and the Eight of Wands – Air and Fire; so there is a "tense motion". When we consider the keywords of the two cards, "Judge" and "Movement" (see *Tarot Fundamentals*) we might just see that there will be a swift resolution. However, considering the two elemental energies, we can also observe that there will be a need to deal with tension throughout the resolution. There must be a constant calmness and patience (water and earth) to equilibrate the air and fire.

This method of two-card reading using the elemental combinations can provide a quick yet profound analysis of the deepest elemental pattern within any situation. We can then suggest the best strategies to bring balance or completion to the situation by equilibrating it with any missing elements.

Another way of applying the sub-elements to a reading is to consider the actual way in which the combination of elements manifests in the real world, providing us a scenic backdrop which casts another light upon the two cards.

Table of Sub-Elemental Manifestation

	Earth	Air	Water	Fire
Earth		Dust	Mud	Magma
Air	Dust		Cloud (Rain)	Flame
Water	Mud	Cloud (Rain)		Steam
Fire	Magma	Flame	Steam	

This table can be used when considering a pair of cards with different elements, by imagining the two cards against a background (or seen through a filter) illustrated by the particular sub-element.

Example
The Queen of Wands and the Two of Pentacles = Fire + Earth, or Magma.
We see these two cards against a volcanic and shifting landscape, with a hidden fire and lots of matter being moved from one place to another. Sometimes slowly, sometimes in a volatile manner. Not a good pair when asking "will my investment be secure and long-term with this partner?"

420

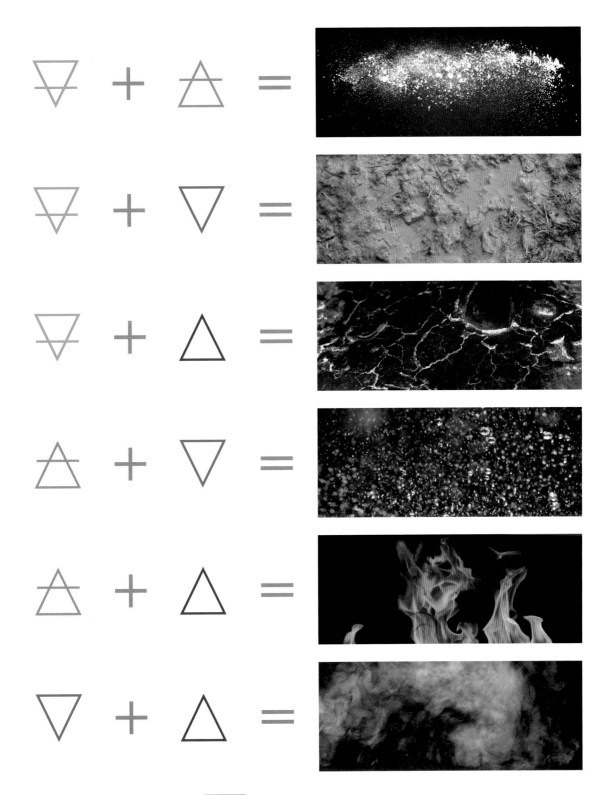

Natural Dignities

Whilst we have looked in this section on "elemental dignities" we have also seen that they are more specifically the "accidental dignities" of their placement in a reading and correspondences.

A more elegant method, which we call "natural" or "essential" dignities" is to simply compare the nature of the two flanking cards together in considering the central card. This relies far more on experience, intuition, and the art of Tarot, rather than a specific set of rules.

It also returns us full circle to the earlier cartomantic methods that we see arising again in Lenormand reading, and on which the Golden Dawn built their esoteric system.

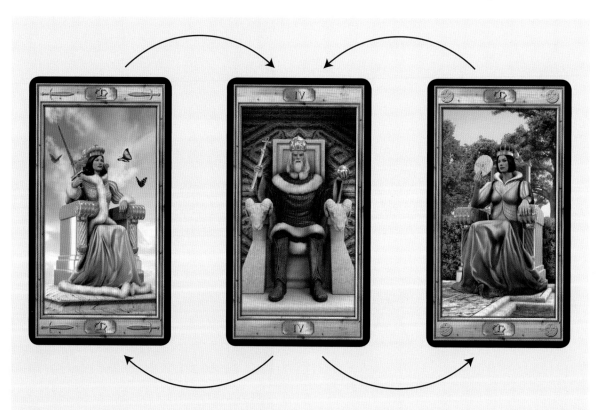

Natural Dignities

The simplified method of the natural dignities is easy to incorporate in a reading.

In a nutshell, when looking at a card, one should also look at the neighboring cards. The center card will influence the surrounding cards, and in turn, it will be influenced by them.

Notes

1. E. Howe, *The Magicians of the Golden Dawn* (London: RKP, 1972), p. 12.

2. W. W. Westcott, An Address to the Sociatas Rosiciana in Anglia, https://www.golden-dawn.com/eu/displaycontent.aspx?pageid=146-address-sociatas-rosiciana-in-anglia.

3. A. Fleming, "Introduction," in D. Küntz, *The Golden Dawn Court Cards* (Edmonds: Holmes Publishing Group, c. 1996).

4. I. Regardie, *The Complete Golden Dawn*, 7th ed. (Woodbury: Llewellyn, 2015). p. 713.

5. *Book T.*

6. Regardie, *The Complete Golden Dawn*, p. 740.

7. From the Kore Kosmou, "Virgin of the World" in the Hermetic writings, a version of which was translated by Dr. Anna Kingsford and Edward Maitland in 1880.

8. M. Katz and T. Goodwin, *Tarot Time Traveller* (Woodbury: Llewellyn, 2017).

9. I. Regardie, *The Complete Golden Dawn*, p. 741.

10. M. K. Greer, *Women of the Golden Dawn* (Rochester: Park Street Press, 1995), pp. 278–290.

11. I. Regardie, *The Complete Golden Dawn*, p. 741.

12. See *Tarot Fundamentals*, pp. 167 and 176 for the basic card keywords.

Fire   Earth   Air   Water

TAROT MAGIC

Magic is the purposeful manipulation of energy and intention to bring about a desired result for the individual. Magic uses symbol, language, action, and ritual to affect the practitioner and bring about desired results. Magical results may present themselves in the form of spiritual knowledge and understanding, physical manifestations such as money and health, or emotional results such as love, forgiveness, or healing. Forms of magical practice are found in all cultures and are often linked with religion in the sacred space where ritual, prayer, and rites overlap.

Tarot magic is powerful. The magical operation can be a simple procedure or an elaborate ritual. The choice is up to the Reader. Tarot's innate structure allows it to be used perfectly in magical practice.

The Magician from the Visconti Tarot, the oldest surviving deck in history. Detail.

Three Essential Magical Tools

Working a spell using Tarot cards is an excellent way to utilize the psychological processes that are involved in magical work. The three essential tools are:

- focusing your intention in a clear and precise way,
- affirming your focus,
- and using a positive point of view.

Justice from the Pagan Tarot. By Gina Pace and Luca Raimondo. Detail. The cards express the Law of Three as a representation of Justice.

The Law of Three

Before you cast any spell, it is of utmost importance that you be sure that you are motivated by good and positive intentions. Ask yourself why you are aiming for this goal. Is it out of spite or for revenge? Would the outcome be hurtful to others? Be absolutely sure your goal is ultimately for the greater good. Negative spells will come back to haunt you. They will bring the opposite of your desired effect.

It is useful to keep the Wiccan Law of Three in mind. This law states that whatever you release to the world will be returned to you three times over. This is true of magic and regular life. Be sure to cast enchantments that empower yourself and the world with positivity. Working with darkness will attract pain and chaos. No one wants that.

In the Pagan Tarot, the Hermit card (detail) represents the creation of a Tarot spell.

Steps to a Tarot Spell

Magic circles were originally used for creating a sacred and protected space with which to cast magic, summon deities, work with spirits/gods, and conjure elements. You don't need to summon a spirit (though nothing will prevent you from doing so if you want to). A magic circle is a wonderful place to cast magic with your desired intention.

1. Secure a private space.
This should be a place where you will not be disturbed by anyone. You should have everything you need gathered and at your fingertips for use during the spell. The space can be indoors or outdoors. Many outside spaces are naturally energizing and can lend themselves naturally to the magical practice. For instance, a grove of willow trees works beautifully for emotional, spiritual, and wisdom magic, a flat rock in a field works well for grounding magic, and gardens make a wonderful space for manifestation and money magic.

2. Cleanse the space.

Whether the space is indoor or outdoor, it should be cleaned. Clutter and mess should be put away so the space is clean and clear to work in. Energetically clear the space. This can be done through the act of meditation or by burning sage or cedar around the corners of the room to cleanse and purify the space.

3. Mark your circle.

This can be done using chalk on the floor or using a string. If performing the spell outside, you may use rocks, stones, sticks, or bones. You can use the entire Tarot deck to create a circle around you if you like. Or you can simply reserve the four aces of the deck to mark the four directions.

4. Place everything you need inside the circle.

Be sure your cards and any other accessories are within reach once you begin.

5. Cast the circle.

This may be done in any way that suits you and your spiritual needs. You may sprinkle salt, light candles, walk with burning incense. Do whatever feels good for you.
The circle may be cast by placing the Tarot aces at the appropriate points with an invocation.
Begin at the East.
Move clockwise.
Light a candle and place it alongside each card after the invocations.

Detail of the Three of Pentacles of the Pagan Tarot: three practitioners join hand to create a circle and cast a spell.

Place the Ace of Cups in the East and state, "I call to the powers of the East, to the suit of Cups, the imagination, emotions, new beginnings, and Water."
Place the Ace of Wands in the South and state, "I call to the powers of the South, to the suit of Wands, of passion, energy, and Fire."
Place the Ace of Pentacles in the West and state, "I call to the powers of the West, to the suit of Pentacles, of manifestation, results, and Earth."
Place the Ace of Swords to the North and state, "I call to the powers of the North, to the suit of Swords, of intellect, reasoning, and Air."

Suit/Element/Direction

While the connection between suit and element is almost always the same in all Tarot traditions, the connection with the direction is not so universally accepted.
In this article, it is used with the following associations:
- *Water, Cups, East*
- *Fire, Wands, South*
- *Earth, Pentacles, West*
- *Air, Swords, North*

A different, widely used attribution is:
- *Air, Swords, East*
- *Fire, Wands, South*
- *Water, Cups, West*
- *Earth, Pentacles, North*

Water   *Fire*   *Earth*   *Air*

6. Perform your magic.
There are many things you can do inside a magic circle with your Tarot cards:
- *State desired intentions.*
- *Meditate on a card.*
- *Perform a reading.*
- *Communicate with other beings via the cards.*
- *Visualize yourself inside a Tarot card.*
- *Perform magical acts.*
- *Carve a candle with Tarot symbols and infuse with personal intentions.*

The ancient stone circle of Stonehenge in England.

7. Close the circle.

Once you are finished, offer thanks to the elements and to whatever energies you have summoned. Close the circle by working in reverse of your casting. Begin at the North, working West, South, and finally East. Thank each element and ace.

8. End with an incantation or affirmation.

Recite an incantation or affirmation three times.
An affirmation is a simple sentence that expresses your will and determination. It does not allow for a question mark, and often begins with the words "I will..." An affirmation generally channels and focus your will in a specific direction. An incantation is a repeated affirmation. The repetition, enhanced by emotion and purpose, further empowers the affirmation's psychological and magical value.

9. Final ending.

It is always nice to finish with the verse, "With love and light and harm to none, I do declare this spell is done."

Belief and Magic

Magic is intimately connected with belief. Most of modern Tarot magic had been developed by Wiccans, as Wicca has a great space for Tarot and magic equally.

However, not all Tarot Readers will be Wiccans. As long as their personal beliefs allow for the use of magic, they can follow the steps outlined by Wiccans, or they can change and adapt the ritual according to their beliefs and tenets.

Many beliefs and religions coexist in the world.

BASIC TAROT MAGIC CIRCLE DIAGRAM

Tarot Magical Affirmations

An affirmation is a short, powerful statement that indicates a desired change in the psyche. Affirmations are powerful because humans tend to be habitual in all things, especially thought patterns. Affirmations challenge and transform old or negative thought patterns which in turn creates new results and positive emotions in the individual's life. Affirmations manifest healing, peace, and new possibilities. The sky is the limit in crafting an affirmation. The goal is up to the imagination and desire of the individual. Tarot affirmations are particularity potent because a Tarot card either inspires or reflects an affirmation. This brings a powerful visual element to the affirmation, fostering a close connection between the Reader and the card.

The front of the Magician Arcana in the Viceversa Tarot, by Massimiliano Filadoro and Davide Corsi.

To create an affirmation:

1. Choose a negative thought, feeling, or pattern you would like to change.

2. Write the opposite of the thought or feeling.

3. Begin the affirmation with either "I" or "My" to make it personal and immediate.

4. Always write your affirmation in the present tense as if it is true at the present time. This invokes a feeling of presence and ownership.

Affirmation First, Tarot Card Second

Affirmations are created based on need, and the appropriate Tarot card is chosen after the affirmation is written. For example:

⟡ An individual feels trapped in negative thoughts and emotions. She creates an affirmation that states, "I attract positive thoughts and encouraging people into my life." The Three of Cups is chosen to reflect the affirmation and desire.

⟡ An individual is ready to give up his poverty cycle and/or move to a higher financial bracket. He creates an affirmation that states, "Money flows freely to me." The Ace of Pentacles is chosen to reflect the affirmation and desire.

⟡ An individual wants to attract a beautiful romantic relationship into his life. He creates an affirmation that states, "I give and receive empowering love." The Lovers card is chosen to reflect the affirmation and desire.

The choice of an affirmation may lead to a specific Tarot card.

The Tarot cards in these pages are taken from the Viceversa Tarot, by Massimiliano Filadoro and Davide Corsi.

Tarot Affirmations Inspired by Tarot Cards

A Tarot affirmation can be inspired by a favorite Tarot card. Readers can use this affirmation to imbue themselves with the qualities of the card, deepen their connection to the card, and invoke their favorite qualities. For example:

An individual is inspired by the Empress card's creativity and desires a new artistic path. The Empress is pulled from the deck and the following affirmation is written, "I embrace, protect, and feed all my creative impulses."

An individual respects the power and control of the Emperor. The Emperor is pulled from the deck and the following affirmation is written, "I place personal boundaries out of respect for myself and follow through on all of my goals."

An individual seeks the intuitive prowess of the High Priestess. The High Priestess is pulled from the deck and the following affirmation is written, "I heed my inner voice, focus on my authentic self, and embrace my soul's calling."

435

How to Use Tarot Affirmations

Once a Tarot affirmation is created, it may be used in a number of ways. It is important to always use the affirmation along with the Tarot card to forge a connection between the words, emotions, symbols, and image.

- Recite the affirmation every morning and every night.
- Repeat the affirmation for 3–5 minutes every day.
- Write the affirmation in a notebook seven times every day.
- Use your affirmation as a mantra to be repeated in meditation.
- Write your affirmation with symbols from your Tarot card and place copies all over your living space where you can see them.
- Use an affirmation to seal a magic spell ritual.

Note: As stated in the beginning, a Reader can practice Tarot magic without a circle. Proper, physical Tarot cards are not even needed as long as the Tarot archetype is clear in the Reader's mind.

The Judgement card from the Fey Tarot, by Mara Aghem and Riccardo Minetti.

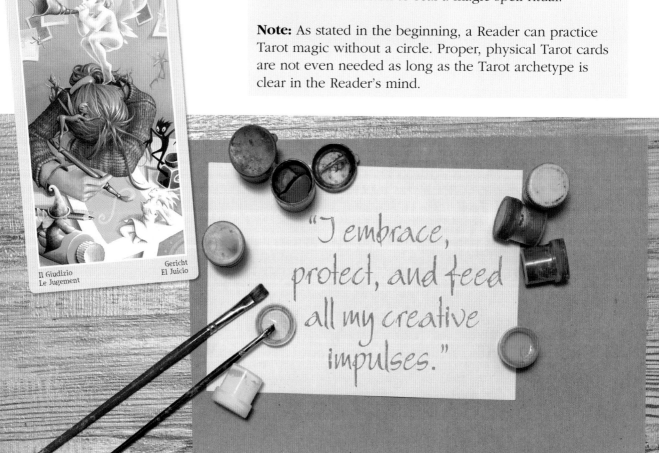

"I embrace, protect, and feed all my creative impulses."

ENCHANTMENT TAROT SPELL/SPREAD

Number of Cards: *5*
Cards Used: *Major Arcana*
Reading Time: *20 minutes*
Purpose: *Create a spell*
Form: *Five cards spread in a simple line.*

Use this spell/spread for yourself or a Querent as a way to focus energies toward a goal. This spread in an excellent first step toward performing a proper magic spell. It can be used as a warm-up.

Belief systems are as unique as the people who hold on to them. Some people believe in fortunetellers and a set destiny. Some are attracted to magic and spells. Simply walking barefoot on the earth is magic to some people. Those who believe in the power of sorcery can affect and manipulate the invisible forces surrounding them.

A spell is cast using three ritual components: a goal, an unwavering and determined attitude, and a model or image that represents a desired goal. Without venturing into the world of beliefs, it is important to consider how many of the psychological techniques used today to increase productivity, self-confidence, motivation, self-esteem, and concentration now bear a scientific explanation. These same techniques were once considered "magic" and used by sorcerers of the past. These techniques are based on three fundamental actions: focus your intentions (get very specific), create a positive affirmation (thus strengthening your determination and will), visualize (develop a mental representation of the desired result).

The mental and physical visualization of your desire becomes the focal point on which to send your energy. It is also a tangible reminder of the objectives that you intend to achieve. Using the Enchantment spread, select a card representing your wishes. The card you choose will consolidate and focus your energy on your intentions and objectives. Tarot's images and symbols are so vivid they work as powerful tools for manifestation.

How this Spread/Spell Works

This spell/spread is unique. It analyzes the fine line between what separates a simple desire to achieve a goal and the commitment necessary to achieve it. Although it uses the metaphor of a spell, Tarot should never be used as a way of shirking responsibilities or negate the fact that each and every one of us is responsible for creating the best possible destiny for ourselves.

We all carry dreams and desires. This spread is crafted with the intention of not only identifying a goal but examining the idea of release. Look at what you are prepared to let go of to make space for something else. This spread also accounts for gratitude and the idea that you must give something back once you have achieved your goal.

Five Arcana from the Viceversa Tarot, by Massimiliano Filadoro and Davide Corsi: Emperor, Fool, Empress, Hanged Man and World.

Preparing for the Spread

Decide on the goal you would like to achieve before beginning this activity. Then select a card that best represents your desire. For example, if you desire a boyfriend/girlfriend you would likely choose the Lovers, for luck you might choose the Wheel of Fortune, to break a nasty habit you would choose the Tower, for a vacation you would select the World, etc. This card will be placed in the first position.

At this point, shuffle the cards and then cut the deck three times to distribute the final four cards.

Card 1 – The Objective: This card is chosen deliberately to represent the objective you or your client would like to achieve.

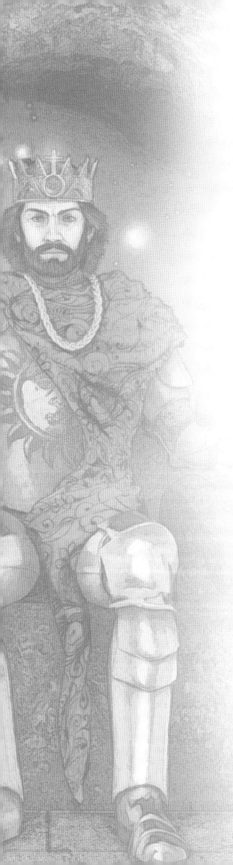

Card 2 – The Sacrifice: This card is what you must release and give up in order to achieve your goal. This should be decided upon and done very consciously.

Card 3 – The Sign: This card represents an event that when it occurs will signify that the desired goal has almost been reached.

Card 4 – The Test: This card is a test of what you or your client must do to prove your commitment to achieve your goal.

Card 5 – The Gift: This card is something you or your client must give in order to show gratitude that your goal has been reached.

Example of the spread:

This reading uses Viceversa Tarot. Patricia, an intelligent Reader, decides to read the Tarot for herself. She is fed up, sick and tired of dating immature men and wants to meet a man who is truly reliable, handsome, and committed.

1 **Objective:**
The Emperor

IV

Using Viceversa Tarot, Patricia intentionally selects the Emperor to represent the man she would like to attract into her life. The Emperor contains maturity, determination, strength, sincerity, and loyalty, which are all qualities she wants to find in her potential lover and mate. Patricia wants someone not only to come into her life but to be someone she can create a life with. The Emperor offers this sort of unwavering stability.

2 Sacrifice:
The Fool

0

The Fool represents innocence, strangeness, and originality. Drawing this card, Patricia realizes if she wants to attract a more mature companion, she must come to terms with the tastes leading her to date younger men who are superficial and inexperienced. She understands that she enjoys the crazy, immature fun of younger men who don't take life so seriously. She enjoys feeling "Fool-like" herself. She realizes she must sacrifice her idea of what it means to be young and free while dating.

3 Sign:
The Empress

III

Patricia associates this card with maternity and motherhood. She realizes that she will know the man has arrived when she sees he will be an excellent father to their children.

4 Test:
The Hanged Man

The Hanged Man represents sacrifice, soul searching, and transition. Patricia is dating a man named Alberto and she knows the relationship is going nowhere. She must break up with him in order to free herself for the responsible man she will attract into her life.

XII

5 Gift:
World

The World represents the completition of a process. Patricia understands that the gift she must make is of complete rebirth. While accepting who she was after college and the men she attracted, she acknowledges that it is time to mature. This decision affects all aspects of her life, not just her romantic sector. She takes her commitments more seriously and engages in life in a new fashion. During the interpretation of this spread, Patricia located not only the correct meaning of each card but also made choices based on what she saw. The fact that she resonates with this spread shows she has reached a new level of awareness. She realizes to create

XXI

The World embodies the desire and need to reach your own "most extraordinary self". Below, a street artist from Russia, expressing her art through colors.

change in her life, it is up to her to do so. Her objective of finding a responsible companion has more to do with a series of changes within herself rather than merely getting lucky. To attract more mature men, she must give up temporary relationships like the one with Alberto. Note how the sign is connected to the goal. In order to embody the Empress, who represents motherhood, it is best that Patricia invokes responsible qualities that will help her to become her most extraordinary self.

TAROT CHARMS

A Tarot card is made into a charm by speaking or singing
over it. You may create the rhyme yourself which is
always more effective or use the example provided.
Select the card you wish to charm. Center yourself, hold
your hands over the card, and recite the following:
Wands, Cups, Swords, and Pentacles play,
Let your magic fill my day.
(Name of card) illuminate me with your powers,
Work this enchantment for 24 hours.

Suggested Charms

Below are suggestions for cards that make excellent
charms. Remember, though, the more personal the card
is to you, the more powerful the charm. To induce the
meaning of any card in your life, create a charm and carry
the card with you all day.

Induce Love and Hot Sex = The Lovers

To Glow with Beauty = The Empress

To Be Magnetic = Queen of Wands

Peace of Mind = The High Priestess

Balance = Temperance

Inspiration = The Star

Intuitive/Psychic Boost = The Moon

Good Health = The Sun

Spiritual Insight = The Hermit

Abundance = Ten of Cups

Happy Family = Ten of Cups

Luck in Business = The Wheel of Fortune

Invoke Change = Death

Outrageous Fun = The Devil

Safe Travel = The Chariot

Action and Power = The Emperor

To Invoke Change = The Tower

Victory = Justice

Satisfaction in Work = Eight of Pentacles

Friendship = Three of Cups

Complete Creative Project = King of Cups

Take Action = King of Wands

Mastery = The Magician

Colors speak the language of intuition. The symbolism of color is not set in stone but deepens our own experience, our mood and our creativity.

Tarot Color Symbolism

Colors have an immediate effect on the subconscious. The study of color theory adds deepened meaning to everyday life and to the Tarot. Pay attention to color to add depth to readings by allowing colors to invoke interpretations, suggest connections, and reveal underlying themes when reading the cards. Color theory can be applied to any Tarot deck. Colors are as powerful to the psyche as Tarot's archetypes. A universal awareness of color symbolism, based on shades and tones found in nature, is hardwired into the human brain. Lush green tones associated with vegetation indicated to primal man that food and water were nearby. The scarlet hues associated with poisonous berries, hot peppers, fire, and blood seemingly trained us, over the centuries, to be wary and alert when encountering the color red. The color blue, encountered with glistening water bodies and clear skies, indicated calmness and clarity as opposed to the greyish/black seen in the sky that suggested threatening storms were imminent and early man should take shelter. Early man was rightfully wary of the color black as it matched the night's darkness which veiled the many dangers lurking in the night from thieves to carnivorous animals and other horrors.

Universal Color Symbolism

Artists, marketing and advertising professionals, and Tarot deck designers take full advantage of the innate, reflexive knowledge and meaning of color. Essential symbolic color meanings are remarkably consistent across all cultures:

White: *unity, light, purity, peace, moon*

Red: *energy, passion, alertness, fervor, fire*

Orange: *warmth, welcome, harvest, home, satisfaction*

Yellow: *caution, consideration, distinction, thoughtfulness, solar energy*

Green: *growth, freshness, attraction, envy, manifestation*

Blue: *emotion, reflection, intuition, coolness*

Purple: *royalty, calm, opulence, wealth, intuition*

Black: *power, mystery, strength, solidity, danger*

Grey: *wisdom, balance, neutrality, formality*

Brown: *earth, security, healing, home, stability*

447

An Esoteric Approach to Colors

The connection between the Tarot cards and color was codified by occultists mainly through the Kabbalah.
In these pages it's possible to see an extimate of the relation between the Sephirot (and numbers), the colors and the court cards.

King Scale

1. Kether *(Crown)* – The brightness of white pervades Kether. In the Page/Princess the white tinges with gold.

2. Chokhmah *(Wisdom)* – Soft blue, grey, mother of pearl grey, white tinged with red, blue and yellow.

3. Binah *(Understanding)* – Deep red, black, deep brown and grey tinged with pink.

4. Chesed *(Mercy)* – Dark violet, blue, deep purple and blue tinged with yellow.

5. Gevurah *(Strength)* – Orange, red, bright red, red tinged with black.

6. Tiferet *(Beauty)*
Pink, gold, light red, amber.

7. Netzach *(Victory)* – Light amber, emerald green, yellow green, brown, green tinged with gold.

8. Hod *(Splendor)* – Violet, orange, rust, yellow-brown tinged with gold.

9. Yesod *(Foundation)* – Indigo, light violet, black-purple, light yellow tinged with blue.

10. Malkuth *(Kingdom)*
Yellow, composite, radiant and composed.

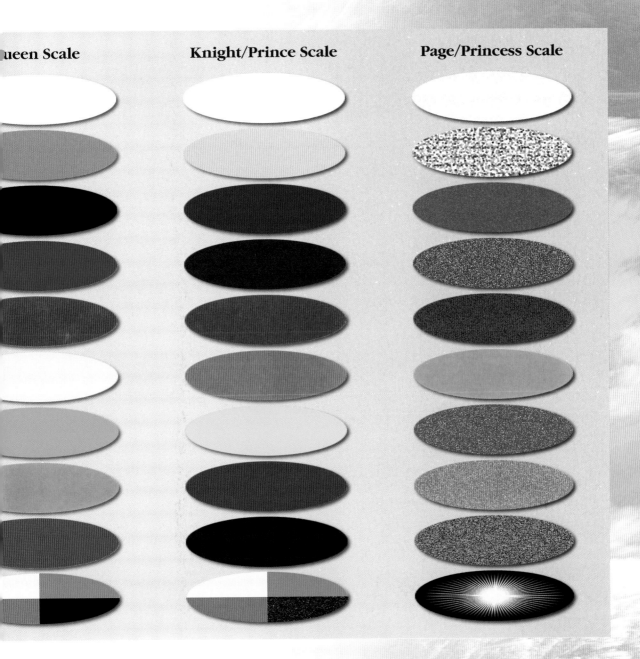

ueen Scale   **Knight/Prince Scale**   **Page/Princess Scale**

The Majors and Color Symbolism

Well-designed Tarot decks contain deliberately chosen illustrations that create a specific effect on the subconscious. This includes color usage. Color, in addition to communicating mood or theme, transmits a great deal of information to a Reader attuned to color symbolism. An awareness of color symbolism will provide a "shortcut" to the meaning of each card.

Some Arcana may have a color dominance: a few similar colors that pervade the whole cards. Others may have a more balanced palette.

Readers will not be surprised to discover the High Priestess often wearing some combination of white (for purity and lunar symbolism) and blue (for reflection). The Emperor's preference for fierce reds and bright yellows is often seen. The Hermit's hair and robes are frequently depicted as grey to mark the wisdom of his age, while the white robes of the Temperance angel marks purity and the Devil's association with red and black indicate passion and wild dangers.

IX

XV

Suits and Colors

Tarot's four suits have become associated with a specific colors over the years. Different esoteric groups have created different color assignments. The Golden Dawn, the turn of the century secret society, created a color system that has proven extremely influential.

The suit of Wands is associated with the fiery color red.
The color red becomes a symbol for many of the qualities associated with Wands: passion, energy, creativity, intensity, action, sexuality, fire.

The suit of Cups is associated with the watery color blue.
The color blue becomes associated with Cups qualities: emotion, intuition, reflection, feelings, depth, spirituality, water.

The suit of Swords is associated with the airy color yellow.
The color yellow symbolizes many of the qualities associated with Swords: quick thinking, decisiveness, logic, analysis, mind, air.

The suit of Pentacles is associated with the earthy color brown.
Contemporary deck designers, preferring more vivid colors, may substitute the color green. Brown and green are linked to Pentacles qualities: growth, practicality, frugality, physicality, finance, earth.

Some cards from the Manga Tarot (by Riccardo Minetti and Anna Lazzarini), the Dame's Fortune Tarot (by Paul Huson) and the Tarot of the Elves (by Mark McElroy and Davide Corsi). These decks were built according to a precise color symbolism.

Color and Deck Design

The Tarot of the Elves is a fine example of a deck suffused with deliberate use of color. The color of the border jewels on every Minor card corresponds to the suit of that card, making it easier for Readers to distinguish one suit from another. The illustrations for each card are tinted with the colors associated with their suit. Red is dominant on Wands cards, blue is seen in the Cups cards, and so on. As a result, skilled Readers can see in a single glance which suits appear or are missing from a spread.

For example, a spread dominated by cool shades of blue will likely represent an emotional or spiritual issue, while a spread dominated by yellow suggests a problem with choices and decision-making.

What Color Can Do for Readers

In addition to surveying the number of Majors and the predominance of suits in a spread, Readers glean important insight by noting the predominance of color. When a Reader is attuned to color symbolism, every aspect of the card, from a character's clothing to the blossoms on a bush in the background, offers clues to meaning.

An awareness of color refines the Reader's tastes, helping the Reader distinguish between well-designed decks and those that may be visually appealing but symbolically weak. Readers can draw on color symbolism when decorating their reading space and or choosing a personal wardrobe. A Reader may wear certain color clothing to invoke the qualities associated with a specific Tarot card—for example, yellow to imbue oneself with Sun qualities, red to invoke the passion of Wands. Note the Querent's color choices as well. What does their color preference tell you about him or her?

What Do Colors Represent to You?

The most important symbolism and associations are the instincts thriving inside of you, not inside a book. Take a moment to list in a Tarot journal or on piece of paper the immediate reaction you have to the basic colors:

White
Red
Orange
Yellow
Green
Blue
Purple
Black
Grey
Brown

Colors can express a landscape even without shape and lines. The colors alone create impressions.

PROFESSIONAL TAROT READING

Remember that professional Tarot reading is a business. To be successful in business one needs planning, organization and commitment. But Tarot reading is also an activity that can deeply affect others, so it needs competence, humbleness and responsibility.

Signs that professional Tarot reading is for you:

- You live, breathe, and sleep with the magic of Tarot.
- You are fascinated by people's behavior, actions, and motivations.
- You enjoy helping, supporting, and empowering people.
- You are comfortable in the role of oracle.
- You enjoy helping others discover their truth.
- You want a flexible schedule and control over your time.

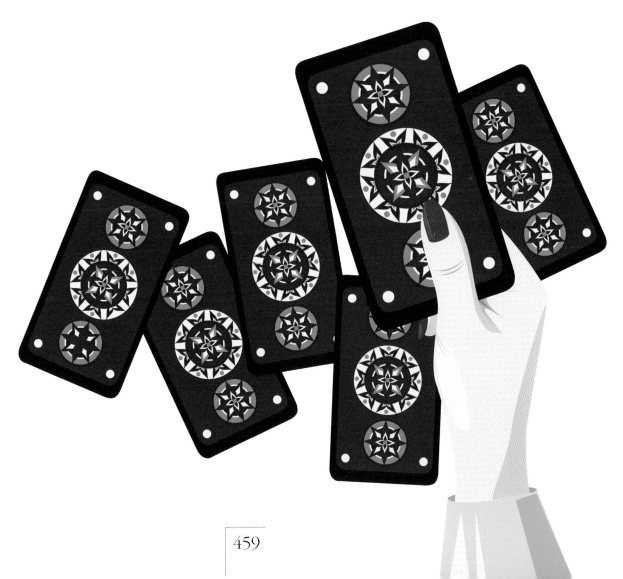

Professional Reading Full- or Part-Time

Tarot reading is an excellent full- or part-time profession. Indulge your passion, help others, and share your knowledge while getting paid for it. Tarot reading is one of the few businesses that has zero startup costs! The practitioner needs only themselves and a deck of Tarot cards. Once the business is up and running, the individual is in complete control of their schedule. This can be especially appealing to female entrepreneurs with small children or individuals balancing work and home responsibilities. Regardless of how large or small you envision your business, once you make the decision to operate professionally, charge money, or barter, it is important to write a business plan. Writing a business plan is an essential piece in the creation or continuation of your business. It is never too late to write one even if you've already been in business for a number of years.

Before starting to read Tarot professionally it is important to make order in that huge wall of endless possibilities.

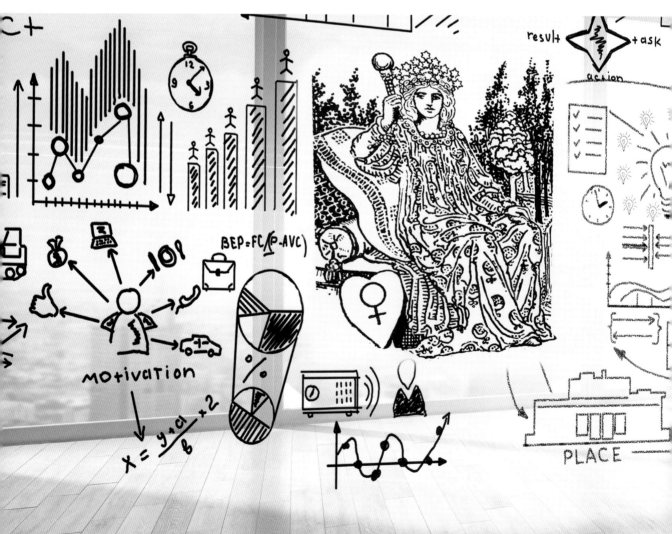

Write a Business Plan

A business plan is a three to five year projection of how your business will operate, grow, and prosper. It is your roadmap to success. Taking the time to create a business plan will inspire, ground, and provide insight. It examines every aspect of your business. It will also save you valuable time in the long run, allowing you to chart your growth as a professional Reader. Do not become intimidated by the writing process. You can always pull a card for information/inspiration!
The plan should be concise, focused, and clear. Think of your business plan as the compelling story of your business. It will contain all the information about how you work, including goals and your personal story. It will help you to bring a logic and discipline to your business in a very "Emperor-like" fashion, setting a groundwork of stability and success.

Business Plan Outline

The creative-minded Reader may create a business plan in a journal and use a free-writing or free-association format to spark ideas when creating the plan. Take time to write, think through, and brainstorm the questions listed below for each part of the plan.
Use Tarot images, art, and visuals for inspiration. This is your plan. Be as creative as you like. Just because it's business doesn't mean it has to be boring.

Executive Summary

| Mission Statement | Products and Services | Future Plans |

Marketing

Company Description

Competition

Operating Procedures

Business

Products and Services

Financials

EXECUTIVE SUMMARY

An executive summary is a snapshot of your business as a whole. This is where you define everything you do. Begin with a mission statement.

Mission Statement

The mission statement is one of the most powerful things a business owner will create. It is often only a few sentences or a paragraph. A mission statement explains the purpose of your business. It explains why it exists and its reason for being. It should contain your business goals and philosophies.

Take your time writing this essential piece. It will encourage you to think deeply about why you are performing your services. Mission statements additionally come in handy when explaining your work to people who are unfamiliar with the metaphysical business world or with your particular set of talents.

Questions to ask yourself while writing a mission statement:

- Why am I in business?
- What is my ultimate goal?
- Who are my customers?
- What is the nature of my business?
- How does my talent add to the world?
- How am I different from my competitors?
- What is my underlying philosophy or value?
- How am I unique and my services unique?
- How do I make the world a better place?
- What problems do I solve for others?

Products and Services

What services will you offer and how will you offer them? This is your opportunity to think about how you serve the public. Think big and outside of the box when it comes to the talents you have to offer. Be specific and list each service and/or product separately. Describe each.

Why not use Tarot cards, and read how each part of your future business plan is going to be? It may be useful.

Samplings of Traditional Tarot services

In-Person Readings

In-person Tarot readings occur when Reader and Querent sit together for a reading. It is an opportunity for the Querent to spend an amount of time focusing on themselves and their issues. Clients and Readers often prefer in-person readings. The physical presence and the intimacy cultivated are a different experience from long-distance readings.

Pros

Client can shuffle the cards, you can observe one another, and a close personal connection can be fostered. Readers can design their reading space and therefore create a full Tarot immersion experience. Reader will have control over the reading environment.

Cons

Client base is limited to Reader's locality. This is an issue for Readers in small towns or rural areas. Reader must incur the cost of renting and finding a suitable reading space.

Reminder

Your reading space should be energetically clear, clean, and comfortable. Your office/reading space is a physical extension of yourself and your business.

Telephone/Video/Skype Readings

Pros

Convenience of Tarot reading over the telephone or computer. Potential worldwide client base, no commute time, true convenience, ultimate freedom.

Cons

Not physically present with the client. Focus at times is an issue regarding outside interruptions on both ends of the

phone including call waiting or random family/friend/pet interruption (if done from home).

Reminder

Disable any call waiting and be sure you have absolute quiet and focus on a phone reading. The Reader who likes clients to shuffle the cards themselves and imbue the cards with their energy should make a plan as to how the client will affect the cards over the phone. One technique has the Reader shuffling. The Reader asks the client to tell them when to stop. Once the shuffling has stopped, ask the client to state a number between one and ten. Count down that number of cards and begin the reading.

Email Readings

Tarot reading via email works particularly well for simple questions.

Pros
Potential worldwide client base, complete freedom.

Cons
It may feel arduous to write a response rather than say it. No physical contact with client (some might say this is a "Pro").

Event/Party Reading

Sociable Readers who enjoy being out, dressing up, and attending events, usually love party readings. Hourly rates are charged to read Tarot at private parties, corporate events, bridal showers, birthday parties, etc.

Pros
Fun challenge to read for many clients in a few hours, good paycheck, free goodies and gift bags, being the mysterious stranger everyone wants to talk to.

Cons
Drunken clients, loud music, potentially late hours, requires high energetic output, line management issues.

Tarot Classes/Salons

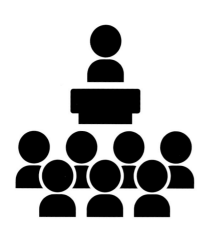

Readers who like teaching and leading group activities will find weekly Tarot classes enjoyable. Classes are an excellent way to foster a community of Tarot lovers. Teaching allows you to indulge in your passions, share your gifts, empower others, and create "Tarot space." Classes may be detailed or perhaps you curate a space or meet-up where people come together to trade readings. It can be as intensive or as loose as suits your personality.

Pros
Regular income once class attendance is solidified, groups of students often form long-lasting bonds, creating Tarot curriculums

expands and challenges your Tarot practice and techniques as you continue to innovate new ideas, class notes become source materials for future Tarot books, the same materials may be used for online classes/workshops, opportunities to travel and lecture.

Cons
Large spaces and seating are required, prep time for classes, notes and materials may be time consuming, you will deal with many personality types.

Outside-the-box thinking
What about a weekly online class? Perhaps you create a series of Tarot teaching videos? What about creating a correspondence course? A weekly email course? An online class can reach the entire world.

Tarot reading is all about people. Each of them will bring their own life into your practice. Make sure the space you will receive them is suitable for you to handle that much energy.

Additional Services

Reiki, yoga, massage therapy, life coaching, energy clearing, spell work, numerology, astrology, past life regression, hypnotherapy—there is an endless variety of additional services you can offer based on your knowledge and abilities. Think about what additional services you want to provide to the public and list them.

Questions to think about:

- What am I naturally talented at?
- What talents do I have that overlap with Tarot?
- What personal gifts do people often compliment me on?
- What is interesting to me?
- What other services mesh with Tarot that I have always been fascinated with?

People interested in Tarot reading may be interested just in fortune telling, or they may have interest in other spiritual practices, like Reiki, astrology, magic, I Ching, etc...

Future Plans

Good things grow with patience and foresight. A little Wands for creativity. A little Pentacles for stability. A little Swords for planning ahead. And a little Cups for being happy with it all.

Future plans are exciting! Where do you see your business in three to five years? Future plans are a great opportunity to stop and ponder your future lifestyle and dreams. It is a good idea to be specific, yet do not allow yourself to become attached to the outcome. Always leave room for the unexpected and you will always be surprised.

Questions to think about:

- Will I be a part-time or a full-time Reader?
- What will my professional/personal lifestyle look like?
- How does work balance with play?
- How will I be growing?
- What directions am I eager to explore?
- What environment do I imagine myself in?

471

BUSINESS

Company Description

Describe the nature of your business and the marketplace you are trying to satisfy. Explain how your services meet these needs. Imagine you are describing your business to a person who has never heard of what you do. This will help you provide a complete picture.

Work environment

- Are you located in an urban area with many sidewalk and storefront Readers?
- Are you based in an artistic, open-minded community where healers and spiritual people abound?
- Are you isolated in a rural community?
- Who are your clients and what do you think they want?
- Will your readings focus on a particular group of people with unique needs?
- Will you specialize in romance readings?
- Will you specialize in readings to open blocked creativity for closed artists?
- Who are you trying to reach out to and who is your ideal client?
- Would you be willing to share office space?
- Will you work from home or in a different space?

List specific consumers or businesses you plan to serve:

- Are you the Reader for a local hotel, mystical shop, or café?
- Would you like to do so?
- Do you work with an online psychic company and/or would you want to?
- Do you want to target a specific group of people with specific needs?

List your competitive advantages

- What makes you and your services special?
- What do you offer that others do not?
- What is lacking from Readers in your area? Discover how you can best offer it.
- How do you bring value to your clients in the best way possible?

Describe your history and why are you drawn to this line of work:

- What is your back story? People want to know.
- What made you want to become a Reader?
- How do you feel you can help people? People are often fascinated by knowing how intuitive entrepreneurs realized they had "power" or "intuition." Build this into your story.

Marketing

Marketing your Tarot business is essential. Marketing and advertising are made simple by knowing who you are and being excited to share your talents with the world.

Your clients

- Who are your clients?
- What age and background are your clients?
- What specific needs are you filling?

Business cards/bookmarks

It is nice to have a card to give prospective clients or have something people can take away from your reading table. Be sure your business card, like your website, is an excellent representation of yourself as a Reader and contact information is clearly available.

Marketing is first of all communication. Listen to the needs of others. Give a message that is effective and short. A card from the suit of Swords may be a good inspiration.

Advertising

Marketing experts say that word of mouth and repeat business are the best ways to attract clients.

- How and where you will advertise? List every single venue you can think of for advertising. Think of your client base.
- Where are they?
- How can you reach them?
- Will you market to party and event planners if you do party readings?

Social media

Social media is ever changing and evolving. Stay current with the latest technology. Decide which avenues are good for your personality and business. Instagram, Facebook, Twitter, Pinterest, etc., are all platforms offering ways to connect with potential clients and/or students. Come up with a basic strategy for your social media and stick to it to reap the rewards.

WEBSITE

The website is like the window of your shop. Make it friendly. make it informative. Make it reflect yourself.

Website

A website is essential. Unless you are operating under a cloak of mystery (and hey, we are talking Tarot, so for some Readers, the more mysterious the better) a good website is the front door to your Tarot business. A potential client should understand who you are in one glance at your website. Be sure to place your contact information on each and every page.

Building your own website:

Pros: Predesigned business templates and point-and-click design tools are making it easier for the small business owner to create their own websites. The Reader has complete control over the look and feel of the site and can update at any time.

Cons: Website creation and keeping up with new technology can be an overwhelming time suck for some personalities. The basic website should include:

Photo
A photograph of you. Hire a professional or have an artistic friend snap some pics on a cell phone camera.

Logo
Use a logo capturing your philosophy or vibe in addition to or in lieu of a photograph. Stock photography agencies can be a simple source for affordable logos or hire a designer or gifted friend create one for you.

Catchphrase/slogan
This is a short, snappy sentence used to describe your business. Slogan generators are available online. Though generic, they can provoke ideas.

What you offer
Make it easy for the client to see what services are available.

Clients and testimonials
Present a list of corporate clients (if you have them) and ask for testimonials from satisfied Querents.

Rates
Do not place rates on your website. You may have different prices for different services and different clients. Most importantly, you will want the freedom to change prices accordingly unless they are set in stone. Corporate entities are often charged a different hourly reading rate than, say a local library event. Don't box yourself in by publishing your prices on your website. Inform clients of your rates when they reach out for your services and you discover what they want.

Ethics
Have a list or section of ethics on your website to help your clients understand how you work.

Blog
You can use a Tarot blog in any number of ways. Use it to promote your business, build your mailing list, and let people know what you are up to. You can use it as an online Tarot diary, sharing your daily or weekly discoveries with the cards, or as a teaching method. Use a blog to increase your online presence. The blog may become content for a future Tarot book.

Social media links
Include social media links to every page of your website and vice versa.

Tarot image usage
Obtain proper permission for any Tarot (or other) photographs or images you use on your website or blog.

Calendar of events
Use to list classes or Tarot events that are open to the public.

Alternate online revenue streams
Once the basic website is up and rolling, you may find a number of alternative revenue streams from things like an online bookshop or an Etsy shop.

Competition

Look at what other Readers are doing with their businesses.

- How and where are other Readers operating around you?
- Is your city full of practitioners offering Tarot services?
- If so, how can you stand out from the crowd?
- Will you operate with an online business?
- How can you differentiate yourself from all the other online Readers?
- Do you live in a place where public sentiment frowns upon divination?

Examining the competition is not about knocking others down. It is about assessing the playing field and discovering how you can add to it. Carving a unique niche is the best thing you can do as a Tarot Reader (and a human).

Operating Procedures

- What are the operating procedures of your business?
- What are your business hours? Boundaries are important. If you work out of a store front, are you available 24 hours a day for readings or Monday through Friday between 9 am and 5 pm? Perhaps you only read Tuesday and Wednesday evenings. Select specific working hours and stick to scheduling appointments during those times.
- What is the legal structure under which your business operates?
- Are you a DBA (doing business as), corporation, partnership? Be aware of local laws. This is important in the event you should be sued or if any legal action is ever taken against you.
- How do you accept payment?
- Will you need a PayPal account?
- Will you only accept cash?
- How do you feel about accepting checks?
- What is your tax structure?

Pentacles can be a useful inspiration when thinking about money. However, the best card for administration and management will probably be the Emperor.

Check with your local small business owners association/administration to discover what types of license are required to own your own business. Some states in the U.S. consider fortunetelling a misdemeanor. Find out any and all rules and regulations.

Contracts, Invoices and W-9s

Readers who read Tarot at parties will want the proper contract and invoice templates to send the client. Have any tax documents on hand and W-9s ready to email at a moment's notice.

Contract

A contract is an agreement between you and the person/company hiring you. The contract should be written simply. *It should include:* your business name, contact number, email, date, the specifics of your event, event date, venue address, your party contact's name and cell number. It should also include any specific information such as requests for how to dress, travel reimbursement, rules you use while reading (such as a twenty-minute break for every two hours of reading), grace period at end of event, etc. Ask the client to return the document with an electronic signature via email. This contract ensures you are confirmed for the event.

Invoice

An invoice is a document describing the services you provide and the amount of money owed to you. Corporate clients run invoices through their billing departments to pay you. It is essential you have an invoice for party readings. An invoice should contain your name, contact number, email, event date and a list of the services you are offering, the number of hours you will be working, and a total amount due. Include any information on how the client will pay you. Invoices can often be linked to your financial software for ease in bookkeeping.

W-9 and other tax forms

This depends on your country of residence and tax structure. Many corporate clients will ask for certain tax documents while processing their payment to you. Be sure you have these ready and available.

Description of Products and Services

List specifically all of your projects and services here. Explain how they are competitive and fantastic. Even include photo-

graphs here if applicable. Be sure to include how much each
product and service costs.

Financials

How much do you project you will make? How will you
manage your funds? How much will you sink back into your
business? Do you need a loan? What is your tax structure?
Every bit of financial information should be placed in this
section of the business plan.

ADDITIONAL THOUGHTS

Where Are You Working?

Home

Will you invite clients into your home? This is an important decision. Consider your screening process, your security, and how you feel about letting strangers into your home space.

Office

Renting a professional office is an ideal situation if you plan on doing many in-person readings and do not feel comfortable having clients in your home. Inquire locally about office spaces rentable by the hour, saving you a pricey monthly fee.

Coffee shop/public space

Many Readers meet their clients in public spaces such as coffee shops, tea salons, parks, hotel lobbies, restaurants, lounges, and even in clubs or bars. Determine for yourself what is most professional and most conducive for you to conduct an effective Tarot reading. This obviously depends on your reading style and the places available to you. Some Readers will not read in public areas, while others are quite comfortable doing so.

Metaphysical shop/bar/lounge

Metaphysical shops and bars often enjoy having Readers available for their customers, hiring Readers for set days and taking a slice of the Reader's fee.

Online psychic website/phone lines

Psychic websites or phone lines will do the marketing for you. The downside is they can take a large commission from your readings. Decide whether you would rather do the advertising and keep 100 percent of the money or if you are willing to split your profits in exchange for their marketing services. Carefully consider the message any online or telephone service sends to potential customers and be sure it

Places have their own energy. Will your place be comfortable and cozy or precise and clean, or spontaneous and artistical?

is in line with your personal code of ethics before agreeing to work with them. Be sure they are reputable.

Recordings of Readings

A client can be overwhelmed at the amount of information flying at them during a reading. Many people will only remember a few of the things you said during a reading. With this in mind, you want to think about how the client can record their experience with you. Will you record the session on a voice recorder? Provide a notepad for your client to take notes? Take photographs of the reading? Will you offer your clients a recording of the reading or may they record the reading on their own devices?

483

STARTING OUT

If you are just starting out there are plenty of places a beginning Reader can get experience. Look for psychic fairs, street fairs, and other opportunities to set up a table and read for the public. People love to know about themselves. Set yourself up and read away!

Local Small Business Support

Free small business support can be found in many places. Local libraries, especially a business library, and colleges may offer free classes, workshops, and lectures for small business owners. Look into your local chamber of commerce. The Small Business Administration, run by the U.S. government, may offer free business counseling and a multitude of support systems for the small business owner. This may even include help with your business plan or loans. If you are female, look into assistance for women's businesses. Online higher education facilities may offer small business classes, sometimes for free!

When all is done, it's time to make the first real step. Your inspiration may be the Magician card.

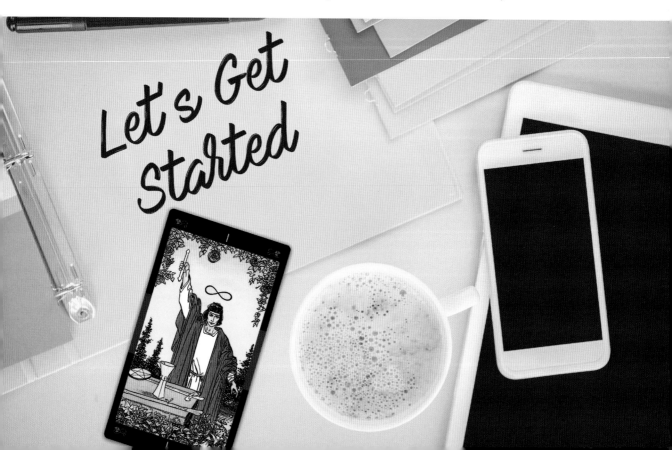

A New Deck Spread

*The true magic comes to life when you cast a Tarot spread.
The cards fly through your fingers, attention is focused and
valuable information rises to the surface. Inside the space of
a spread is where Querents are helped, where discoveries are
made and new card connections are found.*

*Tarot spreads are a place of deep trust. Trust between you,
your cards and your intuition. Trust between yourself and
the Querent. Inside a spread, you must allow your grasp on
knowledge to slip away but trust it will be there to support you
when you need it.*

*Most importantly, you must trust the information as it appears
and trust yourself enough to follow through on it. Because
spreads, like cards, won't change anything unless you are
willing to back up their advice and insight with action and
intention.*

*The first spread will be about creating a relationship with a
new deck. It may be useful for your Tarot practice, but it's not
usually a spread to use for a Querent.*

SEEING THE BEAUTY

Number of Cards: 22
Cards Used: Major Arcana.
Time: 1 hour
Objective: To draw the Reader's attention to the unique details of a new or unfamiliar deck.
Layout: Four rows of cards. In row one, the Fool stands alone, centered above all other cards. In row two, place Majors 1 - 7 (or their equivalent). In row three, place Majors 8 - 14 (or their equivalent). In row four, place Majors 15 - 21 (or their equivalent).

When Readers become too familiar with one favorite deck, they can have a difficult time appreciating, approaching and working with dramatically different alternatives. Seeing the Beauty invites Readers to set assumptions aside and embrace the unique features a new deck has to offer.

As their work together evolves, a Tarot deck and Reader become finely attuned to each other.

With long-term exposure, images from one deck may dominate a Reader's perspective. Before the Reader realizes it, he or she may become "locked in" to seeing certain cards in certain ways. Soon, a reading, which should always be a process of discovery, can become little more than a test of recall. The Reader may draw on the same association, keyword, or symbol every time a card appears.

Readers can fight this tendency by regularly introducing themselves to new decks. When doing so, however, Readers must also be careful not to make their favorite deck a standard by which other decks are judged. When this happens, Readers are no longer able to evaluate a new deck on its own merits; instead, they merely embrace or reject a new deck simply on the basis of how well it mimics a well-worn favorite.

The Seeing the Beauty spread is designed to help the Reader step outside his or her comfort zone, set aside assumptions and preferences and approach a new deck with fresh eyes and an open heart. This spread is recommended whenever the Reader encounters a new deck.

Preparation and Positioning of the Cards

Thumb through the new deck, removing all Major Arcana cards. Begin by organizing the Majors in numerical order if numbers are supplied. If there are no numbers, find parallels between the new deck and a more familiar one using card titles, keywords, images or intuitive connections.

Arrange the cards in four rows, with the Fool centered in row 1, cards 1 - 7 (or their equivalent) in row 2, cards 8 - 14 in row 3, and cards 15 - 21 in row four.

In addition, the Reader will require a notebook or his or her Tarot journal, if one is being kept, and a good pen.

The Reading and the Interpretation

Phase One

The Reader closes his or her eyes, clears the mind, and asks, "What does this deck have to teach me?"

With eyes still closed, the Reader moves an open palm slowly over the array of cards. At some point, the Reader will experience a sensation which many describe as "heat" or "a pull." Others say their hand "feels unusually and suddenly heavy." The Reader lower his or her hand, opens the eyes, and takes note of which card had been selected. This card is referred to as "The Lesson."

1 The Lesson

The card in this position represents a lesson this deck is designed to teach the Reader, a challenge the deck may offer or a benefit the Reader will receive from having worked with the deck.

The Reader interprets this card, making notes in his or her notebook.

Phase Two

Beginning with the Fool and progressing through The World, the Reader examines each card, looking for two specific kinds of details:

1) Features that are similar to more familiar versions of the same card
2) Features that seem to be unique to this particular version of the card

In his or her notebook, the Reader jots down these details. When this exercise is complete, the Reader will create a Synthesis—a short passage recording the Reader's overall impressions of the new deck: likes and dislikes, insights and surprises.

Exploring the Spread

As the Reader moves through the deck card by card, he or she may notice interesting synergies between different cards on different rows.

The rows in this spread represent different levels of mastery. (The Fool, on Row 1, rises above all, and is considered separately.) Row 2 represents mastery over the people and powers of the outer, physical world. Row 3 represents emotional and psychological struggles associated with the refinement of the True Self (the inner world). Row 4 represents progression through the transcendent, spiritual world.

How do cards in parallel positions in various rows compare? For example: how might the third step in mastery over the physical world (The Empress) compare to the third step in mastery over the psychological world (The Wheel) or mastery over the spiritual world (The Star)?

Example of a Reading

Suzanne tends to work with the Universal Tarot. To her, the images of the Classic Tarot appear too delicate and strictly artistic.

The Hermit Represents the Lesson
Suzanne's first impression of the Hermit's is of his advanced age. She realizes that she has resisted the Classic Tarot because she perceives it as an antique: something to be admired, but unsuited for actual use.

Card-by-Card Survey
As Suzanne works through the deck card-by-card, she notes differences and similarities. Her notes are too in-depth to reproduce in their entirety, but her notes on the Lovers are typical of her entries:

Lovers - I'm used to seeing the man, the woman, and the angel in what looks like the Garden of Eden. Here, the angel is a cherub. I like how he is peeking out from under his blindfold so that he can aim the arrow at the younger woman.

The older woman glares up at the angel and puts a restraining hand on the shoulder of her son. The younger woman has caught the son's eye and is holding him by the hand, with her other hand over her heart. This card feels more romantic to me than the Lovers card in the Universal Tarot!

The keyword "Choice" is in the margin. I associate the Universal Tarot's Lovers with choice (whether or not to eat the apple), but here the choice is more a matter of doing what your parents want or what your heart tells you. I wouldn't get that insight from the Universal Tarot.

Universal Tarot

Classic Tarot

Synthesis

After she completes her work, Suzanne is surprised to discover she now perceives the Classic Tarot as a symbolically rich deck – easier to read with, in some ways, than the Universal Tarot. In addition to the ruddy, vibrant color scheme, she also likes the deck's happy, playful images.

What Has Been Learned

Instead of simply comparing a new deck to a more familiar or favorite choice, the Reader must make an effort to approach a new deck on its own terms. Doing so is the equivalent of listening for each deck's unique voice.

The subtle differences among decks – in symbols, keywords, titles, and card order – often become the basis for exciting new insights. Rather than resist those differences, mature Readers celebrate them.

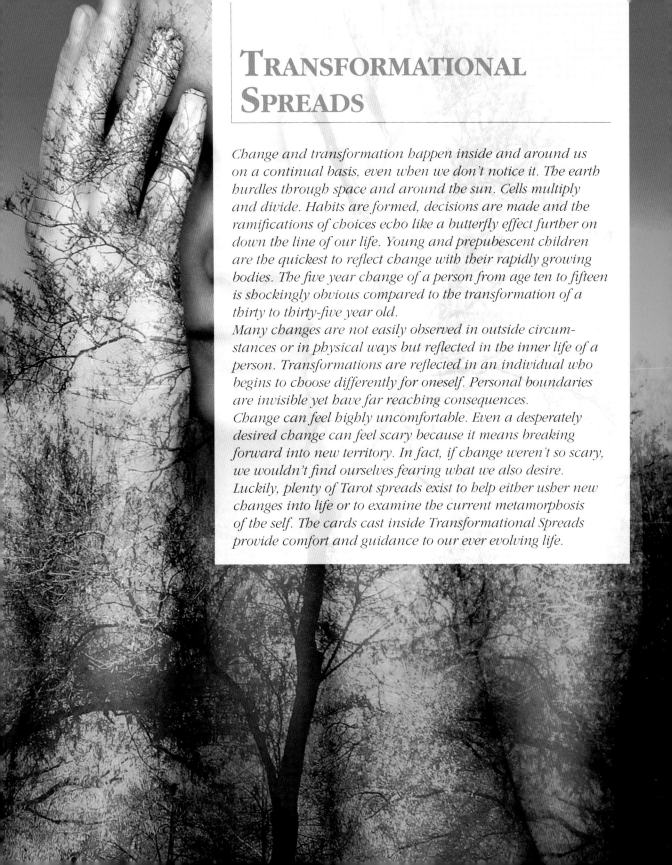

TRANSFORMATIONAL SPREADS

Change and transformation happen inside and around us on a continual basis, even when we don't notice it. The earth hurdles through space and around the sun. Cells multiply and divide. Habits are formed, decisions are made and the ramifications of choices echo like a butterfly effect further on down the line of our life. Young and prepubescent children are the quickest to reflect change with their rapidly growing bodies. The five year change of a person from age ten to fifteen is shockingly obvious compared to the transformation of a thirty to thirty-five year old.

Many changes are not easily observed in outside circum-stances or in physical ways but reflected in the inner life of a person. Transformations are reflected in an individual who begins to choose differently for oneself. Personal boundaries are invisible yet have far reaching consequences.

Change can feel highly uncomfortable. Even a desperately desired change can feel scary because it means breaking forward into new territory. In fact, if change weren't so scary, we wouldn't find ourselves fearing what we also desire. Luckily, plenty of Tarot spreads exist to help either usher new changes into life or to examine the current metamorphosis of the self. The cards cast inside Transformational Spreads provide comfort and guidance to our ever evolving life.

CLEAR RECKONING

Number of Cards: 6
Cards Used: Major and Minor Arcana.
Time: 10 - 15 minutes
Result: Get a full picture of how you feel about something.

People often know what they want to do. Readings are useful to determine how to do it or to gain insight on the effectiveness of a plan. There are times when people don't know what they want to do. They want guidance on direction in a particular area. What do I want from a relationship? What kind of job do I want? What course of study should I pursue? They may feel the need to do *something* but aren't sure what. While Tarot isn't always suited to give such specific answers, it is suited to provide general guidance and food for thought that can lead the Querent to their own answers. These spreads are designed to do just that.

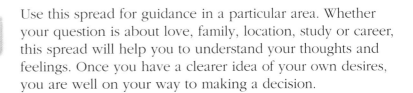

Use this spread for guidance in a particular area. Whether your question is about love, family, location, study or career, this spread will help you to understand your thoughts and feelings. Once you have a clearer idea of your own desires, you are well on your way to making a decision.

Card 1 indicates what you want to do, although you may not admit it. Cards 2 – 5 examine Card 1 in terms of the situation. Card 6 shows your desired outcome. Use cards 2 – 5 to see if the action in Card 1 is sound and is the best path to Card 6.

1 | What do I want (to do)?

What you really want to do. For some reason, though, you are not sure or having trouble admitting this to yourself.

2 | What do I think about it?

What you think about the situation, what your logic tells you. Does what you want to do seem reasonable to you?

3 | How do I feel about it?

Your emotional reaction to the situation. Is your heart urging you to do what you want? Or are negative emotions stopping you?

4 What do you believe about it?

Do you believe what you want is right or wrong? Do you believe you can do it or that you will fail? Does your belief need adjusting?

5 What do I fear about it?

What are your worries and concerns about the situation? Do your fears stop you or are they warnings that you should consider?

6 What do I hope will happen?

What do you hope will be the outcome in this situation? Does it seem the likely outcome if you do what you want?

TRANSFORMATION

Number of Cards: 3
Cards Used: Major and Minor Arcana.
Time: 10 minutes
Result: Accept what is gone, release it and move forward.

Release the past and move on.

The Death card inspires this spread. Death and its implication of permanent change is not always easy to experience. No matter how painful, we all experience change. The cycle of life and death is continual. We can rail against it or we can learn from it.

This spread helps you recognize what is gone. It considers how you can honor and release it. It then shows what transformation occurs as a result.

This three-card spread uses the whole deck. The cards are laid out in a purposeful triangle. Its shape reflects the foundation of death and how something will always rise from the ashes.

1 The Death

This is that which has died. It could be a lost job, a relationship, an ideal or belief, or anything else that was in your life but no longer is.

2 Release

This is advice on how to release what you have lost. It could be about how to mourn it, how to forgive or find peace, or what still remains.

3 Transformation

This is about the transformative process. It can show what you can do to help the process or provide a picture of what is to come as a result of this loss.

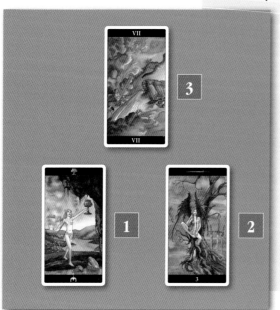

TRANSITIONS

Number of Cards: 12
Cards Used: full deck, with the Major Arcana separated.
Time: 20 minutes
Result: See how the constants in your life evolve as your life changes.

See how things change yet remain the same.

Everyone holds certain values and beliefs to be true. These deeply held ideals shape our lives. This spread identifies three important guiding qualities in your life. The discovery of this spread lies in the fact that you not be aware they exist.

Additionally, you discover how these beliefs have played out in different times of your life. If you dislike how any or all of the truths have manifested, you can use the opportunity to understand yourself better. This knowledge helps you implement change for the better.

Deal the first three cards from the Major Arcana only. Then use the rest of the deck to deal cards 4 – 12.

Cards 1, 2, 3: Truths that shape your life

Cards 4, 5, 6: How these truths manifested in the past.

Cards 7, 8, 9: How these truths manifest in the present.

Cards 10, 11, 12: How these truths will manifest in the future.

Number of Cards: 5
Cards Used: Major Arcana.
Time: 15 minutes
Objective: To help Querent understand the change they are going through.
Layout: One card flanked by a card on the right and left, with two on top, like a pupa surrounded by a chrysalis and moving toward emergence.

CHRYSALIS METAMORPHOSIS

The Chrysalis Spread is a snapshot of change in a person's life. It shows the area being transformed, energies affecting the transformation and the outcome.

Metamorphosis is change and transformation. Like a wormlike pupa enclosed in a chrysalis, it eventually transforms into a butterfly. The pupa and butterfly are different manifestations of the same creature. The transformation occurs in a dark, safe, secret place. It is unseen by the outside world until a brilliant butterfly spreads its wings. Its physicality has changed and it also has newfound ability. What once could only crawl now flies.

Everyone moves through change and transformation. Natural transformations occur during puberty or at key moments in life, from student to professional, married couple to parents. These changes may not always be smooth, nor should they be. When we know what's going on we can smooth the ride.

Transformations will occur without conscious knowledge. Unknowns are involved when we feel an internal transformation, as echoed in the Judgment card. Internal and subtle transformations can be confusing or uncomfortable when we don't know exactly what's going on.

The process of transformation is impacted by a number of factors. The inner life nurtures all change. Outside influences, be they positive like a robust support system of friends and family or negative such as financial burdens,

will impact transformation. Personal ego can be at odds with the change at hand or it can embrace it.

Many schools of thought believe that the transformation process itself never ends and that the process is more important than the outcome. Life is a mutable experience and evolution is the reason we are here. Transformations of the psyche can occur that other people may never notice. Big or small, all transformations can be examined by this spread.

The Preparation and Positioning of the Cards

The Reader and Querent shuffle the deck in turn. The Reader deals the cards from the top of the pile and lays them out, face up, in the positions of the Chrysalis Spread.

The Reading and the Interpretation

The Reader proceeds to interpret the Arcana in each position, keeping in mind the relative meanings. Each card is interpreted individually as a message. The Reader summarizes the entire reading, known as a Synthesis, after the cards have been interpreted.

1 Pupa

This card is the part of the Querent in the process of transforming. It could be a part of their life or a part of themselves.

2 Chrysalis

This card is the innermost part of the Querent that is urging the change. It also can show the reason for the change.

3 Outside influences

This card is outside influences that may affect the change either directly or indirectly. Perhaps it's another person or situation.

4 Desire

This card shows what the Querent's ego desires. This may be in opposition to the change or it may support the transformation.

5 Emergence

This card shows the likely end result of the transformation. It is a glimpse of what the Querent will be like at the end.

Exploring the Spread

This spread creates a map of the change that the Querent is going through. It looks like a pupa surrounded by all the things that can affect it, topped by its eventual goal. More simply, it shows the basic foundation driving the change and the general direction. This does not exist in a vacuum, though, so other elements that can affect or alter the course are shown, too. The outcome, or how

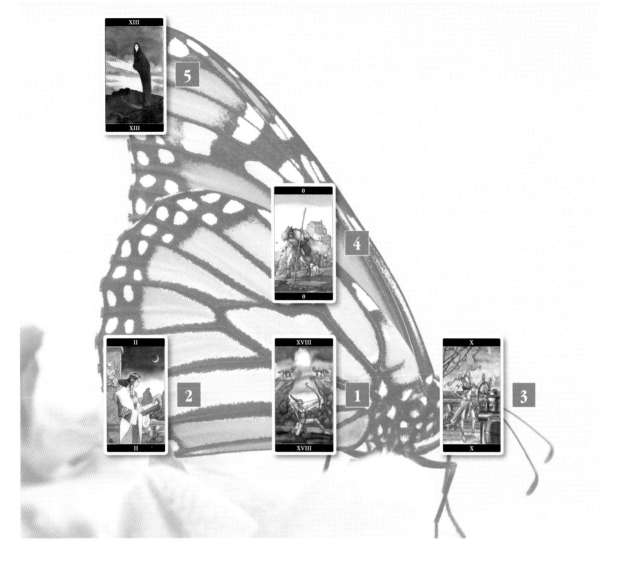

the Querent will emerge is indicated. Having a map of the transformative journey can help ease the way for the Querent.

Also, by being aware of the direction and the influences, the Querent can take more control of the process. If, for example, the outside influences are negatively affecting the situation, the Querent can take steps to neutralize those influences. If the ego's desires are in conflict, the Querent can take that into account and either change the direction or quell the ego. If, by some chance, the emergence is not something the Querent desires, then certainly they can work with the energies and influences present and change the course.

Example of a Reading

Ellen, a woman of 28, is doing well in her career and in her life. Nothing seems wrong…at least on the outside. But she feels like something is going on inside her, like she needs to change something or something is changing. The things that fulfilled her before aren't anymore. Since she's been so content for a while now, this feeling of discontent is unsettling. She's been thinking of doing volunteer work, which she's never done before, and wonders if there is a connection.

The High Priestess is the Pupa

Ellen's inner Priestess is getting vocal! Inner beliefs that she may have ignored in the past are demanding a voice. There are things she knows to be true but she has not acted on. Beliefs at the core of her being want to play a role her life.

Judgment is the Chrysalis

It is fitting that the call to her inner Priestess is this card. She is receiving a higher calling—whether it is from God or her higher self (depending on what she believes). She is being called because she has something more important to do.

The Hierophant is the Outside Influences

Here is a wise teacher, probably one she has yet to meet. This is a person who takes the wisdom of the spirit and applies it to real life. It is someone who can really help her answer the call, whatever it is, in a meaningful way.

The Hanged Man is the Desire

Ellen's ego would probably be quite happy to leave things as they are. Her life has a nice balance and is something she's used to. Her ego would prefer to just hang out and not upset the status quo. Doing nothing at this time is its preferred course.

Justice is the Emergence

By answering her soul's call, Ellen will be planting the seeds of her future. She will have the knowledge and experience to do that wisely and with insight. She'll have a clearer vision of what is right and wrong—at least for her own life.

Synthesis

This is one of those readings that really does flow together beautifully. Ellen is feeling called to do volunteer work and this reading very much affirms that feeling. It is not merely a "doing charity work" kind of thing (although there is nothing wrong with that). It is more. It is part of her transformation. By doing so, she will learn much and have more ways to shape her life, for Justice is the card of karma, of reaping what you sow. As far as energies helping or hurting her process, the Hierophant will definitely lend a helping hand and will probably teach her more than she imagines. Her ego doesn't seem to keen on the transformation nor does it seem actively against it. She shouldn't find too much resistance in herself regarding this transformation.

What We Have Learned

In this reading we learn that a spread can be used to validate or affirm someone's feeling or intuition. Sometimes people have "a feeling" about something but maybe just aren't sure about it, have no logical reasons to feel that way, or don't really understand what it means. In addition, a reading can add clarity to a situation like this, providing a Querent with a clear sense of direction and confidence to move forward.

505

UNDERSTANDING CHANGE

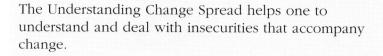

Number of Cards: 5
Cards Used: Major and Minor Arcana.
Time: 15 minutes
Objective: To help a person understand their feelings about a change.
Layout: One card in the center with four cards around it showing how the change (in the center) creates a ripple effect of experiences.

The Understanding Change Spread helps one to understand and deal with insecurities that accompany change.

Metamorphosis is transformation. Transformations can be slow and gradual or sometimes change occurs quickly. We often find ourselves surprised by what is going on in our lives. Transformation is as much about the process as the destination. Whatever happens during a metamorphosis becomes part of the end result. Sometimes, we learn something about ourselves or the world around us. Sometimes we experience a change in the way we think about things. Sometimes, it creates a monumental shift in our belief system.

The Understanding Change Spread focuses on the journey of the Querent. Regardless of the nature of the change, be it an inner transformation or external change in circumstance, it focuses attention on thoughts and feelings so growth and strength are fostered.

Human nature often fears the unknown. People usually want to know about their outcome. This spread includes a card regarding how the change will manifest in the Querent's life.

The Preparation and Positioning of the Cards

The Reader divides the deck into five sections: the Major Arcana, Swords, Cups, Wands and Pentacles. The Reader and Querent shuffle all five decks separately. The Reader deals one card from the top of each pile and lays them out face up in the positions shown below.

The Reading and the Interpretation

The Reader proceeds to interpret the Arcana in each position, keeping in mind the relative meanings. Each card is interpreted individually as a message. After the cards have been interpreted, the Reader summarizes the entire reading, known as a Synthesis.

1 The Change (Major Arcana)

This card represents the change that the Querent is facing. An inner or external transformation.

2 Thoughts (Swords)

Swords represent thoughts. This card represents what the Querent thinks about the change. Thoughts are not always rational.

3 Feelings (Cups)

Chalices represent emotions. This card represents what the Querent feels about the situation. The feelings may be emotional or intuitive.

4 Inspiration or Fear (Wands)

Wands represent passion. This card represents the aspect of the change that either inspires or scares the Querent.

5 Manifestation (Pentacles)

Pentacles represent the physical world and manifestation. This card represents how the change will manifest in the Querent's life.

Exploring the Spread

This spread shows the change and the projected outcome. More importantly, it focuses on the Querent's experience during the transformation. People facing change often feel conflict. In part, it is a natural reaction to change. People's responses to anything new, either in themselves or in their life, will vary. The way someone feels may be at odds with what they think. What inspires them may also frighten them.

It is important to give attention to each card individually. Also to look at the interplay between the cards, especially the Thoughts and Feelings cards. This spread is particularly useful for exploring these different responses because it divides the deck into suits.

Example of a Reading

Frank, a married man in his mid-30s, is facing a dramatic transformation. He and his wife are going to have their first baby. He is very much looking forward to the experience. The time is flying quickly and he's not had time to examine his thoughts and feelings. He thinks that he'd like to write down this reading and explore it on his own and someday give it to his child.

⌒ The Emperor is the Change

Frank's life will certainly become more stable and grounded with the arrival of a baby. Structure and routine will become a way of life. Also, he will become much more of a leader. He will have to look out not just for his own good, but think always of his child.

⌒ The 4 of Swords is Thoughts

Having a baby in the house will, in a way, lead to a retreat from the world. Frank's focus will be more on his home and family and less on social outings and events. As with most Swords, this one is double-edged, as having to stay home can lead to resentment.

The 8 of Cups is Feelings

Frank feels he has, in a way, left his old life in search of something more. He feels having a family will give greater meaning to his life. Part of his transformation to father is the search for something more than himself and his wants.

The 3 of Wands is Inspiration or Fear

As with many people, Frank's inspiration and fear are in this card. He looks forward to the future, hoping for happiness…it is this hope that inspires him. He also cannot help but worry about the future: Will the baby be okay? Will he be able to care for it?

The 7 of Pentacles is the Manifestation

Becoming a father will influence Frank's life in many ways. One way will be in the little, every-day things that he does. Every simple action at home will be filled with more meaning because of his sense of fatherhood.

Synthesis

The 8 of Cups is the most active in the reading. It shows that Frank's desire to be a father is fueled in part by his feelings—his desire for something more, for deeper meaning in his life. Rationally, he realizes that this will change his life. Swords are usually double-edged and while fatherhood can mean a retreat from social obligations and activities, he must be aware that part of him may miss that lifestyle at times. However, the 4 of Swords is a gentle card and so Frank clearly isn't too worried about it.

Frank seeks to have greater meaning in his by a father. What he may or may not realize is that in many ways his life will stay the same. He will go to work. He will do household chores. He will take care of his obligations. But what will be different is everything. Suddenly, all those actions are for more than himself. They are for his child.

What We Have Learned

In this reading we learn that a deck can be used in different ways. It is most common to shuffle all the cards together, or to use only the Major Arcana. In order to focus very clearly on the areas of life represented by the suits, it is a good idea to separate the suits and match the suits with the positions in the spread.

SPREAD LIBRARY

The spreads that follow each have some small particularity that can be useful to the Tarot Reader. Even if the Reader will not use the spread as it is – after all, each Reader approaching this book probably already has a lot of experience with spreads – studying these spreads may supply some additional insights on how to conduct readings and modify your own spreads. The Universal Vision Party Spread, for instance, is an example of a spread that is well suited to parties and noisy, high distraction environments, where entertainment is as important as accuracy.

The Estensi Golden Tarot Spread and the Excavation Spread are jumps into the past. The first is also a perfect example of a deck-specific spread, built to draw forth the strengths specific to a single deck. But both spreads draw heavily from concept rooted in the very soul of human history. Try these spreads on, and you will realize that each of them has a little something unique: a different approach that, when glimpsed, can be part of a Reader's growth.

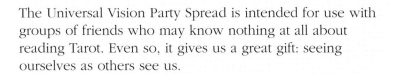

UNIVERSAL VISION PARTY SPREAD

Cards used: Full deck
Number of cards: 6
Time: 10 minutes
Objective: To provide party guests with a positive "universal vision" of how others see them.
Layout: The cards form a pyramid: three rows of cards, with one card on top, two in the middle, and three in the bottom row.

The Universal Vision Party Spread is intended for use with groups of friends who may know nothing at all about reading Tarot. Even so, it gives us a great gift: seeing ourselves as others see us.

Preparation and Positioning of the Cards

Because this spread is an intuitive game, party guests may take turns playing the role of Reader and Querent. No special training in reading Tarot cards is required.
The designated Reader and Querent may volunteer or be selected by random means: drawing straws, rolling dice, or drawing cards. Once chosen, the Reader and Querent shuffle the deck in turn, and the Querent cuts the deck. The Reader then creates the pyramid of cards, dealing them face-down on the table from top to bottom and from left to right.

Reading and Interpretation

The Reader interprets the Arcana in each position, saying whatever pops into his/her head. In addition, other party-goers are encouraged to make suggestions of their own. The funnier the interpretation, the better.
Having interpreted all cards, the Reader summarizes the reading and salutes the good-natured Querent with a toast.

1 The Personality Card

In this first position, we find a one-card summary of the Querent's personality. While turning over this card, the Reader says aloud, "This card represents your overall personality."

513

2 | The Annoying Habit

The card in the second position represents the Querent's most annoying trait, something he/she does that exasperates friends. (This should be one of those little quirks friends indulgently overlook.) While turning over this card, the Reader says aloud, "This card represents something that drives us mad with annoyance!"

3 | The Lovable Trait

The third position represents the Querent's most lovable trait. (Think in terms of good habits or attractive physical features.) The Reader, as this card is revealed, says aloud, "This card represents what everyone loves about you."

4 | The Biggest Challenge

The fourth card represents the Querent's biggest challenge—habits, tendencies, and light-hearted issues from work or relationships. The Reader, revealing this card, says, "This card represents your biggest challenge."

5 The Secret Desire

The card in the fifth position represents the Querent's secret desire, something he/she privately longs to do, but publicly represses. (The more outrageous and risqué the interpretation, the better.) The Reader, revealing this card, says, "This card represents your most secret desire!"

6 The Greatest Strength

The sixth card represents the Querent's greatest strength. The Reader, revealing this card, says, "This card represents your greatest strength—your very best quality of all?

Synthesis

The goal of this reading is not accuracy, but sheer entertainment! Guests should free-associate with the cards, shouting out any and all interpretations. (With the inexperience of the Readers in mind, it is best to use a fully illustrated deck—like the Universal Tarot—for this game.) Spend no more than sixty seconds or so on each card. Keep things light, favoring outrageous interpretations. As the reading progresses, capable Readers and good-natured Querents should be rewarded with applause, cheers, and toasts. It is also fun to "turn the tables"—literally—forcing each Reader and Querent to swap roles.

ESTENSI GOLDEN TAROT

The Estensi Golden Tarot Spread is designed for Querents facing a milestone event in their lives. It shows the major influences that are moving out of and into their lives.

Cards used: Major Arcana
Number of cards: 5
Time: 20 – 30 minutes
Objective: To illustrate the changes the Querent can expect and prepare for as they face a milestone event.
Layout: One card in the middle and four around it (one on top, one on the bottom, and one on each side).

Major life-changing events, while exciting, can be a little scary. Having some idea of what to expect can be comforting. It can also be helpful in preparing the Querent for the changes. Awareness of change allows the Querent to recognize and make use of the new energy entering their life.

The Wheel of Fortune card in the Estensi Golden Tarot of the Renaissance is an interesting card. Each of the figures on the wheel has a motto. The figure on the left has *regnabo*, I will rule. The figure on top has *regno*, I rule. The figure on the right has *regnavie*, I ruled. The figure on

the bottom has *sum sine regno*, I do not rule. These demonstrate life moving in cycles, different events moving in and out of time. While the energy that is currently ruling has the most effect, the energy moving into and out of our lives also has importance. And the energy that is not present is also important, as its absence has an effect as well.

Preparation and Positioning of the Cards

The Reader shuffles the deck. The Querent then shuffles and cuts the deck into four piles with their non-dominant hand. The Reader picks up the four piles in reverse order making one pile again. Dealing from the top, the Reader places the four Wheel cards down. Then the Reader takes the bottom card and places it in the middle of the wheel. All cards should be placed face up.

Reading and Interpretation

The Reader proceeds to interpret the Arcana in each position, keeping in mind the relative meanings. The cards should first be interpreted one-by-one in order. After all the cards have been interpreted, the Reader summarizes the entire reading in a complete discourse, known as a Synthesis.

1 I Rule

This card represents the current energy or situation that has the most impact on the Querent's life. It is the part of their life that is about to change. If it is something that the Querent is happy about, then it is possible that they are more nervous or anxious about the coming change. If it is something they are unhappy about, then likely they are looking forward to a change.

2 I Ruled

This card represents the energy or events that have passed from their life but still have some effect. Consider the Querent's reaction to this card, as it can represent unfinished business, unlearned life lessons, or emotional baggage that can hinder a smooth transition to the next phase of their life.

3 I Will Rule

This card represents the new energy that will be brought about by the forthcoming milestone. Again, carefully watch the Querent's reaction to this, whether positive or negative. In some ways, this (along with the center card) is the most important in the spread and the one that the Querent will likely be most interested in.

4 I Do Not Rule

This card represents energy that is absent from the past, current, and forthcoming situation. The absence of something can be as telling as what is present. It can illustrate a necessary lack of balance in the Querent's life or a potential distraction to the Querent.

5 | The Center

This card represents what will remain constant in the Querent and their life. This is the aspect of their personality or life that will help them stay steady as they face the coming change. Having a stable place is important and necessary so that the Querent doesn't feel adrift or overwhelmed.

Exploring the Spread

Everyone reacts to change differently. Some embrace and welcome it or even actively seek it out. Others resist it as much as possible. But, as we all know, the only constant in life is change. So it is likely that at some time or another, your Querents will be facing it. It is important to gauge their reactions to change in general and to the cards that come up for them, so that you can best convey the information and help them prepare for what lies ahead. Even though we know that the future is not set in stone, there are things that will occur whether we want them to or not. But in the face of these life-changing milestones, we can control our reactions and responses to change. That is where this spread and your skill as a Reader can help your Querents.

As you interpret the spread, pay attention to patterns within the cards. Is there a sequence to the first three cards? What kind of progression is there from what has been to what is becoming? Do things seem to be moving forward or backward for the Querent?

After examining the first three cards in detail, look at the "I do not rule" card. How is this energy different from the pattern created by the first three? How does the Querent react to this card? Does it indicate something that may distract the Querent? Or is it an energy or area of life that is necessarily on the back burner as the Querent focuses on the task at hand? You may be tempted to read this as representing a lack of balance in the Querent's life, something that is absent that the Querent should bring into their life. Resist that urge, though, as it is not meant to be read that way. While there are times in life when balance is desirable, there are times when a strict focus is necessary and balance is not improbable but also undesirable.

As the spread is synthesized, continually refer to the center card. This is energy or characteristics that will serve as the Querent's base or foundation. This is something that has not and will not change. It will in some way affect and influence all the other cards. In fact, if you have trouble seeing a

progression in the first three cards, try looking at them all relative to this card, as if they were different aspects of it. As you and the Querent discuss the "I rule" and "I ruled" cards, identify the ways in which the center card has provided continuity and stability. As you discuss together the "I will rule" card, explore ways in which "the center" will shape that energy.

Example of a Reading

Julie has recently finished law school and an internship. She will begin the search for her first job as a lawyer. This is an important time in her life, one filled with change. She is leaving her life as a student and moving into her professional life. She wants to know what kind of changes she should be aware of and how she can move most gracefully into her new life as a practicing lawyer.

The Devil is I Rule

While working as an intern, she was bound to work for a firm in exchange for experience. She received no monetary compensation. Yet she had no choice … she needed the experience and that was the price she paid. Her current experience is very constricted and controlled by her choice to practice law.

Justice is I Ruled

Julie worked hard in school, carefully balancing attention to her studies and her personal life. That sense of balance left her life when she took on the internship, which demanded most of her waking hours.

The Empress is I Will Rule

In contrast to her years as a student and intern, this card looks like an oasis for Julie. She expected several more years of financial hardship as she established herself. However, this card indicates that abundance and nurturing energy are moving into her life.

520

Death is I Do Not Rule

It is interesting that in a series of significant changes Death, the card of endings, is the energy that is not present. Julie's life phases are not discrete, but rather they are all part of one long journey. No matter how Julie's external circumstances change, there are no endings because she is moving toward the same goal and all these phases are just steps toward that goal.

The Fool is the Center

Julie's ever-optimistic attitude helped her through school and the internship and will serve her well as she seeks the right job for herself. Being on a journey toward a goal made every step of it important and valuable.

Synthesis

The progression from Justice (and the need for balance) to the Devil (imbalance and servitude) to the Empress (abundance) is a positive and welcome one for Julie. Her combination of always being dedicated to her journey with a light heart (the Fool) and seeing all things as moving toward her goal (Death) have led her through some tough times. Yet it seems that the future is bright and that her hard work will pay off. In fact, the combination of the Fool, with its idealistic attitude, and the Empress, with its honoring of the earth, indicates that a future in environmental law might be worth considering.

What We Have Learned

This spread is about reading the large cycles in a person's life. Therefore, it is important to see how the cards flow into each other, as with the first three cards of this spread. Secondly, by relating the center to each card in the spread, we learn how to see how one card can relate similarly and differently to other cards. Finally, we learn that absence of a card or energy can have as much importance in a reading as its presence.

Astrological Houses Spread

Cards used: Full deck
Number of cards: 12
Time: 30 minutes
Objective: Get a picture of your overall life at present and learn about the 12 houses in a natal chart.

This spread is useful in getting a snapshot of where you are in your life at the moment.

A natal chart is a snapshot of the stars and planets at the moment of your birth. It looks like a wheel and is made up of 12 houses. Each house represents an aspect of your life. The planets and constellations fall in these houses and influence your personality and life lessons. Using this idea, we can do a reading based on the houses to get a snapshot of your life at this moment.

This spread uses the full deck and can be done for yourself or a Querent. There are plenty of cards, so plan on taking some time with this one. The 12 cards are laid out just like the houses in a natal chart.

1. First House: Your self-image, personality, ambition, drives, and body.

2. Second House: Your value systems, material possession, and financial attitudes.

3. Third House: The way you communicate, think, and learn; siblings and neighbors.

4. Fourth House: Your mother and father, your roots, your domestic life and family.

5. Fifth House: Creativity, affairs of the heart, fun, hobbies, social life, and children.

6. Sixth House: Your job, responsibilities, work habits and relationship, and health

7. Seventh House: Business and romantic relationships; how you interact with people.

8. Eighth House: Jointly controlled money and assets, taxes, inheritances, obligations.

9. Ninth House: Spirituality, religion, morals; higher education; long distance travel.

10. Tenth House: Your public image, and career; relationships with authority figures.

11. Eleventh House: Friendships; memberships in groups; hopes, goals, and wishes.

12. Twelfth House: Your inner self, dreams, secrets, the past; subconscious; karma.

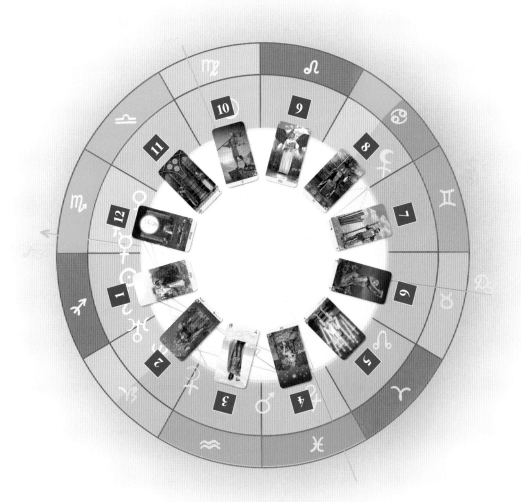

THE THREEFOLD
LAW SPREAD

Cards used: Major Arcana only
Number of cards: 3
Time: 15 minutes
Objective: To anticipate the consequences of an action taken.
Layout: Three cards, arranged in a semi-circle or crescent.

Whatever we sow, we reap! The Threefold Law Spread reveals the consequences of actions, allowing Querents to reconsider strategies that would amplify the negative energy in the world.

The Threefold Law of Return (sometimes called "the Rule of Three") is a simple but powerful Wiccan principle: whatever energy we project into the world returns to us amplified three times. The Threefold Law Spread provides a simple, visual means of predicting the consequences of any action. It can prompt Querents to reconsider hurtful or spiteful plans by revealing how that negative energy will be amplified when returned.

Preparation and Positioning of the Cards

After the Querent relates a plan of action, the Querent and Reader choose a Major Arcana card to represent what the Querent wants to do.

The Reader returns this card to the deck and shuffles. The Querent cuts the deck three times with his or her left hand. The Reader then deals the cards face up into the spread.

Reading and Interpretation

Each card in the spread represents one of three ways the Querent's action will be amplified and returned. The Reader interprets each card, watching for reversals, elemental associations, and other relationships among the cards which may further illuminate the meaning of each card.

Exploring the Spread

Since the Reader and Querent have chosen one card to represent one specific action the Querent is considering, it is entirely possible that this card will appear in the spread. When this is the case, the Querent will receive back *precisely* what he or she plans to do to someone else!

HEAVENLY STAIRS SPREAD

Cards used: Full deck
Number of cards: 5
Time: 20 minutes
Objective: To identify the steps a Querent must take to reach a goal.
Layout: Five cards arranged to resemble a flight of stairs rising from the present (lower left) to the desired future (upper right).

Bridging the gap between the present and the future is a set of Heavenly Stairs—a prescription for action that, executed in sequence, can move a Querent from a state of desire to a state of bliss!

The Heavenly Stairs Spread achieves three things at once:

⌐ It involves the Querent in the important work of identifying how the present situation differs from a desired future.

⌐ It encourages the Querent to define a goal in concrete, measurable, vivid terms.

⌐ It outlines three steps the Querent can take, creating a prescription for action.

Preparation and Positioning of the Cards

Before the reading begins, the Reader presents the deck to the Querent and says, "Look through these cards, taking as long as you need, and find a card that represents you in some way." This card, called *the Significator*, becomes a symbol for the Querent's current circumstance.

Once the Querent finds this card, he/she places it face up on the table.

Next, the Reader says, "Look through the deck again and locate a card that represents what you hope to achieve."

This card, called *the Goal*, represents the Querent's desired future. When this card has been located, the Querent places it face up on the table.

The Reader places the Significator into the first position and the Goal in the fifth position. The Reader then collects the remaining seventy-six cards and shuffles them as usual. After shuffling, the Reader passes the deck to the Querent, who cuts them with his/her left hand. Finally, the Reader deals three additional cards into the second, third, and fourth positions in the spread, creating a staircase between the present situation and the desired goal.

Reading and Interpretation

The Reader proceeds to interpret the card in each position. While the Reader should point out the specific and relative meanings of each card, it is also important to ask the Querent to explain why he or she chose the Significator and Goal cards, as this may reveal a great deal about the Querent. Having interpreted all the cards, the Reader summarizes the entire reading in a complete discourse, known as the Synthesis. In this case, the Synthesis may be expressed as a prescription for action: "By taking these three steps, you can achieve your goal!"

1 The Significator

This card, deliberately chosen by the Querent, is a self-portrait. When the Reader sees this card, the Reader thinks, "This is an insight into how my Querent sees him/herself."

2, 3, and 4 The Three Steps

These three cards, selected at random by the Reader, represent three steps the Querent can take to achieve his/her goal. As the Reader reveals these cards, the Reader thinks, "This is a step the Querent must take in order to achieve the goal."

5 The Goal

This card, deliberately chosen by the Querent, illustrates the goal the Querent hopes to achieve. When the Reader sees this card, the Reader thinks, "Here is a symbol of what my Querent desires the most."

What Has Been Learned

Note that the Heavenly Stairs Spread provides Querents with concrete steps, but that the interpretation of these cards and their meanings is more fluid, flexible, and interactive than usual. When first interpreting each card, embrace any and all possible interpretations that occur to you or the Querent; you can always revise your interpretations later in the reading. Note, too, that this spread is designed to provide specific steps to be taken in a specific order. Critics often disparage the Tarot by claiming that it provides nothing more than vague generalities. Readers may silence such critics by challenging them to scale the Heavenly Stairs for themselves!

THE EXCAVATION SPREAD

Cards used: Majors only
Number of cards: 5
Time: 15 minutes
Objective: To help the Querent identify things from their past that are affecting their present.
Layout: Four cards laid out in a vertical column with the fifth card crossing the top card.

> The Excavation Spread reveals layers of forgotten experiences, thoughts, beliefs, or emotions that still affect the Querent.

Ancient cultures lay shrouded in mystery. Traces of their existence are gleaned from archaeological artifacts. We learn about history through recovered, studied objects.

People's lives are like that too. An event will happen and have great significance later in a person's life. By excavating our lives, so to speak, we can see what happened in the past that is directly affecting our present. We can see patterns. We can see how cause and effect play out in our lives. And these patterns are not just interesting, they are useful. If we are happy with the way our lives are going, by recognizing the pattern that formed the foundation of the present, we continue to work with that energy as we build for the future. If we are not content with our lives, we can examine the causes. We can then move forward in a more favorable direction by healing, transforming, or channeling the energy from our past.

Preparation and Positioning of the Cards

The Reader and the Querent shuffle the deck in turn. The Reader deals the cards 1, 2, and 3 from the bottom of the pile and lays them out in the positions of the Excavation Spread, face down. Then cards 4 and 5 are dealt off the top of the pile, face up.

Reading and Interpretation

The Reader proceeds to interpret the Arcana in each position, keeping in mind the relative meanings. Cards 4 and 5 are interpreted first as giving a snapshot of the Querent's current situation in relation to their question. Then cards 3, 2, and 1 are revealed in reverse order. After the cards have been interpreted, the Reader summarizes the entire reading in a complete discourse, known as the Synthesis.

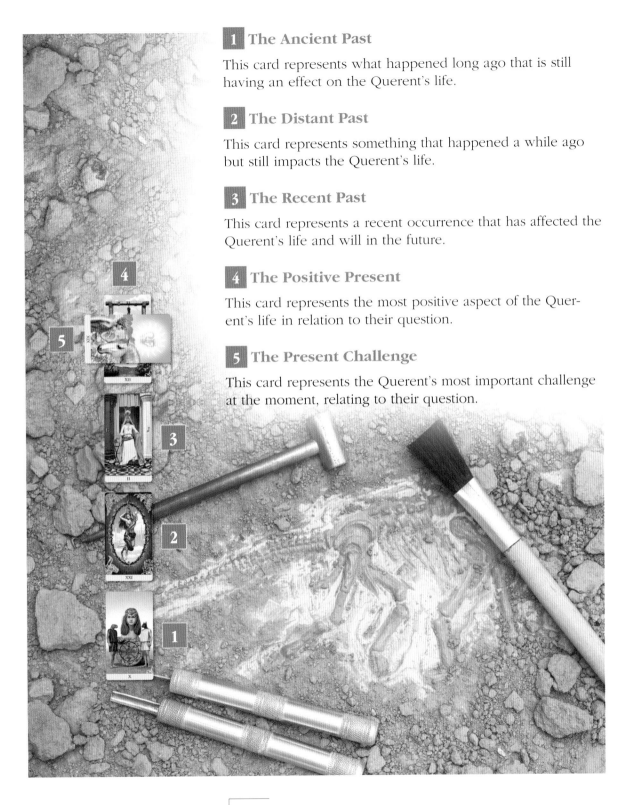

1 The Ancient Past

This card represents what happened long ago that is still having an effect on the Querent's life.

2 The Distant Past

This card represents something that happened a while ago but still impacts the Querent's life.

3 The Recent Past

This card represents a recent occurrence that has affected the Querent's life and will in the future.

4 The Positive Present

This card represents the most positive aspect of the Querent's life in relation to their question.

5 The Present Challenge

This card represents the Querent's most important challenge at the moment, relating to their question.

529

Exploring the Spread

This spread seems very simple. And in some ways it is. But as with a real excavation at an archeological site, the work can be slow and painstaking. And once something is gently unearthed and cleaned off, it may take some detective work to find out what it really is. Then comes the work of fitting it into the big picture.

And that really is the key to this reading. Each of the pieces of the past must be handled gently. There is no telling what is buried deep within a person. They may not even know. If they've repressed a memory or experience, it may be painful to see again. Also, it might be difficult to determine what the revealed card actually is. The card name and basic meaning might be useful, or they might actually be a hindrance. In this reading, in particular, it is important to have the Querent examine the images and pay attention to their intuition and emotional responses.

As you and the Querent work your way up the cards, tie the previous card to the next card. See how each card influences and shapes the next as its effects are assimilated. As the spread is interpreted, a thread from the past to the present should be clear.

What We Have Learned

In this reading, we learn that the Reader can provide the basic interpretation of the card to get things started. But with a reading like this, the Querent plays a major role in the final analysis. Working from the basic meanings, the Querent looks at the images as if they were mirrors. In them, he sees his reality reflected back. What he sees may not be what the Reader or deck designer intended, but that is okay. Sometimes it is surprising where the continuity from one card to the next is found. In this case, it was in the bases of the cards and not in the main images. Just as when examining a small piece of history, you don't always know what is going to be important or hold the key.

Past Life Spread

Cards used: Full deck
Number of cards: 9
Time: Up to 1 hour
Objective: To reveal details of a past life and explore their impact on the present day.
Layout: A diamond consisting of five columns of cards, containing one, two, three, two, and one cards, respectively.

The Past Life Spread explores the mysterious realm of past lives. It weaves stories about former selves and reveals their connections to a present incarnation.

Preparation and Positioning of the Cards

The Reader and the Querent shuffle the deck in turn. The Querent cuts the cards once with the left hand (symbolizing the past) and once with the right hand (symbolizing the future). This done, the Reader deals the cards.

Reading and Interpretation

The Reader proceeds to interpret the Arcana in each position, keeping in mind the relative meanings. Having interpreted all the cards, the Reader summarizes the entire reading in a complete discourse, known as the Synthesis.

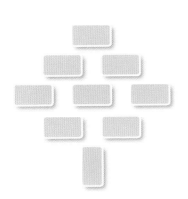

1 Former Self

This card is a former incarnation, a defining quality that may be considered this former self's signature. Some aspects of this card will suggest gender, as well. As the Reader reveals this card, the Reader thinks, "This is who my Querent was."

2 Former Goal

This card is the former self's greatest hope, what he or she wanted to accomplish. As the Reader reveals this card, the Reader thinks, "This is what my Querent wanted to achieve."

3 Former Obstacle

This card is an impediment to reaching the former goal, an obstacle that hindered progress. As the Reader reveals this card, the Reader thinks, "This is what my Querent struggled with again and again."

4 Life Lesson

This card is the life lesson the Querent was meant to learn in this former incarnation. As the Reader reveals this card, the Reader thinks, "This is the insight gleaned from a past life."

5 Verdict

This card indicates the Querent's success. As the Reader reveals this card, the Reader thinks, "This card tells me whether the Querent achieved his or her goals in this previous incarnation." This card may also suggest something about the way the former incarnation died.

6 New Mission

This card is the Querent's new mission. Something he or she elected to explore in his or her present incarnation. As the Reader reveals this card, the Reader thinks, "This card tells me why the Querent returned to earth."

7 Present Goal

This card is the Querent's current goal, what the current incarnation is designed to teach the Querent. As the Reader reveals this card, the Reader thinks, "This is the lesson assigned to my Querent in his or her current incarnation."

8 Present Obstacle

This card is the Querent's current obstacle. A situation or concept that again and again threatens to disrupt progress. As the Reader reveals this card, the Reader thinks, "This is what my Querent struggles with now."

9 Present Self

This card is the Querent's present-day incarnation. A quality or trait that defines the Querent as clearly as card 1 defined the former self. As the Reader reveals this card, the Reader thinks, "This is who my Querent is today."

Synthesis

Astute Readers will quickly note the dualistic structure in this spread and begin to see how this structure reveals relationships between past and present lives.

What relationships exist between cards 1 and 9? Do the numbers suggest progress or retreat? How has the core or essence of the Querent been changed or refined by experience? What parallels exist between the former goal (and obstacle) and the current one? How might the interaction of these themes be used to explain present-day attitudes, preferences, or emotional triggers?

How might the degree of success (card 5) in learning a former life lesson (card 4) have impacted the mission (card 6) assigned to the Querent in his or her current incarnation?

What Has Been Learned

Spreads like the Past Life Spread encourage a radical shift in the Querent's point of view. The spread's power lies in its ability to suggest new explanations for the motivations and fears that speed or hinder our progress in the present.

This spread will provide a great deal of food for thought for those who take the concept of past lives seriously. That said, use of this spread does not require a belief in reincarnation or suppressed past life memories. If nothing else, the concept of the past life may be used as a metaphor for the unconscious, for repressed motivations, or for shadow aspects of the self that the Querent would prefer to project elsewhere.

When Querents who do not believe in past lives are encouraged to "make one up," using the cards in this spread as a basis for their story, the story they tell inevitably has bearing on the situation they are dealing with now.

THE PYRAMID SPREAD

Cards used: Full deck
Number of cards: 8
Time: 20 minutes
Objective: Learn how to make the best of favorable situation.
Layout: Eight cards laid out in the shape of a pyramid.

In a favorable situation? Now you can discover how to make the most of it.

The ancient Egyptians, the inspiration for The Egyptian Tarot, hardly need an introduction. Who hasn't heard at least something of their remarkable culture and society? By making smart use of irrigation and the Nile River, the Egyptians created a food surplus, which led to benefits and marvelous developments in many areas of Egyptian life. Among their social and cultural developments were writing, art, religion, medicine, trade, architecture, and military skills. They made good use of a fortunate situation and it paid off with effects and ramifications they could not have imagined when they irrigated their first field. While the ancient Egyptians may or may not have known what they were getting into, you can use Tarot to get a glimpse of what you are getting into. If you find yourself in a favorable or fortunate circumstance with an eye to making that circumstance into something even greater, this spread will be very useful.

This spread is laid out like a pyramid, not because it is about preparing for the afterlife, but because it is a strong symbol of ancient Egypt. Also, it is a good representation of something with a strong foundation that reaches up toward lofty goals. It is, in short, a good representation of a fortunate situation with lots of potential. It builds an answer in layers. The bottom row shows the foundation—that is, things that are in place now. The second row shows potential action—that is, things that you can do or draw on to further your plan. The final row (and card) is the outcome.

1 Physical resources

This card shows the physical or tangible resources available to you at this moment.

2 Energy

This card shows the energy, ability, or particular strength that you have or is available.

3 Challenge

This card shows a challenge, problem, or weakness that must be solved.

4 Other people

This card shows other people or their attitudes/energy that affect the situation.

5 Help

This card shows help or additional resources that are available if you seek them out.

6 Inspiration

This card shows where to find inspiration both for guidance and encouragement.

7 Advice

This card shows advice regarding an action that you should take or it could be a warning.

8 Outcome

This card shows the probable outcome if things remain as they are and the advice is followed.

Exploring the Spread

This spread builds the answer to the question in layers, so it can be easily read as linear and chronological. There are other associations that can be made, as well. For example, when interpreting card 5, Help, see how it relates to card 3, Challenge, as it may help solve the problem. Or card 7, Advice, may be the solution to the problem in card 3 or it may be the best way to use the physical resources in card 1. As an experienced Reader, you're becoming more and more used to seeing these kinds of relationships between the positions in a spread.

535

Example of a Reading

Diana is thinking about setting up an ambitious online business. She feels that she is in a good position to do so. However, there are a few obstacles that may be overwhelming, or they may be insignificant. Diana wants advice on how to take best advantage of her situation. She has time, some resources, and many ideas right now.

 The 2 of Cups is the physical resources. There are some meager physical resources available acquired through a partnership. They are, though, more emotional or imagined than tangible.

 The 7 of Pentacles is the energy. Diana has great skill in looking over a situation and making assessments as to what works, what doesn't, and what pays off the best.

 **The 4 of Wands is the challenge.** The challenge for Diana is one of celebrating too early, being content with a temporary achievement, or stopping work too soon.

The Chariot is other people.
Other people potentially involved are eager to take control and drive this project. They are more in charge than Diana.

The Hermit is the help.
Diana should withdraw for a time and use her skill of assessment here. Perhaps a teacher or mentor will come her way.

The 10 of Cups is the inspiration.
The project's main inspiration may be emotional or creative. The fulfillment and drive would be that rather than monetary.

The Knave of Wands is the advice.
Either start over, learning more about the business being considered, or work as an apprentice in order to gain experience.

The 10 of Swords is the outcome.
Staring her own online business is not the best use of her situation. It will deplete her resources with nothing to show for it.

Synthesis
Diana thought that she was in a fortunate situation, having free time, lots of drive, and great ideas. She has a clear picture of what worked for other businesses and what didn't. But her resources were not tangible and her ambitions were not realistic. If she did partner with someone or others with the needed experience and resources, she would find herself in the backseat of the project. In short, the end result would fall far short of her expectations and dreams. Instead, the reading advises (with cards 5 and 7) that she table her plans for a while and put herself under the mentorship of someone with more experience.

ADDITIONAL CONTENT

The following section of *Tarot Compendium* would not have been possible without the contribution of our Kickstarter backers.

Three very important authors have agreed to share some of their wisdom for this book, and provide an unique contribution and point of view to our work. Tarot is a never-eneding journey, and we know that no book, however big and well done, could ever be able to contain it all. As it was said in the previous volume, Tarot is not a journey to learn but one to experience. Still, it's thanks to authors like Kim, Theresa and Nei that we can have a little spark of the journey still to make, of different directions, inspirations and points of view.

In any case, we hope you enjoy these bonus chapters.

Taking Tarot Outside the Box

with Kim Huggens

Kim's article is illustrated by the incredibly beautiful images of the *Illuminati Tarot* and of the *Tarot of the Apokalypsis* she created with Erik C. Dunne. She leads us, the Readers, outside the mold of the beaten path.

Her intuition on Tarot runs from complexity to simplicity and to complexity again with surprising clarity and powerful insights. She is able to provide continuously different points of view and expand on them. Everything is different, but yet familiar and practical, combined with easy exercises that are sure to bring new energy to your way of reading Tarot.

The Art of Teaching Tarot

with Theresa Reed

Theresa is one of the most respected teachers in the whole USA and anyone that has ever read one of her books will know how clear and synthetyc her teachings can be, while staying at the same time warm and complete.

Theresa's guidelines about teaching Tarot can be invaluable to anyone who would follow in her footsteps, but also to students everywhere in the world.

Her essay is gives perspective not just on the how but also on the way we could or should approach the teaching of Tarot.

Sacred Geometry

with Nei Naiff

Nei Naiff will bring us on a long and detailed journey about the symbolic shapes of Sacred Geometry. Thanks to his teachings it will be possible to see patterns in spreads where before we could see none.

Each shape is a concept, but also a pattern, and carries alongside a pace. By tuning into it and looking at a Tarot spread like a living thing, an additional layer of wisdom can be found.

Nei Naiff's unique perspective is very different from the Sacred Geometry chapter already contained in this book and will complement it perfectly.

Kim Huggens

Kim Huggens is the author of *Tarot 101: Mastering the Art of Reading the Cards* (Llewellyn, 2010) and the co-creator, with Erik C. Dunne, of *Tarot Apokalypsis* (Lo Scarabeo, 2016) and *Sol Invictus: the God Tarot* with Nic Phillips (Schiffer, 2007). She is also the author of the companion book to the *Tarot Illuminati*, by Erik C. Dunne (Lo Scarabeo, 2013) and the expanded *Complete Guide to Tarot Illuminati* (Llewellyn, 2013). Kim has been reading and studying Tarot for 23 years, and has given talks and workshops on Tarot internationally. She also has a passion for mythology, folklore and ancient history, and has published several papers on Graeco-Roman religion, magic and necromancy. She is a freelance proofreader and editor, and has edited three anthologies for Avalonia Books: *Memento Mori* (2012), *Vs.* (2010) and *From a Drop of Water* (2009). She often delivers lectures on her academic research interests – malefic-erotic magic in the ancient world – in the UK.

In her spare time, Kim enjoys live action roleplaying (LARP), tabletop RPGs, sword fighting, and writing. She currently lives in Cardiff, UK, with her partner, cat, library and collection of armour and shields.

TAKING TAROT OUTSIDE THE BOX

Even for the most experienced among us, reading Tarot can sometimes feel like a paint-by-numbers exercise. We become so accustomed to the images on the cards that the meanings begin to solidify to the point of habit. We are asked the same questions over and over again by different querents, so the common tendencies of human desire, fear and hope become plain to see, engendering in our minds rote responses.

"What is Tarot?" is rarely an idle question. As the answer changes, so it changes our way to approach the cards, read with them and create our story.

Before we know it, we begin to feel tired of ourselves as readers, bored with our readings, as if we are hitting a brick wall with our progress and learning.

This isn't helped by the vast number of books that promise unique insight into the cards and the practice of reading, only to go over the same content again. An understanding of the symbolic systems of the Tarot – numerology, Kabbalah, astrology, the four elements, etc – is useful as a foundation to your knowledge of the symbolic landscape that populates the card images, but should not be the pinnacle of one's understanding of the art. In order to move from being a good Tarot reader to being a great one, we need to take our understanding one step further and learn to read, and relate to, Tarot outside the box.

Here we will explore three areas in which we can do this:
- Accessing symbols
- Kindling your readings to life
- Transformative Tarot.

These areas will be explored with a variety of hands-on exercises and techniques to accompany the theory.

In learning to access the symbols in Tarot card imagery in new ways, we gain a broader and deeper perspective on both the cards and human experience. We also learn how to make our readings more dynamic, unique to every question and querent, and how to engage with them more fully. In learning how to (re)kindle the fire of life into our readings, we step outside our comfort zones and discover new ways to use the Tarot and to approach the questions we are asked, as well as identifying innovative ways to encourage active participation from our querents. Finally, in using Tarot as a tool for transformation, we allow ourselves to grow through our use of the cards, taking them up not only for divination and insight but also for full, courageous and conscious awareness of, and engagement with, oracular opportunity, self-transformation and magic. In these three ways, we can move beyond simply laying out cards statically in a spread and interpreting the symbols based on rote meanings, and challenge ourselves to an empowering and innovative relationship with the art of Tarot.

Accessing Symbols

The point at which many people feel they have progressed from being beginners to experienced readers is when they move beyond interpreting the cards in a reading as individual, distinct points and instead interpret all the cards as a whole, drawing links between them and weaving a cohesive story. The cards of the Tarot have often been likened to the pages of a book, and we must remember that to read only one page of a book leaves us with a limited understanding of the wider story. When we read for others – and even for ourselves – we will never be given the whole book, as we are reading only certain aspects of the life of the querent, but if we pick out the threads of meaning in each separate page and relate them to each other, we begin to see the themes, plot and characters of the wider story more clearly. In order to do this, we need to be able to take the rote meanings of the cards we have learned in books, and our understanding of the fundamental symbolic systems of the cards, and craft them into a holistic reading. We need to employ new ways of engaging with symbolism in the cards and accessing it.

Four maxims should be remembered when considering the vital role that symbolism, and our method of accessing it, plays in a Tarot reading. These maxims can be represented pictorially by the four Aces of the Tarot suits.

1. Symbolism is the language spoken by Tarot (Ace of Swords).
2. A picture is worth a thousand words (Ace of Pentacles).
3. There are no accidental oracles (Ace of Cups).
4. Every meaning is a unique moment that cannot be recreated (Ace of Wands).

The first maxim asks us to consider what a symbol is. The word comes from the Greek σύμβολον (*symbolon*), which comes from συν (*syn*, "together") and βολε (*bole*, "throwing or casting"). It means throwing things together, one thing representing another thing. A symbol is a representation of something rather than the thing-in-itself. It is a representation of concepts that might not be easy to define, as well as a

Ace of Swords   Ace of Pentacles   Ace of Cups   Ace of Wands

The four Aces of the *Tarot Apokalypsis* by Kim Huggens and Erik C. Dunne.

means by which attention and energy is invoked and directed. When we think of symbols, we often instantly look to occult and arcane systems, imagining glyphs of astrological importance or complicated magical alphabets. In fact, symbols can be anything. Symbols can be iconic and recognized by a great percentage of the world, such as the Statue of Liberty, or they can be more subtle and specific, such as Tibetan prayer flags, an eight-rayed star, or a white lily. They are commonly embedded in cultural values, yet many of them have almost universal application. Often, symbols can be seen as purely decorative.

Symbolism isn't only the language spoken by Tarot, but by us: our lives are guided by it. When we stop our cars at a red light, it is a colour symbolising an action that tells us to do so. When we write our names, the letters we use represent sounds that make up a greater concept. When we are presented with a choice of public bathroom, it is a symbol that guides us to a space with wheelchair access or baby changing facilities. Even the vital safety measures in place for the use of hazardous substances use symbols to alert us to risks or actions that must be taken. As such, when we look at the imagery on a Tarot card, we must be aware that anything in that card can be a symbol, not just the traditionally arcane images. We must also remember that symbolism does not

549

A single symbol can contain a very wide range of concepts and meanings. A symbol is at the same time a shared code and a suggestion. It is a hint, like an empty dress, and our mind will fill in what is missing.

just represent concepts, but evoke feelings – a collection of images is used by an artist to engender in the viewer a certain attitude or experience.

This leads to the second maxim, which reminds us that a single symbol contains within it a varied landscape of meaning, and that these meanings might not be the same from one moment or reading to the next. It is for this reason that we must accept that, sometimes, the meanings we have learned in books or from symbolic systems are only a small part of what a symbol denotes, and an even smaller part of the overall reading. This is also why studying symbolism can prove tricky in the global village that is our world. What one person in the western world understands as the meanings of a black cat may differ to what somebody in the Arabic world understands them to be. Where white is a colour of innocence and life in Western culture, worn by a happy bride on her wedding day, in China it is a colour of death, worn by the deceased and mourners alike. As such, learning how to access symbols and how to interpret them and read them, rather than only what they mean, is vital.

The third maxim reminds us not that everything happens for a reason, nor that there is no such thing as coincidence, but rather that meaning can be found in all things. As meaning is created by the mind, we must ask ourselves why our mind has chosen a particular thing to create a particular meaning from at that particular time, instead of something else. What our mind chooses to note and ascribe importance to is often the most telling of things. In this sense, Tarot reading could be considered a form of aleatoricism, which is the use of chance and random occurrence in the process of creating art or media. The word derives from the Latin *alea* (the rolling of dice), which was the root of *aleator* (gambler). In aleatoricism, artists "discover" a poem, piece of music or artwork through a mode of random generation. It can be seen to have a strong connection to the art of divination, in which we create meaning through otherwise random occurrences – illustrated cards drawn at random.

The final maxim is vital, yet most often forgotten by readers. Often when we read Tarot we are so desperately trying to remember the meanings of the cards that we lose sight of what they actually mean. We fall into the trap of thinking that there are a definite number of meanings for each card, and that a reading is a cut-and-paste job founded on our ability to recall what we have read. It isn't. Every reading is unique, a moment in time that can never be recreated. It is a sacred, divine, magical moment when one or more people connect with symbolism and imagery in a distinct point of time, in a distinct location, with a distinct question, state of mind, experience and sense of self. If we accept that we are changing all the time, then each time we come to the cards we are different and our perspectives and mind will be different.

We must, therefore, practice techniques and exercises that train us to think creatively about symbolism and meaning.

Invoking and Evoking meaning

Symbols function by both invoking meaning and evoking it. When a symbol **invokes** meaning, it draws upon traditional symbolic understanding that is often found in culture, symbolic systems, religion or history. It is meaning that is traditionally considered to be associated with that symbol, and may not necessarily have an emotional connection with the individual. When it **evokes** meaning it pulls out of the individual a personal response to the symbol, based on experience, understanding, aesthetics, feeling and moment. A single symbol can both invoke and evoke meaning at the same time, but not always.

Example

The symbol of a red lion in Tarot is often intended to invoke meanings related to alchemical symbolism of the Red King, and thus the planet Mars, the Divine Masculine, or the active component of a project. However, in any given reading, the reader (or querent) may not feel that this invoked meaning is applicable at the time, and instead find a different meaning being evoked: perhaps the querent works in a pub called the Red Lion Inn? Perhaps this particular lion reminds them of their red setter dog? Perhaps the red lion has always been symbolic to them of courage and strength? Or perhaps it simply evokes a particular feeling or emotion in the reader or querent?

Many Tarot readers have experienced a moment where a querent has found significant meaning evoked by an image on a card in their reading. While the reader rambles on about how the dragon in the card is a reference to St. George and the Dragon, and therefore a beast that must be slain or tamed, the querent stops them mid-sentence and says that they have been having recurring dreams about dragons for the past year. Perhaps the reader is explaining the traditional meaning of the Ten of Pentacles, and the querent shakes their head: "No," they say, "the man in that card reminds me of Santa Claus. I know what that means. I need to give something back to my family. I need to sort out a will."

We need to be open to responding to symbols that evoke meaning, as we often view this as secondary to the invo-

The High Priestess of the *Tarot Apokalypsis*, alongside a real pomegranate.

cation of traditional symbolic systems. However, it is the evocation of meaning through symbols that often proves most meaningful in a reading and speaks most powerfully to the querent.

In this High Priestess from the *Tarot Apokalypsis*, the symbol of a pomegranate is prominently held out by the priestess. It is intended to invoke the meaning of mystery, with its traditional association with the Mysteries of Eleusis. It is also a symbol of fertility, as it contains hundreds of seeds within it. It is commonly found in renditions of this card. However, the pomegranate symbol might evoke in a reader a variety of other meanings: here, they might associate it with the loss of fertility, due to the way the seeds and juice are falling away from the fruit; they might see in it the offer of secrets or the process of being tempted by something.

Ace of Swords

In this version of the Ace of Swords from the *Tarot Apoka-lypsis*, two ravens feature prominently and draw the eye of the viewer. In this deck, the suit of Swords is represented by ancient Scandinavian culture, and the Norse gods make themselves known. The two ravens here, therefore, are intended to invoke a connection with Odin, the Allfather, and his wisdom and knowledge. He sends the two ravens out every day to find out what is happening in the world, bringing information back each night so he might know all. However, a reader may find that these ravens evoke other meanings for them: they might see the open beak of the one on the left and hear, in their mind, its squawk, equating that with gossip and chatter, or mental noise preventing them from getting work done or maintaining focus.

Exercise: Invocation and Evocation of Meaning

~ Choose a few symbols that you are familiar with from traditional symbolic systems, or a few from the following list: *dove, lion, ram, star, rose* (white and red), *cat, red, water, moon, sun.*

~ Note down the traditional (invoked) meanings and associations of your chosen symbol (you can refer to books if you like).

~ Now assess the symbol without reference to traditional symbolic systems: what feeling or imagery does it evoke? How do you relate to it? Does it evoke any memories or ideas?

~ Compare the invoked and evoked meanings. In some cases, you might find similarities; in other cases, they will be very different. Both are right.

Every Tarot image is a complex symbolic landscape for us to decode – like the cryptex in *The Da Vinci Code*, the Lemarchand boxes from the *Hellraiser* film series, or the labyrinth to be navigated in Greek mythology. How do we decode the mystery? How do we solve the puzzle? How do we find our way through the labyrinth? We may follow the cryptic ravings of an old academic as in the *Da Vinci Code*; we may apply logic and cunning to open the fiendish puzzle box; we may even use a skein of silver thread and the advice of a goddess to find our way through the labyrinth. All are valid ways to solve the clues that a Tarot image shows us.

Focusing on Symbols in a Reading: The Three-Symbol Reading

It can be easy to forget to look at the symbols in the cards during a reading, getting distracted instead by trying to recall the traditional meanings of the cards and applying them to the question or the spread. However, when we take the time to look only at the symbols in the images, free from the bounds of traditional rote meanings, we can begin to branch out into more authentic interpretations. A useful method of training oneself to focus more on symbols in a reading is to take the idea of a Tarot spread and create it with a single card, using a single symbol from the card for each spread position. This technique is not only an exercise to change the way you approach Tarot readings, but is also a useful and concise reading method in itself. It is as easy for beginners to use as it is for experienced readers, so it can also be a great way for beginners to start exploring symbolism and learn how to put together an interpretation of a reading.

There are many things in a reading that can be distracting. Focusing on the cards first, and on the symbols on them second, can be very helpful.

10 of Pentacles

First, ask your question (if you have one – this works just as well for general readings). Shuffle the deck and draw a single card. Now, let your eyes rest on a single symbol in the **foreground** of the card. This symbol represents what is most prominent or obvious at this time, the most pressing matter, what is most influential on the question, or the clearest way forward. Next, let your eyes rest on a single symbol in the **mid-ground** of the card. This suggests influences, events or circumstances that are acting upon you but that don't yet have clear manifestations. Finally, let your eyes rest on a single symbol in the **background** of the card. This suggests any hidden influences or unexpected events or circumstances that you are unaware of that are playing upon you or the question. You will likely discover that the interpretation you receive from this exercise is very different to what you would have received had you looked up the traditional meaning of the card, but it will be just as useful and accurate.

Example reading for Summer:
Ten of Pentacles, Tarot Illuminati

In the foreground, the resting dog suggests that the most pressing matter for Summer is asking where her loyalties lie and who she can trust. In the mid-ground, the child hiding behind his father's robe suggests that there are those who know things or have seen things but are not coming forward, keeping the truth partially hidden or obscuring it with white lies. Finally, beyond the scene in the background, the green forest suggests that what is happening will continue to happen naturally, and that Summer will have very little control over events. Perhaps she can't see the wood for the trees, or is missing the bigger picture by focusing too much on the immediate, or unimportant, things. Together, these symbols suggest that although she is distrustful of those she perceives to be hiding things from her, they are only doing what they feel is best for her and, although she may wish to explore this further, she should accept that there was no malicious intent.

XVII. the Star

Example reading for Josh: The Star, Tarot Illuminati

The sparkling water flows freely onto the earth in the foreground of this card, evoking the meaning that Josh's life is currently, on the surface, feeling nourished and blessed.

He is growing and learning all the time. In the mid-ground, the leafy tree suggests that opportunities will soon open up for him to branch out further from his current position, hopefully growing great things from the nourished earth that is his foundation. However, in the background the mountains are steep and forested – they would be difficult to navigate, suggesting that although these opportunities will be available to Josh, they will be extremely challenging, and he may lose himself in them. He should consider carefully the path he wishes to take at this time. What else will he find in those forested mountains?

Example reading for Jakub:
King of Swords, Tarot Apokalypsis

In the foreground, Jakub is called to the circle of runes, suggesting that a quest for knowledge is of foremost importance to him, and his studies are the most pressing demand on his time. In the mid-ground, Odin's crossed arms suggest that, despite his best efforts, something is blocking him from progressing any further, and he feels trapped and frustrated by this. It is unclear what is causing this obstacle. In the background, the icy forest is reminiscent of Jakub's environment in the academic world: he is unaware of the freezing of some resource he requires – such as funding – or a detached attitude from tutors to his research that is causing a go-slow or a feeling of being unable to move forward. He'll need to identify the source of the blockage and the unfriendly environment before he can progress.

King of Swords

The environment we live and work in is not something detached from our inner self. They always influence each other.

In all three example readings, certain aspects of the traditional meanings of the cards were touched upon – the concept of loyalty in the Ten of Pentacles, nourishment and blessing in the Star, and knowledge in the King of Swords. However, these traditional associations were not relied upon, and the readings provided more specific information that would rarely be found in a traditional interpretation of the card meanings – such as the freezing of resources in the King of Swords and friends hiding things from each other in the Ten of Pentacles. To many Tarot readers, the thought of straying from traditional interpretations of the cards can be terrifying, but the above readings are accurate, profound and applicable to the querents.

Identifying a Theme:
Three Symbols, One Card

In order to identify a prominent theme in a card, we can look to its symbolism. This technique allows us to move beyond memorizing card meanings and instead reach a deeper understanding of the subtler nuances of a card, basing our perspective on the symbolism and imagery. This helps us embed the card's meanings more thoroughly in our minds and can allow us to deliver more engaging and personal readings. It is also a useful technique for beginners who want to get to know a card, or for those who are facing reader's block when it comes to a specific card.

Take the card you wish to explore, or choose one at random, and lay it in front of you. Pick three symbols that come to you first as you look at the card image. Remember – anything can be a symbol – from the facial expression of a figure in the card, to the way light plays on the water; nothing is accidental if your eyes fall on it rather than on something else. When you have identified three symbols, ask yourself the following questions:

- Do these symbols share something in common?
- Do they differ significantly?
- How do you feel about these symbols?
- Do they fall into a category, e.g., animal symbols, man-

To see the symbols: focus!
The symbols will come to you.

Queen of Pentacles

XVIII. the Moon

made items, heavenly bodies, oceanic things, they are all the same colour...?

~ Are they all in the same part of the card, e.g., are they all worn by a figure, are they all situated in the sky?

~ Can you sum them all up with a single word?

These questions will either allow you to pinpoint a dominant theme in the card or highlight some challenges and dichotomies represented by the card.

Example: Queen of Pentacles and The Moon from Tarot Illuminati.

In the Queen of Pentacles, the rabbit, the bunch of grapes and the fruiting tree are chosen. The rabbit is a symbol of fertility, as it reproduces rapidly and frequently. The bunch of grapes and fruiting tree suggest the fruits of one's labours and the sweet things in life. Together, these symbols suggest a theme of the card: abundance. All the symbols are found in nature – none are man-made – but all may be cultivated or nurtured by man, suggesting that this card represents abundance that must be nourished and grown through our own efforts. However, in The Moon the three symbols chosen highlight a dichotomy rather than a theme: the dog, the wolf and the moon. Here, the dog suggests nature being tamed, whereas the wolf represents the wild, the untamed, the unnerving. The moon is full, so it evokes associations with madness (lunacy), but it bears the serene face of a woman within it, evoking feelings of peace and blessing. To me, this denotes a dichotomy of the wild versus the tamed, and the challenge many of us face as we grow older: being required to apologise for our wild, our wolf, and being expected to instead be obedient and serene like the dog, despite our desire to howl at the moon.

Illuminating a Symbol: Chasing the Story

Sometimes we find that we are having trouble with a particular symbol and what it means, or that a symbol consistently recurs in our readings or lives. Perhaps we notice a symbol that has recurred in a number of cards, or it has simply caught our eye. It can be useful, in situations like this, to find the story that the symbol is telling throughout the Tarot.

559

To chase the story of the symbol you wish to explore, look through every card in the deck and put aside each one that includes that symbol. Depending on the symbol, you may end up with only a few cards, or a great many, which in itself can tell you something about that symbol. For example, you might only find a *sign of benediction* in the Hierophant and Ten of Swords, but a *horse* can be found in all the Knights, the Chariot, Death, the Sun and Six of Wands. (This will change depending on the deck you use.)

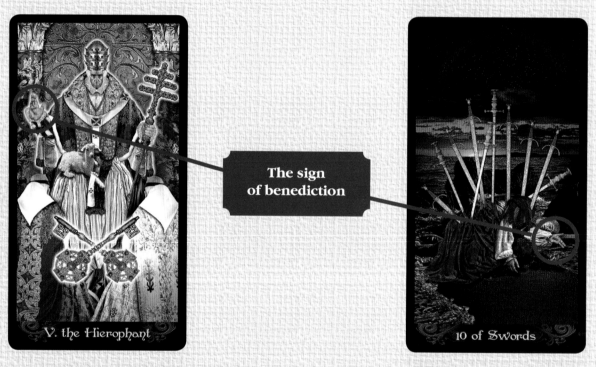

The sign of benediction

V. the Hierophant

10 of Swords

Take some time to consider the traditional meanings and associations of the cards that bear this symbol. A few aspects you could consider include:

◦— Do the cards have anything in common?

◦— What is different or similar in the way the shared symbol is presented in each card?

◦— What role does the symbol play in each card?

◦— How does the symbol inform or modify the meanings and associations of each card?

◦— How does its presence in these cards make you feel?

◦— Have the cards you have identified changed your response to the symbol?

Finding out the cards that share this symbol not only highlights some of the meanings of that symbol and of the cards, but can also start to reveal some of the Tarot's inbuilt (invoked) mysteries. Why, in the Thoth Tarot, for example, are the *lion* and *eagle* important symbols in the Empress, the Emperor, Lovers and Art?

You can expand this technique to a **storytelling reading**. When you have removed all the cards that feature the symbol you are exploring, shuffle only those cards and then lay them out (or, if there are a lot of cards, lay out the first five). Then, using the card imagery and the meanings that you know, but always being inspired by the image rather than memorized meanings (because that is the landscape and context of the symbol whose story you are telling), create a story from the beginning to its conclusion. Begin with a traditional story opening – "Once upon a time", for example – and end with a traditional ending. Tell the story of that symbol, how it evolves from its appearance in the first card to its ending in the last. How does that story relate to your life, and what do you think the symbol has been telling you? For example, you might discover in the story that the horse in all the Knights, the Chariot, Sun, Death, etc, appears to have been urging you to take action.

Storytelling is a form of creative activity that can also be used just for fun.

What's your story?

Breaking Free from Habitual Interpretations: Cut-up Tarot

One of the biggest drawbacks of even some of the most experienced readers is that we can fall into the trap of interpreting the cards as distinct entities in a reading, rather than as a whole picture. When we do this, it becomes difficult to see the links between the cards or the ways the symbolism interacts between the cards. One way to train ourselves out of this bad habit is to take a leaf out of the book of cut-up theatre, which is a form of *aleatoricism* (discussed earlier). The concept can be traced to at least the Dadaists of the 1920s, but was popularized in the late 1950s and early 1960s by writer William S. Burroughs, and has since been used in a wide variety of contexts. In the context of Tarot, it allows us to view a Tarot reading from a purely symbolic perspective, removing our pre-conceived, pre-learned ideas of Tarot meanings.

With cut-up technique, a poet, for instance, takes pages from a literary work and cuts sentences, blocks of text and words out, then rearranges them at random. An example of this was performed in the 1920s during a Dadaist rally, in which Tristan Tzara created a poem on the spot by pulling words at random from a hat. Later, it is believed that cut-up technique was rediscovered by Brion Gysin in the 1950s, when he placed layers of newspaper as a mat to protect a table top while he cut papers with a razor blade. Upon cutting through the newspapers, Gysin noticed that the sliced layers offered interesting juxtapositions of text and images. He began deliberately cutting newspaper articles into sections and randomly rearranging them. A book – *Minutes to Go* – was born from his experiment. In the 1960s, William S. Burroughs said about cut-up technique:

"When you cut into the present the future leaks out."

This is exactly what we do when we read Tarot, but without the scissors: we cut into the present so that we can gain a glimpse at the future. In this technique, we will use cut-up theory to encourage us to view many cards as one coherent whole, cutting out a new card from those we have placed on the table.

562

You will need:
- ∽ A pack of Tarot cards of your choice (although this exercise can also be done with pages from magazines, any oracle deck, photos, etc. Note that it does work better with borderless cards).
- ∽ A frame of some kind. This can be a picture frame, or you can cut out a frame using plain paper; this technique works best with A5 frames, sometimes slightly smaller, and sometimes slightly larger, depending on the purpose of the technique (eg, how in-depth the question and desired answer is).
- ∽ Optional: a camera

Take the deck/images and place them face up on a flat surface. Swirl them around and mix them up. The idea is to not only shuffle them to obtain the randomness of cards that every Tarot reading should provide, but also to ensure they are in a variety of positions. It doesn't matter if they are so well mixed that some cards are hardly visible beneath a mish-mash of other cards, but try not to leave large gaps of blank space.

When you have a sufficient mish-mash of cards in front of you, without thinking and without looking too closely at the content of the images, allow yourself to be drawn to an area and place your frame over one part of the mish-mash. This framed part is your reading – it is your new aleatorical Tarot card. If you wish to remove all other stimuli, you can also take a photo of this framed area and refer to that.

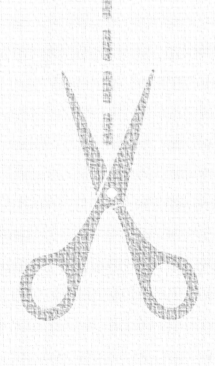

In interpreting this cut-out Tarot reading, your goal is to interpret the image purely on its own merits, not on the merits of the cards it is created from. That it is a conglomerate of the Hierophant, Two of Swords, Four of Wands and Queen of Cups does not matter; what may matter, however, is the presence of any of the words of the card titles. If "Hiero" has found its way into the frame, try interpreting what it means. Don't be afraid to play with words. "Hiero" could be a link to the sacred through the original Greek, or it could seem to you to be a "hero", or perhaps even a name – "Piero".

When you have analysed the imagery from your aleatorical image, give it a title that summarises the meaning it invokes/evokes, for example:

- Cutting Through to Action
- Inputs and Outputs of the Mind
- The Decline of the Feminine
- Resources Lost in Chaos

Cutting Through to Action

Inputs and Outputs of the Mind

There are many more ways in which you can access symbols in the cards during study, or in a reading, in order to deliver a more accurate and profound interpretation of the cards or gain a deeper understanding of the mysteries of the cards. Most importantly, these ways should be a variety of theory and practice – it is through practice that the skills of Tarot reading and accessing symbols are honed.

**The Decline
of the Feminine**

**Resources
Lost in Chaos**

Kindling your Readings to Life

It is easy to take Tarot seriously. As we become more experienced, we begin to ascribe to it a set of principles and practices that encourage a particular approach. Many of us hope to create a successful business from offering professional reading services, so we make our use of Tarot serious and standardised. We put a lot on the Tarot's plate – Tarot is a tool for immense transformation; it can change your life; it offers a way to explore various aspects of yourself and life; it is a journey into the self, a descent into your soul, the Underworld, an immersion in the Universe; Tarot is magic. While all of these are true, they make it easy to forget that Tarot should still be fun, innovative, passionate and daring.

When we view Tarot only as serious business, we start to judge ourselves and our readings. This creates fear and doubt – fear of failure, fear of not keeping up with others, fear of getting it wrong. We begin to ask ourselves if what we are doing is "the right way", which is aggravated by books that tell us what we should and shouldn't do with Tarot. The Tarot world is full of well-defined rules that we think make Tarot easy but in fact just encourage our fear and doubt.

There is no "right way". There is only "your right way".

This does not mean that Tarot should be for entertainment purposes only, but that it should be for entertainment purposes also. We must always try to maintain our sense of fun so that our passion for the Tarot does not die. When we have passion for our art, our readings also become passionate, and we engage our querents more easily in the process of transformation. When we are passionate about a reading, when we have kindled our readings to life, we no longer second guess ourselves and our interpretations. Instead of having an interpretation come to mind that is very different to the accepted meanings of a card and ignoring it, only to discover later in the reading that it was correct, we feel certainty like a fire coursing through our blood. Our revelations in a reading should not be ordinary and rote, but should burn with passion. There are three ways we can attain this passionate approach to Tarot:

- Change the way we think about Tarot.
- Use methods, techniques and skills that encourage passionate readings.
- Engage with, and immerse ourselves in, the reading process and the dialogue we create with the cards.

The following techniques and exercises will help us develop this approach.

Removing the Fear of Not Knowing: Finding your Tarot Voice

With this exercise, the goal is not to remove unknowing or uncertainty, because these are natural, but to not let fear of them override our confidence in a reading. Doubt, in the wider sense of the term, is essential for an enquiring mind, but the fear of it holds us back and prevents us from taking risks and responding more intuitively to a reading. It encourages us to rely on book meanings as a crutch, using them to support ourselves in times of uncertainty.

Every Tarot lover is looking for their own voice. This voice may differ from the voices of others, but each of them is a contribution to the overall expression of Tarot.

One way in which we can remove fear of not knowing and become more confident in our readings is to find a voice with which we can project certainty. For those who have been reading for a long time, finding our confident Tarot voice might be easy – each of us has our own style in which we deliver our readings. However, for those who are still uncertain, new to Tarot, or who wish to reflect more deeply on their Tarot voice, we can turn to the cards themselves for inspiration. To many people, confidence and certainty are represented in the Tarot by cards such as the Emperor, the Queen of Swords or Wands, the King of Wands, or the Magician, but the ability to not fear comes from a different place for each person, and could be any card of the pack. Knowing the nature of our Tarot voice and the way we deliver our readings can also be a firm foundation for confidence and the first step in embodying engaging readings, allowing us to play to our strengths.

Exercise: Finding Your Tarot Voice

Shuffle your deck. Imagine that there is a fire in your heart, and as you breathe in you feed its flames and increase its heat. The flames course through your body, permeating it, each breath making the fire grow hotter and bigger, until it begins to take hold of your hands and the deck that you are shuffling. Ask for your voice of certainty and of power now to be revealed. Pull a single card from the deck. This is your confident Tarot voice.

Study this card. Ask yourself what it means for the source of your confidence. What actions do you need to take to project confidence and build it up? How does this card represent the way in which you deliver readings (or should try delivering readings)?

"I deliver readings by removing all extraneous information and getting straight to the heart of the matter. I do not sugar-coat my readings, even if it will hurt the querent. My confidence comes from knowing that by doing this I will make way for profound realisation and truth."

XVI ✦ The Tower

"My Tarot voice is one of compassion and kindness. It is from this that I gain my confidence: through reading for people, I am helping them and guiding them towards healing. My certainty comes from my deep wisdom and understanding of human emotion."

Ace of Cups

Princess of Wands

"In my Tarot readings, I enter into my power fully and embody my best self. The voice of my readings is of passion and life, and my confidence is infectious: I inspire others with it."

This Tarot voice may not always remain the same. It might change from reading to reading. Why not pull a card before each reading to signify you, the reader, the voice of that reading? Let that card show you what power source you can draw upon for that moment.

Removing the Fear of the Mind Blank: Finding the Keys to a Reading

Another thing that increases our fear and doubt and prevents us from kindling our readings to life is the mind blank that often comes at the beginning of a reading, just after the cards have been laid out. The moment when we stare at the cards and, briefly, have no idea what they could mean, can be the moment when fear of failure creeps in. It can create panic and doubt in our own skills and knowledge, which starts the reading off on the wrong foot. Instead of letting this happen, this moment of blankness can be utilised as a space in which the foundations of the reading can be set.

Finding the keys to a reading is also a matter of choice. There are many options, but only some will be used to give life to the reading.

Although intuition plays a vital role in a Tarot reading, the numbers do too. The mind blank at the beginning of a reading offers you a chance to analyse the cards before you – not for interpretation or symbolism but for a basic headcount.

571

The prevalence of a certain suit or colour, for instance, can inform your reading before you have begun to tackle the symbols and spread. Some things to take note of in this still, quiet moment prior to interpretation include:

⟜ Which suit is most prevalent? This might suggest the area of life the reading is most concerned with, or point to an overwhelming influence of a particular feeling, behaviour or concern. Imbalances of suits can also be significant: no Cups in a relationship reading? Only one Pentacle in a reading about money? Consider what the lack of something, or the dominance of a suit not usually associated with the subject matter of the reading, suggests.

⟜ Do Major or Minor Arcana dominate? If the Major Arcana are the majority, perhaps this is a reading in which a greater number of big issues are involved, whereas more Minor Arcana might suggest lots of smaller issues. These might also indicate the difference between a situation that is easily controlled by the querent (Minors) and one that is out of their hands (Majors).

⟜ How many Court Cards are there? Perhaps a large number of Court Cards indicates that there are lots of people involved in this situation.

⟜ What numbers stand out and what does this mean numerologically? Are there lots of Fives? – conflict could be important in this reading. Perhaps there are many Aces and Ones? – the reading might be about the beginnings of something.

⟜ What colour is most striking and prominent? Perhaps the dominance of reds indicates an active, martial aspect, or the overwhelming "blueness" refers to an emotional reading.

During this moment of quiet reflection and taking stock, you might also notice patterns or other interesting things about the cards that stand out, free from the symbolism and interpretation of the images. By doing this, you will find that before you've begun to interpret the individual cards and their relation to the question, you have a general insight into some of the important themes of the reading.

Example reading using Tarot Apokalypsis.

In this spread, the dominant suits are Wands and Swords, suggesting that the reading may generally be about projects, goals or ambitions related to intellectual pursuits. There are also two Fours and two Aces. Numerologically, the number Four relates to manifestation and foundation, while the number One relates to beginnings and instigation. This suggests that the reading might be about how the querent is moving from the early stages of their project to the stages of fruition and manifestation. There are also a lot of Court Cards – this might suggest that there are many different people, or roles, involved in the project; whether this is a help or hindrance can be explored more in the actual interpretation of the spread. There is only one Major Arcana card, suggesting that this issue will be one of the everyday, mundane world, rather than one concerned with lofty concepts or spiritual ideals. Finally, the dominant colours are red and blue, evoking imagery of fire and ice – perhaps the querent currently has a hot-and-cold relationship with this project?

This technique is particularly useful in larger spreads where more cards are used, and can provide a framework for a more detailed interpretation, as well as begin to guide your interpretation of the cards.

4 of Swords

XIX · The Sun

Prince of Wands

King of Wands

Queen of Swords

4 of Wands

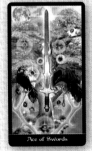
Ace of Swords

Queen of Cups

Ace of Pentacles

Making Your Readings More Dynamic: the 78-card Pick-up

Often, we find that it is difficult to get to the heart of a reading or to feel engaged by the issue the reading is about, especially if it's a question we've heard dozens of times before. This seeps into our readings and can make them dull or prevent us from being confident in their delivery. One way in which we can make our readings more dynamic and encourage an intuitive and outside-the-box approach to Tarot reading is the 78-card pick-up technique.

Those familiar with throwing runes will see some of the influence behind this technique. With runes, rather than drawing single stones and laying them out in a spread (though this is done, it is not necessarily the most common method), the stones will be gently tossed on the reading area – this might be a bare space, or one covered with a reading cloth that is separated into areas representing different aspects of life. The reader will not only interpret the individual meanings of the runes but also where they have landed and how they have landed in relation to each other. Applying this to Tarot, we can break our habitual modes of

Runes are usually made from 24 stones, crystals or staves with engraved ancient norse symbols.

reading by breaking convention: instead of laying down a number of cards in a spread, we take the whole pack (or part of it, if you have small hands) and bend the short edges back (similar to how you would bend a poker deck for a riffle shuffle) so that when we let the cards go from our hands they spring forward in a fountain, falling to the floor. When this is done, before you should be a large spread that you can walk around and through, becoming part of that reading as you move between the cards. You will need to use both your traditional knowledge of the cards (invoking meaning) and an intuitive response to the imagery and patterns (evoking meaning) to interpret this spread.

As you walk among the cards, ask yourself the following questions and consider how they might be interpreted:

- What overall shape have the cards formed? Are they in a straight line ahead of you? Perhaps they are spread out in a puddle? Are there distinct sections in the pattern with gaps between them? Does one group of cards form an arrow pointing to another group of cards?
- Are there patches of colour, or are the colours evenly spread out?
- What types of cards can be seen closest to you and furthest away from you?
- Are there one or two cards that have fallen far from the main group? Which cards are they?
- Are some cards face down? How many of them? Do you feel this means they should not be read? Or are these the cards that represent hidden forces?
- How wide an area do the cards cover? If a small area, perhaps the issue is very focused; if a wide area, perhaps it is more general or affects many people/parts of the querent's life.

When you have gained a general understanding of the pattern of the cards, you can begin to interpret individual cards and how their meanings relate to their position among the other cards. You can also invite the querent, if you are reading for somebody else, to walk among the cards with you, entering into their own spread. This can help to engage the querent in interpretation. This technique also encourages you to see the links between cards in a reading and break free from habits that are holding you back.

Delivering the Goods:
Three-Sentence Readings

When we are uncertain of our interpretation, it can be tempting to try to pad it out in order to hedge our bets – the more we say, the more likely we are to be accurate on at least some points, and the more likely a querent is to find something that rings true. However, this approach does us a great disservice and trains us to doubt ourselves, allowing us to be drawn unknowingly into the world of cold reading and Barnum statements (which are not necessarily bad, but which many readers try to avoid due to the negative press they have received in the industry). These sorts of readings also do the querent a disservice, as they run the risk of throwing so much information at them (some of which might be irrelevant) that they find it difficult to take away the vital messages of the reading.

In order to wean ourselves off this approach, create more confidence in our readings and ensure the vital information is delivered and impactful, try condensing the reading down to three sentences. In those three sentences, you need to convey as much of the useful information as possible without losing anything important. Consider the language you use.

Ask yourself:

- Is it impactful?
- Is it persuasive?
- Is it concise?

A good reading is a useful reading, not an accurate reading.
This is because the reading ends only when the querent has incorporated it into their life and gained something from it.

These three sentences can also be used as a conclusion to a normal reading to tie it together and ensure the most important messages are remembered. If you want a challenge, try this exercise using increasingly larger spreads, and try to practice creating concise overviews and conclusions that can be used to end a reading and refocus the querent on the most important messages.

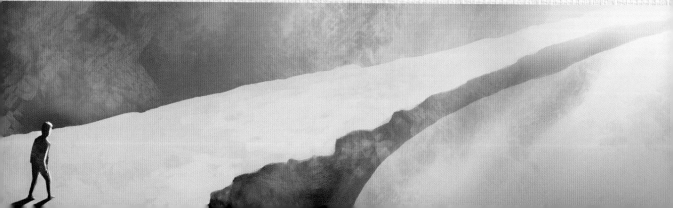

Example reading for Sophia using the Tarot Apokalypsis.

A significant emotional loss (*5 of Cups*) forms the foundation (*at the bottom of the spread*) of a calling towards a spiritual journey and draws you into the darkness of your Self (*8 of Cups*). However, do not be afraid of this darkness (*9 of Swords*): travelling through it, you will find a light of guidance and illumination (*the Star, at the top of the reading*). Look to history and established wisdom (*Princess of Swords*) for an idea of how to push through this dark time.

If you use this technique as an exercise, write down the three sentences you have created so that you can look back at them. When reviewing them, ask yourself what aspects of the cards you left out and why. This will give some insight into your Tarot voice, concise language and how to avoid repetition. You might also find it useful to record a full interpretation of the reading first and then create the three sentences, and compare the two to see how you condensed the reading down.

II ✦ The High Priestess

The High Priestess from Tarot Apokalypsis depicts Persephone seated at the entrance to the underworld in which initiates are transformed; the card is inspired by the ancient Greek Eleusinian Mysteries.

Transformative Tarot

The most common and widespread use of Tarot is as a tool for divination and fortune-telling. With these uses, it is not just a mundane tool but also one of reflection, questioning and spiritual guidance – Tarot readers quickly learn that the spiritual world and our inner lives are not separate from the everyday world. However, the Tarot can be more even than this, and can form the foundation of continuous initiation into mystery. With Tarot we can attain knowledge and understanding, wisdom and insight. With Tarot we can look into the past, present and future and use the information to choose the path before us consciously. With Tarot we can make informed choices.

But Tarot offers us more than this: the step forward from all these things is transformation.

We are constantly undergoing transformation on all levels – we can't help it. On a cellular level our bodies are constantly breaking down and destroying themselves, renewing what has been lost. Intellectually and emotionally, we learn something new every day. Each experience is a learning opportunity. We take in new stimuli and respond according-ly, our behaviour changing over time based on experience. Our physical, emotional and intellectual transformations inspire spiritual transformation (and vice versa), and we can use Tarot to help us through these changes. In this context, Tarot serves many functions:

 1. It helps us to choose consciously the **moment**, **moti-vation** and **mode** of our transformation.
 2. It helps us engage with our subconscious and uncon-scious, transferring our choice of transformation from the conscious to the place where it acts in our inner landscape.
 3. It allows us to take control of our transformation and become active participants in it rather than passive followers.

The three aspects of transformation – moment, motivation and mode – are engaged with as needed. The moment of transformation refers to its temporal aspects – it takes place during, and as a result of, a specific moment in time

XIII ✦ Death

Death is usually the card that indicates transformation.

that brings with it specific experiences. The motivation of transformation refers to our reasons for undergoing transformation, which are informed by all aspects of our lives. The mode of transformation refers to the way in which we achieve that transformation, the approach we use. Not all techniques of transformation engage all three aspects of it.

The imagery and organisation of the Tarot is designed to help us access and engage with our less conscious thoughts and to explore with awareness our conscious thoughts. It speaks in the language of symbolism, and thus helps us to integrate on all levels any transformation that we undergo. The landscapes of each card are a direct reflection of the landscapes of our inner world as well as the landscape of the wider universe: *As above, so below; as without, so within.*

Every card of the Tarot has been designed to express some smaller part of the Greater Mystery. Each card is one star in the firmament of stars that represent Unity. Thus, every Tarot card stands before us, as the High Priestess does, as an Initiator into that Mystery, both barring the way and opening it when we are ready.

In the Greek mystery cult of the goddess Demeter at Eleusis, initiates would enter the Telesterion – the initiation hall – much like that which the High Priestess of the Tarot guards, and undergo a threefold rite of transformation:

1. *Dromena* ("things done"), a dramatic re-enactment of the Demeter/Persephone myth.
2. *Deiknumena* ("things shown"), a display of sacred objects, in which the hierophant (high priest of the cult) played an essential role.
3. *Legomena* ("things said"), commentaries that accompanied the *deiknumena*.

Combined, these three elements were known as the *apporheta* ("unrepeatables"); the penalty for divulging them was death.

Transformational Tarot is a combination of these three things, although we often, as readers, only focus on the *legomena*, with a brief foray into the *deiknumena*. When we put all three parts of the mysteries together in our Tarot practice, we create something that can be so profound that it is unspeakable: not because it is wrong to speak it, but because the change occurs on such a personal and profound level that we often cannot put it into words.

To explore transformational Tarot, we'll look at some ritual and magical techniques that can be applied to the Tarot to initiate us into the deeper mysteries of self and the universe. This will help us to turn our usual divinatory practice into an oracular opportunity for powerful transition.

Affirmations and Intention Setting

Engaging the **moment** and **motivation** of our transformation.

Intention is possibly the most powerful force available to an individual.

Giving the querent an affirmation or helping them set an intention can be a great way to conclude a reading, make it transformational and engage yourself or the querent in proactive, informed, and continuous transformation. It is also useful to begin other transformational work with this technique, which can take your Tarot readings from simple divination to life-changing events.

Sometimes during a reading a particular card will speak more loudly than others or resonate more with the querent. It may represent the heart of the matter, or offer profound advice for moving forward. This card can be used to create an affirmation or set an intention for the querent to take away from the reading with them, helping them transform the moment of transformation they experienced during the reading into a long-term plan. Alternatively, a card could be pulled from the deck, or chosen from the deck (or the reading) to represent what the querent can aspire to or the intention/goal they can set. In order to create an affirmation using this card, the querent needs to be very clear about what they want or what their goal is.

There are (broadly) four types of affirmations:

- **Habit change (specific)** – quitting smoking, limiting procrastination, stopping stress eating, not making excuses, complaining less, remembering names, etc.
- **Attitude building** – enhancing self-esteem, being more responsible, engaging in positive thinking, being more compassionate, etc.
- **Motivational** – having more energy, belief, trust, desire, purpose, etc.
- **Situational (broad)** – achieving better grades, getting a new job, maintaining a loving marriage, improving health, paying more attention to friends, etc.

An effective affirmation should fulfil three criteria:

- ✐ It should be **Positive**
- ✐ It should be **Personal**
- ✐ It should be stated in the **Present Tense**.

The first is because positivity creates transformation, and speaking in negatives (such as "I will not fail") is not as powerful for the mind. The mind easily discounts "not" in a sentence, so "I will not fail" quickly becomes "I will fail". Further, by repeating such a sentence, we are placing the focus on what we do not want, rather than what we do want, which makes us less motivated. The second – that the affirmation should be personal – is because we can only ever make affirmations for ourselves, not for others. We cannot control how others think or change how they feel – we only have power over our own perceptions and reactions. The last – that the affirmation should be stated in the present tense – is a powerful tool for triggering the mind into believing that the change is happening now, rather than in an unknown future time. It urges us towards action straight away and makes us aware of what we can do now to create the change we want to see.

The process of creating an affirmation:

- ✐ **1.** Begin the affirmation creation by placing the chosen card in front of you and the querent and discussing what the card means. You may already have explored this in detail during the reading, so you can draw upon how the card relates to the querent's question and their life at this time.
- ✐ **2.** Visualize/imagine the eventual goal in personal, real terms. The querent could visualize and describe showcasing their artwork in a gallery, shaking hands with a boss of the company they want to work for, trekking through the rainforest on the trip of a lifetime they want the courage to take, or embracing the sister they've been too afraid to reconcile with.
- ✐ **3.** Brainstorm the goal and what might be needed to achieve it, as well as any imagery that the querent associates with it.
- ✐ **4.** Using your discussion and brainstorm, choose a pronoun (I, my...).
- ✐ **5.** Continuing to use your discussion of the card, choose a verb in the present tense (am, feel, will, act, speak, give, offer, receive, etc) or, if you have chosen "my" as a pronoun, a noun appropriate to the goal ("My will..." "My body...").

6. Go from there to complete the affirmation. This is a creative process, but the Tarot card you are using should be kept in mind. What does it represent? What is the figure doing? How are they acting? What is their demeanour? What does the environment offer? What resources are available to the figure in the card? You should end up with a sentence that is positive, personal and present, which encapsulates the querent's goal or intention.

Examples

0 ⬧ The Fool

2 of Cups

10 of Swords

The Fool:
*"I embrace
the new beginnings
being offered to me and
accept opportunities
with joy."*

Two of Cups:
*"I love
compassionately
and use my emotional
experiences to heal
others."*

Ten of Swords:
*"My wounds are
learning opportunities,
and I transform through
suffering to freedom."*

IX. the Hermit

Princess of Cups

Queen of Swords

The Hermit:
*"I shine my light
out into the world and
share my wisdom with
others."*

Princess of Cups:
*"I am inspired by the
everyday world and create
powerful artwork from my
experiences."*

Queen of Swords:
*"I express
myself clearly and
enjoy public speaking."*

The querent can take this affirmation away with them – you could write it on your business card or a piece of paper, or they could simply remember it. Perhaps, if you have a deck that is missing a card or two, you could write the affirmation on one of those cards.

This affirmation can be used by repeating it a certain number of times upon waking in the morning, when you are looking in the mirror, every time you step into your workplace, whenever you start your car, whenever you sit down at your keyboard or sit at your easel, or walking home after dropping the kids off at school. It should be made repetitive and part of a routine. You can perhaps put a copy of the affirmation on your wall, ceiling, mirror or work desk for added reminders throughout the day.

To make this affirmation even more effective, there may be something that comes from your discussion or visualization that relates to an action or gesture you do every day. "I wear my achievements with pride" or "I surround myself with protection" could relate to the action of putting on a coat or jacket; "I take the reins of my destiny" could be the act of steering a car; laying down to sleep could be the action that reminds you of the Ten of Swords and its affirmation. Pair the affirmation with these actions. Eventually, you will find that you have performed the repetition of the affirmation with the associated action so often that only the action is required to transform your state of mind. This is a powerful tool for turning your everyday world and the most mundane of tasks into an opportunity for positive change.

Sigilisation and Triggers for Transformation

Using the **motivation** of transformation to create the **moment** of transformation repeatedly.

The technique of sigilisation can be used as a standalone technique or as an extension of an affirmation. Sigilisation is the act of making your intent, will and desire into an abstract symbol that can be used to bypass the doubting mind and be plugged directly into the creative mind, the subconscious, or unconscious. The sigil can be seen as a seed that is planted, there to grow to fruition as a manifested goal. Importantly, sigils are a form of symbol, so they function in a similar way to the symbols found in the Tarot, and they can be used in conjunction with Tarot to create transformation.

The traditional method of sigilisation is as follows:
1. Form a sentence using positive phrases in the present tense (affirmations), such as "I am my ideal bodyweight" (rather than "I wish to lose 10lbs").
2. Remove from the sentence all the vowels and any repeated consonants after the first one. "I am my ideal body weight" becomes MYDLBWGHT.

585

3. Combine the remaining letters through a series of iterations into a "magicalish" glyph. How they are combined is up to you, and you may go through several possibilities before you discover the one that feels right. At this stage, the glyph – or sigil – does not have to look anything like the original string of letters.

4. Activate the sigil. There are several ways of doing this. Some people pray over the sigil. Others perform ecstatic trance dance while focusing on the sigil. Some chant while focusing on it. Others engage in sex magic and fire the sigil off into the universe at the moment of climax. The important thing is to make sure that the sigil is embedded in your mind.

5. Forget the sigil. Destroy the copy or copies of it you have made, thus removing it from your conscious mind and allowing it to work more fully in your subconscious. Alternatively, you could take the opposite approach and continually be reminded of the sigil, as one would with an affirmation. Both ways are effective.

Always remember that symbols have power.

To use this technique with Tarot we use symbols instead of a sentence.

- **1.** Take a card that represents your goal.
- **2.** Write down several symbols that stand out to you.
- **3.** Remove any symbols that begin with a vowel.
- **4.** Remove any symbols that are found more than twice in the image.
- **5.** Remove any symbol that ends in a vowel.
- **6.** Make very simple line drawings of the remaining symbols – simplify them as much as possible.
- **7.** Combine these into one symbol to create your sigil.

In this way, you can extend your affirmation practice using a card to a powerful magical technique that will drive your subconscious towards your goal more effectively.

Self-Initiation and Dedication

Engaging the **moment** and **mode** of our transformation.

When we begin to undergo transformation, we often push forward from the beginning with a burst of energy, which later trails off. We find that our transition also loses its power, so we get stuck and stop moving forward. Tarot readings can be a bit like this: querents receive readings and leave feeling empowered and positive about what they can do to engage with their lives and make the changes they need, only to find that two weeks later they have returned to their old selves. Many querents use Tarot as a brief balm to soothe their tired spiritual muscles, quickly returning to the old habits that gave them so many aches and pains in the first place. But it is important to remember that while Tarot should be a fun way of providing ourselves with entertainment, making choices, or gaining insight, it can become too easy to use it to decorate the walls of our cages to give ourselves fleeting happiness and peace. But many people leave it like that, and forget to use the Tarot to get back home. How can we help ourselves and our querents turn a resolution from a reading into self-initiation and dedication, ensuring the transformation is long-lasting and profound?

587

Using the philosophies of Aristotle's habituation theory and the Hindu practice of bhakti yoga, we can attain greater unity with the cards that represent goals given to us during a reading. Aristotle's habituation theory states that a person can become virtuous by habitually practicing virtuous deeds; after enough habitual practice, they cease to just be virtuous deeds and become deeds performed by a virtuous person, as the person has taken virtuousness into themselves. A querent might come away from a reading with the realization that some of their problems are caused by a lack of compassion towards others, resolving to practice compassion more actively in their everyday lives, yet after a brief time they may forget to do this and veer from their course, giving themselves no time to habituate the practice of compassion. Taking a card that represents compassion – perhaps the Ace of Cups or the Six of Pentacles – and dedicating a certain amount of time to letting that card lead their lives, might allow their resolution to become habit more quickly.

The Hindu practice of Bhakti yoga is devotional yoga. It is designed to bring the devotee closer to their chosen deity, and eventually attain true unity with it. The Bhagavata Purana (7.5.23–24) teaches nine primary forms of bhakti:

1. **śravaṇa** ("listening" to the scriptural stories of Krishna and his companions)
2. **kīrtana** ("praising", usually referring to ecstatic group singing)
3. **smaraṇa** ("remembering" or fixing the mind on Vishnu)
4. **pāda-sevana** (rendering service)
5. **arcana** (worshiping an image)
6. **vandana** (paying homage)
7. **dāsya** (servitude)
8. **sākhya** (friendship)
9. **ātma-nivedana** (complete surrender of the self).

One way we can use Tarot to kickstart and continue our transformation is through applying these nine principles of bhakti yoga to working with the cards. It can be a continuation from a reading, affirmation, or intention setting, and is also a useful and profound way to learn more about the cards.

Yoga can be a whole journey by itself, independent from Tarot.

First, choose a card that represents your resolution (or that you want to develop a greater understanding of). Keep it near a place where you, every day, have time to yourself, and once a day take that card and spend time with it. In this time you can examine it, speak to it, journal it and more. Let it tell you what affirmation, goal, or aspect of your resolution you are to explore today. Keep that intention in your mind as you go through your day. As you continue this practice over time with a card that represents your goal, spend several days on each of the nine bhakti yoga practices, in order.

589

1. To "listen" to the card, read about what others have said about it.

2. To "praise" the card, write your own meanings of it, write poetry about it, create your own version of it.

3. To "remember" or "fix your mind" on the card, memorize it until you can see it and pick out every detail in your mind's eye. Study it, and you will find details coming out that you didn't know of before.

4. To "render service" to that card, perform acts in your everyday life that carry the message of that card or a particular aspect of it.

5. To "worship the image", collect as many versions of the card as you can, collage them, keep a scrapbook of them, and then collect images of that card's message in action.

6. To "pay homage" to that card, create a shrine to it. Surround it with items that represent the message of that card.

7. For "servitude", actively perform worship/offerings to that shrine, perhaps using the poems, hymns, and praises you have written.

8. For "friendship" of that card, carry it with you wherever you go, and imagine it as a person walking with you, living your life with you. Undertake conversations with it in your mind's eye (or out loud, if you wish). Allow it to take on a personality.

9. By the time you reach the stage of "complete surrender of the self", the messages of the card should be so embedded in your life that you are acting on them without a second thought, thereby achieving habituation of your desired transformation or goal.

Through this, you can also create an effective self-initiation. Using this practice, you live the principles and the mysteries of that card every day and are constantly aware of it, surrendering yourself to it, immersing yourself in it. You can discover more not only about the card but also about its mystery and about yourself.

Pathworking, Vision Quests, Meditation and Reflection

Discovering the **motivation** and **mode** of our transformation in our chosen **moment**.

Pathworking is a commonly recommended technique for gaining a deeper understanding of the Tarot and the mysteries that it holds, but it is also a useful technique for self-reflection and exploration both on a spiritual, psychological and emotional level. It is best known in the form developed by Carl Jung, called active imagination, a meditation technique in which the contents of the unconscious are translated into images, narratives or entities separate to the self.

The unconscious can spark a visual journey within the self.

"[Y]ou choose a dream, or some other fantasy-image, and concentrate on it by simply catching hold of it and looking at it. … You then fix this image in the mind by concentrating your attention. Usually it will alter, as the mere fact of contemplating it animates it. The alterations must be carefully noted down all the time, for they reflect the psychic processes in the unconscious background, which appear in the form of images consisting of conscious memory material. In this way conscious and unconscious are united, just as a waterfall connects above and below."
Carl Jung, The Conjunction, Collected Works, Vol. 14, par. 706.

Jung goes on to say that instead of merely observing the sequence of events, the individual takes part in the scene, as if they are not the controller of the fantasy sequence, but a participator or character therein, becoming "an acting and suffering figure in the drama of the psyche". As the scenes in which the pathworking or meditation take place are symbolic, the landscapes of the cards of the Tarot provide a rich world to explore, allowing discovery of the self and the universe. You can use the technique to initiate yourself into the mysteries of a specific card – this is particularly good for the Major Arcana, which represent abstract, universal mysteries. Instead of an initiation rite being performed in the real world with actual implements and rituals, it is performed in the creative mind, in the subconscious, in the imagination; the rite is just as powerful here as in real life, while being unburdened by mundane limitations (cost, physical space, etc).

The technique for pathworking with a Tarot card is simple, and parts of it will be familiar to those who have practiced guided

It may be difficult to journal visual and spiritual experiences. It may be useful to utilize symbols and associations to make appropriate notes. Tarot card images can also be used.

meditations previously. The main difference between guided meditation and pathworking is that the former follows a script that the meditator simply imagines, while the latter is not scripted and is created actively by the imagination or subconscious.

1. Prepare the space and the self (this may be done in any way you wish).

2. Set your goal. What is it you wish to gain from this pathworking? What do you wish to discover? You can choose a symbol or image that you will set as the signpost of finding your goal during your pathworking.

3. Visualize the starting point for the pathworking – in this case, the starting point is the image of the chosen Tarot card, memorised so that it can be seen clearly in the mind's eye.

4. Project into the visualized scene. Imagine the Tarot card opening up like a doorway, allowing you to step into the scene.

5. Experience the main vision. Interact with the scene you find and explore it more deeply. Allow the landscape to expand beyond the card you have memorised and be populated with landmarks, beings, places, sensations and experiences.

6. Arrive at your destination point. This will be represented by the symbol or image you have chosen as a signpost of your goal, or you will simply know when you have completed your journey.

7. End the pathworking. This is traditionally done by imagining yourself returning through the landscape you have explored, back the way you came.

Many people find it helpful to journal their experiences. You may find that one pathworking of a card raises more questions or highlights new areas of that card to explore – this can be done with subsequent pathworkings of the same card.

It is interesting to note that since the 22 Major Arcana cards are embedded with the system of the Kabbalistic Tree of Life, and each card represents a path on this tree, they can be used to pathwork the Tree of Life. The Tree of Life is considered to symbolically represent the entire universe and its mysteries, encapsulating a mystical system of attaining spiritual enlightenment. In this system, the Major Arcana are pathworked in order beginning with the World nearest the base of the tree (and therefore closest to our experiential, mundane world) and working our way back up to unity with the Fool at the top of the tree (and therefore closest to divine oneness).

The Tree of Life is an abstract construct. But any tree can become a symbol for it.

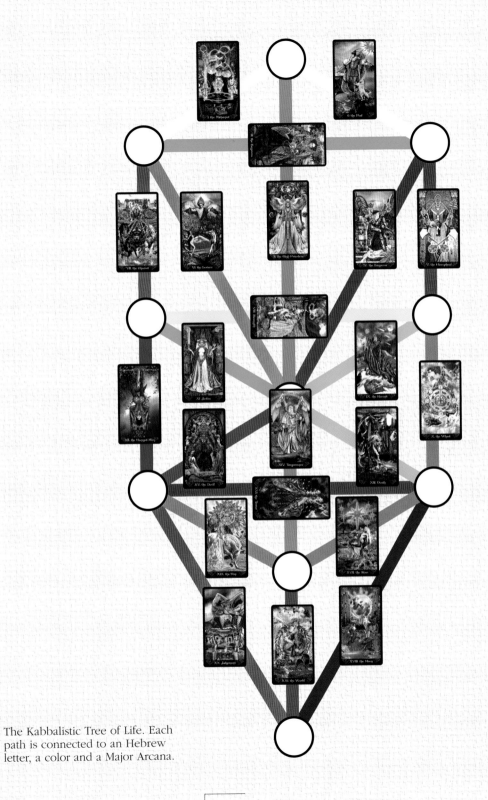

The Kabbalistic Tree of Life. Each path is connected to an Hebrew letter, a color and a Major Arcana.

Atavistic Resurgence
and Tarot Card Reversals

Awakening the **motivation** through **mode** and **moment**.

"Atavistic resurgence, a primal urge towards union with the Divine by returning to the common source of all, is indicated by the backward symbolism peculiar to all Sabbath ceremonies, as also of many ideas connected with witchcraft, sorcery and magic. Whether it be the symbol of the moon presiding over nocturnal ecstasies; the words of power chanted backwards; the back-to-back dance performed in opposition to the sun's course; the devil's tail – are all instances of reversal and symbolic of Will and Desire turning within and down to subconscious regions, to the remote past, there to surprise the required atavistic energy for purposes of transformation, healing, initiation, construction or destruction."

Kenneth Grant, Hidden Lore: Hermetic Glyphs.

Transformation, as expressed by the Death card of the Pagan Tarot.

XIII DEATH XIII

LA MORTE
LA MORT

LA MUERTE
DER TOD

Many people avoid reversals in their Tarot readings because they can be hard to read, hard to analyse, and unpleasant to look at: who enjoys looking at upside-down artwork? However, the reversed card(s) in a reading can be a turning point for transformation. In the above quote, Kenneth Grant – based on the work of occultist and artist Austin Osman Spare – has given us a clue as to what else we could use reversals for: turning the Will and Desire within and down into the subconscious region, where the deeper, more primal and unconscious energy lies. Once the Will and Desire are there, they can use this energy for transformation, initiation, healing, etc. Will and Desire are vital for any transformation to take place.

A reversed card that speaks loudly in a reading, or is alone, might suggest that it should be used for atavistic resurgence, whereby a greater unity or understanding can be gained by "going backwards" to a point of origin or a deeply rooted state of being. This reversed card can help us discover the nature of both our Will and Desire and direct us to a source of immense energy otherwise ignored and untapped within us.

We can utilize a reversed card to move the reading from divination to engagement and transformation. The technique uses similar methods to sigilisation, but takes it one step further by "burying" the sigil somewhere deep within the self, where it can awaken the dormant atavistic energy within.

The technique for using a reversed card for atavistic resurgence:

1. Have the reversed card in front of you. Whether you choose to work with it upright (so you can more clearly see it) or reversed (as that is how it fell) is up to you.

2. Ask yourself: What is my Will? Let your eyes fall on one symbol in the card.

3. Ask yourself: What is my Desire? Let your eyes fall on another symbol in the card.

4. Merge these two symbols together to create a unique sigil. As with the sigilisation technique discussed earlier, the two symbols do not have to be distinguishable in this sigil.

5. Memorise the sigil you have created until you can clearly visualize it in your mind's eye.

6. Pathwork with the sigil, using the reversed card itself as the gateway into the pathworking. Take the sigil with you, as if you were carrying it. Allow yourself to descend deep into your active imagination with this pathworking, exploring the landscape thoroughly. Try to go as far as you can into this inner world.

7. When you have gone as far as you can into this inner world, place the sigil there. Imagine yourself burying it in there, and then return without it.

8. An alternative method to this is not to use the card as a gateway but to use a memory from your past, and to take the sigil "back in time", placing it at a point in your past where you feel the challenge, blockage or problem began.

This technique can use Tarot and symbolism to instigate profound change in your life.

"...It is like Aristotle's view that men being initiated have not a lesson to learn, but an experience to undergo and a condition into which they must be brought, while they are becoming fit (for revelation)."

Synesius Dio 1133

*Transformational Tarot
can be seen in the
Three of Pentacles. The
three figures in the traditional images of the card,
or the three pentacles
themselves, are symbolic
of the three alchemical
ingredients required for
the Great Work: Sulphur,
Mercury and Salt. These
also represent blood, sweat
and tears, or mind, body
and spirit.*

Transformational Tarot can be seen in the Three of Pentacles.
The three figures in the traditional images of the card, or the
three pentacles themselves, are symbolic of the three alchemical
ingredients required for the Great Work: Sulphur, Mercury and
Salt. These also represent blood, sweat and tears, or mind, body
and spirit. Together, they remind us of what must be put into a
process of transformation in order for it to be effective. There is
a clear structure prescribed in a great many systems throughout
the world for effecting transformation – the Tarot itself has become allied with some of them (such as alchemy and Kabbalah).

However, the Tarot is also a versatile, creative and engaging tool
for enabling us to become active participants in our stories, our
transformation and our lives. It combines the threefold parts of
initiation – dromena (things done), deiknumena (things shown)
and legomena (things said) – to create a phenomenal, personal
and profound change in the self, and by extension in the
world. By taking Tarot outside the box, we can effect change in
ourselves and the world in accordance with our will – we can
create magic. With Tarot, we are always enacting an initiation:
the cards are the initiators standing at the temple doors, letting
us pass. We must remember that transformation through Tarot is
not about lessons to be learned but things to be experienced.

Theresa Reed

Hey! It's me, Theresa Reed.

As a Catholic schoolgirl with a superstitious mother and a grandma who felt omens like other folks feel arthritis, it's not too surprising that Tarot, astrology, and other intuitive arts would become my driving fascination—and my life's work. I picked up my first Tarot deck at age fifteen and kick-started my career by performing readings on my little sister. (Most of her questions were about the cute boys in class. Some things never change.) Thirtyish years later, I've done readings on thousands of clients—from teachers to recovering addicts to new mothers to angst-ridden teens to small-business owners and powerhouse CEOs. In addition to doing private, confidential Tarot readings, I also lead Tarot workshops, speak at Tarot conferences, cohost a podcast for spiritual business owners, and dip my toes into lots of other Tarot-licious projects.

THE ART OF TEACHING TAROT

Just as Tarot is a calling, so is teaching. Not every Tarot reader will want to take on the role of instructor, but for those who do, it can be a rewarding path. It's a chance to share your experience and wisdom - and to help others understand the cards.

While book learning can suffice (and in some cases, may be the only thing available), there is nothing better than a live class with a seasoned pro. With a teacher by your side, you have the chance to ask questions and get hands-on practice. This speeds up the learning curve and offers a chance to go deeper, faster. You can't get that from a book. An experiential approach is far better.
If you've been reading Tarot for a while, at some point, you may feel called to teach. It's also possible that you may come across more than a few clients who are interested in learning more. They might even request that you start teaching.
It may seem intimidating (just like learning Tarot cards), but with some solid strategies and a bit of courage, you, too, can start teaching Tarot.

Teaching is important. There are limits to what one can learn only from a book.

The call to teach

Let's begin by discussing the call to teach. As I stated above, not everyone is interested in teaching. After all, it's a big task. Lesson plans, homework, tests, not to mention dealing with student dynamics – this is no small feat.

But for those who feel the pull, none of that matters. The responsibilities and burdens become par for the course. The call to teach Tarot is a passionate invitation from your heart and soul. When that call comes, you cannot deny it. You know you must answer it, even if you're not sure you're ready.

Teaching Tarot is a hero's journey. It's a mystical adventure with the chance to spark curiosity and wonder in the minds and hearts of your students. Also, it's an opportunity to shine a bright light on the cards, unravel the mysteries within, and leave a legacy.

It requires pure devotion. Devotion to the cards, the craft, and your students.

It's that devotion that makes a good teacher extraordinary. If you feel that down to your marrow, then you're ready to teach Tarot.

What makes a teacher great

While devotion and passion are necessary elements, there are two other qualities that make a Tarot teacher great. One is knowing your stuff. Which means you should have a fair amount of experience. A thorough understanding of the cards is a must. You should not be reliant on only books. Reading with diverse audiences and situations will also make you a better teacher. If your body of knowledge is weak, it will undermine your student's learning. They deserve an experienced teacher who knows what they are talking about - not someone who just "wings it."

The second thing you need is compassion. Here's why: a compassionate teacher who cares about their students and their experience is going to forge a better connection with

A teacher, or a guide, can be an important person in the life of others. It can be a joyful responsibility.

them. The holier-than-thou teacher looking for guru-worship or a pedestal to perch on is unapproachable. These types may exude an aura of confidence that some might find appealing, but most students will just find that attitude off-putting. A caring teacher who takes the time to make her students feel heard and respected is a more effective one.

The role of the teacher - take your seat

The role of the teacher is that of a guide or mentor. It's a position that must be treated with respect, both by the students and the teacher. Which means that, although you want to be friendly, it's important that you create clear boundaries immediately or you risk problems with the students.

Boundaries are important because they help to maintain a respectful atmosphere. They also protect you from the small percentage of students who might be problematic. While it may be rare that a Tarot student turns out to be a trouble-maker, it does happen. And when it does, it can disrupt the learning experience for everyone else.

You'll need to get clear on what your policies are - and then you need to enforce them. For example, if you insist that homework be done before the next session, then that needs to be mandatory. No exceptions, period. If you create rules for your classroom, but don't follow through, then they are not rules. Consider what policies might be important for you, then outline them for your students. Be sure to also outline the consequences as well. Students need to know that there are repercussions when rules are broken, and they need to understand what those might be. An example might be this: "If you miss three classes, you will be dropped as a student. This series requires participation and missing too many classes will hinder your experience as well as the experience of your classmates."

You'll also want to be clear on your availability. Can students talk with you after class hours? Will you allow for after class discussions? Are you available for consultations via email? If so, to what extent? Keep in mind that, while an open door policy could be helpful for your students, you also run the risk of a needy one taking up a lot of your free time. You are not required to be available 24/7.

Socializing with your students could also be problematic, because this can blur lines. Keep this to a minimum, and you'll avoid potential issues. Find the balance between being friendly without being friends. It's not easy, but it will keep drama to a minimum.

Where to teach

With the advent of the internet, the possibilities of teaching are immense. You are no longer relegated to a physical classroom, although some may find that route to be preferable. Online offers opportunities to teach via webcast, conference line, or teleseminar. If you are thinking about teaching online, you'll want to do your research to find a medium that makes the most sense for you. For many modern Tarot readers, this is the way to go, because you can reach more people and it's convenient.

A physical classroom requires a bit of legwork and research. Will you teach in your home? If not, how about a library or a coworking space? There are many options, some free, others not. Look for a space that meets your needs - and your budget. You'll want to make sure the room is welcoming and comfortable with plenty of space as well as access to a bathroom. Tables are vital for teaching Tarot - a cramped coffee shop with tiny tabletops will prove to be a hassle. Big surfaces that allow you to spread out the cards is a must.

If required, you'll want to have WI-FI available as well as pens and paper. If you're doing a PowerPoint presentation, you'll also want to make sure you have access to a screen and projector. Refreshments and snacks are optional but at the very least, consider having water, coffee, and tea.

The environment, both phsyical and social, will likely affect the quality and the flavour of your teaching.

SETTING UP FOR SUCCESS

Whether you're online or in person, you'll want to set yourself up for a successful class. That means: creating your material in advance and going through a practice run before you step foot in the classroom.

Your material may include: teaching notes, the syllabus (the outline of what you're teaching), any necessary handouts, as well as slides if you're doing a PowerPoint presentation.

In order to be successful it's necessary to focus on the target and be confident of yourself.

A clear syllabus creates a template for a successful learning experience. This begins by determining what your goal is.

For example, if you want to teach an introductory class on the Major Arcana to complete newbies, you would need to develop your curriculum to reflect that. You certainly wouldn't add in advanced techniques and a complex history of Tarot art because it wouldn't make sense.

Determine your goals and then outline how those goals might be reached. Would your class involve lectures? Would there be time to practice? Is there going to be Q&A with you? What steps might you need to lead the students through to reach your goal?

Next, outline the class or lesson plan (you'll need a lesson plan if you are teaching an ongoing series). Make sure the class follows a logical plan that leads directly to the goal.

Example

If you teach a class on Major Arcanas, you might want to begin with an introductory lecture about the Major Arcana with a PowerPoint presentation (if your class is live). From there, you might have to allow a little Q&A followed by a series of practical exercises. A short period of Q&A can smooth out any issues or additional questions that came up during the practice round. This can be finished with assignments or a recap of what has been learned.

Make an outline for yourself - and another one for the students. I recommend having a handout or, if your class is online, a slide with the syllabus outlined.

Class length

The class length will vary but in general, a two-hour class seems to be the best. Too short, and the material feels rushed. Too long, and boredom sets in. Two hours leaves enough time for lecture, practicum, and Q+A, plus a little break.

Set the tone

Your number one concern is to make sure that your students are comfortable. Remember: learning a new skill can be scary - especially if you're in a group of strangers. A good teacher creates an environment that feels safe and secure.

Which means beginning with a warm introduction. Take a minute to introduce yourself and briefly describe your Tarot background. It also bears mentioning: a smile goes a long way to make people feel relaxed.

Set expectations immediately. Let students know what the class is about, how the day is going to proceed, and any policies you may have. This gives your students a clear idea of what to expect going forward. Plus, it also sets the tone for you as the teacher.

A typical class might follow this structure:

- **Introduction**
- **Housekeeping** (structure of the class, policies, breaks, location of restroom, etc.)
- **Lecture**
- **Practicum**
- **Q&A**

If this is an ongoing series, expectations for the next class should be discussed.

- **Closing.**

What you're really doing

The key word for teaching is "inspiration". It's not about knowledge, or information. That can be supplied by a book. It's about vision.

You might think teaching is simply passing on information. While sharing knowledge is a large part of the teacher's role, the truly great teachers don't just teach. They INSPIRE. This is what you should be aiming for every time you open up the doors to your Tarot classroom.

HOW CAN YOU DO THAT?

Be passionate!

Bring your passion for Tarot front and center. Remember: you want to EXCITE your students and get them jazzed about Tarot! If you don't care, why should they? A teacher who is enthusiastic about the material is an effective teacher.

Be creative!

Come up with interesting, memorable assignments that will keep your students engaged – and talking about the lessons long after they are done.

Come up with exercises that drive the point home in a fun, practical and useful way. Above all, be as interactive as possible. In fact, encourage it between the students with interesting exercises that get them shuffling and talking.

Your students have their own passions. Their passion, their creativity and their heart will respond to your teachings.

What to avoid: dry, linear lectures. You may think you sound scholarly, but you're probably boring your students to tears and chances are, they won't retain much if they're not interested.

Teach from the heart

Make it personal. Share YOUR stories. Don't be afraid to be vulnerable with your students. Students love a teacher they can relate to. The most effective teachers are personable.

It's not about you – it's about THEM.

While sharing your stories is a way to drive a point home or make a connection, don't waste your student's time by going on a diatribe about your life. Remember: you're here for them. Share your stuff sparingly – and mostly to make a point.

Make their experience awesome by putting the spotlight on them instead. Let them share their stories and experiences!

Keep it simple

Even if you're teaching a complex subject, avoid overwhelming by keeping things simple. Break your subject down into manageable chunks. A convoluted method, curriculum, or exercise will only make students confused - and want to give up.

Reinforce the information

If you want the key points of the lesson to stick, you will need to repeat them. Don't overwhelm with too many things - stick to three important points per lesson and repeat, repeat, repeat.

Allow time for questions and feedback - when students have time to ask questions or give feedback on exercises, the information is better absorbed.

It is important to reinforce the information. So: Reinforce the information!

Homework is a great way to keep the learning happening long after class is over. Have a short homework assignment to give the students some follow up work. This way, they have something to work on to reinforce the lesson.

Listen

A good teacher listens. From time to time, stop talking and give your students the floor. They may have an insight to add or an experience to share that might be relevant to the lesson - or the other students.

Talking to students

Most students who come to Tarot are adults. It's rare to find a child in a class. Which means: don't talk to your students like they are children. Treat them like adults. They deserve your respect as much as you deserve theirs.

You can be an authority without going the authoritarian route.

That being said, if a problem does arise with a rogue student, nip that in the bud immediately. If a student is being disrespectful, take them aside and let them know that you won't tolerate it. Set a firm boundary and stick to it. You might be able to avoid drama altogether if you set strong policies for your classroom and state them immediately before the class begins.

Teaching, as many other things, may start as in a school, with the flow of information and communication going in a single direction from the teacher to the students. But the more teaching grows, it will become more akin to sharing, as the students do not look anymore to a teacher but to a guide.

Pay attention to your students

As you are going through the lesson, pay close attention to your students. Are some extroverts taking over the class? Are there some who hang back, perhaps afraid of asking a question? Do you notice one student who seems to be grappling with a particular part of the class (look for furrowed brows and an exasperated expression). Be alert for students that need extra help - and those who need to be the center of attention.

For students that seem to be struggling, ask if they have questions. Allow extroverts to have their moment in the spotlight, but be sure to encourage those introverts to participate, too (I will often call on an introvert just to make sure they have a chance to share).

Attention is the first and foremost form of respect.

616

Cheer them on!

Always recognize their efforts. Acknowledge - and acknowledge often. When you praise a student, you're giving them the greatest gift ever: confidence.

Be a fan of your students!

Constructive criticism

While it's important to applaud success, don't fear criticizing a student. That being said, make that criticism constructive. Saying "Brian, you're totally wrong. That interpretation doesn't make any sense" humiliates the student and serves nothing. Instead, use the criticism sandwich: start with positive feedback, correct, more positive feedback.

"Brian, you're making an excellent point. But let me show you how you might look at the Devil card differently. Thanks again for your sharing your ideas - I like the direction you're exploring."

This is the way to criticize without making the student feel bad - or making you look like a jerk.

Treat each student like an individual. You cannot use the same approach for everyone.

Some students learn best through hands-on activities. Others love a lecture. Some may prefer simple exercises, while others want details, details, details. You'll also encounter students who learn quickly and others who don't. This can be challenging!

The best bet is to have a variety of exercises that will work on every sort of learning style: a bit of lecture, some visual aids, and plenty of practicum covers every learning style.

That being said, if you notice a student who seems to be having an issue, reach out and ask what's going on. Find out what they need so that you effectively teach them.

Step by step. All good things grow step by step.

WHEN A STUDENT DOESN'T GET IT

On occasion, you may come across a student who just doesn't get it. It might be that the material is too hard - or that the way you're teaching isn't right for them. Try to find out what the issue is, and then deal with it swiftly.

For students who are struggling, you might want to take a little time after class to address their issue.

For those who just don't get it, you may want to discuss a different class for them so that they don't get lost... or hold the rest of the class back.

Learning should not be a burden, but it cannot be always easy.

In my experience, the students who had the hardest time were the ones who didn't do their homework. They would come to class unprepared every week, which slowed things down to a crawl and frustrated the other students. Eventually, I would have to ask the student to leave because they dragged the whole class down.

Furthering your own education

A good teacher never stops learning, which means it's also important for you to remain a student yourself. Take classes, read books and magazines, attend Tarot conferences, and learn from other Tarot teachers. Keep up with all the industry news and trends. The more you learn, the more effective you'll be.

Everyone will always be a student.

Wrap up

In conclusion, Tarot needs more dedicated teachers, so now is the time for more readers to step forward. This is a sacred role, and it must be treated as such. Be as serious and passionate with your teaching as you are with your Tarot cards. Do that and you will inspire the next generation of Tarot readers - and leave a legacy behind.

What will the cards say about the idea of teaching? Believe in yourself and ask Tarot.

623

Nei Naiff

Nei Naiff, the spiritual name of Claudinei Santos, "One who wins by truth and purity", was born in Jundiaí, in Spain, on the fourth of November 1958, and resides in the city of Rio de Janeiro since the 1980s. He is a writer, a Tarot expert, an astrologer and a therapist. He has technical training in archivology and industrial chemistry, and also higher education in trade administration as well as a degree in Portuguese and English Literature.

He travels the world teaching Tarot and reading professionally for literally thousands of students and querents. For more than 40 years he dedicated himself to esotericism and for over 30 he was a professional Reader and therapist. Still he considers himself only a seeker, an eternal apprentice whose motto is: SELF-KNOWLEDGE IS THE ONLY EVOLUTION!

SACRED GEOMETRY

I started my first Tarot advanced courses in Brazil, in 1991.
The idea was to share knowledge with professional tarotists
who were willing to question all what had been written
about the arcana. It was Tarot for those who knew it. Ideas
were popping into my head because much of what I had
studied in books or learned with other masters didn't work in
practice – I needed to discuss, ponder, synthesize. Astrology
and numerology books are ancient, with unquestionable
well-structured teachings, but most of the Tarot books
were written from the 20th century on and each author
contributed with a part of this knowledge. It shows that
Tarot is in transformation and all of us can contribute to its
development.

In my career as a Tarot teacher I noticed that there's a major interest in learning all one can about the cards in a hermetic plane, but only few know the path of study for the Tarot reading: the way to build the SPREAD (layout, method, reading technique), the energy of the form. Spreads are usually used as if they have random disposition and then the readings are made without a guiding principle; new ways of reading are intuited or the existing structure is altered and yet, no one can explain why the spread is read that way. These issues make the learning of a new spread confused for most tarotists specially when they find many different books with the same spread presented in different ways, as for example the CELTIC CROSS or the ASTROLOGICAL SPREAD.

Take note

Not all the spreads widely taught (in books, lectures, courses) follow this topic's methodology. *Which one is right?* All of them are by the structure – geometric form; only a few by the reading system – *house meanings and the direction of the reading.* All of them work perfectly in the spiritual plane although the nearer it is to what it is showed in this chapter, the more accurate the answer will be.

Geometry is the canvas on which the universe is painted.

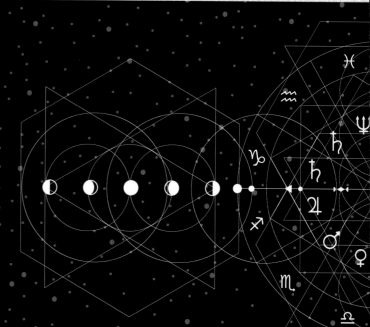

How about to get to know the spread's form to better understand the importance of the layout's construction? What is sacred geometry?

GEOMETRY (Greek word: measurement of the earth) is the fundamental tool that permeates and weaves the foundation of everything, everything that exists is based on this science. In antiquity, it was so sacred an art that only a few chosen could use it. It was a mix of math, engineering, physics, astronomy, astrology, numerology, philosophy. Not every priest was a geometer, but every geometer was a priest! This multiple content for this important work lasted until the middle of the 16th century and it was related to the hermetic axiom:

> *Quod est inferius est sicut quod estsuperius, et quod estsuperius est sicut quod est inferius, ad perpetranda miracula rei unus.*
>
> (Emerald tablets, 8th century)

So, imitating the sacred art by forming nature, Man carved the stones building his temples and dwellings because there was the need to unite functionality with the beauty of the universe. He intuited that with the circle (symbol of the macrocosm, divinity) and the square (symbol of the micro-

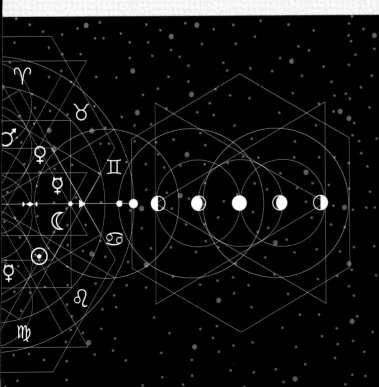

cosm, man), he'd form all the structure and measurement necessary for an edification, observing in these proportions the manifestation of God and the Earth in its most perfect symmetry. All the sacred buildings until the 16th century were conceived the same way: a place was chosen, then a date (usually summer solstice). During the sunrise the geometer laid his staff on the ground whose shadow would project another point in the land, allowing them to find the axis that would represent the main entrance to the temple (east) and the place for the altar (west). Then the point where the staff was laid and the other, found at the end of its shadow, would be used to trace two circles and by their intersection (bisector), the axis north and south could be found. Finally, the geometer established the square necessary for the foundation so all the construction was proportional to the base; doors, walls, windows, domes and ceilings were defined by the cardinal directions. Absolutely everything should be in harmony among each other (Pythagoras' golden ratio, golden

Notre Dame de Paris, the Parthenon in Athens and the temple of Amon-Ra in Egypt.

number), we have as examples of buildings based on sacred geometry: Tabernacle of Jeovah, Shivas' Sanctuary, Amon-Ra temple, the Parthenon, the French Gothic Cathedrals, among hundreds of others.

In the most ancient oracles, at the interpretations of geometric figures prevailed in the fire, sand, clouds, entrails. Geometric forms have also great importance in magical and religious rites and not by mere chance. The neophyte must have the body facing east-west to gesticulate geometric figures and to say magical words, like to cast a magic circle or to form a pentagram for protection. The integration divinity-earth made the symbols of faith (Egyptian ank, the cross of Christ, David Star, the Chinese Tao, pentagram, etc.), as they refer to the geometric form that they were associated with – the symbol of the circle, the cross, the star. With the passing of time everything became analogais and united to the sacred geometry: *the temple, the ritual, the oracle.*

PACE

How would projects be if there was no mental and physical direction? What if there were no cardinal points and the numbers? Have you already imagined social life without plans and purposes? The answer is simple: nomadic man didn't have the necessary ability to settle down, to build, to grow, to thrive. He was always wandering off, searching for a paradise full of food to consume everything and then go searching for another, on and on. When he finally acquired the sacred geometry, the proportion and quantity knowledge, he was able plan and build his own oasis! Yet, nobody builds a house starting by the roof, nor do we reap a fruit without planting its seed! For the Tarot spreads (layouts, methods, techniques) it wouldn't be different, because the process of reading is the very similar: if there is no logic and an ascending direction, there will not be a satisfactory result and if the direction is not obeyed, the reading could be contradictory. So, the numeric sequence of the arcana in a spread must be interpreted step by step (1 – 2 – 3, etc.), except in certain situations.

Take note

We do not turn all the cards at once just to see what the last one is. It is a waste of time because all of them are extremely important in a reading.

The most remarkable aspect of the sacred geometry in a spread is the way it is built – where it begins and ends, the exact shape of how it is established. If we look carefully to the direction that the spread suggests we will be able to see the creation of a geometric form that's very important for the understanding of the oracle. From this symbolic way, we extract the interpretation rhythm, a necessary pace to establish a good reading. The oracular rhythm will enable the reader to qualify it and understand which spread will be more appropriate for each situation as well as the improvement of the arcana's concept and meanings during a reading. The rhythm, in fact, shows the directional movement of the arcana – which goes where and how they go – revealing hidden features.

Rhythm of the circle and the triangle

1. In the ternary forms (triangle) or decennial (circle) that symbolize respectively balance and elevation, the clockwise sequence of cards or the cards on the right side of the reader refer to the future or present-future and it will be the active part of the situation, the exterior, the advance, the emanation, the projection or the arcana creative energy. The counter clock sequence, or the cards on the reader left side, shows past or present-past actions, it will be passive, inner, receptive or the arcana fecundated energy.

2. The circle radius upper part and the upwards triangle top reveal the unknown, the active, the projection, the actions from the present to the future. The circle radius lower part or the downwards triangle top is what is known, the conscious, the passive, the actions from the present to the past.

3. The **empty** circular spread (with no central card or coordination axis) will be a timeless one, a past situation or a distant future. With a central card (central point symbol, axis) it will contain time attributes, active, present and near future manifested.

4. The triangle top to the **right** symbolizes an exterior force, changeable, present-future, projections. With the triangle top to the **left**, it indicates an interior, unchangeable force, present-past, conscious.

The concept of pace is necessarily linked to the concept of time. But how can it be expressed in geometry?

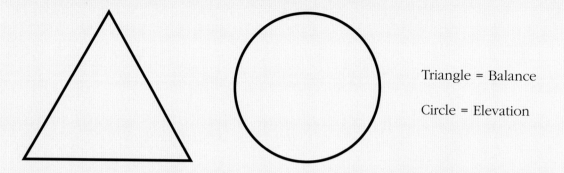

Triangle = Balance

Circle = Elevation

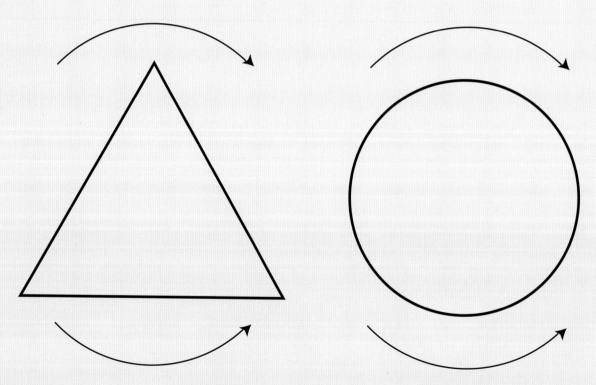

Clockwise rotation = active, progressive
Counter-clockwise rotation = passive, regressive

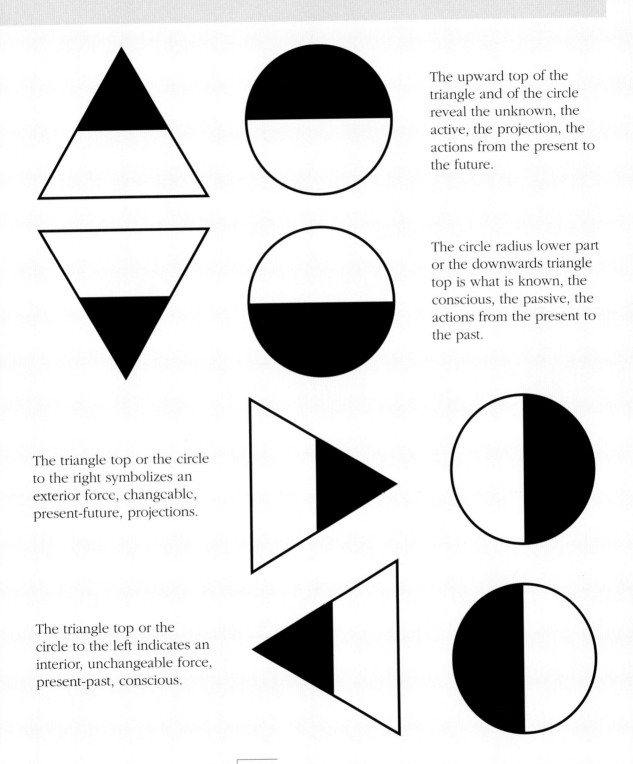

The upward top of the triangle and of the circle reveal the unknown, the active, the projection, the actions from the present to the future.

The circle radius lower part or the downwards triangle top is what is known, the conscious, the passive, the actions from the present to the past.

The triangle top or the circle to the right symbolizes an exterior force, changeable, present-future, projections.

The triangle top or the circle to the left indicates an interior, unchangeable force, present-past, conscious.

633

Rhythms of the square and the cross

1. In the binary (cross) and the quaternary (square) forms, that symbolizes the clash of the opposite (active-passive), all that is in the **upper** part is known, clear, conscious, present action. All that is in the **lower** part is unknown, unconscious, future advancement.

2. The horizontal line indicates the present situation, passive, unchangeable. The vertical line, changeable, future, active. The central point indicates strength, will, balance, facts union.

Geometry and meanings: square and cross

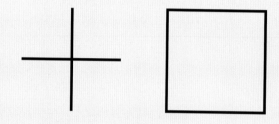

Cross = Binary
Square = Quaternary
All that is in the upper part is known, clear, conscious, present action. All that is in the lower part is unknown, unconscious, future advancement.

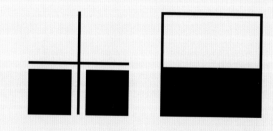

The horizontal line indicates the present situation, passive, unchangeable. The vertical line, changeable, future, active. The central point indicates strength, will, balance.

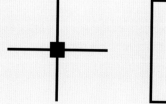

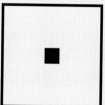

Why does the tarotist read one spread better than another?

Why would a spread work for its creator but do not give good answers for other readers?

Why do some spreads not work properly?

Knowing the sacred geometry will allow you to understand what spread is better structured.

Example

If in a circular design the lower cards refer to the future, it will not be properly built! If in a cross shaped form the lower card refers to the past, it will be broken! If the left card of this same layout refers to the future, the reading will fail!

The way a spread is built also has its **symbolic force**, so it must follow its esoteric and occult symbolism. The **reading system** and the **interpretation rhythm** will provide soul and vigor to the spread's structure and together they allow the reader to make a fail-safe Tarot reading. Whenever the geometry is used, conscious or unconsciously, its power, energy and symbolism are still present. We'll observe the meaning of each geometric form that a spread contains in the next section.

The Circle... the planet, the temple, the flower.

Circle

Concept

It is certainly the first geometric figure drawn by man, since this form is abundantly found in nature and easily detected by sight: the sun, the moon, a flower, a tree top; everything that is round, round shaped or semicircular in the visible surface of the Earth. The planets Sun and Moon were considered deities so it was natural that the circle was used to represent something sacred superior to man, containing principles of eternal rebirth, with no beginning and no end. So, the first structures made by man before he settled down were in circular shapes: the rounded dwelling with bet stones, the megalithic temples, the circle dances around the fire.

Symbolism

The circle has properties of perfection, homogeneity, beauty. It symbolizes the cosmic sky, the macrocosm, the universe, totality, the spiritual realm and man together. Also, the sacred

manifestation as a way to preserve the latent power. It can be depicted as in the Egyptian uraeus, the Greek oroborus, a swag, a mandorla.

Structure

The circular spreads are not suitable neither for objective nor specific situations. They have proportions that contain several life fields with no need for questions. Consequently, every oracular structure in circular shapes will channel simultaneous aspects of the material, sentimental, mental and spiritual life in total interaction.

Spread

Astrological Spread.

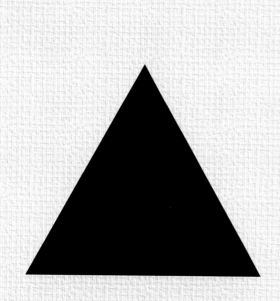

The Triangle... the pyramid, the arrow, the mountain.

Triangle

Concept

Every organic realm grows visibly upwards (straight up) searching for light as if it wishes to reach the sky, to meet the creator (circle). For the ancient priests the solar deity (circle) shed light onto his own creation, so they understood that the triangle (formed between the creation and its shadow) would be the balance between Man and God. In the ancient cosmovision the earth's surface was in the center of the universe. However looking at the image of a triangle, it was believed that the magical formula to reach the sacred was found in it. So, the second manifestation in buildings was the construction of triangular forms: ziggurat (Babylonian and Sumerian cultures), pyramid (Egyptian, Mayan, Olmecan cultures), pagoda (Indian, Chinese, Japanese cultures).

Symbolism

As we have analyzed in the trilogy's first book (p. 145) the ternary principle, the same will be employed here – Man's

mental structure is binary based (like a straight line) but he searches for the ternary (triangle), the necessary balance to ascend mentally and spiritually. For this reason, the ternary (the triangle) is the universal walk for totality and to meet God (the circle). We can broadly analyze the symbol of the triangle as: harmony, proportion, beauty, development, evolution.

Structure

The triangular spreads are suitable for advisement or specific situations. They have proportions that establish directions to be taken. Usually, these forms are not appropriate for objective questions, only situations. All in all, beyond triangular spreads, we'll also find hidden triangles in others of different shape, but these cases just show the development of correlated facts (Astrological Wheel, Labyrinth). The triangle evokes other analogais shapes: the star and the pyramid.

Spreads

The Star of David, Little Master Advisement, Pyramid, Week Spread.

The Square... the square, the palace, the television.

Square

Concept

With the discovery of the triangle man could plan and build all kinds of edifications. This achievement took hundreds or even thousands of years. Nowadays it's very easy to write theses or try to throw light on something, however even with all the technology available it still takes a long time to get to a conclusion. So, just try to figure out what it would be for a nomadic man that had nothing but the horizon and the zenith to behold. It is believed that the square is the only geometric figure drafted by man since this shape is not found in the visible nature – mountain, hole, tree, flower or fruit are not square shaped! Although it is strictly seen as an earthly, human and material symbol, it (the square) will never oppose the celestial and spiritual (circle) shape, instead it will be complementary.

Symbolism

According to occultism, the square is the manifestation of the circle. Therefore, being the Earth (square) the center of the Universe (circle), nothing more natural that the religious

altars, temples, dwellings, villages, cities were made in their basis or lower parts by a perfect square, double or triple, always built on hills or rounded flat lands with domes in the center of their structures – man always tried to be in harmony with the sacred. The square is a figure that translates the idea of solidification, stabilization and perfection. It's not by mere chance that the cube is the representation of the alchemists' philosopher's stone.

Structure

The square shaped spreads are suitable for practical and dynamic questions based on the earthly and material conditions; the square analyses opposed and separated questions, different from the circle that shows how they interfere in one another. Similar to the circle and the triangle, it is not appropriate for objective questions because it has designations for the oracular houses. We can also find hidden squares in circle spreads, showing new perspectives for orientation.

Spreads

Grand Master's Advice, Personal Square, Labyrinth.

The Cross... the Christian cross, the crossing, the sign.

Cross

Concept

We don't know if the figure of the cross or the square was the last sacred geometry's creation, it might even have been the first! However, it is not considered the most important symbolically, but it would be natural if it has preceded all the geometric forms since probably the nomads followed the line of the sun or of some star. Speculations aside, the cross is a symbol of the cardinal and spiritual direction. In all ancient cities, the temples and sacred places strictly followed the cardinal points: the main door was always facing east where the sun light came out, the temples, altars and sacred deposits were built on the west where the gloom (night) resides so they can be enlightened. In the north-south axis there should be windows and doors for the devotees and passers-by, because they meant the flowing sacred energy, dual and intermediary between heaven and Earth. Nowadays, we can still see a little bit of the sacred geometry in gothic churches – the main front door is only open during the cults and faces east, northeast, southeast (never faces north, south, west, northwest or southwest); the side doors are permanently open, the windows are always sideways, the sacristy is in the back and the main altar is under the main dome.

642

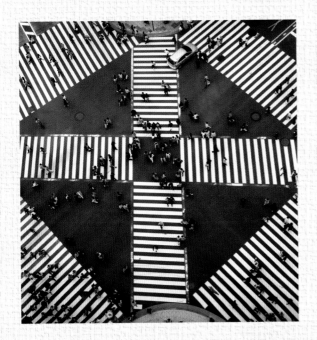

Symbolism

The cross divides the circle in four parts, suggesting it is the intermediate world (cross, direction) between heaven (circle, divinity) and Earth (square, human). The cross is the universal sign of duality or harmony and with the star (triangle, evolution) became one the most ancient symbols that are still alive. Persia, India, Egypt, China or Crete were the first to use it to establish direction, not only geographic but also spiritual. Far from being a symbol of suffering as in Christianity, the cross represents inner balance more than sacrifice. It is the personal decision for one of the four elements, the cardinal points or the harmony between them that would be the cross-interception point.

Structure

All the cross shaped spreads are excellent to make any question because they analyze all the elements of an objective or generic question, what is for and against, pointing out a result, guidance or a solution.

Spreads

Peladin, Celtic Cross, Crossroads, Temple of Mars, Belief,

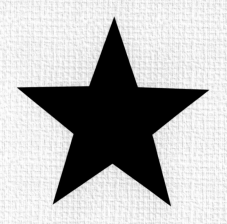

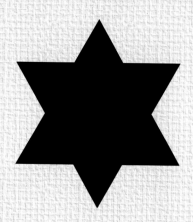

Stars may have different number of
points. That changes their symbolic
meaning.
However, the stars in the universe
do not actually have points.

Star

Concept

The star is formed by several triangles, not being a sacred
geometry basic form. However, it has such deep characteristics that it is typically used to express countless spiritual
concepts, including Tarot spreads.

Symbolism: its celestial aspect makes it naturally the symbol
of the spirit and, particularly of the conflict between the
spiritual (light) and the material (darkness) forces. The
darkness of the night (similar to our fate and thoughts)
brings something not visible but noticeable, because the
light of the stars reveal a fixed point in this dark vastness,
bringing brightness, reference and direction. In each hour,
however, it is found in a different place in the night sky,
always offering new ways like the sacred light beacon that
enlightens the soul.

Structure
All the star shaped spreads give direction, guidance, clarify
and reveal direction of the question. This shape has similar
characteristics to the triangle, that by similar to it assumes the
same characteristics of the reading.

There are three stellar forms:

1. Pentagram
The five-pointed star
In Ancient Egypt, it was the human soul, prayer and faith ideogram. In the Coptic Age, it showed Science and Knowledge, universal meaning. In the Middle Ages, the perfect symbol of the human power in the spiritual realms. Michelangelo has painted human proportions through a five-pointed star. Nowadays is the perfect symbol of the microcosm and the Earth.

2. Hexagram
The six-pointed star
Also called David's shield, Seal of Solomon or Flaming Star: this kind of star made by two entwined triangles or six lines traced from a central point, appears in many civilizations, always bearing balance between inferior and superior forces, the union between humanity and divinity, spirit and matter. The hexagram with a central point indicates, according to the hermetic tradition, the creation of the world, because it refers to the seven planets, the seven metals, the seven colors of the rainbow, the seven musical notes. Symbolically, it used to be the dream of the occultist Wiseman of Renaissance: the reduction of the multiple to the unified, the sacred sciences' universal key. Today it's the perfect symbol of the macrocosm and of the universe.

3. Reshit
The seven-pointed star
It was developed in the Chaldean culture as a symbol of the universe and, subsequently, the Hebrews formulated the creation of the world according to the kabbalah.
In ancient Greece, it was also used by Orpheus and Pythagoras to represent the cosmic lyre and music of the spheres that meant earthly, planetary and human harmony. It represents God's Will and always announces a cycle full of involution or evolution.

Spreads
Star of David, Week Spread.

Tarot Compendium Glossary

Adept: A person who has attained a special level of knowledge or skill within an organization.

Affirmation: A short, powerful statement which indicates a desired change in the psyche.

Alchemy: An ancient science attempting to turn base metals into gold. This quest was often understood as a personal quest for self-transformation. Alchemical images may have influenced the development of Tarot.

Angel: A higher order and a truth that cannot be denied.

Arcana: Plural form of Latin word "arcanum," meaning deep secrets or mystery. Tarot is divided into Major Arcana (twenty-two cards) and Minor Arcana (fifty-six cards).

Arch: Passage, movement, threshold.

Archetype: Describes a set of personality traits, ideal example, or a symbol universally recognized by all people. Collective thought patterns that are innate and inherited and often expressed via dream, art, and myth.

Armor: Defense and shows experience in battle, the ability to persevere.

Baphomet: A Knights Templar idol, according to legend. The appearance of the Devil card in Tarot is often based on Baphomet.

Bat wings: Indicate a darkness and death.

Binah: Hebrew word meaning understanding and numbered three on the Kabbalistic Tree of Life.

Bird: Indicates a spirit capable of guiding the souls of the dead in the afterlife. In ancient times the souls of men were painted as birds.

Birth Cards: Created by Wald and Ruth Ann Amberstone, Birth Cards are a pair of Major Arcana cards that mark an individual's essential personality and polarity. Birth Cards are found by reducing the numbers of an individual's birth date.

Black: Color used in Tarot decks to communicate themes of power, mystery, strength, solidity, danger.

Blindfold: Initiation and inner thoughts.

Blue: Color often used in Tarot decks to communicate themes of emotion, reflection, intuition, coolness, and the suit of Cups.

Boat: Passage across watery depths, sometimes the boundary between life and death. Boats denote all things spiritual, material, and energetic.

Bonifacio, Bembo: Most likely the painter of many early Tarot decks including the Visconti-Sforza.

Book of Thoth: The Tarot deck created by Aleister Crowley and painted by Lady Frieda Harris.

Book T: A Golden Dawn secret manuscript written by Samuel Liddell Mathers.

BOTA: Builders of the Adytum, a modern mystery school in Western tradition created by Paul Foster Case. Their Tarot correspondence course has greatly influenced modern Tarot usage and understanding.

Bow and arrow: A weapon that can hit from a distance in a subtle and penetrating way. The arrow is also a phallic symbol.

Bridge: Passage and chance to move to a new reality. Crossing, structure and pathway.

Brown: Color often used in Tarot decks to communicate themes of earth, security, healing, home, stability.

Bull: Powerful, potent force.

Butterfly: Transformation, connection to the spirit world, higher energies.

Caduceus: Health, prosperity and peace, attributed to Mercury as messenger of the gods.

Cartomancy: Fortunetelling with cards. This includes but is not limited to Tarot, regular playing cards, gypsy cards, angel cards, and so on.

Castle: Stability, home, and success.

Cat: Feline energy, mystery, and aloofness. Independence.

Chesed: Hebrew word meaning mercy and numbered four on the Kabbalistic Tree of Life.

Child: Simplicity, naive and carefree, but also the dualism inherent in every individual.

Chokhmah: Hebrew word meaning wisdom and numbered two on the Kabbalistic Tree of Life.

Claws: Animal nature.

Clerics: Represents two different ways to address spiritual authority, prayer and supplication.

Clouds: Mystical visions and manifestations, also transformation.

Coat cards: Another name for court cards.

Columns: Recall the Temple of Solomon, the Jewish sovereign known for fairness in judging. The names of the pillars were Boaz ("in him is strength"), and Jachin ("God decides" or "God sets").

Court cards: The Minor Arcana cards without numerical attribution. Usually they are depicted as royal figures.

Crawfish: The dark and unreal thoughts that take form in the depths of the mind, slowly rising to the surface.

Cup: Receptive container that can hold anything, symbol of suit of Cups.

Decan/decante: A ten-degree segment of the zodiac.

Devil's hand gesture: The gesture is similar to that of the blessing shown on the Hierophant card, but in this case indicates a guide that leads to a wrong path.

Dignity/dignified: The value or worth applied to a card determined through a number of different factors, usually the cards surrounding it.

Divination: Worldwide practice of inquiry regarding future events or matters. The process of obtaining knowledge of secret or future things by mechanical means or manipulative techniques including (but not limited to) astrology, Tarot cards, palm reading, crystal gazing, rune casting, numerology, tea leaf reading, etc.

Dog: Loyalty, base instincts.

Dove: Symbol of the Christian Holy Spirit of peace. In a general sense, a the dove represents innocence, beauty, and simplicity.

Dualism: The idea the universe is composed of opposites or contrasting aspects, such as dark and light, good and evil, matter and spirit. For many, the goal of Tarot is to harmonize such contradictions.

Ein Sof (or Ain Soph or Ayn Sof): The Kabbalistic space of the universe that contains the nature of the Deity/God.

Elemental dignitics: A mcthod of interpreting cards in a spread using correspondences among the elements (suits) to identify cards that either strengthen or weaken each other.

Elementals: Relating to or being an element. In Tarot and astrology these are Earth, Air, Fire, and Water.

Embrace: Expresses friendship, harmony, and bonds of brotherly love.

Emerald Tablet: A foundation text of alchemical and hermetic thought.

Esoteric: Intended for or understood by a select, small group of people. Private. Confidential. Secret.

Face cards: Another name for court cards.

Fire: Manifestation of divine wrath that unexpectedly affects beings with the fury of human nature. One of the four elements. Creativity and destruction.

Fish: Visions, symbol of Water and the suit of Cups.

Flag: An announcement of transformation.

Free association: A free-form word/image technique created by Sigmund Freud to uncover authentic truth and true feelings.

Freemasonry: An esoteric system using complex rituals. The Rider-Waite deck uses a great deal of Masonic imagery.

Garland: Represents nature, fruitful and changeable. In particular, the leaves are tied to rationality, the flowers to sentiment.

Gevurah: Hebrew word meaning strength and numbered five on the Kabbalistic Tree of Life.

Grapes: Intoxication, pleasure, joy, and abandon.

Grass: Life reborn after the frosts of winter, fueled by spring rains.

Gray: Color often used in Tarot decks to communicate themes of wisdom, balance, neutrality, formality.

Green: Color often used in Tarot decks to convey growth, freshness, attraction, envy, manifestation, and Pentacles.

Halo: The spirit, chakras, aura.

Hand: Demonstration of power, dominion, and transference.

Heart: Traditionally considered the seat of feelings, emotions, and passions.

Heresy: Religious ideas that conflict with the official teachings of the church.

Hermetic Order of the Golden Dawn: The most influential magical group to spring from the 19th century. The Golden Dawn used Tarot as their symbolic key within their esoteric and magical workings.

Hermeticism: Esoteric philosophy of self-transformation attributed to the ancient philosopher Hermes Trismegistus.

Hod: Hebrew word meaning splendor and numbered eight on the Kabbalistic Tree of Life.

Holy Grail: A sacred object in literature and certain Christian traditions identified as the dish, plate, or cup used by Jesus at the Last Supper. The Grail symbolizes perfection, and some consider the Grail imagery the source of Tarot and its four suits.

Horn: The connection between the divine and the earthly world.

Horse: Power, speed, and assistance. Often indicates the speed at which something will happen.

Human remains: Symbolize the memory of life and all things that are not essential abandoned.

Intuition: A quick and ready insight. Instinctive knowledge of or about something without conscious reasoning.

Kabbalah (also Kabalah, Cabala, Cabbala, Cabbalah, Quabbala, Quaballah, etc.): A system of Jewish mysticism explaining the nature of the universe.

Kether: Hebrew word meaning Divine Will and numbered one on the Kabbalistic Tree of Life.

Key: Secret knowledge.

Knights Templar: Order of Knights whose enemies accused them of occult practices, including divination and worship of a demon called Baphomet.

Lantern: The inner light that illuminates the road and shows the way.

Law of Three: This law states that whatever you release to the world will be returned to you three times over.

Lemniscate (sideways figure eight): Eternal cycle. Ying and yang.

"Le Monde Primitif": Massive 18th century work by Antoine Court de Gébelin. It contains the first mention of Tarot as a secret doctrine from ancient Egypt.

Lightning: Divine intervention and flashes of insight.

Lily: Purity and innocence.

Lion: Brute force.

Magic: The purposeful manipulation of energy and intentions to bring about a desired result for an individual, using symbol, language, action, and ritual.

Major Arcana: The first twenty-two cards of the Tarot deck numbered zero through twenty-one.

Malkuth: Hebrew word meaning kingdom and numbered ten on the Kabbalistic Tree of Life.

Meditation: Method of stilling the mind and body to gain spiritual awareness.

Minor Arcana: Fifty-six Tarot cards often referred to as pip cards or minors. Minors consist of the Aces through Tens and the court cards.

Moon: Femininity, monthly cycles, ebb and flow, the renewal of nature, the continuous transformation, feminine intuition.

Mountain: Attainment, challenge, man's movement to higher realms. The symbol of ascension.

Mystery School: Mystery Schools claim there is hidden meaning behind outer words and symbols that can only be experienced, not taught. The schools guide an individual through a series of rites that begin or "initiate" a transformation of consciousness. This awakens organs and subtle energies within the body activating abilities of which the general populace are not generally aware. (Mary K. Greer definition)

Netzach: Hebrew word meaning victory and numbered seven on the Kabbalistic Tree of Life.

Night: The dark side of consciousness. The sleep of reason, dreams, the unconscious.

Nudity: The purity of physical, moral, intellectual, and spiritual innocence. Truth.

Number cards: Forty Minor Arcana cards with numerical value from Ace through Ten.

Occult: From the Latin word "occultus" meaning hidden, mysterious. From the 15th century was used as a verb to conceal. Used in the 19th century to describe supernatural and magical practices and beliefs.

Orange: Color often used in Tarot decks to communicate themes of warmth, welcome, harvest, home, satisfaction.

Personality card: Based on teachings of Mary K. Greer, the personality card shows the purpose of an individual's current lifetime.

Pips/pip cards: Pips are small symbols on suits of Tarot packs to define the nature of the suit. Swords will show swords, etc. Therefore pip cards are the cards using pips, Ace through Ten of all suits.

Pitchers: The ability to contain, store, and distribute food for the body or spirit. They are a reference to the miracle at the wedding of Canaan.

Pool of water: Expresses what is hidden in the mind of man; memory or the unconscious.

Processional three-rod cross: Indicates the ability to drive through the three theological virtues: faith (dogmas), hope (prayer) and charity (benevolent actions). Can also represent fate, fortune, and destiny.

Purple: Color often used in Tarot decks to communicate themes of royalty, calm, opulence, wealth, intuition.

Querent: The person who seeks the reading and the one who is asking questions and seeking advice and insight.

Ray: Symbolizes the creative or destructive power of the Sun, whose heat can give life but also take it.

Reader: The person who lays out and interprets the cards.

Red: Color often used in Tarot decks to communicate themes of energy, passion, alertness, fervor, fire, and the suit of Wands.

Reversal/reversed: Term used to describe a card that is upside down in a reading.

Rider-Waite Tarot: The world's most popular Tarot deck, designed by Arthur Edward Waite and painted by Pamela Colman Smith. The name "Rider" refers to the original publisher.

Rope: Binds individuals to things or persons.

Sacred geometry: Examines the mystical properties of patterns and shapes.

Salamander: Symbol of fire.

Scales: A balancing, expressing an opinion, and the ability to weigh things with common sense.

Scepter: Power in the material world.

Sepher Yetzirah (also Sefer Yetzira, Sefer Jetzira, Book of Formation and Book of Creation): An ancient text of mysterious origins considered the first mystical text describing the Kabbalah.

Sephirot (singular, Sephirah): The ten circles of divine energy that form the Tree of Life.

Shadow self: A psychological term coined by Carl Jung. Describes the place where individuals store desires, wants, and needs that they do not like, approve of, or want to acknowledge.

Sickle: The harvest, which happens with a clean cut, is the allegory of death and is the inevitable end of each cycle.

Significator: A card chosen at random or intentionally to represent the person who is receiving the reading.

Skull: The death of intellectual abilities and the vanishing of thought.

Solar crown: The clarity of thought and intelligence illuminating the spirit.

Soul card: A soul card shows the individual's purpose across many or all of our lifetimes. Based on teachings of Mary K. Greer.

Star: A symbol of Ishtar, the Babylonian goddess of love, identified by the Greeks as Aphrodite and by the Romans as Venus. Indicates beauty.

Suits: The four parts of the Minor Arcana, which vary greatly in modern Tarot. The most common are Cups, Pentacles, Wands, and Swords.

Sun: Energy, the male element, the light that defeats the darkness, truth and intelligence, clarifying any doubts.

Supernatural: Of or relating to an order of existence beyond the visible universe, especially if relating to a god, demigod, spirit, or devil.

Suspension: Out of time, timelessness, altered state.

Sword: Strength and the desire for conquest. Symbol of the element of Air.

Synchronicity: The existence of two or more meaningful events having nothing to do with one another yet supposedly meaningful. A coincidence of events.

Taro River: A river in Northern Italy near the region of the first known Tarot decks.

Tarocchi: The original Italian name for the Tarot cards and the game played with them.

Tarock: An Austrian version of Tacocchi, usually played with a smaller deck.

Tetragrammaton: The four Hebrew letters (Yod, He, Vav, He) that stand for the name of God and constitute a central theme of Kabbalah.

Three-tiered tiara: The ability to direct one's thoughts through the material, psychological, and spiritual.

Throne: Solidity and concreteness.

Tiferet: Hebrew word meaning beauty and numbered six on the Kabbalistic Tree of Life.

Tomb: Death and resurrection.

Torch: Physical vitality and fire of the passions.

Tower: A phallic symbol. Also family, home, the human body, and, in some cases, the church. It is a direct reference to the Tower of Babel. Man's attempt to touch the divine.

Tree of Life: A mystical concept that explains the universe as described by Jewish mysticism. An arrangement of the ten Sephirot and the connecting paths among them.

Tree: Life, knowledge, and communication between the earthly world and the celestial world.

Trumps/triumphs: The Major Arcana. Tarot cards numbering zero to twenty-one. Called trumps because each card is more powerful, or "trumps" the previous. Corruption of the Italian "trionfi."

Unconscious: Parts of our personality or mind of which we are not directly aware.

Veil: The fabric preventing sight beyond. Inaccessible knowledge.

Walking stick: Prudence in moving, aid in walking, or a defensive weapon.

Wall: A limit, a boundary between two dimensions, and a protection. It also indicates the foundations from which to build.

Wand: Linked to the element Fire, the symbol of desire, the instrument of magic.

Water: Fertility and anything that refreshes the body, mind, and soul. Life and regeneration.

Western Mystery School/Order: Organizations created to provide its members with an experience of self-transformation, union with the divine by providing structured initiation ceremonies, ritual, meditative and contemplative work.

Wheel: The passage of time, and the ups and downs of fortune.

White lily: The primordial goddess, psychic integrity. The alchemical lily represents incorruptible and eternal nature, the noblest thing.

White wings: The ability to rise above the material dimension and seek heaven.

White: Color often used in Tarot decks to communicate themes of unity, light, purity, peace, lunar qualities.

Yellow: Color often used in Tarot decks to communicate caution, consideration, distinction, thoughtfulness, solar energy, and the suit of Pentacles or Swords.

Yesod: Hebrew word meaning foundation and numbered nine on the Kabbalistic Tree of Life.

Young man: Indicates inexperience, but also energy, life, passion, and ingenuity.

655

LO SCARABEO